959.053 Sch
Scholl-Latour
Death in the ricefields :

W9-BLH-036

MORRIS AUTOMATED INFORMATION NETWORK

0 1029 0099949 5

ON LINE

WITHDRAWN

APR 29 1985

399

MORRIS COUNTY FREE LIBRARY

Parsippany-Troy Hills Public Library
Lake Hiawatha Branch
Nokomis Ave. & Hiawatha Blvd.
Lake Hiawatha, N J 07034

DEMCO

Death in the Ricefields

Death in the Ricefields

An Eyewitness Account of Vietnam's Three Wars,
1945-1979

Peter Scholl-Latour

Translated by Faye Carney

St. Martin's Press
New York

Copyright page

© 1979 by Deutsche-Verlags-Anstalt GmbH, Stuttgart.
All rights reserved. Printed in the United Kingdom. No part
of this book may be used or reproduced in any manner
whatsoever without written permission except in the case of
brief quotations embodied in critical articles or reviews. For
information, address St. Martin's Press, 175 Fifth Avenue,
New York, N.Y. 10010.

ISBN: 0-312-18619-3

First published in Great Britain in 1981 by Orbis Publishing
Limited, London. First published in German as *Der Tod im
Reisfeld: Dreissig Jahre Krieg in Indochina*

First U.S. Edition

10   9   8   7   6   5   4   3   2   1

Contents

5

THE SECOND INDOCHINESE WAR
The Americans

THE THIRD INDOCHINESE WAR
The Chinese

7

Foreword

This book has been written from memory and gives a purely personal view of the events described in it. During my thirty years in Indochina I discovered that subjective reporting is often the most honest way of getting closer to reality or – if it is not too big a word – the truth.

P. S-L.

Gloom over Saigon

Ho Chi Minh City, August 1976

The monsoon rain had been falling non-stop since early morning, and the view over the Saigon River was blurred by the dank, humid air. One or two rusty old freighters stood tied up at the quayside, but there was nothing of any real size. During America's military involvement the Red Cross ship the *Heligoland* had been berthed here. At first it had flown the German flag, very discreetly, to show its support for the American cause, but later on public opinion had changed dramatically and support for the USA had steadily waned. A few lights were beginning to appear here and there in the haze, and their reflections shone on the wet pavements of the Rue Catinat. The Rue Catinat used to be the smart shopping street in Saigon in the days of French colonial rule. Its name was later changed to Tu-Do Street (Freedom Street) and it became the American red-light district, packed with bars and brothels. Recently the victorious Communists from the North had rechristened it Dong-Khoi (Street of the People's Revolt). That left the South Vietnamese wondering exactly who was meant to have risen in revolt.

As we were visitors from the West the new Communist authorities had installed us in the Majestic Hotel. During the long years of the first and second Indochinese wars – the first involving the French, the second the Americans – we had always stayed at the Continental, which had been a kind of army camp for war correspondents from all over the world. Now, however, the Continental had been taken over by party officials and bigwigs from Hanoi. In the old days the terrace of the Continental had been the regular haunt of the livelier members of the press, the place where they got together to swap stories and pick up girls. Recently it had been screened off from public gaze by iron railings,

11

Now members of the new regime could sit and enjoy their meagre privileges in peace. From my hotel window in the Majestic I could look out onto an endless vista of mangrove swamps, through which the Saigon River wound its way like a fat yellow snake.

A troop carrier packed with soldiers from the Vietnam People's Army heaved slowly away from the bank and steamed off in the direction of Vung Tau. It eventually disappeared from sight round a bend in the river, taking with it its cargo of Vietnamese revolutionaries in their green uniforms and pith helmets – a quaint souvenir of colonial days. That evening I had no idea where these reinforcements were heading: the disputed border with Cambodia.

The tropical night descended with its usual suddenness. Upstream the dying sunset split the sky into vivid bands of colour, setting everything ablaze with a fiery glow. It reminded me of the last days of the fighting, when the beleaguered city was on the point of collapse. The last surviving defenders of Saigon, a courageous band of Catholic paratroopers, had been surrounded in Xuan Loc and the army of the North had stood poised to deliver the final blow to the capital. Now, as I gazed out over the city, I saw the concrete memorial to Marshal Tran Hung Dao, military leader and national hero, silhouetted against the crimson sky. This huge statue had been left standing by the Communists, and so it stood where it always had, looking out over the harbour. The legendary Tran Hung Dao was evidently still considered part of North Vietnamese history. He had once saved his country by defeating the Mongolian emperor, Kublai Khan, when he drove back the invading Chinese armies at the Bach-Dang River in Tonkin. Centuries later he was still revered as a symbol of Vietnam's struggle for independence against China. And now, in the last few days, he had suddenly become a topical figure again. Rumours had begun to fly in Hanoi and Ho Chi Minh City (as Saigon was now called) about the inevitable clash that was coming with Peking, and Marshal Dao was once again hero of the hour. Our interpreter from Hanoi quoted a wise old Vietnamese proverb to us: 'When the danger from the south is averted, the threat from the north is twice as great.' Then she added mysteriously: 'The Chinese have grey bellies.' It was a remark that carried sinister implications.

We strolled along the Street of the People's Revolt together with our colleagues from the camera crew. The mopeds and Hondas that had been a trademark of the brash consumerism of the old pro-American regime were still very much in evidence, though goodness only knows how their owners managed to get hold of petrol. All the bars and vice dens in the town had been closed, and members of the business community were resignedly waiting for the retail shops to be taken over any day now. The inevitable trishaws were still parked outside the shops but they waited in vain for customers.

Now we were out in the street again, we could talk freely about our plans for the day and our impressions of the city. Back in our hotel rooms we always had to be careful in case we were bugged. Since our arrival in Saigon we had been aware of an atmosphere in which we were clearly regarded as spies, or at least with great suspicion. It hung over us like a dead weight. We knew that every step we took was being closely watched, and ever word we uttered listened to. The security forces were probably waiting for us to make one false move so they could clamp down on us – and if that happened we would be lucky to get away with having our travel visas revoked. In the course of thirty years as a foreign correspondent you acquire a kind of sixth sense for situations like this, and I had noticed that our official escorts from Hanoi were keeping their distance. They had seemed very friendly at first but now they were suspicious and on the defensive.

Practically everyone you saw on the streets of Saigon looked grave, bitter or apprehensive. As for us, we couldn't so much as bring ourselves to say the new name, Ho Chi Minh City. It seemed to stick in the throats of the Red party officials, too; even they balked at linking the name of their esteemed revolutionary leader with a town that so obviously hankered after the 'evil' ways of the past. The black market still flourished, however. You could still buy illicit and shoddy American goods, and the effect these had on the rugged peasants from the North is not hard to imagine. The contents of the PX store must have looked like the inside of Aladdin's cave to the soldiers of the Red Star. A tailor in the flower market offered to make us each a complete new outfit of clothes for a ridiculously cheap price – payable in US greenbacks, naturally. All the shopkeepers and second-hand dealers in the city knew only too well this was just a brief respite before the final blow fell. Every morning they had to face the possibility of being bundled unceremoniously onto a lorry together with a few of their possessions and household utensils. They would then be taken to the wilderness of the New Economic Zones where they would be forced to help build the brave new Socialist Republic.

During my time in Saigon I deliberately made no attempt to contact any of my old acquaintances, for fear of putting them at risk. None of this seemed to deter our old camera-assistant, Cuc, when I accidentally bumped into him in the street. Cuc was a burly half-Cambodian who was renowned for his irrepressible good humour. When he saw me he hugged me in full view of everyone, then whispered in my ear: 'If only I'd got away while I still had the chance!' He told me he was driving one of the huge red American limousines that people had used for weddings in happier times. Now these flashy monsters sat idle in the evening haze of the monsoon rains, as alien as dinosaurs of a bygone age.

From behind the steamed-up shop-front, the owner of the last surviving hairdressing salon in Saigon beckoned to me as I was walking by. The rest of the women in Ho Chi Minh City had had to knuckle under to the puritanism of the new commissars; she, however, had decided to proclaim her individuality and courage by continuing to wear make-up and smart clothes. The national dress of Vietnamese women was the *ao dai*. It was like a brightly-coloured butterfly wing, chaste and seductive at the same time, and it captivated every visitor to Indochina. Now the new regime had banned it altogether from the streets of Saigon. High heels were also prohibited, as were mini-skirts, which were denounced as a 'counter-revolutionary provocation'. None of this seemed to matter in the hairdresser's on Rue Catinat, however. The proprietor made sure her girls continued to look smart in their skimpy white garments. When I entered the shop they all seemed to be giggling and chattering without a care in the world, just like the old days. Yet everyone knew the shop would be closed in a few weeks at the very latest. The woman suddenly became serious and began telling me about her relatives in Paris and her family's attempts to emigrate to France. 'If only they realized how easy it is to bribe these commissars. Clean-living puritans my foot!' I had a sudden mental picture of a member of the hairdresser's family standing outside the doors of the consul general, queueing up every morning as soon as the curfew was over in the hope of being granted a joint exit visa. It took nerve to do this, not to mention a certain desperation, because the name of every applicant was recorded by police informers and the security forces.

In the hairdresser's I had come across a rather unusual character, a young Vietnamese man who looked about twenty-five. I had been very struck by him at the time, though in any other circumstances I would not have given him a second glance. In the days when General Thieu was in power he would have been described as a cowboy, but this was just a way of getting in a dig at the Americans. He had on a pair of cowboy boots and what must have been the tightest jeans in Saigon. He wore a loud check shirt open to the waist to reveal an assortment of chains and pendants dangling on his chest. The thing that really stood out about him, though, was his neatly-groomed, shoulder-length hair. He sat sprawled in the hairdresser's chair, having his nails manicured and talking away as if nothing at all had changed. I wondered what would happen to this last cowboy, who looked more like a caricature of a typical Vietnamese pimp. Would he be spirited off the very next day to some re-education camp? Was he perhaps being used as an *agent provocateur* by the Communist secret police? Or was this simply his own way of putting on a bold front before he finally went under? I remembered a Frenchman who had been in a concentration camp once telling me that two kinds of prisoners in the camps were braver than all the rest. They were a certain breed of aristocrat – and the pimps.

Our official escort from the Information Service had warned us to be on the look-out for pickpockets and possibly even muggers on the streets after dark. He wasn't joking either: that day an East German diplomat had been robbed in broad daylight. So we heeded his warning and took care always to walk in the centre of the road. The traffic, which had never been very heavy, had virtually disappeared long ago. At every crossroads stood soldiers or policemen with Kalashnikov rifles at the ready. We had originally planned to eat out that evening at My Canh, a river-boat restaurant. It had been blown up by Vietcong frogmen during the war and several Americans and their Vietnamese girlfriends had been killed or wounded. However it turned out that the restaurant, which used to be run mainly by Chinese, had been taken over by the authorities that very day. So we searched out the last private French restaurant in Ho Chi Minh City, a place called Valenco's. It was owned by a Corsican in his early fifties called Dominique, a familiar face to every war correspondent in Saigon. Rumour had it that he had once belonged to the now defunct Corsican Mafia which reputedly had controlled the business world in Saigon in the days of French rule. While the Corsicans certainly made a small fortune dealing in piastres, they were pretty small fry compared to the big-time speculators and financiers who ran things in the predominantly Chinese city of Cholon, a short distance from Saigon.

Entering Dominique's bar I instantly felt as if I had stepped back thirty years. Groups of young Frenchmen with short army haircuts sat at the tables looking as sunburnt as soldiers who had just come back from the paddy fields. They were employees of a big French firm that had been contracted by Hanoi to carry out test drillings for oil around the Mekong and the coastal region of Cochin China. The young Frenchmen had come to Dominique's bar in search of a piece of home. They seemed to be enjoying themselves and were making a fair amount of noise.

Dominique, who looked rather like the French film actor Michel Piccoli, was standing gloomily behind the counter. His face brightened when he saw me come in. The arrival of an outsider from the West, and an old Indochina hand as well, was something of a consolation for him. He had been visited by the authorities only that morning, and now had to pay a hefty sum in back taxes if he wanted permission to return to France. Dominique was determined to leave, no matter what it cost. He admitted he had backed the wrong horse. He had bargained on there being a place for a business like his in the new Socialist Vietnam and had been rapidly disabused. He gave vent to his feelings in a bitter tirade on politics and politicians in Indochina and his native France. 'What a fool I was voting for Mitterrand and the Left in the last presidential elections! But mark my words, when I get back to Corsica I'll start a campaign against those Red devils!' Between the rapidly thinning bottles of brandy and apéritifs on the shelves stood a bust of Napoleon, and next to the mirror behind the bar hung the motto 'I'm Corsican and proud of it'. We talked about old friends we had known from both Indochinese wars. Some had gone on to make a success of things, others had come to grief in the upheaval that followed de-colonization. The conversation was very nostalgic and it left me feeling terribly morbid and worldly wise compared to the happy-go-lucky young oilmen enjoying themselves at the other tables.

A pretty Eurasian girl called Violette was sitting at the cash desk. I had a message to pass on to her from someone in Hanoi. A member of the French delegation there had got her a provisional permit that would allow her to return to France. 'I don't suppose it'll be enough,' she said. Violette never stopped flirting, no matter how bad the situation was. She joined us at our table and explained that she needed money to get an official exit visa. Boats were few and far between these days, since even fishermen were allocated barely enough fuel for their cutters. Recently she'd heard people talking about an escape route through the highlands of Annam and Laos; apparently some of the Montagnard hill-tribes were in revolt there. But the journey was said to be really hard going and most people died *en route*. Violette reckoned she would most likely end up being sent to some drab new settlement in the plain some day – always assuming she was lucky enough to avoid being sent to a re-education camp. Dominique, with whom she had lived, couldn't protect her for very much longer.

There was another girl in Valenco's that evening. She had been flirting with the young Frenchmen at the other table, and you got the impression that she was on very intimate terms with one or two of them. Her name was Vanh, which means 'cloud' in Vietnamese. She had a scarf tied round her forehead which made her look slightly rakish, rather like a pirate. She had a typically Oriental face with beautiful high cheekbones, and she moved with the animal grace that comes only with a perfect figure. She was dressed in jeans and a T-shirt. 'I'm going around looking like a hooligan,' she laughed as she came to our table. 'When my father was Chief of Police at Cam Tho I used to wear the smartest dresses in town. But now he's either dead or in prison, and I have to fend for myself – any way I can.' It didn't take much intelligence to work out why the daughter of a senior police officer under the old regime was able to work as a hostess in the last remaining Western bar in Saigon. Vanh probably had to report every morning to one of the dour, grim-faced officials in the security services. She would have to repeat to him everything she had heard the French oilmen say, at table or in bed.

One thing she could report was that these oilmen, like many other young Frenchmen of a similar age and background, had come out to the new, reunified Vietnam as Socialists or Communists. Yet it had taken only a few weeks in the Democratic Republic of Vietnam to turn these erstwhile members of the French Left into rabid anti-Communists. The Frenchmen talked to us about the crowded prison camps they had seen in the Mekong Delta. They described the repression of the local population that was going on there and the tyranny and corruption of party cadres. They had had first-hand experience of how incompetent and over-blown State-run industry could be. They found that armed resistance was still occurring in areas where the Buddhist Hoa Hao sect was active, and they had heard artillery fire at Vinh Long while searching for oil in the bed of the Mekong River. What they did not realize, though, was that the third Indochinese war – the bloody confrontation between Vietnam and Cambodia – was already under way, and they had been the first outsiders to inadvertently witness it.

The door opened and a frail old man in threadbare clothes came in, accompanied by a gust of damp night air. He was carrying a guitar, and after greeting Dominique he sat down and started singing in French in a thin, husky voice. He began with a French song that had also been popular in Germany in the thirties, *'Il était un musicien qui jouait dans un café. . . .'* He followed this with a tune whose words were to make an indelible impression on me: *'Adieu, le temps des amours, adieu, le temps des aventures.'* Hearing the song sung like this by an old man begging for a few piastres was almost unbearably moving. I made arrangements for him to come back next day so we could film him for our documentary. He promised he would, but he didn't turn up for the appointment and we never saw him again.

Three new customers came up to the bar, Vietnamese this time. They must have been informers or plain-clothes policemen. No local person would normally dare enter this place, well known as a haunt of foreigners from the West. The French began to throw hostile glances in their direction. Dominique was so nervous he dropped a glass and it shattered into pieces on the floor. The faces of the two girls remained totally blank. Whenever members of the North Vietnamese security service or secret police appeared, the reaction was always the same. Whenever there was an incident, or an arrest, or even just a routine check, the locals would don a mask of inscrutability behind which they hid their fear and contempt and loathing. 'That's the Bo-Doi,' whispered Vanh. Bo-Doi had once been a term of pride in Vietnam and eventually even the Western press had taken it up. According to French newspapers it meant 'barefoot soldier', but this was a mistranslation. The name meant, in fact, soldiers who operate in the plains and jungles – in a word, guerillas. Although it originally had overtones of respect and prestige, since the victory of the North Vietnamese it had come to be used by the people of Saigon as a swear-word and general term of abuse. Bo-Doi was now synonymous with 'yokel' and 'harsh oppressor'. It was equated with the primitive savages from the North who had carted off anything vaguely resembling consumer goods and had taken over the key positions in the city. And the name had an additional pejorative sense for the bar-girls of Saigon. Bo-Doi to them meant all those Communist soldiers and officials who had become homosexual from having spent so many years fighting in ascetic, all-male communities – types who could only react with shocked helplessness when confronted with the charms of the Saigon flirts.

On the way back to the hotel we happened to pass a couple of prostitutes standing at the top of the Street of the People's Revolt. One came up and greeted us in Russian; she had obviously mistaken us for visitors from the Soviet Union. When we arrived back at the Majestic we took a final look inside the hotel dining-room. The old waiters there became extremely friendly towards us, albeit in a melancholy way, the moment they found out we were from the West. The same thing happened with everyone we spoke to in Saigon. Behind the display of warmth there probably lurked the faint hope that the door had not closed on them forever, that maybe one day it would open again and allow them access to a better, freer life.

Only one table in the restaurant was occupied now. A group of Russians, engineers by the look of them, were sitting at it together with the inevitable Vietnamese escorts. They were dressed unfashionably and their coarse faces looked even less prepossessing beside the fine features of the Asians. Their movements were clumsy, but they were careful never to raise their voices. It wasn't that these Soviet workers looked at all off-putting – it was simply that they seemed to go around with a perpetually worried look. Not one was laughing or joking. 'How on earth are we meant to believe in Lenin when his followers always look so depressed and down in the mouth?' a Swedish diplomat once said to me in Hanoi. The Vietnamese interpreters at the Russian table were clearly on their best behaviour too.

As I gazed out into the darkness from my hotel window that evening I caught something of the mood of fear and anger and, above all, sadness that hung over Saigon. The footsteps of a heavily-armed Bo-Doi patrol rang out in the street below. I thought of all the other times I had looked out from my hotel room at the far bank of the Saigon River and the area of marshland the locals called the Rungsat. During the French and American wars first the Viet Minh and then later the Viet Cong had taken up position in the mangrove swamps across the river. Once or twice the enemy had aimed rockets at the heart of the city from their base in the Rungsat. On those nights, I remembered, the sky above the dark plain had been lit up by signal rockets like a carefully-timed firework display. Tonight, over by the headland that used to be called comics' corner, the only flicker of light came from a lamp that cast a tremulous yellow beam onto the murky waters of the Saigon River. It was here, during the winter of 1945–46, that I first set foot on Indochinese soil.

THE FIRST INDOCHINESE WAR

The French

'You are Going the Wrong Way!'

On board the *Andus*, Winter 1945

The 26,000-tonne troop ship *Andus* was on hire from the Royal Navy. In those days the French forces, their morale and equipment, were still adversely affected by the Fall of France in 1940 and much military hardware had to be bought on credit. The British crew of the *Andus* hardly knew what to make of it all. The war was over, but here they were transporting a French colonial army to the Far East to fight. The French troops had the unenviable task of trying to win a few battles to make up for the national defeat at home. And the pressure on them was even greater now that the war against Japan was over. In the end, not a single French unit had taken part in that conflict, despite de Gaulle's strenuous attempts to involve his troops in the fighting.

Another troop ship of the same tonnage followed behind the *Andus*, keeping well in sight of her. It was flying the Dutch flag alongside the Union Jack and was taking Dutch colonial troops out to Djakarta. As the *Andus* sailed through the Red Sea it met whole convoys of troop ships heading in the opposite direction, back towards Europe. Victory pennants flew from their mastheads and British veterans of the Burma campaign stood on deck. They were on their way home to their native land, back to peace and the old nine to five routine. If you looked through binoculars you could just make out their sunburnt faces, reddened by the tropical sun. Even at this distance you could detect their happiness, their obvious relief at having survived the twin perils of the jungle and an implacable enemy. The British troops waved cheerily to the French and Dutch as they sailed past. Then an English voice came booming through a megaphone. 'You are going the wrong way!' it said, with just a hint of mockery. 'What's up with these Britishers now?' grunted a portly French major. He obviously didn't think it funny.

The situation was, in fact, quite ludicrous. Britain's Labour government had only been in power a short time but had already decided to turn its back, once and for all, on the old dreams of Empire. Kipling or no Kipling, the Indian sub-continent was to be abandoned to its own devices and would soon become independent. After one or two initial setbacks, the British Army in Burma had distinguished itself and the campaign had ended on a high note. The troops could now leave the stage like conquering heroes, proud of their achievement. When it came, the British departure from Delhi would be graced by the presence of Lord Mountbatten, who imparted the appropriate degree of style and dignity to the occasion. However, these sentiments were not at all shared by the French and Dutch, respectively first-round losers and lucky last-minute winners in the colonial stakes. They, unlike the British, were determined to hang on to their empires. They still clung stubbornly to the mirage of former glory in Indochina and Indonesia.

The young French officers on board the *Andus* felt demoralized at the prospect of arriving on the scene too late and having to play second fiddle in Indochina. Quite a few had already served under de Gaulle with the Free French and had been declared traitors to their country by the Vichy government. Others had joined up in North Africa when the Americans took over. Most of them had lived through the humiliation of the German occupation. Now they wanted to wash away the stigma of defeat in the waters of the Mekong and the Red River. Deep down they were fearful of arriving in Indochina and finding the country already pacified and loyal to France. What they all thirsted for was exotic adventure and stirring experiences. Every one of them down to the last second lieutenant had probably read Sartre, but even if they hadn't all were existentialists in uniform in their own way. All were seeking roads to freedom, *Les Chemins de la Liberté*, in a tropical battle-torn Saint Germain-des-Prés of the imagination. One of them wrote in his diary: 'Oh to find a piece of earth not covered with tarmac . . .'

There were two companies of legionnaires on board the *Andus*, and roughly two thirds were German. Most had been prisoners of war in France, where they had nearly starved to death. They had signed up for a posting to Indochina for one of two reasons – either because they had abandoned any hope of being reunited with members of their family who had gone missing in the East or, quite simply, because they wanted to eat well again. There were some, too, who had served with the SS during the war and wanted to avoid the de-Nazification programme going on in Germany. In the evenings the German legionnaires would sing old Wehrmacht songs about Erika and Heidi and Lore and Försterwald. They would have been surprised to learn that their former enemies, the French, would one day take over their old Teutonic military songs. Who would have believed that, twenty years after French troops had had to listen to endless choruses of 'Madelon', a new generation of recruits would be marching past to the strains of the 'Blauer Dragoner'?

The most interesting among the legionnaires were the Belgians. They were, in fact, Frenchmen who had lied about their nationality so they could serve in the Legion, which admitted only foreign nationals. They were quite different from the thugs and common criminals who used to use the Legion as a bolt-hole from the law before 1939. These fictitious Belgians were actually French collaborators who had served on the German side during the war, either in the French Volunteer Legion (which took part in the 'Crusade against Bolshevism') or, in the closing stages of the war, in the Charlemagne Brigade of the SS. De Gaulle had offered the chance of rehabilitation to all ex-collaborators provided they were not accused of having taken part in operations against the Resistance: if they were prepared to do five years' service with the Foreign Legion in Indochina they would be allowed to return home again with the slate wiped clean. The 'Belgian French' were thoughtful and serious-minded compared to the German legionnaires. Somebody in the German contingent was always sounding off about his excellent war record, and at times it seemed as if every one of them was a former U-boat captain and recipient of the Knight's Cross. Towards the end of the war the remnants of the Charlemagne Brigade had fought several rearguard actions to try and halt the Russian advance into Pomerania. They had been almost completely wiped out in the process, but the survivors had been granted the privilege of defending Hitler's bunker underneath the Chancellery.

The regular army volunteers for the Far East, who heard the news of the Japanese surrender while waiting in their embarkation camp at Marseilles, had felt a real sense of anti-climax. Those who had fought on the eastern front reacted quite differently however: they were genuinely pleased. I talked to a youthful legionnaire who came from one of the leading families of France and was

25

concealing his true identity behind the anonymity of the white kepi. He whispered to me: 'Indochina isn't the end of the road. It won't be long before we find out the real destination of this mission – Vladivostok and the Far-Eastern provinces of the Soviet Union.' The struggle between East and West, soon to be dubbed the Cold War, was already under way. On board the *Andus* we could talk about little else as we sailed through the phosphorescent waters of the Indian Ocean, on course for Malacca.

The cabins on board ship were stuffy and overcrowded. As we headed East the night air became increasingly hot and humid. In the evenings the troops would stay on deck till the last possible moment, trying to get a breath of fresh air. They would play cards or peer into the darkness. The women serving in the auxiliary force, the AFAT, used to hang around the lifeboats in the late evening, waiting for gallant officers to come and chat to them. Then all they had to do was push back the tarpaulin covers on one of the boats and they had a ready-made love-nest between the rowers' seats and the rudder. Most of these army girls seemed quite unembarrassed at being surrounded by so many men. They tended to wear a lot of make-up, and some were so free-and-easy in manner that they were soon suspected of having good reasons for wanting to get out of France. Some may well have had affairs with German soldiers during the occupation. Others had probably worked as prostitutes in a Wehrmacht brothel. There was, in fact, a fair amount of squabbling and jealousy over women on board the *Andus*.

One evening a narrow-chested cavalry lieutenant, who had a blond moustache and pale skin, and would have looked more at home in a novel by Proust, quoted some lines of a poem by Heredia. 'Like a flight of hawks . . . Weary of enduring their proud misery . . . Drunk with a brutal and warlike dream . . .' So ran the over-blown lines of the 'Conquistador', which every French schoolboy must have had to learn. '. . . Leaning over the bows of their white caravel, they discovered at night those new constellations that rose out of the depths of the ocean into an unknown heaven . . .'

Buddha Astride the Tiger

Cochin China, Spring 1946

The military convoy drove out of Saigon and headed for the rubber plantations of the neighbouring province north-west of the city. We could now see more definite signs of the guerilla war being fought in the area. The surface of the tarmac road had been cut into by deep trenches; apparently the Red commissars forced local peasants to dig them every night under cover of darkness. The French had christened these ruts in the ground 'piano keys', because they were so regular and even. Over in the east the morning sky was beginning to turn a greenish yellow. We drove on in the direction of Tay Ninh. After travelling a short time we suddenly saw, beyond the palm trees and interminable ricefields, a black mountain. It rose menacingly out of the flat plain. This sinister-looking cliff-face was the Black Virgin and it marked the border with Cambodia. None of us could have guessed at the time that the Black Virgin would one day strike awe into the hearts of American GIs, like some avenging Fury.

We got out of our vehicles and left the road, walking deeper into the jungle. Above us packs of monkeys flitted through the dense branches of the bamboo trees. The chirping of the birds gradually died away as the heat grew more intense; the green vegetation turned black in the strong sunlight and the air began to shimmer. We were out on patrol with a French commando unit – just one more routine operation as far as they were concerned. The soldiers walked along the dykes that divided up the bare paddy fields, a procession of figures silhouetted clearly against the sky. Suddenly a shot rang out from somewhere. In those early days of the war, the Vietnamese guerillas had few weapons and even less training, so the unit was not in any great danger. In fact the only time the French really sustained any losses was when they came up against rebels who had been reinforced and trained by members of the 'Kempeitai', the Japanese military police who were wanted in Saigon for war crimes.

We continued marching for several hours in a dog-leg curve that led around the foot of the Black Virgin, heading in the direction of the Cambodian border. By this time the sun had baked the paddy fields to the consistency of hard brick. The commandos stared at the ground in front of them as they walked. The cracks in the clay soil and the parched stalks of the rice plants danced before their eyes with a hallucinatory clarity. Beads of burning sweat trickled down their faces. Suddenly shots were fired at us again, this time from a farm hidden in the bamboo. The soldiers quickly established the direction of the shots. They fixed bayonets on their Sten guns, specially adapted for hand-to-hand combat. Then they charged the thicket, firing from the hip as they ran. Shadows darted across the paddy field. The French had already set up their machine gun, and as the figures came within its arc of fire they toppled to the ground.

We went over to look at the men who had been shot. They looked oddly pathetic lying there – little yellow dolls with twisted limbs. Old-fashioned Lebel rifles lay on the ground beside them and their thin, stringy legs stuck out of their shorts. The outfits they were wearing could hardly be called uniforms, but they all had a scrap of red cloth with a yellow star – the badge of the Indochinese revolution – sewn onto their black smocks. The badge told us one thing: these dead peasants were not members of the Cao Dai. The Cao Dai was a strange religious sect also fighting the French in this region; its main shrine, a hideously ornate building, was in Tay Ninh. No, the badge identified the men as belonging instead to the Communist Liberation Front of Vietnam. It was this organization, calling itself by an assortment of different names, that would keep the rest of the world guessing for the next thirty years.

The people of the surrounding villages had fled as soon as they saw foreign soldiers approaching. The villagers lived in simple rectangular huts, each furnished with a wide bed made of wooden planks and a few mats on the floor. Despite the lack of furniture, every home had its ancestral altar. The huts were spotlessly clean and tidy, and a European would have found them perfectly habitable. The soldiers filled their water bottles from the wide-bottomed pitchers that stood outside every hut. The water in them was slimy and lukewarm; it was hardly surprising that cases of amoebic dysentery were on the increase.

Before we resumed our march the soldiers set fire to the hamlet. One match was all it took to set the straw roofs alight. The water buffalo left behind by the peasants were shot. A little Cao Dai temple went up in flames too. I managed to catch a glimpse of the interior through the smoke, and I saw the bare table that served as an altar, with all the saints lined up in a row (Cao Dai was a syncretic religion and a rather confused one at that). I spotted a tiny statue of a pot-bellied Buddha made out of earthenware. The figure was sitting astride a tiger and holding out its little hands with an impish smile.

The next attack on the commando unit killed one man and wounded two. In retaliation, the French killed ten Communist guerillas and left their bodies floating in the stagnant water of a nearby irrigation ditch. A briefing was held afterwards in a large farmhouse. Colonel Ponchardier, known as the Pasha to his men, was not at all happy with the way things were going. As he saw it, this was no way to fight a war. He was a stocky little man, built like a wrestler, with more than a passing resemblance to the actor Lino Ventura. In the past he had done such things as training a special unit to make a joint parachute jump over Singapore with the British SAS. Not surprisingly, he found the war in Cochin China something of a come-down after that. It would have been impossible for anyone who didn't know Ponchardier to single him out from the rest of his men as he sat there, stripped to the waist, with his green jungle-hat clamped on his head. The Pasha never let his sub-machine gun out of his sight, and he always had an ancient car horn clipped to his belt. When he went into action he would toot it from time to time – his way of sounding the recall. With his small unit of 150 men, the Pasha reported directly to the French commander-in-chief in Indochina. His troops refused to salute any officers outside their own unit. They evidently thought they were a cut above the other regiments in the Expeditionary Force which had come out to Saigon after them.

As a young officer Ponchardier had joined up with de Gaulle's Free French in 1940. While working for the French Resistance during the occupation, he founded an organization called Sosias. His brother Dominique had helped him (they looked uncannily like each other, and *sosie* means 'double' in French). Among other exploits, he successfully freed a group of Resistance fighters being held prisoner by the Gestapo in Amiens, backed up by an accurate bombing strike by the RAF. Dominique recorded the adventures of this oddball pair of swashbuckling heroes in his book, *The Pavements of Hell*. He describes, among other things, the strange sensation a Resistance leader experiences when he strangles a traitor from among his own ranks with his bare hands. Some years after the end of the Algerian campaign, Pierre Ponchardier, by now an admiral (he originally came from the French Fleet Air Arm), was killed in an aeroplane crash over French Senegal. As for Dominique, he rose to become ambassador to Bolivia and high commissioner in Djibouti. But his biggest success, as far as he was concerned, was his best-selling spy series based on the adventures of the Gorilla. The Gorilla, as de Gaulle once remarked when he received his ambassador, was probably none other than Dominique himself.

Ponchardier's commando unit had a reputation for being a tough bunch of thugs and mercenaries. But it did include one or two respectable people, sons of 'good' families who were trying to kick over the traces and break away from their strict middle-class background. The unit had its fair share of characters. There was one, for instance, who was an expert on China. He had an enormous eagle tattooed on his chest, and he could tell amazingly funny stories about the Sons of Heaven (a nickname for the Chinese). Then there was the pair of Parisian spivs who, it seemed, were involved in the prostitution business before they joined up. Everyone reckoned they were there only because they wanted to cash in on the commando's entitlement to claim spoils of war inside the combat zone. There were also one or two mavericks from a news agency who had baled out over the hill country around Tongking after the Japanese surrender. While in the north they had met up with the demoralized remnants of the former French army in Indochina which had recognized Pétain during the war and been smashed by the Japanese in March 1945, just when they were thinking of going over to the Allies. The outlying provinces and ethnic minorities of France were well represented in the unit, too – there were Alsatians, Corsicans, Bretons and Basques. It was hard to imagine how these men would manage to readjust to normal civilian life when they were eventually demobbed. Even the Pasha seemed to think some of them were a bit dubious. 'Next time I form a troop,' he grumbled to me, 'I'll choose nice respectable lads. They've got more guts and stamina than crooks in the long run. Crooks soon run out of steam.'

The officers in the unit went on to have fairly chequered careers. There was Captain Quilici, for instance, who always reminded me of a Corsican *bandit d'honneur*. When I ran into him again twenty years later, he was serving as a paratroop colonel with the marines in Chad and was on a tour of inspection of the northern oases in the Tibesti-Enedi desert. Then there was Lieutenant Augustin, who looked very much the religious type, even in those days. You came across this kind of thing quite often in the French officer corps; the links between the sable and ciborium go back a long way. After the Algeria débâcle he turned his back on the army and gave up the glamorous life of soldiering to become a lay brother in a Dominican monastery. In the end, though, the officer who had the most amazing career of all was Captain Trinquier. He had served with the colonial infantry in Shanghai, which was a French concession in those days, before joining Ponchardier's outfit. The Pasha wasn't too keen on this exquisitely dressed young man with the Mediterranean good looks. Even in the jungle the captain was never seen without a silk cravat, and he tended to stand out from the others because of his refined way of talking. In the closing stages of the war, Trinquier went on to organize pockets of resistance behind the Viet Minh lines, working among a pro-French hill-tribe, the Meo. He was also responsible for the savage repression of terrorists in the Algiers casbah in the late 1950s in Algeria. At the time, though, nobody in the unit would have believed him capable of anything so daring. After the generals' coup against de Gaulle, Trinquier was discharged from the army and he ended up serving as a colonel in Moise Tshombe's forces in Africa.

We resumed our march. After a time we suddenly saw a group of Cambodian peasants coming towards us in single file. We could tell at once they were Khmer because they had dark skin and curly hair and were wearing sarongs tied round their hips. When they caught sight of the French troops they knelt down and put their hands together in an age-old gesture of obeisance.

Now, at last, we were beginning to see signs of human habitation, the first we had encountered since entering Cambodian territory. The houses were built on piles along the banks of rivers or streams. Even the landscape began to take on a different appearance, with solitary, windswept sugar-palms rising high above the paddy fields. At the next village we stopped to take on porters. The powerfully-built Cambodians were delighted to hire themselves out to the French if it meant there was a chance of Vietnamese being killed. The Vietnamese and the Cambodians had been bitter enemies for centuries. When we first ran into action the porters panicked at the sound of firing. But they soon got used to it and ended up breaking out into child-like laughter every time shots were fired.

In the distance we could see the old French fort of Tay Ninh. It looked like a toy castle in the evening sunlight with its embrasures, merlons and towers. The fort dated back to the early period of colonization, when the first French conquerors in Cochin China had waged war against the river pirates. Inside the fort there were folding camp beds, each with a mosquito net, for us to sleep on. Darkness fell quickly and the night was clammy and airless. Someone had managed to get hold of some red wine, which the soldiers drank with their rations. After a while the casements of the old fortress began to echo to the sound of drunken revelry.

Earlier that day, during the afternoon, a squad of Special Police from Saigon had arrived at the fort to interrogate some prisoners. When we arrived we learned that the police, who were mainly Eurasian, had tortured the suspects by holding their heads under water until they confessed. This particular form of torture was known as the bathtub. Another method used electrodes and a small generator, but it hadn't yet been used in Indochina. The Asians were rumoured to have terrifyingly sophisticated ways of forcing stubborn prisoners to talk – so woe betide any European who got himself captured by guerillas. Several times we had come across the bodies of French soldiers floating in rivers and lakes. The corpses had been impaled on bamboo stakes with their testicles stuffed in their mouths.

While the men inside the fort enjoyed their drink and shouted for Cambodian girls to be brought to them, outside on the fringes of the jungle the advance guards stood at their posts in twos or threes. To the men out there, isolated and surrounded by danger, the jungle seemed to echo with the sounds of the entire animal kingdom. The smaller an insect was, the more noise it seemed to make. In the silences between the bursts of sound they could hear faint dartings and rustlings as nature pursued its remorseless round of hunting and killing. Only the fear of being laughed at prevented the guards from firing wildly into the invisible world of pattering, buzzing and screeching fauna teeming all around – and which provided cover for enemy scouts to creep up on them undetected.

In a turret room inside the fort the commando officers busily digested the information passed on to them by an intelligence agent from Saigon. The expert from the Intelligence Service was half Chinese and had an alert, birdlike expression. He had supervised the torture sessions earlier that day. By this stage in the war the French had lost most of the illusions they had had when they first came out to Indochina. In 1945 de Gaulle had had liaison officers parachuted into the areas where the Vietnamese were in revolt; some had been sent in even before the Japanese had surrendered to the Allies. The theory behind this, according to Paris, was that anti-Japanese guerillas in Tongking and Cochin

China would welcome the French as friends and liberators. Unfortunately, however, things did not go according to plan. Most of these courageous men died soon after being parachuted in, but not before being subjected to the most excruciating torture. The survivors – men, for example like Pierre Messmer, a future French prime minister – were imprisoned by the Communist guerillas in bamboo cages so the local populace could spit at them and pelt them with rotten eggs. They were the lucky ones, however, and were grateful to have got off so lightly.

The man from the Intelligence Service told the French officers about the recent change in the political situation in the Tay Ninh area. Initially the Expeditionary Force had been expected to encounter most opposition from those groups and sects that had collaborated with the Japanese, no doubt in the hope that they might eventually grant them independence. In the provinces around Tay Ninh, the main opposition came from the million and a half followers of the Cao Dai religion, while in the Mekong Delta itself, on the edge of the Plain of Reeds, the opposition was concentrated among the Hoa Hao, a militant Buddhist movement of about 600,000 members. Both sects had their own private militias, ready to go into action. Lately, it appeared, these rather muddle-headed religious fanatics had begun to see the arrival of the Communist revolutionaries as a threat to their own existence. In addition they still felt an instinctive antipathy towards the materialistic ideology of the Can Bo, the Communist commissars who went about stirring up the local peasants with missionary zeal. Because of this shift in attitude, the sects were now anxious to reach an agreement with their erstwhile colonial rulers – on the one condition that the French respected the autonomy of the Cao Dai and Hoa Hao. The sects would clearly be useful allies for the French, if only because they alone seemed to possess the necessary spiritual motivation to withstand the ideological onslaught of Communism.

In April 1945 the Japanese had declared the emperor of Annam, Bao Dai (meaning 'Guardian of Greatness'), head of state of an independent kingdom of Vietnam. The anti-Communist Vietnamese could still vividly recall the humiliation of seeing this puppet ruler being installed. In order to remain in power, Bao Dai, who had been emperor since the age of twelve, had to rely on the backing of the pro-Japanese Dai Viet Party and the mandarins in Hue. Despite their support, however, he only managed to hold out a few weeks against the guerilla leader from north Tongking, the man with the goatee beard who had proclaimed in Hanoi the new Democratic Republic of Vietnam and who went by the name of Ho Chi Minh.

Ho Chi Minh was no stranger to the French Intelligence Service. He had gone to France for the first time as a young man and worked in a photographic laboratory; by 1920, when the French Communist Party was founded in Tours, he was already official Far East representative. Later he went on to work his way through the ranks of the Comintern. In World War II he took up the fight against the Japanese, operating out of the South China border region with a small band of faithful followers. At that time, ironically enough, Ho Chi Minh was receiving support from the American secret service, the Office of Strategic Services. The OSS, which was based in the provincial Chinese town of Kunming, was supplying financial and military aid to the Viet Minh, the national coalition of Vietnamese Communists.

In those days, just after the end of the war, Colonel Ponchardier still had hopes of being called on to do great things with his commandos. A campaign by the British had enabled the French to gain a foothold in the southern half of Indochina. North of the 16th parallel, however, in Tongking, Annam and northern Laos, Chiang Kai-shek's Kuomintang divisions had been entrusted with the task of disarming the Japanese. What had happened, in effect, was that the Chinese had established themselves as the new occupying force in the north. It was obvious to all that they had not the slightest intention of handing back their unexpected conquest to the former colonial administration. If it had been left to President Roosevelt – a committed and romantic anti-colonialist – not a single French soldier would ever have been allowed back into Indochina. But Roosevelt died just when Japan surrendered, and the British were happy for the French and Dutch to retain their former possessions, particularly as they had been left in a state of complete chaos and disruption by the Japanese. Perhaps at that point in the proceedings the British should have tried to divert the tide of Asian nationalism by setting up a buffer zone in Indochina and Indonesia. Great Britain (still regarded as 'perfidious Albion' by the French) could then have instituted a system of government there based on the far-sighted and liberal model of the Commonwealth.

That night in Tay Ninh the French paratroop officers knew only too well that the fate of Vietnam was not going to be decided either in southern Cochin China or in the mud of the Mekong Delta. The

real battleground would be the rugged and inhospitable north –
then still called Tongking – where the forces of Chiang Kai-shek's
Nationalists and Ho Chi Minh's Communists now confronted
each other in a tense and uneasy truce. The Pasha had just received
a secret report from General Leclerc instructing him to prepare
his commandos for a possible parachute jump over Hanoi.
However the operation was to be delayed until a sufficiently large
French invasion fleet could be assembled off Cap St Jacques,
ready to sail for Tongking. The officers in the unit greeted the
news of the operation with mixed feelings. The last time they had
carried out a series of practice jumps over the airstrip at Bien Hoa
they had found out, too late, that the parachutes had been badly
damaged by the effects of the climate and lack of proper care.
There had even been a couple of serious accidents because of the
lack of auxiliary parachutes. And to make matters worse, Paris
seemed to have underestimated both the fanatical fighting spirit of
the Vietnamese and the strength of the Chinese presence in the
north.

During the early morning there was a sudden heavy shower of
rain. The sun had already dried the wet ground by the time I
arrived outside the shrine of the Cao Dai, a massive yellow
building in the style of a French cathedral. The vegetation on the
steep slopes of the Black Virgin glistened deep green in the early
morning light. When we first arrived in Tay Ninh we had not
expected things to have got back to normal quite to the extent they
had, and we were surprised to find the cathedral more than half
full for the morning service. The 'pope' of the Cao Dai had fled to
Thailand, but the majority of the clergy – including a college of
cardinals and several bishops – had stayed on. The French left the
sect very much to its own devices, and it was allowed to carry on its
bizarre rituals in the huge echoing nave more or less undisturbed.
Inside the cathedral, in the place where the high altar would have
been in a Catholic church, there was an enormous eye. It was set
inside a triangle surrounded by rays, and it stared out over the
congregation. The priests wore silk robes of blue, red or yellow,
depending on their rank; these tapered off to a pointed, Ku Klux
Klan-style hood at the top. The ordinary worshippers were
dressed in white. The low murmur of prayers that rose from the
congregation reminded me of Christian litanies and Buddhist
Sutras. The congregation bowed repeatedly during the service,
gongs were sounded at regular intervals and clouds of incense
floated up through the air towards the mystical eye.

The strange religion of the Cao Dai had been founded comparatively recently, in the early 1920s. The saints in the pantheon who were particularly venerated included Buddha, Confucius, Jesus Christ, and, amazingly enough, the French poet, Victor Hugo. Crude effigies of all these prophets, made out of garishly coloured plaster of Paris, stood at the entrance to the cathedral. The thing that most amused French visitors was the statue of Victor Hugo, who had evidently been included in the roll of Cao Dai saints because of the humanist message of *Les Misérables*. Hugo, wearing the green dress uniform of a member of the French Academy, gazed over the palm grove that grew outside the cathedral. I noticed that the bearded face below the three-cornered hat bore a striking resemblance to the traditional portrait of Karl Marx, and I felt strangely moved by the similarity between the two men. When all was said and done, nobody could afford to dismiss the Cao Dai lightly. After all, every religious institution that was ever founded has some peculiarity or other. One thing was certain: the Cao Dai were not going to be a permanent feature of the religious scene in Vietnam. But in its fanatical devotion, its search for models abroad, and its commitment to nationalism the sect was similar to the underground religion of Vietnamese Communism. This tenacious ideological faith had already seized a share of power in Hanoi, and the number of followers in the Mekong Delta was increasing all the time.

The French were convinced they knew how to handle the people of Annam. In Cochin China there had grown up an indigenous middle-class of doctors, lawyers and plantation owners who had adopted the French language and way of life and even, in some cases, French nationality. Yet at the bottom of the social scale, below this élite minority, there lived a people who were probably known only to ethnologists who specialized in the Far East and a handful of missionaries. These were the subsistence rice farmers, or Nhaques as they were contemptuously called, who had served as baggage-train soldiers in World War I. They had not been allowed to enlist as fighting troops because they were thought to be unfit for combat duty. When the French Expeditionary Force first arrived in Vietnam, its members were told by so-called experts – those incorrigibly foolish colonial representatives, universally referred to by the respectable English term of 'old hands' – that the Annamites never fought at night because they were afraid of ghosts and tigers. In fact, as soon became obvious to the troops, the Vietnamese were the toughest fighting race in the whole of Asia, and their natural element was the dark.

Underneath the sectarian nonsense of Vietnamese religion there often lay a core of deadly serious political intent. A classic example of this was the strange congregation of the Saints of the Coconut Palm, which we came across on the banks of a branch of the Mekong River. Apparently one day a hunch-backed Annamite businessman suddenly had a divine call to found a new religion. The hunch-back, who developed the habit of meditating on a coconut palm, soon collected a large following. His disciples wore brown habits and lived a life of bizarre ritual and harsh self-discipline. Because their prophet's physical deformity prevented him from sleeping on his back, they always lay on their sides as an expression of their love for him. The main shrine was located on a pile settlement in the middle of the river, but the ornate churches of the Brown Fathers were to be seen all the way to the suburbs of Saigon.

I saw a huge globe of the world placed on a broad platform in the middle of the river. On this globe Vietnam had been enlarged to several times its actual size so that it stretched to the very edge of the Pacific Ocean, from Kamchatka to Australia. I asked a pious-looking old man, who had seven hairs on his chin in the traditional manner of a Taoist saint, what this map of Vietnam signified. He replied, in surprisingly fluent French: 'When Vietnam is united, and free once more, and Cochin China, Annam and Tongking are one state again, then we shall be as great and as powerful as the map on the globe shows.' What no French administrator or colonial official had managed to grasp was that the religious ferment in this strife-torn country heralded the dawning of a new era, a new Vietnamese nation. But then could any proconsul or centurion in the Roman province of Syria ever have imagined that the spiritual unrest among the local Jewish population would eventually usher in the end of imperial rule, and bring about a total shift of consciousness in the classical world?

As the commando unit was driving back to its regular billet in a rambling old Chinese house half-way between Saigon and Cholon, our column was held up by an unusually large crowd blocking the road. A long procession of troops from the combined services was marching three abreast through the streets of central Saigon. They carried no weapons and they were led by officers. We asked somebody in the crowd what was going on. It seemed that a small group of French pacifists and left-wing anti-colonialists had distributed leaflets demanding the withdrawal of French forces from Indochina. The pamphlets accused the Expeditionary Force of having *honneur et profit* inscribed on its flag instead of *honneur et patrie*. The troops taking part in the demonstration had already wrecked the protesters' printing press. Now, as we waited among the crowd, we heard a chorus of voices coming from the direction of the Rue Catinat, chanting, 'de Gaulle for President!' In January 1946, de Gaulle had surprised everyone by resigning as leader of the provisional government in France. He had then retreated in high dudgeon to his country home at Colombey-les-deux-Eglises in protest at the fresh outbreak of inter-party squabbling that was threatening France's parliamentary government with collapse. As a result the army in Indochina, which contained a strong Gaullist element, suddenly found itself without a spokesman. The situation was made worse by the fact that the parties of the French Left were beginning to stir up opposition to the campaign in the Far East. The French Communists were not the only ones who supported the Vietnamese Nationalists, if this incident was anything to go by. 'De Gaulle for President!' The cry went up a few more times, then a squad of military police chased the demonstrators back to their barracks without much difficulty. Twelve years were to elapse before the same cry – this time taken by a vast crowd in the forum of Algiers – was to usher in the fall of the Fourth Republic.

Uncle Ho's Pact with the French

Haiphong, Spring 1946

The Bay of Halong lay shrouded eerily in mist. Gradually it lifted a little to reveal a host of limestone cliffs, their fantastic shapes rising steeply out of the still, green waters of the bay. A cold drizzling rain fell continuously. The troops taking part in the French landing stood shivering by the ship's railing, wishing they were back in the heat of Saigon. One or two junks loomed out of the mist, and soon more came to join them. The flat-bottomed boats had whole families on board, crowded into primitive living quarters. Their dark brown sails made the junks look more like bats flitting over the surface of the water. The Vietnamese boat-dwellers evidently wanted to make contact with the foreign invaders. They were dressed in rags, and judging by the way they pounced on the scraps of food that fell from the ship's hatches, they must have been famished. They even fished empty tin cans out of the water and hoarded them like a precious find. On first acquaintance, the fisherfolk of Halong seemed to be fairly well-disposed towards us, and they talked non-stop. The soldiers tried making friendly overtures to the young girls, but when they managed to coax a few smiles out of them they were horrified to see that their teeth were painted black.

For three days now the fleet had been lying off the northern port of Haiphong. General Leclerc had already gone ashore to try and negotiate with the leaders of the Chinese Nationalist army. Back in February Chiang Kai-shek's government had already agreed in theory to the replacement of Chinese forces by the French Army. It appeared, however, that the Generalissimo had very little control over the warlords in Yunnan province, and their armies had invaded Tongking, pillaging and looting as they went. The Chinese Nationalist hordes had descended on northern Vietnam like a plague of locusts. They had plundered and raped and generally behaved like a conquering army, carrying all before them. Not surprisingly, they were none too pleased at the thought of having to withdraw and relinquish the territory that had just been handed to them on a plate.

On the fourth day the sound of artillery fire echoed round the strangely beautiful Bay of Halong. The French High Command had finally lost patience with the Chinese. A commando assault troop landed on the coast, and the cruiser *Le Triomphant* sailed up the estuary of the Red River heading for Haiphong harbour. The cruiser was fired on by coastal batteries, but it quelled the resistance with a few salvoes in return. The white flag was raised above the Chinese emplacements and the battle was over. When the French went ashore they were surprised to find that the enemy guns had been fired by Japanese prisoners of war, as the troops from Yunnan had no idea how to operate them.

I never tired of watching the Chinese Nationalist troops on the move. They were fairly tall in comparison with the Vietnamese, and they wore sky-blue uniforms with thick puttees. When marching they preferred to sling their boots over their shoulders and go barefoot. Unlike the Tongkingese, who would crowd inquisitively round new arrivals and bombard them with questions, the Chinese maintained a psychological distance between themselves and the French, a barrier of reserve that was never completely lowered. And for all their shiny new lorries from General Motors, and the physical exercises they did with much bellowing and shouting every morning in the parks of Haiphong, the Sons of Heaven seemed more like a medieval rabble than a modern, disciplined army. When it came to looting they made no distinction in Haiphong between the native Vietnamese and the prosperous Chinese business community. The latter, for their part, made no attempt to conceal the repugnance they felt towards the marauding hordes, and they gave free rein to their innate Confucian disdain for all things military.

The Japanese prisoners of war in Haiphong were totally different. The Japanese army had remained a disciplined body, and officers would strut about among the ranks like cocks of the walk. Later, when the time came to sail home, they gathered in their thousands on the quayside, ready to board the American cargo ships that were to take them back to the Land of the Rising Sun. The Japanese had suffered defeat, the first in their history.

Slowly it began to dawn on the French administrators and Far East experts who had returned to Tongking that the world was completely changed, that powerful and uncontrollable forces had been unleashed. The first man to make a realistic assessment of the new situation in Indochina was General Leclerc de Hautecloque. Leclerc is portrayed in one of Hemingway's novels as a typically arrogant member of the landowning aristocracy, but the description is unfair both to the man as an individual and to his record as an army commander. It was Leclerc who, in 1940, assembled the first unit of Free French troops in Central Africa. He spent the next three years crossing the deserts of Chad and Libya, not stopping until he reached the shores of the Mediterranean. In the summer of 1944 he landed on the Normandy beaches with his Second Tank Division, and General Eisenhower allowed his unit to be the first Allied division to enter Paris. The General got precious little thanks from Leclerc, however; in the winter of 1944–45 the Frenchman, acting against the express orders of his commander-in-chief, led his troops over the Vosges mountains and into the Rhine plain. He advanced on Strasbourg and there, fulfilling a romantic vow he had made under the palm trees of the Oases of Kufra, he hoisted the tricolour over the cathedral.

This slim, headstrong man, who never went anywhere without his walking stick, was now dealing with a very different type of rebel – the revolutionary leader Ho Chi Minh. Very few Frenchmen in Indochina at that time realized the deeper implications of the secret talks that went on between Leclerc and Uncle Ho, as he was known to his followers. Admiral Thierry d'Argenlieu, who had been sent to the Far East on de Gaulle's orders, was no exception. Before the war, d'Argenlieu, an ardent Gaullist from the start, had been abbot of a Carmelite monastery. Now he was appointed French High Commissioner in Indochina, with full administrative powers. During his time there he conducted himself like a latter-day crusader. He opposed anything that vaguely hinted of compromise with France's enemies and was soon dubbed the 'Bloody Monk' by the left-wing press in Paris.

Ho Chi Minh realized that a continuing Chinese presence in Tongking would strike a far worse blow to Vietnam's hopes of independence than any temporary deal struck with the French. After all, French colonial rule had lasted just under a century, but the Vietnamese people had been fighting for 2000 years to resist domination and total assimilation by China. There were also immediate political considerations to be taken into account. The Kuomintang Chinese now found they were having to deal with a Marxist government led by the Viet Minh United National Front. Not surprisingly, the Chinese Nationalists were suspicious of Ho Chi Minh's National Assembly, as it belonged to the same ideological camp as their arch-enemy, Mao Tse-tung. The situation was further complicated by the existence of a group of middle-class Nationalists in Indochina who modelled themselves on Chiang Kai-shek's Chinese party. In 1931 this group had sparked off a rebellion against French rule that had to be savagely put down by the colonial authorities. During the thirties the Communist Party in Indochina had succeeded in building up a tiny network of cells with the help of French Marxists. Ho had to bide his time until events in World War II gave him an opportunity to go into action with his guerilla force, which by this time was far better organized than his middle-class rivals in the Nationalist Party of Vietnam. The VNQDD (the initials stood for Vietnam Quoc Dan Dang) had returned to Hanoi in the wake of the Kuomintang Chinese, who forced Ho Chi Minh to make room for them in his government. Ho agreed to this with some reluctance, for he had an intense hatred of these 'class enemies'. During the winter of 1945–46 clashes between the Viet Minh and the VNQDD were numerous. As Ho saw it, his whole future now depended on French troops ousting the Chinese from Tongking.

General Leclerc saw the Marxist Ho Chi Minh as a potential ally for France. Since France's defeat in 1940, her colonial empire had become a thing of the past. The intention now was for the introduction of a new era of liberal relations between metropolitan France and her overseas territories. Ho Chi Minh proposed that the Democratic Republic of Vietnam should continue to exist as part of a joint confederation with France. He was prepared for Paris to retain control of such matters as diplomatic representation, defence and finance, pending further negotiations. In the end both sides came to a rather odd arrangement by which a French force was to be sent into the area north of the 16th parallel to save the Tongking Communists from being encircled by the combined forces of the Chinese Kuomintang and the Vietnamese VNQDD. The government of the Fourth Republic, which had just been given a mandate in a recent referendum, agreed to allow the Viet Minh a free hand in the north. France also obtained assurances that Chiang Kai-shek's forces would quit Vietnam.

Both parties well knew that they had made a pact with the devil. There was no great love for decolonization among the French Army, and the majority of right-wing officers loathed the Viet Minh commissars. However, in accordance with the terms of the agreement, the Chinese finally marched back across the border into Kwangsi and Yunnan, laden with the spoils of victory. Thereupon the first action of the revolutionary committee of the Viet Minh was to wipe out their rivals. The French, perhaps unwisely, did not lift a finger to stop the liquidation of these anti-Communist forces. In years to come they would bitterly regret the loss of these potential allies in the struggle for Vietnam. The French colonels were secretly itching to get their hands on the Viet Minh. They wanted nothing more than to re-establish the *pax franca* in the Far East by military force.

The Vietnamese, on the other hand, made no attempt to disguise their real intentions. It seemed that on every inch of wall or road the magic words *Doc Lap* were painted in huge red letters. *Doc Lap* meant 'independence' in Vietnamese, and only a fool could have imagined that these fanatical, Marxist-inspired Nationalists would ever settle for anything less than full sovereignty over Vietnam. Ho Chi Minh and his followers would never submit to French rule in Indochina, no matter what the terms. There were other, equally insistent wall inscriptions calling for the Unification of the Three Ky, the three parts of Vietnam – Tongking, Annam and Cochin China. The Viet Minh revolutionaries knew that, if it came to the crunch, the leading French financiers connected with the Bank of Indochina would pull out of the overpopulated Red River region in Tongking and abandon its starving masses to their fate. The French would be equally prepared to write off the inhospitable mountain region of central Annam. But the Viet Minh knew that these influential moguls would never consider abandoning their interests in Cochin China, in particular the lucrative rubber plantations in the south and the fertile rice plain of the Mekong. These important wealth-producing areas would be formed into a separate republic under French control.

During the weeks that followed the declaration of the new republic in the north, some strange sights could be seen in Haiphong. The official flag of the country was now the Viet Minh's red banner with its yellow star, and it was flown beside the French tricolour on all public buildings. The new Democratic Republic now had its own army, with its own distinctive reddish-brown uniforms and green pith helmets. The men were mostly armed with weapons captured from the Japanese. Uncle Ho's pint-sized troops went out on joint patrols with French colonial infantrymen. These reluctant comrades-at-arms had been more or less thrown together by fate, and no love was lost between them. The French staff officers felt it was beneath them to have to fight on an equal footing with the Viet Minh, who were little better than snipers after all. The French knew for a fact that the Viet Minh military leader, Vo Nguyen Giap, had learnt everything he knew about military strategy from history textbooks. And Giap's professed admiration for Napoleon merely won him condescending smiles from his French allies.

The spell of cool, rainy weather suddenly came to an end. In the space of a week the temperature in Tongking rose sharply and the place sweltered in the heat. The air was now so clear that the rugged foothills in the distance looked close enough to touch. Everyone was slowly beginning to realize that North Vietnam would be a grim country to fight a war in. As for Haiphong itself, apart from two well-laid-out squares that would have done credit to a French provincial town, it had little to commend it. Still, spring had come, and the jacarandas and flamboyants were blooming in all their purple and crimson glory.

At that time I was staying in a house beside a canal in a fairly drab district of Haiphong, where the outskirts of the town merged with the monotonous expanse of rice paddies. Every night we could hear revolutionary battle-songs coming from the nearby villages. Through our telescopes we used to watch the Viet Minh militia exercising in the distance. They often used bamboo sticks because they were short of rifles. Then one morning the mutilated bodies of three French engineers were found in the canal, floating out to sea. The days of the phoney truce, the so-called '*modus vivendi*', were numbered. A week later I was ordered back to Saigon. I duly embarked on the French cruiser *Tourville*, which was lying off the Bay of Halong. As I went on board in the fading redness of the setting sun, a breathtaking sight lay before me. The still waters of the bay shone like pure gold in the evening light, and the black limestone cliffs loomed up like prehistoric megaliths. As the evening star sank in the west the junks sailed past, making broad sweeping curves on the water, like insects circling a flame.

The Changing Face of the War

Saigon, Spring 1951

Four years later I sat on board the Paris–Saigon plane, a DC-4 that took three days and two stopovers to reach its destination. Most of the other passengers were powerfully-built men of military age. All had army crew-cuts but were dressed in civilian clothes. The Indian authorities had been wary of letting the plane stop over in Calcutta, and the last thing they wanted to see was a French uniform. Back home, the Paris press had splashed the bad news from the Far East across every front page. First of all the plans for the defence of the Red River Delta had been leaked to the enemy. Then the French Chief of Staff, who went by the ominous name of Revers (the word means 'defeat' in French), decided at the last minute to evacuate the border garrisons whose job it was to defend Tongking against attack from the Chinese provinces to the north.

These border outposts had been under threat since Mao Tse-tung's victorious armies marched into the southern Chinese provinces of Kwangsi and Yunnan. The new People's Republic of China had publicly declared its support for Ho Chi Minh. It was already sending supplies of equipment to its Communist allies across the border, and the successful methods that had been employed in the war against Chiang Kai-shek were being used to train the Vietnamese Revolutionary Army in Nanning. Recently a French column of 3000 men, retreating from the border town of Cao Bang, had been ambushed as it climbed the hairpin bends of a mountainous jungle track. The entire force had been virtually wiped out. The garrison at Lang Son narrowly escaped a similar fate by taking to their heels and leaving all their supplies and equipment behind. Mao's victory in China meant that the French cordon sanitaire in northern Indochina could no longer hold. In the past, public opinion in France had veered between a complete lack of interest in the Far East campaign and fierce criticism of it. Now the Paris press was preparing to break the news of the decisive defeat of the Expeditionary Force in the Red River Delta. Pamphlets put out by the French Communist Party labelled the war in Indochina *la sale guerre* (the dirty war) and in the port of Marseilles dockers blacked ships bound for Saigon. It meant that reinforcements for the army in the Far East had to embark under cover of darkness. Even coffins of the dead shipped back to France had to be unloaded in secret.

This time round I had come to Saigon as a reporter. When I arrived in the city I didn't have to search very long to find the Pasha. I came across him sitting in an apartment on the Rue Catinat, sweating profusely and tinkering fondly with a complicated-looking radio transmitter. Anyone would have thought it was a time bomb, the way he handled it. Since I last saw him he had been awarded his first two admiral's stars, but you would never have guessed it by looking at him. He was in the process of forming a new commando unit of marine fusiliers. 'Don't hang around in Cochin China,' was his advice to me. 'It's all just routine stuff here now, and nobody's bothering very much. You want to go to the north – that's where the real action is. We're throwing all we've got at them right now.'

Two days previous to this, forty Viet Minh battalions had launched a major assault on the stronghold of Vinh Yen. Wave after wave of troops had been hurled at the fort, but the attack had collapsed in the face of heavy French artillery fire. Shortly before this the Revolutionary Army had overrun the military base at Vietri, and so they thought Vinh Yen was more or less in the bag. Confident of victory, they had committed half of their entire strength to the attack, and they had ended up losing 8000 men in a battle that lasted five days. Giap, the Viet Minh chief of staff, was a shrewd guerilla leader. He had wisely balked at the risk of fighting a pitched battle at Vinh Yen, but he had been overruled by the politburo of the Communist Lao Dong Party which represented the hard-liners in the Viet Minh. As it turned out, the Vietnamese Communists had been very unlucky: they had suddenly found themselves faced with a new French commander-in-chief, General Jean de Lattre de Tassigny. De Lattre de Tassigny was the kind of leader who would visit the front lines in person to sustain the morale of his men. He made several sweeping changes in the army in Indochina, including the reorganization of the existing French divisions into mobile combat groups known as *groupes mobiles*. His main contribution, however, was to step up the involvement of the air force, which had been hurriedly reinforced with American equipment. The air force was, in fact, to play a crucial role in the Vietnamese conflict. Viet Minh strategists had not considered that napalm would be dropped on their forces. The other new factor in the war was the attitude of the Americans. Mao Tse-tung's decisive victory had left the Communist guerillas with access to a vast area of impregnable hinterland behind the Chinese border. Until recently the belated colonial venture of the French in Indochina had been a thorn in the flesh of American diplomats. But now the United States was up to its neck in the Korean conflict, and the French could count on American help and support against the new threat from the north.

The face of Saigon had changed drastically in the four years since my last visit. The last traces of squalor and pollution that had followed in the wake of the Vietnamese revolutionaries' short-lived takeover had disappeared quite some time ago. Now Saigon looked more than ever like a sleepy French prefecture, basking in the tropical sun. The selection of goods on offer in the shops on the Rue Catinat was sufficient to satisfy the most discriminating tastes. The Corsican Mafia and various other speculators were currently growing rich on the proceeds of the trade in piastres. The piastre, the official currency of Indochina, was being bought up by racketeers at ludicrous black market prices and then transferred to banks in France at several times the official rate of exchange. Meanwhile young graduate officers from the military academy at St Cyr were bleeding to death in the ricefields. This was bad enough for the French soldiers on leave in Saigon, whose haggard faces showed the ravages of malaria. But what really made them angry was the sight of fat staff officers who spent the afternoons sunning themselves on the terrace of the Continental, knocking back brandies and soda. Then in the evening, to add insult to injury, these backroom boys would get off with all the best-looking Vietnamese tarts in the place. In the meantime the troops who were actually out fighting in the field had to make do with the delights of Buffalo Park, a huge piece of open ground at the top end of the Boulevard Galliéni. Buffalo Park was a big army brothel where nearly 1000 prostitutes from Annam and Cambodia plied their trade amid a great deal of shrieking and giggling. The girls were crudely made-up and scantily clad but, in the main, were extremely pretty. Any soldier who got past the guards on duty at the gate and entered the inner courtyard would be greeted by an unbelievable sight: all those women! It seemed too good to be true. Then, before he knew what was happening, his trousers would be literally ripped from his body.

And yet Saigon, the town that managed to be bourgeois and brazen at the same time, was not entirely untouched by the war. In the daytime all bars and restaurants had to be protected by close-meshed iron grilles because the Viet Minh assassination squad had a nasty habit of throwing grenades at men in uniform. At night signal rockets would flicker in the sky over the Rungsat marshes on the far bank of the Saigon River. At such times it was better to steer clear of Cholon, which was a short trishaw-ride from Saigon. Cholon had a close-knit Chinese community of a million people, most of whom were making more out of the war than all the French put together and who were going about their business as if the shooting and killing concerned them not at all. In the gambling dens of the Grand Monde, the red-light district of Cholon, the woven mahjong baskets were only for the benefit of less well-off punters. The rich Chinese preferred to gamble on the latest electronic machines. They would bet huge sums in an evening, their faces never betraying the slightest flicker of emotion. Next to the dens and fleshpots of the Grand Monde was the stinking, rat-infested river bank with its miserable rows of shacks huddled on top of one another. There were hundreds of houseboats along the water's edge, jammed up beside one another. The Viet Minh commissars were as much at home in this squalid district as the proverbial fish in water.

I left Saigon early next morning, heading south. Here in Cochin China, too, the war had taken on a new appearance. The tarmac road to My Tho and Can Tho was lined with wooden watch-towers – a sight reminiscent of Roman camps. These towers were positioned within seeing distance of each other so that sentries could send signals along the line. They were supposed to date back to an invention of General Galliéni, the commander responsible for pacifying Madagascar in the nineteenth century with his 'oil-spot' strategy. The emplacements around these rather anachronistic fortresses were protected by a fence of razor-sharp bamboo stakes. As this system of defence tied down too many troops at one time, the French High Command decided to replace their own men with local auxiliaries – anti-Communist volunteers. These new allies of the French, who wore the traditional black costume of the subsistence rice-farmers, were not regarded as particularly trustworthy. As a result, the French lance-corporals and NCOs, whose job it was to protect them, had a particularly nerve-racking time at night trying to keep them out of the clutches of the Viet Minh. As soon as it got dark the rustling and creeping and banging would start up out in the ricefields. A blast of noise would suddenly emerge from the darkness, silencing the bullfrogs, then loudspeakers would start blaring out Communist and Nationalist battle-songs and propaganda slogans. Occasionally sentries in these isolated forts came up with suitable methods of psychological warfare to get back at the enemy. A bearded sergeant from the Auvergne, for instance, used to play his scratched old records every night, and with the aid of an amplifier would send a selection of Viennese waltzes belting out in the direction of the invisible pioneers of world revolution.

At this stage in the war the French still had a relatively firm hold on Cochin China. This was due partly to the fact that the militant sects of the Cao Dai and Hoa Hao had made their peace with Paris and saw to it that Viet Minh infiltrators inside their territories were ruthlessly hunted down. The sects were driven by the same sort of motivation as the Communists, and they proved to be equally skilled at guerilla warfare. The Hoa Hao, in particular, would resort to any form of atrocity to achieve their ends. In Ben Tre province these sects were reinforced by a contingent of troops led by a Catholic Eurasian called Colonel Jean Leroy. Leroy was a tough customer and definitely not the type to stand for any nonsense. Again, in the area around Saigon and Cholon, the French had entered into an alliance with a band of river pirates called the Binh Xuyen. This gang of cut-throats took charge of policing the region in return for receiving a share of the profits from the gambling dens of the Grand Monde in Cholon. The Binh Xuyen were feared and hated by the locals. They were ruthlessly efficient, and all kinds of gruesome reports circulated about the methods they used to make people talk.

I met up with the Pasha again at Tan-Son-Nhut airport when I flew with him on a special flight to Hanoi. 'You see how low we've sunk,' he said with a wry laugh. 'Who would have believed, back in Tay Ninh, that one day we'd have these crazy Cao Dai for our friends and allies?'

The Arrival of the Aristocrat

Hanoi, Spring 1951

The cold, drizzling rain glistened on the runway at Gialam airport, east of Hanoi. The new fighter-bombers recently delivered by the Americans stood lined up at the edge of the strip. The French were still using a fleet of old Ju 52s to transport troops and equipment. Hanoi itself was situated on the far bank of the Red River (an apt name, as things had turned out). Over its swollen waters stretched the iron curve of the Paul Doumer Bridge, which had been regarded as a miracle of modern engineering in the days of the Third Republic. The bridge, however, was totally inadequate to cope with modern-day military traffic. For one thing, it was always clogged up with the overloaded rickshaws and buffalo teams of the local people. To complicate matters, the railway lines to and from Haiphong travelled across it too.

This one communication link over the Red River was guarded by a large contingent of black colonial troops. They were always referred to as the 'Senegalese', even though most of them came from the Upper Volta. These blacks stood shivering in the damp, raw air. Their eyes were as big as saucers in their coal-black faces as they looked morosely upon the endlessly moving, ant-like columns of Vietnamese. The inhabitants of Hanoi were so tiny that they barely came up to the shoulders of the bean-pole Africans. Soon after their arrival in Indochina it had become clear that these Africans were not cut out for fighting a guerilla war in Asia. They felt homesick and frightened in this hostile foreign land. Like everyone else, they had their Vietnamese whores to keep them company, but their women were completely ostracized by the locals, who were extremely racist. Sexual jealousy and

49

rivalry was common in the black units and there were frequent reports of stabbings among the men. The French officers would have dearly loved to send them back to Africa. They were really only any good as guards, and even then they could only be used during the day.

Compared to Saigon, Hanoi was a quiet and sober city. The whole pace of life seemed slower somehow. As we drove from the main shopping centre to the Chinese district we passed the Little Lake, in the middle of which stood a tiny Buddhist temple. Its painted walls were the only spot of colour to relieve the drabness of that grey, rainy day. We passed a pathetic little fair with one or two barefoot children standing about inquisitively, but even that seemed incapable of spreading any cheer. The jeep that had come to pick me up at the airport drove through broad, tree-lined streets. The avenues were a tribute to the skills of the French town planners who had designed them, as were the ochre-coloured palaces in the administrative quarter; apparently the Governor-General used to live in one of them. We passed a fortress built on the lines of a gloomy Vauban casemate. I was told that European civilians had taken refuge in it during the Viet Minh uprising in December 1946. Eventually we turned into a handsome-looking block of two-storeyed villas with yellow, lime-washed walls. A sentry stood guard at the entrance, looking a trifle bored. I arrived at the press camp and was shown by a sergeant into a spacious room containing an enormous bed with a mosquito net. I then introduced myself to the duty officer, who also happened to be in charge of running the establishment. Major Roëllec was a plump, good-natured Breton, full of the joys of living. The tropical sun seemed to have had no effect at all on his pale skin, and his receding hair made him look older than his years. Once, when out in the rice paddies, he had got a piece of shrapnel in his backside. Somebody had just to mention this wound and a flurry of feeble jokes would come from the crowd of reporters, who were predominantly French. Roëllec was a hard drinker and was forever boasting about his sexual exploits too. When I met up with him again, fifteen years later, he was serving as a paratroop colonel in Laos.

Large notices had gone up all over the bar of the press camp giving details of the briefing then in progress. Julien, an AFP correspondent whom I knew from my Paris days, told me in a hoarse whisper that the bar had not been done up specially for the reporters' benefit. Seemingly our compound had been a high-class brothel before the war, and some of the amenities dated from that time. The French captain giving the briefing had an off-hand, rather arrogant manner. His coolness probably stemmed from the fact that he had practically nothing to report but bad news. He might equally well have been feeling an overpowering (and typically French) antipathy towards the small band of Anglo-Saxon war correspondents who had recently arrived in Hanoi after the battle of Vinh Yen. The Americans and British were keeping a critical eye on the desperate struggles of the French Army in Tongking. They were convinced they could have conducted the war more efficiently themselves and even believed they could have won it in a fairly short time. In fact the Americans would have been quite unbearable had they not been somewhat subdued by developments in the Korean War, which had begun the previous summer. The British correspondents were mostly veterans of the Burma and Pacific campaigns. Some had served as officers, and they shook their heads disapprovingly over these Gallic cocks who were so unlike Kipling's idea of a soldier. The French laid bets as to which of the British reporters was in fact a member of the Intelligence Service.

The military briefing was fairly short and uninformative. The captain announced that they were to be honoured with a visit from General de Lattre de Tassigny, Commander-in-Chief of the Expeditionary Force and High Commissioner for Indochina. The general, it appeared, would be dining with them the following evening. This announcement made no impression at all on the British and the Americans, but it provoked a buzz of excitement among the French. De Lattre was no ordinary general. When still a young officer his name had been entered in the German military records of the 'Foreign Armies – West' section. After the collapse of France in the summer of 1940 de Lattre, a landowner from the staunchly Catholic department of the Vendée, offered his services to Marshal Pétain's pro-Nazi government. What is more, his signature – *horresco referens* – even appeared on the document issued by a Vichy military court condemning de Gaulle to death. De Lattre was rehabilitated in 1942 when, after a futile attempt to halt the German advance into southern France, he made a dramatic escape to North Africa. Once there he worked tirelessly to organize the First French Army, which landed at Provence in the summer of 1944. De Lattre then marched through Burgundy into Alsace, where he fought several bloody battles and won back some of the glory that France, stunned by defeat, so desperately needed.

During the closing weeks of the war the First French Army

battled its way through the Black Forest until it reached Lake Constance and the Vorarlberg, adopting *en route* the rather grandiose motto of 'Rhine and Danube'. As a military leader de Lattre inspired as much fear among his own officers as he did among the enemy. During his time in occupied Germany he began to assume the manner of a Sun King, and it wasn't long before he became known to one and all as le Roi Jean. In Sigmaringen, so the story went, he roundly condemned the Crown Prince of the Hohenzollerns to his face for his 'unworthy' behaviour – and then drove him out of his castle, leaving him to make his getaway on a bicycle. De Lattre would have been a lot happier if the French had been blond and blue-eyed and if they had jumped to it a bit quicker. The sloppiness you always find among French troops used to drive le Roi Jean mad with fury. His unexpected arrival in the staffs and barracks of Swabia was guaranteed to send everyone into a panic. All in all this man with the strong, aristocratic profile seemed to have a quite staggering gift for imposing his will on others.

So far the same career pattern had been repeated in Indochina, where de Lattre had inherited a desperate situation at a critical time. He knew from the start that he would win no laurels in Tongking and that the most he could hope for was a military victory. In effect, what this vain and hot-headed man was doing was committing professional suicide. At the time, however, he and his doctor were the only ones who knew that he was suffering from a terminal illness. When he arrived in Saigon the first thing he did was to order the entire officer corps in Tan-Son-Nhut to fall in. The men were to wear regulation dress of tropical whites. When this dazzling white group lined up for inspection, the general's gimlet eye singled out a portly colonel who, for some reason, had turned up wearing khaki. 'You will be sent home to France on the next plane,' he snarled at the unfortunate man. Then, turning to the officers at his side, he remarked: 'There are too many colonels and not enough lieutenants here.' How right he was.

The battle of Vinh Yen had brought this French aristocrat and his men into the thick of the action. Since his arrival at the front his popularity with the troops had grown. Back in Hanoi staff officers could be seen scurrying round the barracks' yard picking up litter and scraps of paper whenever one of de Lattre's inspections was due. This, of course, could hardly fail to endear him to all the privates and NCOs at the front.

When Major Roëllec heard about the imminent arrival of le Roi

Jean his first impulse was to dragoon the reporters in the press camp into sweeping and dusting the place. As it was, he had to make do with chasing the gang of kitchen boys up and down stairs like frightened rabbits and prodding the cleaning women into frenzied activity. Nevertheless the grand old man of the French war correspondents, Max Olivier of *Le Figaro*, insisted on checking his colleagues' fingernails to see if they were clean, which made him none too popular. The French press seemed more strongly represented in Hanoi than in many an editorial office in Paris. There was Olivier, a Protestant giant of a man from the Cévennes who never allowed anything to ruffle his composure. He could tell fascinating tales about his time in India, where he had covered the granting of independence. His most vivid recollection of that period was Gandhi's funeral. It was a scene he could never forget – the raised funeral pyre of the murdered Mahatma, with hundreds of thousands of frenzied people crowding round, weeping and howling. Again and again the mass of people had surged forward to the pyre, like a stream of molten lava, and huge Sikh policemen had tried to push them back, tearing into them with their clubs, smashing skulls and shoulders. Shortly after leaving Hanoi, Olivier was to meet a Korean girl from a good family at a Protestant service in Seoul. He married her and took her back to France with him, and they settled down happily.

Julien, the man from AFP, was an uncomplicated, happy-go-lucky individual whose main aim in life, apart from work, seemed to be his never-ending amorous escapades. He was a slightly built man, rather donnish in appearance, so that people tended to take some of his stories with a pinch of salt. It was common knowledge that he had a beautiful Eurasian mistress back in Saigon – not that he allowed this to cramp his style while he was working in Hanoi. Fate caught up with Julien one day. He was in bed with the wife of a French air force pilot when, on the very same day, her husband was shot down. This coincidence had such a profound effect on Julien (whom nobody would have believed capable of such emotional depth) that he promptly married the widow, and from that day forward became the most dutiful husband in the whole of Indochina.

Another reporter worthy of mention was Max Motte, the correspondent for *Le Monde*. Motte had earned a reputation among the military for being a dangerous left-wing intellectual, purely on the strength of his penetrating analyses and pessimistic forecasts. Only a handful of people knew, for instance, that he had once eked out a living giving judo and karate lessons in Saigon. Nobody at the time could have foreseen that in his seventies he would rise to become editor-in-chief of a thoroughly bourgeois Parisian newspaper, nor that he would devote most of his leaders to attacking left-wing terrorism and advocating the restoration of the death penalty. Perhaps the most interesting character of all, though, was a phlegmatic old-timer called Lulu Bodard. Bodard was a living relic of the glorious and turbulent days of the old Chinese Empire, before the takeover by the Communists. He had grown up in Szechwan, in the very heart of China, and his autobiographical novels about his exotic childhood brought him a certain amount of fame in later life. Even in Hanoi he was always full of tales about his experiences among the Sons of Heaven. His stories tended to revolve around the poverty of the masses, the vagaries of the warlords, the wisdom of poor people and whores but most of all, the indescribable, teeming, self-seeking, boundless vitality of this vast nation. Sometimes he would hold court in a draughty hut in the Chinese district. There, seated on the mat, he would watch as the pellets of opium slowly melted. On those occasions his anecdotes would take on a power that transformed them into something approaching literature.

De Lattre surprised everyone by turning up at the camp in civilian clothes. He took pains to be scrupulously polite towards the crowd of pressmen and generally treated us as equals. He paid particular attention to the Americans. He spoke appalling English and his accent made him sound like a caricature of Maurice Chevalier. The impression he created, however, was anything but ridiculous. The Yankees, whom he won over with surprising ease, were struck by his amazing resemblance to Douglas MacArthur, his counterpart in Korea; seemingly the likeness was not only in looks but in attitude as well. De Lattre made it plain that he was under no illusion about his role in Indochina. The French army would be unable to make any impact at all unless it were part of a major show of force involving all the countries of the Free World. Here the general was playing the trump card of a Franco-American alliance as the only possible answer to the Marxist revolution that had taken place on the Chinese mainland. Ultimately, though, he realized that such an undertaking was doomed to failure. 'When the Chinese come . . .' he would say, shrugging his shoulders in a gesture of defeat. De Lattre had a plan in mind that involved flying to Washington to win public support for France's involvement in Indochina. He also hoped (though this would mean swallowing his pride) to appeal to Congress to grant additional military and economic aid to his forces.

After de Lattre had gone, a lieutenant turned to the British and Americans. 'We've just received a cable from Saigon saying an American journalist by the name of Graham Greene has turned up there. Does anyone know who he is?' His question was greeted with roars of laughter.

The Vietnamese cleaning women came in to clear the tables. They were dressed in baggy black trousers and shapeless white tops, and they kept their flat straw hats on their heads even when they were indoors. Major Roëllec had evidently got hold of the ugliest women he could find to wait on the reporters. Apparently when the press camp was first opened he had employed young Vietnamese boys to do the work, until the day one of the prettier ones was indecently assaulted by a lonely war correspondent – with his consent, naturally, and on payment of the appropriate fee.

In the evenings officers and correspondents alike used to go to the local dance hall in search of women. The hall, called the Paramount, was a short distance from the Little Lake and had a red neon light above the entrance that shone out onto the deserted street. The only sound to be heard were the ringing footsteps of passing army patrols. Occasionally one or two trishaws would draw up, attracted to the red glare like mosquitoes to a lamp. Inside the Paramount everyone danced the Chinese tango while the band played sentimental tunes. The hostesses demanded a plastic token from their partner in return for every dance. These had to be bought at a counter, like gambling chips in a casino. The girls were all dressed in the *ao dai*, the demure national costume. Their heavy make-up distorted their lovely faces into lewd masks and showed them in their true colours – these were obviously not nicely brought up convent girls. Inside the dimly lit Paramount three or four couples would usually be circling the floor looking intensely bored. The damp night air crept steadily in through the gaps in the windows. The girls would sit next to one another on a row of chairs, their expressions vacant, like hens on a perch. As soon as they were asked to dance and one of their tokens was cashed, they would break into radiant smiles. The girls themselves always insisted that they were not prostitutes. They would only agree to sleep with clients they liked or who had danced with them for a minimum of three nights. Otherwise they were afraid of appearing 'cheap'.

The Fighting Bishop

Phat Diem, 1951

The Catholic churches loomed above the straw roofs of the villages like mighty castles. Phat Diem province was the Catholic stronghold in the coastal area around the Gulf of Tongking, and it lay under the shadow of the Cross. Our native escort of five soldiers, who were supposed to be protecting our river-boat against attacks by the Viet Minh, heaved a sigh of relief when we were out of the danger zone. The government of the anti-Communist State of Vietnam had been helped into power by the French, and wherever we saw the flag of the new administration (three horizontal red stripes on a yellow background) flying over towns in the Red River Delta, we had to be ready for anything. The French had installed Emperor Bao Dai as head of state and were trying to bolster him up against Ho Chi Minh; here in Phat Diem his flag was lowered as soon as darkness fell. Night-time, in fact, was when Red commissars took over. Every time something moved out on the flat dykes of the paddy fields our guards released the safety-catch on their rifles and peered nervously into the mist. Artillery fire could be heard in the distance.

Now that we could see the yellow and white flag of the Vatican fluttering over the massive church buildings, we knew we were safe. We were entering the diocese of Bishop Le Huu Tu of Phat Diem, a man with a reputation as a fighter. The Communists had a fair idea of what he was like too, since this former adviser to Ho Chi Minh had fallen out with the godless Marxists. Monseigneur Le Huu Tu, who was a Trappist, would have nothing to do with the French either. He was a committed Vietnamese patriot and always deeply suspicious of any representatives of the old colonial power. He had had some experience of the officials of the Third Republic, and as far as he was concerned every Frenchman was a potential Freemason in disguise.

Like all the other churches in the delta, the cathedral of Phat Diem was a massive building with a tower that soared into the sky. But unlike the others, it was built entirely of wood and was decorated with Chinese motifs. We were greeted by Le Huu Tu's adviser, a Belgian priest. 'You've arrived at an interesting time,' said the Flemish Father. 'There's a kind of investiture struggle going on here at the moment. The new governor of Tongking,

Nguyen Huu Tri, is a member of the conservative Dai Viet Party, and he would like to force our bishop to confine himself to religious duties and keep out of politics.'

A huge crowd was gathering outside the church. The mass of circular straw hats looked like a crop of mushrooms from above. It had been raining steadily for days, and the Catholics of Phat Diem were standing ankle-deep in cold mud. The entrances to the big square in front of the cathedral were guarded by the bishop's own soldiers. Le Huu Tu had his own small army which he personally commanded; its banner was the flag of the See of Rome, and it followed the regulation drill of the Viet Minh. The precautions the bishop had taken were strictly necessary. During the last Corpus Christi procession some Communist guerillas had mingled with the worshippers and then, when no one was expecting it, had started shooting into the crowd. To his great disappointment Le Huu Tu had had to send for a French unit from a neighbouring town to come and restore order. On the cathedral roof, below the yellow and white flag with its keys of St Peter, the colours of the State of Vietnam, France, the United States and Great Britain fluttered together in the breeze. The French were not at all happy about the Anglo-Saxon presence – particularly as the town's young Vietnamese students took to greeting every European newcomer with a coy smile and a few phrases of garbled English. Now that France had been defeated – a defeat which in Le Huu Tu's opinion was inevitable, ordained by God – the Catholics of Tongking looked to America as their new and invincible patron.

Le Huu Tu walked up the ramp at the entrance to the cathedral, wearing the white habit of the Trappist order. He was a raw-boned, ascetic man whose eyes burned with a holy fire. Physically he was very similar to Pham Van Dong, the subsequent prime minister of Communist Vietnam. Choirboys were lined up in front of him, holding aloft his coat of arms, his mitre and his staff. The bishop blessed the people and they knelt down in the mud. Then he shook hands with the notables and guests present. When a French cavalry major who was acting as liaison officer kissed the bishop's ring, Julien, who came from a socialist, anti-clerical background, had to choke back his indignation. One or two Buddhist priests in grey robes had also appeared beside the Catholic clergymen surrounding Le Huu Tu; oddly enough, they did not look at all out of place in this setting. The bishop stepped forward to the microphone. On both sides of the steps, soldiers wearing wide-brimmed slouch hats presented arms and unshouldered their weapons. The people rose to their feet and proceeded to unfurl banners – a trick they must have learnt at Viet Minh rallies.

The Belgian priest translated the bishop's speech for us. Monseigneur Le Huu Tu began to explain the new political situation in Tongking to the members of his diocese. He made no secret of his contempt for Emperor Bao Dai, newly affirmed as head of state. In the past, Bao Dai had always given in to the stronger side, whether it was the French, the Japanese or the Communists. Pursued by Ho Chi Minh's forces, he had fled to Hong Kong, where he had set himself up in business – and he would have done better to have stayed there. Unlike Bao Dai, the shepherd of Phat Diem had stuck by his flock through thick and thin. Admittedly Monseigneur Le Huu Tu had made a temporary pact with Ho Chi Minh, purely for tactical reasons, but he had consistently spoken out against Marxist ideology. In 1949 the Viet Minh had planned to extend its scorched earth policy to the Catholic provinces of Phat Diem and Bui Chu in order to thwart the advancing French forces. The Christians, led by their chaplain, had responded by taking up arms and putting an end to the Communist threat. But now new dangers lay ahead for them.

The French had finally given up playing their separatist game in Cochin China and had appointed a head of state to govern the whole of Vietnam. The man they chose was Trang Van Huu, a wealthy landowner from Saigon who had both French and Vietnamese citizenship. He was a typical representative of the Cochin China middle classes, and came in for strong disapproval from all sides. Bao Dai regarded Trang Van Huu as a puppet of the French, so installed as governor of Tongking a man who seemed better suited to political in-fighting. This was the Dai Viet politician Nguyen Huu Tri. The new governor had already had a brush with the French police before the war because of his militant nationalism, and in the end he had had to flee to China. Recently he had publicly declared his support for the total separation of Vietnam from France, and had come down firmly on the side of the Americans. He might have made an ideal partner for the West in the struggle to stop the spread of Communism in Asia if his Dai Viet party had had a broader base of support among the people. Unfortunately his following was small, and the mandarins who had rushed to grab all the sinecures going in his new administration were largely discredited among the population. There was no doubting Governor Tri's patriotism. The only problem was that, in order to realize his policy of national independence and self-determination in the face of the Communist threat, he needed the support of that very French Army he wanted to throw out of the country. Now he was trying to bring the diocese of Phat Diem inside his narrow sphere of influence by depriving Monseigneur Le Huu Tu of his political rights. The official story was that he was carrying out a policy of centralization, but, given the circumstances, this was a quite ludicrous pretext.

The bishop acted the part of the loyal subject submitting to authority as if he had been treading the boards all his life. Speaking in the strange, high-pitched language of the country, he declared: 'I am ready to obey the directives of the governor of Hanoi. I am prepared to lay down temporal responsibility for my beloved diocese and devote myself exclusively to my pastoral duties.' At this point a storm of protest broke out. The crowd knelt down again and shouted in unison (they were obviously well rehearsed): 'We do not want a foreign ruler! We shall follow our bishop and submit to his priestly authority!' Then Le Huu Tu, his face slightly flushed, spread out his arms and gave his blessing. The bells of every church in the vicinity rang out, and the police band of Phat Diem struck up a march in which the sound of French bugles and Chinese gongs mingled oddly together.

The journey back to Hanoi was tough going. The roads were virtually impassable because of the notorious 'piano keys', and the holes had to be filled in every morning by a bulldozer. The Viet Minh had begun systematically mining all communication links and so we placed sandbags under the seats of the jeep, though they didn't offer much effective protection against a blast. There seemed to be a great deal of energetic building and mixing of concrete going on around the delta area and at all the checkpoints we passed. Apparently General de Lattre had given orders for a permanent line of defensive fortifications to be built to put a stop to Communist attacks. These defences were to be a faithful copy of the old Maginot line, and, not surprisingly, this caused a certain amount of sarcastic comment from the soldiers. They were particularly angry at the scandalous profits being made out of the project by one or two French contractors. Right from the start, the grey pillboxes standing forlornly in the ricefields seemed to invite disaster. They were protected by barbed wire and were manned mainly by black colonial units. Nobody trusted the 'Senegal negroes', who were scared of the dark and terrified of the guerillas, not to try and make a run for it during the night, so they were locked up in their bunkers every evening and were only let out again at daybreak.

Near Ha Duong we came across a battalion of the newly-formed Vietnamese National Army. The French did not rate these troops very highly and they let their Asian allies know it. This, in turn, meant that the Vietnamese soldiers lost confidence in themselves, and when the time came for them to go into action they had little heart for fighting. 'Just look at that,' the captain travelling with me said in disgust. 'Instead of combing the ricefields and travelling light like the Viet Minh, those National Army soldiers always follow the roads and load themselves up with equipment and weapons so they're completely immobile. They should go barefoot instead of wearing marching boots.'

That evening I was invited to dine with de Lattre de Tassigny. His wife had flown out to join him in Hanoi, and everyone took this to indicate a further deterioration in his health. His son Bernard, a young lieutenant, also joined us at table. (Bernard was to be killed a few days later in the rugged hill country around Hoa Binh.) There was also an American colonel present. He was full of blustering optimism, and kept on paying Madame de Lattre clumsy compliments that got on the general's nerves. De Lattre was not in a particularly good mood that evening anyway. The experiment with Governor Tri had not been a success. The French might just have got away with installing an enemy of France as governor of Tongking, but when the man also proved incapable of mustering any support worth mentioning against the Communists, it became clear that they had backed the wrong horse. The afternoon of that same day Nguyen Huu Tri had organized a mass rally outside the Opera House. It had taken place in the drizzle that always fell at that time of the year, and the whole event had been something of a washout. The grey-haired mandarin, whose face had a touch of the Indian about it, had eventually fallen out of favour with the high commissioner.

Two days previously de Lattre had had a meeting with Bao Dai, the head of state, on board his yacht in the Gulf of Tongking. It had apparently been a fairly stormy encounter. The stout ex-emperor had the reputation of being both extremely intelligent and totally unscrupulous. He was a descendant of the great Gia Long, who had first brought the French to Hue to free him from his dependence on China. De Lattre had asked Bao Dai to try to do everything he could to help his country. But he was wasting his breath. The man he was dealing with was an indolent playboy who reacted like an outraged prima donna to every suggestion that was put to him. In the end, so one French eye-witness reported, the head of state had an expression on his face like that of a rickshaw coolie who has been paid with a banknote and refuses to give any change.

During the meal General de Lattre did not touch his food and he had nothing to drink except a glass of water. 'The other day,' he said, 'I gathered the students of Saigon around me. I told them we were perfectly willing to hand over full control of Vietnam to the Vietnamese, but I expected some degree of patriotic commitment from the young people of this country, particularly the intellectual élite. These privileged sons of the local bourgeoisie can't expect the sons of French peasants and French working men to go on risking their necks forever just to prevent Communism taking over in Asia. So I raised my voice to them. "Messieurs," I said, "I despise any of you who go on pursuing your own pastimes and pleasures while your people are suffering or dying around you. I would have more respect for you if you went over to the other side and fought for the Viet Minh against us." '

I have one last memory of the war during that period. At de Lattre's suggestion I had travelled to the coastal province of Thai Binh where Operation Mercury was in progress. Two regiments of the Viet Minh 320th Division were reported to be encircled there, according to military headquarters in Hanoi.

The clouds were low in the leaden grey sky, and a biting cold wind was blowing from the north. The legs of the little boys, sitting astride their buffaloes like Mowgli, were blue with cold. The soldiers who made up the army of the French Union were a motley crew. The Moroccans wore thick wool jellabas with brown stripes. You could pick out the Algerians by their turbans. Who would have known at the time that the seeds of the Algerian Revolution were being sown in those paddy fields? It was while they were in Indochina that the Maghrebis became infected with the virus of nationalism. When we came across a lorry with the red and green insignia of the Foreign Legion on it, as often as not it would be snatches of German that carried over to us on the breeze. And by this time as much as a third of the strength of some French colonial infantry units was made up of Vietnamese. This growing predominance of native troops in the Expeditionary Force was known as le jaunissement ('the yellowing'). Metropolitan Frenchmen were definitely a minority among this hotch-potch of soldiers.

At the front-line command post of the 10th Mobile Group the

road petered out. Nearby we could hear a battery firing at irregular intervals. The command post was located in an ancestral temple. Despite the thick clouds of cigarette smoke the scent of incense still hung in the air. Outside two platoons of paratroopers were advancing on the last line of villages before the coast. They waded through the water in the rice paddies, walking some distance apart, sometimes sinking up to their knees in the pale green stems of the plants. Shots were fired at them from the outskirts of the village but the firing was only sporadic and it stopped altogether when they reached the first mud huts. The paratroopers showed us an underground fox-hole where the Viet Minh had dug in; a thirteen-year-old European would have been lucky to squeeze inside it. A soldier said: 'When we comb the villages, they pull hunks of turf or brushwood over their heads and we can pass close to them for hours without spotting them.'

A few soldiers with minor wounds came towards us along the narrow, slippery embankment. They were covered in mud from head to foot. At a crossroads, paratroopers with machine guns at the ready were stopping and checking a stream of refugees who suddenly seemed to have appeared out of nowhere. The civilian population was pouring in now from every conceivable direction. The Viet Minh had herded them all together in the few remaining square miles of land on the edge of the coast, the idea being that they could disappear among them and smuggle themselves through the French lines if necessary. The guerillas of the Viet Minh 320th Division had, of course, donned the traditional black peasant costume before infiltrating the delta region.

The French soldiers gave the young men among the refugees a thorough going-over. The tell-tale papers were easy enough to find – military documents, regimental orders, Communist battle-songs, tracts, photos of Ho Chi Minh, even a picture of Marshal Stalin. The weapons, however, lay buried somewhere in the ricefields. By a sheer fluke the soldiers managed to track down the political commissar of a regiment. He was hiding in a fox-hole when the mine-detecting device in his wristwatch accidentally went off and gave him away. Now the man stared gloomily into the distance and refused to say anything.

A thin drizzle was falling on the line of refugees. The Thai Binh region is one of the most overpopulated in the world, and the scene there was one of abject misery. The women with young children suffered most; some had not eaten for days. Grave-faced village mandarins, sporting the thin goatee beard and black turban of their caste, moved among the huddled peasant women in their brown tunics. There were shaven Buddhist monks, and even an occasional Catholic priest in pith helmet and cassock, leading his parishioners as if he was drilling a company of soldiers. Nearby the powerful buffaloes stamped their feet restlessly. When it was almost evening the sun finally broke through the clouds. Its rays were reflected in the rice paddies; the glistening surface of the moisture-laden air seemed to merge. From a distance the black chain of refugees looked as if it was suspended between the sky and water like a mournful flight of migratory birds in an imaginary Chinese painting.

Crossing the Chinese Border

Lai Chau, 1951

The pilot of our Ju 52 was a coffee-coloured Martinican who radiated cheerfulness and self-confidence. At one time the plane had served in Goering's Luftwaffe, but now it flew over North Vietnam, picking its way gingerly through the wisps of low-flying cloud. In between the gaps in the grey haze you could just make out the Black River below us, its banks and gorges overgrown with vegetation. We were flying over Viet Minh territory in the direction of Lai Chau, a mountain hide-out in the highlands of the west Tongking, on the border with Yunnan and the kingdom of Laos. Lai Chau had recently been declared the capital of a new Thai Federation. The Thai hill-tribes had been fighting off pressure from the Vietnamese in the plain for centuries. Consequently the French had found an instant ally in the racial minorities who inhabited this remote mountain region. Its only link with Hanoi was by airlift, and a German legionnaire was standing at the ready by the rear door of the Ju 52, tying up parcels of food and ammunition. Those French support bases in the Thai region that had been cut off by the Viet Minh had to be supplied by parachute drop.

The plane came to a standstill in a large field. A few Thai soldiers wearing felt hats and blue pyjama-suits stood around at the edge of the landing-strip like extras in an Asian bandit film.

They were unenthusiastically holding back a crowd of inquisitive locals, and I was immediately struck by the peasants' brightly coloured clothes and their narrow slit eyes. Arriving in Lai Chau was like stepping inside a picture-book Asia, exhilarating, strange and exotic.

Colonel Coste, with whom I was travelling, was a blond, placid man who originally came from the north of France. He was planning a tour of inspection of the French garrisons along the Chinese border that would take about fourteen days. The Thai Federation lands were the last part of Indochina occupied by French forces that directly bordered China. The only other point of immediate contact was the small town of Mong Cai on the Gulf of Tongking, where the local Nung people actually spoke Cantonese. I had visited Mong Cai a few days before, and had gazed across the narrow river marking the border. I saw a huge propaganda painting on a pagoda wall on the far bank of the river, just beyond the cordoned-off bridge. The poster showed victorious soldiers of the People's Liberation Army holding red flags aloft like a team of relay runners. They seemed to be competing in a race against a team of blue-clad workers. At the finishing tape the glorious symbols of the Communist revolution beckoned them on, while an avuncular-looking Mao acted as referee.

The French administrator in Lai Chau received us in his residence – another white building that looked like a toy castle. He was official adviser to a Thai prince called Deo Van Long and he lived with an extremely self-willed Chinese woman. When Coste and I went to take a siesta, we had to listen to a domestic tiff on the other side of the thin partition. It seemed that the Chinese woman had wanted to take one of the French military vehicles to go shopping for food and clothes in Hanoi. She had been told she could not have it, and now she was ranting on in a shrill voice about this apparent slight to her person. The administrator tried vainly to mollify her. 'Who the hell do you think you are anyway?' yelled the woman, who seemed to have picked up a fair smattering of soldiers' slang. 'You call us yellow monkeys and you think of yourselves as white men but you're not – you're red-faced brutes. Ugly red crabs, that's what you are, and I don't see why I should let you treat me like a cow.'

That evening she reappeared, elegant and demure once more, to entertain us to a superb Chinese meal. She wore an expensive-looking, high-necked evening-dress with side-slits that nearly reached her hips and showed off her long, slender legs. She had an aristocratic complexion the colour of pale ivory, and the sunburnt face of the administrator did, in fact, look rather like a beetroot in comparison. She had a beautiful Yao girl with her who helped serve the meal and acted as joint hostess. She wore the traditional native costume of her tribe: a huge black turban on her head, heavy silver chains and pendants on her feet, and a short black pleated skirt that stopped above the knee. Even the black puttees on her legs would have been pounced on by any of those Paris couturiers who are always on the look-out for exotic ideas. The Yao girl was well aware of her own beauty and was not in the least coy or prudish. She posed for the obligatory photos with the professional air of a model going through her paces.

After the women had retired the administrator gave us a slightly knowing leer and began playing some of his records. These turned out to be a unique collection of 'blue' drinking songs. Next he took down from the shelf his prize collection of pornographic photos, handling it reverently like some exquisite antique. Coste reckoned afterwards that he used it to console himself because his Chinese bedmate was so coldly contemptuous towards him. You certainly met all kinds in those lonely outposts.

For the past eight hours our small contingent had been travelling northwards over steep mountain tracks. The path was cut into the rock like a flight of steps in places, and the sturdy mountain ponies would kneel on the raised step with their front legs, then jackknife with their rump in order to clear the obstacle. The unit had recently been joined by a French captain from Gascony. He was a gaunt man with a thick Pyrenean accent who was always cracking jokes. His huge nose, which the Asians viewed with a mixture of horror and derision, had earned him the nickname of Cyrano. We had been given an escort of three Thai guerillas, all of them sullen and obstinate characters. They had probably been highway robbers at one time. Then there was Ko, a smiling, inscrutable Chinaman dressed in civilian clothes. Ko was an intelligence agent, and he had tortured so many Viet Minh prisoners in the course of interrogation that we knew we could count on his loyalty. Another redeeming feature was his staggering local knowledge, both of the terrain and its inhabitants.

Before we finally left the valley of Lai Chau behind us Coste pointed out a path that ran in a south-westerly direction. 'This is our only road link with the outside world that isn't controlled by the Viet Minh,' he said. 'The trail goes to Laos, and it's only passable in the dry season. About half-way between here and Luang Prabang, the imperial city on the Mekong River, there's a Thai village called Dien Bien Phu. It's in a fertile valley, and we've got a small garrison stationed there.'

Towards evening the sky began to clear. We rode along the valley until we came to a village. The huts stood on the river bank, looking clean and welcoming. We held our legs high out of the water and drove the horses through the fast-flowing ford, swaying about in the saddle like monkeys. We felt very relieved when we arrived safely on the opposite bank, where the village elders were waiting. The village had organized an official reception for us, and we were led off to eat straight away. Meanwhile the guerillas saw to the horses and unloaded the pack animals; we had brought along two light machine guns, a mortar and some ammunition for protection. We squatted down on the wooden floor of the communal dwelling and ate our meal of minced buffalo meat, which was served with the glutinous rice that grows in the highlands. Throughout the meal we were served with a fierce and extremely alcoholic brew called *shum*, which was made out of sugar cane and tasted like schnapps. A young Thai woman knelt behind every European. Whenever we laid down our chopsticks for a moment they would place the bowl of shum to our lips (they had surprisingly strong arms) and force us to drink the muddy liquid in one go. When the last drop had disappeared everyone seated round the table would shout '*Kampei!*'

The mountain Thai have the same ethnic origins as the Thai population in Siam. They also speak a very similar language, and could make themselves understood in Bangkok without any difficulty. In the late Middle Ages the Thai were driven out of Yunnan and the mountains of southern China by Kublai Khan, the Mongol emperor, who pushed south in a great mass migration, conquering all before him. The Thai eventually ended up in the present-day Menam plain, where they intermarried with the dark-skinned Mon and Khmer tribes and became converted to Buddhism. In contrast the majority of the mountain Thai in the uplands of Indochina were still animists and had only assimilated one or two basic Confucian beliefs.

The full moon had risen, and we realized we had arrived in the middle of a religious festival. One of the wizened old men of the tribe, presumably the village shaman, summoned the young girls down to the river. The girls formed a semi-circle facing the full moon. They were dressed in tight white bodices that identified them as White Thai, and distinguished them from the neighbouring Red and Black Thai. Their black skirts fell long and straight to their bare feet. They each wore a green sash tied round their hips and their beautiful hair was woven into heavy knots. A gong was sounded inside the communal dwelling and the girls began to move in a graceful, rhythmic step, rather like a slow-motion samba. All the time they were dancing they remained facing in the direction of the pale, chaste disc of the moon; clearly the inviting movements of their hips were intended for its benefit. 'It's a fertility dance,' said Cyrano in a whisper.

Two days later we made a halt in a Yao village that clung perilously to the side of a steep hill. The Yao tribe lived mainly on dry rice and the proceeds of bartering. Up here in the mountains the Yao women were less well dressed, and certainly less bold, than their flirtatious tribal sisters in Lai Chau. They did, however, wear the same intricately embroidered clothes. Two richly decorated straps draped over their shoulders represented a pair of dog's paws. The Yao, who were also known as the Man, believed they were descended from a mythical dog. According to the legend, the dog took up residence in the imperial court of China in order to set free the emperor's daughter. In those days China was being terrorized by a terrible monster. The emperor sent all his bravest warriors to kill it, but none of them was equal to the task. In the end the emperor promised to give away his daughter and half his kingdom to anyone who could rid China of the scourge. Eventually the legendary dog, the ancestor of the Yao, succeeded in killing the monster. Faithful to his word, the emperor handed over his daughter, but when it came to dividing up the kingdom he had a trick up his sleeve. Certainly the dog would get half of China, but nobody had said how the split was to be made, vertically or horizontally. So in the end the dog, and its descendants, got the mountainous top half of China, while the fertile valleys and rice plains of the south were kept for the Han people, the true Sons of Heaven.

We carried on through dense jungle until we came to Phong To, the seat of a Thai prince who was highly respected in the area. As we rode through the humid undergrowth we were plagued by leeches that dropped onto us from out of the trees. When you saw these loathsome parasites on your skin your first reaction was a feeling of revulsion. You had to stifle it, though, and most important of all, you had to resist the temptation to pull them off, otherwise they left festering wounds. If you held a lighted cigarette to them, they would usually drop off by themselves.

We stayed in Phong To for three days, and it was one long round of dancing and feasting and revelry. The Thai women were even lovelier and sweeter-natured in this part of the country. The aged prince, whom the colonel always addressed as His Excellency, had the wise and dignified bearing of a character in an Oriental fairy tale. In the evening we smoked opium while we waited for the girls to dance for us. We went to bathe under a waterfall and when we got back found mounds of flowers piled up on our sleeping mats. We felt as if we had stumbled on the mythical paradise of Shangri-La.

The war was never very far away, though. Cyrano would spend long hours crouched over the Morse telegraph, keeping in contact with the handful of French officers and NCOs who were roaming the highlands with their bands of guerillas, left entirely to their own devices. The Viet Minh had set its commissars to work on the various members of the Thai Federation and had achieved one or two successes with individual tribes. The higher we climbed, the bleaker and more inhospitable the landscape became. The grass was regularly burned off at this time of year to clear the ground. This method, which was part of the Rai system of cultivation, frequently led to huge steppe fires breaking out, and once or twice we had to gallop to safety to avoid the flames. At such times we relied completely on the instinct of our horses to get us out of danger. They would pick their way along the edges of precipices, as sure-footed as mountain-goats. At night we wrapped ourselves up in the parachutes that had been issued for the outposts, but our teeth still chattered with the cold.

Up there in the mountains lived a wild, hardy race of tribesmen called the Meo. At that time the Meo (who are also called the Miao in China) were known only to ethnologists. Since the war in Laos, however, they have caught the imagination of newspaper readers all over the world. The Meo of northern Tongking inhabit a region of bleak mountain peaks, where everything is shrouded in mist and drizzle for the greater part of the year. The women's costume was similar to that worn by the Yao, only far more colourful. As we travelled further we came across more and more of these Meo women. They were sturdily built and carried heavy baskets on their backs. Their mouths were stained red with betel-nut juice and they were usually seen smoking a clay pipe. Despite the loads on their backs they had strong calf muscles and could run up very steep slopes. The red aprons and silver buckles they wore were priceless examples of folk art. The men always dressed in black pyjamas, with black skull-caps on their heads. The weapons they used were ancient muzzle-loaders or flintlock rifles. It was safest not to tangle with these picturesque warriors, however. In those days they practised the old tribal custom of eating the liver of their slain enemies.

The Meo, who, as their name suggests, worshipped the cat as a sacred object, were Tibetan in origin. That, at any rate, was what the captain from Gascony told us, but I think he was mistaken. The legends of the Meo people all speak of their endless journeying from a land where night lasted half the year and water turned to stone. The Meo must originally have migrated to South-east Asia from Siberia.

Life among the Meo was a good deal less friendly and civilized than with the Thai. When we got to the outskirts of the village of Yao-San we were stopped by three warriors covered in dirt from head to foot. They were waiting to escort us to the communal dwelling in the centre of the village. As we rounded a bend in the road our eyes were greeted by a glorious sight: in the evening haze a vast field of poppies spread out before us, glistening with every colour of the rainbow. The Meo are the biggest producers of opium in the whole of South-east Asia. Meo women were standing in the midst of the poppy field, harvesting the opium. They would make a cut with a tiny knife in the swollen base of the flower and a viscous white sap would trickle out.

Most Meo tribesmen had thrown in their lot with the French. Colonel Coste took thick bundles of piastre notes out of his saddlebag and distributed wages to the men, the last band of guerillas this side of the Chinese border. We did not touch any of the food the Meo offered us, just to be on the safe side, but we were not allowed to refuse their opium. Inside the hut where we smoked, an oil lamp cast a dim reddish glow. An old man, presumably the shaman of Yao-San, picked up a pair of bagpipes and began to play. The noise he made was terrible, shrieking and caterwauling. Then he began to revolve slowly. The rhythm of the pipes got faster and faster, and gradually the old man went into a trance. Suddenly he put down the instrument, stammered a few words and collapsed in front of the house altar. The rest of the Meo sat spellbound, watching with fixed expressions on their faces. We, too, felt strangely carried away by it all – probably because of all the opium we had smoked.

At last we reached the Chinese border. The opium we had smoked the night before took its toll on the final leg of the journey, particularly as we had to climb the steeper slopes on foot. We could see the border fort of Ban Nam Kum lying far beneath us in the valley; it would have been impossible to defend in the event of a major attack. The fort was occupied by a dozen Thai guerillas and a solitary French NCO, whose skin was tinged yellow with malaria. Left on his own in this bleak, hostile part of the world the man had become a crank. His sole interest in life seemed to be his pea plantation. He looked unshaven and unkempt, and discipline among his men was not all that it might have been.

The fort had been visited by some Nationalist troops from across the border in the Chinese province of Yunnan. They were a sinister-looking bunch and were led by a Chinese feudal lord from the area. He was a stout man and had a disconcerting habit of giggling for no apparent reason. He had got together his tenant farmers and armed them in an attempt to fight off Mao's forces, who were advancing from the district capital of Mong Tzau. His motley troops were reinforced by a handful of professional bandits. They claimed to be members of the Kuomintang, but their political motives seemed suspect to say the least. The wealthy Chinaman had a private word with Coste while the pack animals were being unloaded. So the two machine guns and mortars were eventually handed over to the last surviving Chinese border troops in Yunnan. The code was: 'We've brought you some tinned milk'. Even the colonel had to smile at his own optimism in describing the beleaguered Chinese troops of Ban Nam Kum as a 'strategic buffer zone in the battle front of French Indochina'.

As we supped our noodle soup at breakfast, the Chinese guerilla leader asked me if I wanted to pay a visit to the headquarters of the rebellious forces in southern Yunnan. The headquarters were in the town of Muong Long, just over twenty kilometres away on the other side of the Nam Kum River. He said he would assign someone trustworthy from his unit to escort me there and back. I put the idea to Coste, who was all in favour of it, but he strongly advised me to be back in camp before nightfall. He said he would send a Thai guerilla along to act as interpreter.

We rode through the Nam Kum River, whose dark green waves were crested with foam. Nothing else marked the frontier between Tongking and China. At this time of year the scenery over the border in Yunnan looked just the same as on the Indochina side – the mountains bare and the rice paddies dried up. Even the little bamboo houses were identical. We rode the horses at a gallop along a narrow jungle path. The creepers blocked out most of the view overhead, and all we would see through the trees was an occasional glimpse of leaden grey sky. White flowers as big as clenched fists gleamed in the undergrowth. We passed peasants working in ricefields and wearing straw hats shaped like pots. They stood stock still in amazement at the sight of a white man. I tried hard to memorize the route we were taking. There was no knowing what condition we might be in on our journey back, and the advance guard of Mao's People's Liberation Army was rumoured to be only forty kilometres away.

All of a sudden we found our way barred at a turning in a path by two heavily armed figures. They wore dark blue outfits and had ammunition belts slung diagonally across their chests. Turning a deaf ear to the assurances of our escort, they accompanied us as far as the first huts of Muong La, glancing at us suspiciously all the time. The headquarters were housed in an imposing mud building, around which were encamped a number of wild-looking fighting men. They had on the same distinctive dark-blue costume of the region and wore felt hats, turbans or black skull-caps on their heads. The only way you could tell they were actually soldiers was by the identity tags on their chests, which gave the number of their unit and the name of their commander, a certain Colonel Liung. Their pockmarked faces had a sullen and hostile expression. Soon women and children began streaming out of the huts to join them. Only the opium smokers stayed where they were, lying on mats. It was like something out of *Ali Baba and the Forty Thieves*.

A gaunt man with fine features came up to us. He raised his hand to his soft hat in greeting, and introduced himself in broken English as a major in the Nationalist army. He apologized for not being able to extend a more hospitable welcome. He told us the latest news of the Communists' position: they were apparently heading in this direction from Mong Tzau and getting closer every day. They had already attacked the village of Muong La with mortar fire. The major was obviously anxious to dissociate himself from his rather sinister-looking comrades-at-arms. It appeared we had just missed his superior officer, Colonel Liung, who had had to ride on to the next base. The major got his company of barely 100 men to fall in, after a fashion, and he showed me their weapons. They mainly used American M-17 Winchesters, but they also had a few Mauser carbines that had probably found their way to China at the time of the German military mission to Chiang Kai-shek. The men pointed proudly to the two mortars in their possession, only one of which was operational. The major seemed to be the only professional soldier among them. The others were mainly bandits – a traditional and perfectly respectable occupation in Yunnan. They were supplemented by a few peasants who came from the private militias of feudal lords opposed to the decree of collectivization that had gone out from Peking. Looking at the motley crew before me, I felt the whole charade of Nationalist resistance had to end soon.

The major looked a sympathetic character and quite out of place in the midst of this gang of robbers and farmhands. He asked me to address a few words of encouragement to his men. I ended up having to make one or two idiotic remarks about the common destiny of the Free World and the worldwide campaign against Communism, which my interpreter duly translated for me. The whole thing made me feel a complete fool. When I had finished, we hastily drank a cup of tea with him before leaving. Dusk was already falling by the time we mounted our horses. We were relieved that nobody tried to stop us, far from it in fact – the outposts even waved goodbye as we passed. We rode at a fast trot, taking the way we had come. Before we reached the river marking the border we stumbled on a group of Chinese Thai girls. They were picking flowers in the woods and collecting them in large baskets. I sat quite still on my horse while two of them covered me with flowers from waist to neck. Then they presented me with a bunch to take on the rest of the journey and stuck a few sprays between the horse's ears for luck.

We decided to travel back to Lai Chau by river. Every so often we had to keep stopping to carry our narrow dug-out canoes across the rapids. When we finally took our leave of Phong To, our Shangri-La in the mountains, the cheerful Thai girls splashed us with buckets of water. To borrow a quotation from Rilke's *Cornet*, 'for a long time afterwards the white bodices shimmered among the greenery'.

I heard a follow-up to the story two weeks later in Hanoi. Just three weeks after we left the border area a Red Chinese battalion overran Muong La and wiped out the Nationalist guerillas there. Mao's troops then crossed the border into Tongking, captured the fort at Ban Nam Kum without a single shot being fired, and headed back to China, carrying off the solitary French officer. They had got as far as Phong To. They seized the year's opium harvest from the fields around the Meo villages then, without more ado, turned round and rode back to Yunnan. A troop of Moroccan Tabors were quickly dispatched to confront the Chinese invaders, but they had already disappeared over the border. The incident caused a great deal of head-scratching in Hanoi as people wondered why the People's Liberation Army should have made a sortie into Tongking. I always like to think they did it in retaliation for my visit to Muong La. The Chinese Communists must have known about it after all, and they almost certainly put my motives down to something far more sinister than professional curiosity.

The Aftermath of Dien Bien Phu

Hanoi, Summer 1954

The stronghold of Dien Bien Phu had fallen. The French defeat in Indochina was complete. Navarre, the commander-in-chief of the French forces, had gambled and lost. He had concentrated 16,000 of his troops in this godforsaken river-basin populated by Black Thai tribesmen. Until then the village of Dien Bien Phu had been known only as a miserable stopping-off point between the Tongking highlands and the Laotian side of the Mekong plain; now it was famous throughout the entire world. The French had dug in behind a circle of fortifications with the aim of drawing the Viet Minh Army into a frontal attack. For years military staff in Hanoi had dreamed of confronting the enemy in a pitched battle and destroying him. The French were so weary of the constant strain of guerilla warfare that they were prepared to take the colossal risk of being cut off in this remote hollow. Unfortunately General Navarre had seriously underestimated both the skill of the Viet Minh commander, a former history teacher named Vo Nguyen Giap, and the doggedness of his troops. Any military expert you cared to ask would have sworn it was impossible to transport artillery overland through the mountain jungle to Dien Bien Phu. Yet the Viet Minh managed it by dint of a superhuman physical effort. The French defences, which were not designed to withstand anything heavier than a mortar attack, collapsed under

73

the first salvoes fired by the besieging army. The French High Command in Indochina seemed retrospectively bent on confirming the truth of Clemenceau's remark that war was too serious a business to leave to the military.

The bourgeois coalition government in Paris was as much to blame for the defeat as the military, however. The Mouvement Républicain Populaire, which had once ranked as one of the progressive forces in French politics, now clung blindly and inexplicably to the mirage of its colonial heritage. At the last minute Georges Bidault, the foreign minister, even tried to persuade the Americans to drop tactical nuclear bombs on the Communist positions around Dien Bien Phu. But only a year had passed since Washington had reluctantly agreed to the armistice in Korea. For the first time in its history the United States had not emerged victorious from a war; it had had to agree to a stalemate in the form of a return to the situation existing before hostilities broke out. In the circumstances not even John Foster Dulles was likely to support the idea of nuclear intervention in Indochina. When the red flag with the yellow star was finally raised over the last French bunker, the reaction of the Western press, and even of the French public, was an ignominious sense of relief. The deadly escalation of the 'dirty war' had been prevented. Technically the French Army still held the Red River delta area, but it would be just a matter of weeks before it was totally defeated there, too. General Giap was massing his troops for an offensive against Hanoi.

Journalists had poured into Hanoi from all over the world. Previously the war in Indochina – unlike the Korea campaign – had had a very bad press from the international news media. Even a section of the Parisian press was ashamed of the belated French colonial venture. But now the final curtain was about to fall, and the vultures were gathering. The heat during those summer weeks was unbearable. The rice paddies in the Red River plain were under water, and evaporation from this man-made lake turned Tongking into a turkish bath. The mood in the press camp was strained. The chubby Major Roëllec had been replaced by a new commanding officer by the name of Garde. He was a wiry man with a crew-cut of black hair and was respected by everyone in the camp. Nobody could have then suspected that seven years later this officer would be one of the OAS conspirators in Algeria, and would plot to overthrow, and even kill, de Gaulle. The daily briefing was stormy. The American correspondents were astounded that Nam Dinh had been evacuated. This meant, in effect, the withdrawal of troops from the entire southern delta area, and it had already led to the resignation of Governor Tri.

'After an alignment of the front at Phu Ly our troops have taken up new defensive positions at Hadong,' said the military spokesman.

'What?' asked a thick-set American. 'You mean you've abandoned Hadong too?'

The French officer protested: 'There is no question of withdrawing from Hadong.'

'You mean it'll be evacuated the day after tomorrow,' the American retorted sarcastically.

Most questions centred on the plight of the French prisoners taken at Dien Bien Phu who were being escorted to Viet Minh internment camps in a gruelling forced march across hundreds of kilometres of mountainous jungle. The American journalists had written about a 'death march' in their reports, but the army censors had changed it to an 'exhausting march'. The Americans were furious at this toning-down of their language. 'What's that supposed to mean, an "exhausting march"? To an American an "exhausting march" means walking three blocks!' I was to be reminded of this scene later when the US Army took over from the French in Indochina, ten years too late.

Hanoi had become a fortified army base. Official buildings were cocooned in barbed wire. A sense of imminent departure hung in the air, a mood of farewell you could feel in the tree-lined avenues and the well cared-for villas. French civilians were packing their bags and getting ready to leave. They discussed the latest reports from Geneva, where the new French prime minister, Pierre Mendès-France, was negotiating with the Chinese representative, Chou En-lai, and the Viet Minh delegate, Pham Van Dong (later to become prime minister of a reunited Vietnam). When the time came to swallow the bitter pill of defeat, the conservative right wing in France had stepped aside to make way for the radical, progressive Mendès-France. PMF, as he was called, could never be accused of capitulating to the enemy. He fought tooth and nail over every clause in the ceasefire agreement. He even set a deadline for the end of the ceasefire, otherwise – so the threat went – he would send massive reinforcements of French conscripts to strengthen the Expeditionary Force. Mendès-France even compelled the respect of the old colonials in Hanoi, for they realized just how desperately he was bluffing. The French army in Tongking was on the point of collapse.

At night the booming of artillery salvoes could be heard on the outskirts of the city. From the hotel terrace you could see the flashes of gunfire flickering on the horizon. The ragged rhythm of a Chinese tango wafted from a bar next door. And so, against a background of dance music and gunfire, the French community in Hanoi waited for the final blow to fall.

A Visit to an Outpost

Son Tay, Summer 1954

For the last ten days, Son Tay, the outermost point in the western defences of Tongking, had been like a ghost town. The European troops had abandoned it to the Vietnamese National Army, and now the locals knew only too well what fate lay in store for them. 'Today it's the Nationalist Vietnamese, tomorrow it'll be the Viet Minh,' said the Chinese shopkeepers as they loaded their belongings onto ancient lorries and made off in the direction of Hanoi. And so we pulled out of Son Tay, driving past boarded-up shops, heading for the Viet Minh lines. A short distance out of town we left the rice plain of the delta behind us and found ourselves driving through rolling steppe country. In the distance we could see the fantastic shapes of the peaks of the Tongking highlands, their rocky faces overgrown with vegetation. This was ideal country for raids and surprise attacks, and we could see the road had already been torn up in several places by exploding mines. It was here that the last French outposts in Indochina were stationed, and it was here that the Viet Minh infiltrated every night, often in battalion strength.

Hoa Lao, the most westerly base in the area, was sited on a flat hilltop. The dug-outs went back deep into the ochre earth, but they were poorly protected overhead. A French sergeant lived here entirely on his own, with just fifty native militiamen for support. Five days ago he still had as many as 100 men under his command. The other fifty troops had since gone over to the enemy. 'Sometimes they disappear during the night,' said the sergeant morosely. 'Lately they've started coming to me demanding to be discharged, just like that. I don't try to stop them going in case they try to cut my throat while I'm sleeping. Anyway, you can hardly blame them for deserting. They're only thinking of the long term, and I shouldn't think we'll last out here for more than a few days at most. In the end we'll either have to withdraw or be smoked out.'

The sergeant did not appear to be nervous. People probably got nervous back at headquarters in Hanoi, inside the citadel. But out here nature was harsh and unforgiving, and the danger was real and tangible. In the end all you could do was to meet it head-on and stare straight into its blankly indifferent face.

Machine-guns in the Ricefield

Route 10, Summer 1954

The shooting started at 11 pm sharp, just as the lieutenant had predicted. First of all a single shot rang out from about 300 metres away in the ricefield. Then a burst of machine-gun fire came from the lower dyke. The red trail blazed in the darkness and then vanished into a small clump of trees. Gunfire then started coming from all directions. Still it was impossible to make out what was happening.

I was with a company of Algerians stationed on the dyke; luckily they had been in Tongking long enough not to lose their cool in all the shooting. I was told this (rather pointless) nightly firework display was organized by Bao Dai's Nationalist troops, together with the local militia from the next village. They were a completely different kettle of fish from the Viet Minh – the Viet Minh you never saw but could feel all around you. Now the Viet Minh meant business; they only fired when it was worth their while. Evidently it must have been worth their while attacking the nearby base of Ngoc Tao, for now, as we watched, we could see flames leaping high into the sky above it.

The Vietnamese Nationalists must have requested a barrage, because shells began pouring out of Son Tay. They landed a few hundred metres in front of us, sending up fountains of mud that were silhouetted against the clear and starry tropical sky. Then the firing stopped, as suddenly as it had begun. A jittery Bao Dai soldier sent up one final signal rocket. It lit up the sky, then the night came into its own again. Things were anything but quiet, however. The continual sound of yapping dogs came from the countless villages around us. Enclosed in their bamboo stockades, the villages rose above the shimmering waters of the flooded ricefields like dark islands. Crickets and other insects began a loud metallic chirping and the bullfrogs croaked monotonously to one another.

The lieutenant set off on his rounds. The Algerians were positioned in small groups on the outskirts of the village. They huddled together, whispering to each other in their guttural tongue. 'That makes the third night running we've spent out here,' said the lieutenant, cursing to himself. 'Now the raids have been stepped up in this sector we have to be on guard all the time. Yesterday our battalion commander was shot out of his jeep in broad daylight. We've had reports of large-scale Viet Minh movements to the south of here. Apparently they're going to try and cut the road from Son Tay to Hanoi right here. God, if only this damned war would end!'

The village elder sat squatting inside an improvised command post, a bearded North African standing guard over him. The lieutenant was holding him hostage. Practically all the men of military age had already deserted the village. The women had taken refuge in the village school, apparently because they were frightened of the Algerians. And yet, according to the lieutenant, the Algerians were a fairly well-behaved bunch – you just had to know how to handle them. The North Africans always had a swarm of coolies in tow, and they seemed to be on very close terms with them. The coolies were either deserters from the Vietnamese army or prisoners who had been sentenced to digging trenches. Nobody bothered to stand guard over them. 'What would be the point of their trying to escape?' asked the lieutenant. 'They'd never have it so good back where they came from, and they'd still be coolies.' I heard stories about North Africans falling asleep on sentry duty and Vietnamese coolies standing in for them at the machine-gun emplacement.

I awoke next day to see the early morning sunlight stain the water in the ricefields a deep blood-red. The hills around the delta were shrouded in purple haze. The dark green leaves of the banana plants looked almost black. Sergeant Kalifa handed me his binoculars. With them I could see one or two black dots moving about at the far end of the dyke. It seemed that the Viet Minh were just as interested in our movements as we were in theirs. A patrol was organized to link up with the Vietnamese battalion in the neighbouring western sector. Travelling over the tarmac road we took care to avoid freshly dug-up areas, which might have concealed mines. We saw a thin column of men coming towards us. There was a tense moment, then the North Africans identified them as Nationalists, superbly armed but poorly turned out. 'Thank God I'm not assigned to that lot!' said the lieutenant. 'I'm much better off with my Algerians, even though they're vulnerable to all the enemy propaganda thrown at them. Only the other day I came across some leaflets lying around that urged them to desert. The Communists are forever going on about "solidarity among oppressed colonial peoples" and telling everyone to "unite in the common struggle". I know very well my *Tirailleurs* talk about it among themselves, though they always shut up as soon as I appear. Most of these pamphlets must have been printed in Moscow; luckily they're written in Arabic, so only a few of the men can read them.'

Not long before this I had come across an inscription in German on the wall of an abandoned church. 'Legionnaires, give up this senseless and criminal struggle! Come over to our side, the side of the Vietnamese people, and we guarantee you will be allowed to go home to your families.' Apparently one or two deserters from the Legion had, in fact, been returned to East Germany via Peking and Moscow.

The Last Engagement

Hung Yen, July 1954

Around midnight somebody screamed 'Look out!' The armoured cars and half-tracks which were drawn up in a barricade around our position fired their guns. Rockets illuminated the night. A dozen shells struck near the French command post. Wounded men called for the medical orderly. I crouched in the rectangular dug-out where my camp bed was sheltered, set up under the mosquito net like a catafalque. The shooting ended abruptly. The colonial infantry along the road to Hung Yen had just experienced the last action of the French war in Indochina. That same hour the signatures had been put to the ceasefire agreement in Geneva.

When the sun rose and the dead Viet Minh soldiers of the 42nd Regiment lying in the barbed wire had been counted, the officers gathered round the radio. Naked from the waist up, a fat colonel with a rolling, southern French accent sat like a vicious temple dog in front of the tent. A refined woman's voice on Radio Hanoi coolly announced the conditions of the French surrender in Tongking. The 17th parallel was to become the new demarcation line between Communist Vietnam in the north and the opposing Nationalist Republic in the south. The French withdrawal from Tongking would be carried out in stages over several months. This was to give anti-Communists in the north a reasonable time to withdraw to Saigon. Two years after the ceasefire, the ultimate fate and possible reunification of Vietnam were to be decided in free, supervised elections in both halves of the country.

Not a word was uttered as we listened to the news. The faces of the men remained expressionless. The location of the demarcation line on the 17th parallel, which put the old imperial city of Hue out of reach of the Communists, meant that France had fared better than expected. This could be put down to the stubbornness of Mendès-France, but also to the influence of the chief Chinese delegate, Chou En-lai. Chou had exerted pressure on the Viet Minh delegation and urged conciliation. Was his intention in doing this to keep the Americans out of Indochina, or was he attempting, even at that early stage, to prevent the rise of an over-confident Vietnamese state on China's border? The French officers on the road to Hung Yen suspected nothing of the struggles going on behind the scenes at the Geneva conference. They didn't think the anti-Communist state had a chance of lasting. The troops had received the news of the ceasefire without enthusiasm, but without protest either. The dominant feeling was one of resignation. The colonial infantrymen knew they would leave behind a part of themselves in this exotic and alien country, which they secretly felt committed to by an unrequited love. They looked out across the paddy fields where the farmers, behind their buffaloes, were busy ploughing furrows in the fertile mud once again, as though the bombing of the nearby tomb of their ancestors a few hours before had never happened. At the edge of the brown pool, where pretty children were laughing and bathing, a bright blue bush was in bloom. The soldiers pondered the scene, fixing the picture firmly in their minds before having to return to the grimy drabness of the industrial suburbs of their native land.

We felt apprehensive about the return journey to Hanoi. Countless mines buried in the roads had not yet been removed. Columns of smoke rose into the air at regular intervals every time a vehicle exploded. The stoical calm everyone had displayed until the ceasefire came into force had vanished. Now the words on everyone's lips were: 'Just so long as I'm not the last man killed in this war.'

The fat colonel looked as though he had just woken up from a deep sleep. He had not uttered a word, not even a curse. When the time came for us to go he suddenly seemed to recover his powers of speech. He shook hands and said: 'I won't say goodbye to you for good, because this isn't the end. We're bound to meet up again in North Africa before long.' How right he proved to be.

An Exchange of Prisoners

Hai Thon, Summer 1954

The exchange of prisoners began immediately after the signing of the Geneva Agreements. The Viet Minh had dispatched part of the French garrison captured at Dien Bien Phu to make the long journey on foot to their stronghold in the coastal province of Thanh Hoa. (The French had never managed to gain as much as a foothold there in ten years of fighting.) The French Navy assigned an LSM landing-craft to transport 100 Viet Minh prisoners to an agreed rendezvous in the enemy zone.

The captured Viet Minh looked a fairly well-disciplined bunch. The French nurses on board ship were the worst affected by the heavy swell. They were shocked to discover that the Vietnamese soldiers had formed very intimate relationships during the long years spent behind barbed wire. In charge of the group was a second lieutenant from the 320th Division who had lost an arm in the fighting. Since this was the first transport ship to take part in an exchange, it carried sick and wounded prisoners in the main. The official spokesman for the group was a thin young man who had received severe napalm burns, but he had made a surprisingly good recovery. He claimed he was a private but he was, in fact, a political commissar. Speaking in halting French, he told us he was convinced that the neo-colonial regime was doomed to collapse in South Vietnam. President Ho Chi Minh would, he said, bring peace and justice to his people. All the prisoners here, he assured us, were prepared to sacrifice their lives in the future, should it prove necessary. The lecture we got from the ex-student with the fanatical glint in his eyes could hardly be described as original.

A more tragic case was the Catholic soldier from Phat Diem province who had had a leg amputated. He wanted to have nothing to do with Communism, but seemingly Uncle Ho had formed a broad patriotic front where there was room for Christians and Marxists both. On the whole, the mood among the prisoners on board the landing craft was one of apprehension rather than enthusiasm. They were probably wondering what sort of a reception they would get from the Communist authorities the next day.

At dawn we sailed into the estuary of the Son Ma River and ran aground on sandbanks three times. Eventually a big junk drew up with the flag of the Red Cross flying from its mast. Three Viet Minh officers in vivid green uniforms stood at the side of the boat. According to the terms of the agreement they should have been unarmed, but we could see a couple of guns sticking out from under a tarpaulin cover that had slightly slipped. The tall captain of the corvette who was supervising the French end of the exchange said with a wry laugh: 'It's really touching to see how much faith they have in us.' Then he jumped into a small boat and rowed ashore with the medical orderly, while a native pilot guided our ship to a flat area of the river bank. The wretched little fishing village of Hai Thon lay huddled out of sight behind the dense undergrowth on the bank. The blue mass of the Thanh Hoa mountains shimmered on the horizon.

The large door in the bow of the landing craft was slowly lowered into position with a terrific clatter. The prisoners fell into line and prepared to disembark. We jumped onto bamboo rafts that had been brought up to the craft, then we waded the last few metres onto the shore. About thirty Viet Minh soldiers and officers were waiting to greet us. There were no insignia or decorations on their uniforms. A short distance behind them local civilians crowded round, dressed in their brown and black peasant clothes. Inside the bamboo reception hut was an improvised conference table with a yellow cover. At one end a picture of Ho Chi Minh hung in pride of place below the red flag with the yellow star, like an image on an ancestral altar. The Viet Minh delegates introduced themselves. Their spokesman was an ascetic-looking major. The tone of the discussion that followed was cool and polite. It was agreed that the Viet Minh prisoners should be brought ashore first and then 100 French prisoners would be released. The first soldier to come ashore was the second lieutenant of the 320th Division. He walked up to the major and gave his name. The major hugged him so tightly and so awkwardly that the lieutenant nearly lost his footing. The Viet Minh reception committee was visibly moved when the prisoners drew up on their rafts and, on command from their political commissar, gave three cheers for Ho Chi Minh, the revolution and victory. Each cheer was rewarded by enthusiastic applause from the people of the fishing village. The captured Viet Minh were now pretending to be far more ill and exhausted than they in fact were. The peasant women hugged their prisoners, supported them, fanned cool air onto them with their wide-brimmed hats, and stroked their faces. In no time at all the returning heroes had ripped off their French army fatigues and changed into Viet Minh uniform.

We were able to move about freely and have a fairly relaxed conversation with the representatives from the other side. They were interested in events taking place in Europe and were surprisingly well-informed. The talk ended abruptly when the French caught sight of their own prisoners. The battle of Dien Bien Phu, the tiring march to Thanh Hoa and the ravages of disease had all taken a terrible toll. Many of the men were lying on improvised stretchers under a long thatched roof. Very few were able to walk. They welcomed the party of Frenchmen with grateful, feverish looks. No, they had not been badly treated. But the long march on foot through the jungle had been gruelling and a lot of men had died on the way. They had received the same medical attention as the Viet Minh soldiers, but it was nowhere near adequate for a European. Nearly all of the prisoners were suffering from dysentery and malaria. The French nurses now shot looks of hate at the Vietnamese nursing staff. The walk back to the river bank was very subdued to start with. Before the French prisoners boarded the landing craft they said they wanted to make their own personal demonstrations of patriotism and faith, as they had seen the enemy do. They had not come prepared with any speeches, though. One group yelled 'Hip hip hooray!' as if they

83

were at a football match, and a soldier hobbling with a wounded leg shouted 'Vive la France!' as if he were de Gaulle himself.

The voyage back to Haiphong was hard going. A strong wind had blown up over the Gulf of Tongking, and the flat landing-craft was battered by the waves. The survivors of Dien Bien Phu described the battle, the failure of their command, and the terrible shock they got when their poorly protected positions suddenly began to be bombarded by enemy artillery. One Thai battalion had been overrun immediately. The remaining coloured troops of the French Union had refused to fight and had sought cover. The French paratroopers and the legionnaires were the only ones who had really fought to the last. The paratroopers spoke contemptuously about officers in other units who had not stood by their men. But the legionnaires, who were 80 per cent German, had gone to their deaths like heroes in some ancient saga.

There were two exhausted lieutenants who kept themselves apart from the rest of the group. They had been taken prisoner by the Viet Minh way back in 1950, at the evacuation of Cao Bang. They had been harassed for years by the Communist commissars. Not a day went by when they did not have to endure several hours of political schooling and re-education. In order to survive (and also because they were prompted by a certain intellectual curiosity), the inmates of the French officers' camp played along with their captors and pretended to be partly won over to Marxism and anti-colonialism. (This was in sharp contrast to the more rough-and-ready NCOs, who tended to turn a deaf ear to the Communist propagandists.) However bad the living conditions were in the prison camps, in the long run the most unbearable thing was, according to them, the pedantic dogmatism, the presumption of ideological superiority, the know-all schoolteacher attitude of the yellow-skinned preachers of world revolution.

'By the end of a year we felt like we were guinea pigs they were carrying out brainwashing experiments on. It was far more unpleasant and far more humiliating than being hungry or ill,' said one lieutenant.

'We did learn one thing, though,' said his companion. 'We know now that the campaign we fought was ridiculously behind the times. Here in Asia, and tomorrow probably in Africa, we're up against an ideological war, and we'll only be able to maintain our position overseas if we use the same propaganda methods and the same crude indoctrination techniques on the coloureds that the

Viet Minh tried out on us. Maybe we should use the same methods to re-educate our people back home, so they learn the meaning of patriotism and loyalty and discipline again. We've been betrayed by the politicians and parties of the Fourth Republic. They've let us down badly. But we're willing to teach them all about "revolutionary renewal" if they want.'

The voice of the second lieutenant was husky, and it now sunk almost to a whisper. When he finished talking his whole frame was suddenly racked by a fit of coughing. The nurse handed him a clean handkerchief and when he took it away from his mouth it was stained with blood. The sea had become so rough by this time that the occupants of the boat – with the exception of the crew – were all feeling seasick. Soon we were all hanging onto the railing, letting the warm wind blow in our faces while we vomited into the inky black darkness.

Flight Across the 17th Parallel

On the road from Hanoi to Saigon, Summer 1954

The sky above the Red River delta was empty. No more white plumes of smoke from burning villages. No more black clouds from napalm bombs. The war was over. The passengers pressed their faces against the windows of the Dakota as it took off, in an effort to catch a final glimpse of Hanoi. There were quite a number of women and children on board. You could tell the colonial officials who had done long service by their skin: it had the colour and texture of parchment. They gazed down for the last time at the chequerboard of ricefields, glistening in the evening sun. In the past they had often had occasion to curse this country with its debilitating climate and its inscrutable people, its diseases and its sleepless nights. But now the thought of leaving it, and the memory of defeat, brought a lump to the throat. The officers of the Vietnamese National Army on board were turning their backs for good on their homeland to go and fight in the South. The future for them was uncertain to say the least. As we flew over the cliffs around the Bay of Halong, dusk was already falling.

The evening before we had eaten out in the Chinese district of

Hanoi. The Sons of Heaven had been unusually silent for some reason, and their silence had infected us in turn. Afterwards we sat for a long time in Marianne's bar, a favourite haunt of reporters. The almond-eyed Marianne had once spent some time in a convent at Nam Dinh. It still showed when she chatted with customers behind the counter. She acted as if she was not the least bit worried by the Communist takeover that was due any day now. She pored over a large map of Europe, trying to pick out the sleepy little town in central France where she planned to begin her new life. Her waitresses sat perched on their stools, giggling and apparently unworried as usual. In a few weeks' time they would be eyeing customers in the dance halls of Saigon and Cholon with all their grace and charm. But in their hearts they would be thinking of their relatives in the North. Soon there'd be no more expensive dresses or Chinese tangos or carefree living for them – only a brown worker's uniform and the daily grind of forced labour. Outside, French tank patrols clanked and rattled their way through the deserted streets. They drove past banners put up by a Viet Minh advance party only that morning. The banners called on the people of Hanoi to stay where they were; nobody had made any attempt to take them down. Now the Communist agents were coming out into the open and were suddenly all over the city. They would ride into a residential district on their bicycles, take out their notebooks and draw up lists of all the houses and offices that could be used as accommodation for the Communist staffs and government bodies.

Half-way between Hanoi and Saigon the pilot made an announcement over the loudspeaker system. 'We're now flying over the future demarcation line along the 17th parallel and the Ben Hai River. You can see it clearly in daylight.' The night was moonless, with only the occasional flash of gunfire to break up the darkness. The ceasefire was due to come into force a few weeks later in central Annam, to allow time for scattered units in the jungle to be notified. Until now the Ben Hai River, which marked the new border, had been known only to geographers. The peasant rice-growers on its banks still irrigated their fields communally, as they had done for centuries. Soon, however, they would only be able to wave to each other across the barbed wire. And eventually the day would come (and it was closer than most people realized) when the bamboo huts and ancestral graves of peacetime would have to make way for the concrete bunkers of an iron wall.

Prelude to a New Tragedy

Saigon, Summer 1954

The French tricolour had been lowered over Saigon's town hall, and the white stucco building now flew a host of Nationalist Vietnamese flags – three red stripes on a yellow background. The giant portrait of Bao Dai had disappeared from the gabled wall. Although he had not yet officially abdicated as emperor and head of state, his days were clearly numbered. Bao Dai, the fat, ageing playboy who used to go hunting in Alsace and water-skiing on the Côte d'Azur while his country was bleeding to death, was now universally despised and rejected. A new man had taken over the reins of the State of Vietnam, soon to be baptized South Vietnam. He was Ngo Dinh Diem, a mandarin born in Hue and who had already earned himself the nickname of The Incorruptible. This morning Ngo Dinh Diem had presented his new government to the people of Saigon. There had been two companies of the National Army all lined up in dazzling white uniforms, but the local people had stayed away. The bulk of the crowd of 300 spectators probably consisted of secret police.

Ngo Dinh Diem was an uncompromising patriot and a dedicated opponent of French rule in Indochina. The last High Commissioner, General Ely, had only agreed to his appointment after pressure was put on him by the Americans. Diem belonged to one of the most respected families in Annam. In 1933 he became a minister at the court of Hue. Later his Nationalist tendencies gradually hardened as a result of constant opposition – opposition to the French, to the Japanese, to Ho Chi Minh, and finally to Bao Dai himself. Diem was not proving an easy ally for the Americans either, or so the rumour went. That morning the new Prime Minister had worn a white suit and black tie. He was a stout man, with glossy hair parted over a fleshy face. He laid a wreath on the improvised ancestral altar and walked back to his escort, moving with the characteristic waddling gait of senior mandarins.

Diem was heavily influenced by the Confucian tradition at the court of Annam; nonetheless, as was soon to become apparent, he was also a fanatical Catholic. His elder brother was archbishop of Hue. One of his younger brothers, Ngo Dinh Nhu, ranked as one of his closest advisers. He had thrown himself into the study of modern Catholic philosophy and was reputed to be a staunch

87

advocate of the doctrine of Personalism. Most of the ministers in the new cabinet originally came from the North, and this in itself was a clear indication of Diem's determination not to formally recognize the partition of his country. As a Catholic, Diem regarded it as a personal tragedy that more than a million Catholics risked coming under Communist rule as a result of the division of Vietnam. A huge exodus of refugees to the South had already begun, and in the coming months the French fleet was to be kept fully employed ferrying whole communities of Christians to the safety of the South. The latest rumour going the rounds in Saigon was that you no longer had to pass the old exams for the mandarinate; under The Incorruptible's new regime a Catholic certificate of baptism was all that was needed.

The few French officials who attended the ceremony – with no great show of enthusiasm it should be said – stared mesmerized at a radiantly beautiful Vietnamese woman who kept close to the Prime Minister's side, like a cat stalking its prey. Madame Nhu was the sister-in-law of Diem, the straight-laced bachelor. She had been brought up by Catholic nuns and was reckoned to be one of the most influential women in the new regime. Her intelligence, her ambition, and her militant feminism attracted a lot of comment. 'You know the old Chinese proverb,' a French administrator murmured to me. 'The educated man builds the town, but the educated woman destroys it. Remember this piece of Oriental wisdom next time you do a report on Madame Nhu.'

At that time the Viet Minh were gradually taking over the running of the North, and the atmosphere in Saigon seemed more frivolous and happy-go-lucky than ever before. During the last weeks of the war the Viet Minh had rushed their regiments into the South, getting as far as the Mekong Delta by dint of forced marches. They had even marched at night, using torches to light their way. Yet the Geneva Agreements had laid down that all Communist units were to be withdrawn to the North after the end of hostilities. Much to everyone's surprise, Ho Chi Minh now appeared to be honouring the terms of the agreement fairly conscientiously. Admittedly the political commissars were still at their posts, but they were simply standing by. They had gone underground for the time being, and they seemed to be concentrating on organizing their network of secret Communist cells in preparation for the uprising to come. The signal from Hanoi was expected any day now.

In Cholon, Saigon's twin town, police rule was still in the hands of the Binh Xuyen, the river pirates who had got fat on the proceeds of opium smuggling, prostitution and extortion. Law and order in the great metropolis of the South seemed to be deteriorating fast in the hands of these none-too-wholesome types. The French had given *carte blanche* to the gangster boss of the Binh Xuyen, 'General' Le Van Vien, and he had exploited his powers ruthlessly. His henchmen always went about heavily armed and wore distinctive green berets. The locals feared them more than they did the Communist guerillas. In fact their cruel and underhand methods had succeeded in stamping out active Communist resistance in the town. It was common knowledge that Ngo Dinh Diem could not tolerate the idea of this gang of thieves and cut-throats being in charge of law and order in Cholon. After all, Diem was a mandarin, and he had inherited the mandarin's cherished belief in the ultimate authority of the state – a belief that was worlds away from the semi-feudal, semi-religious jigsaw puzzle that made up the French power structure in the Mekong Delta. The French secret services knew all about the private talks that had gone on between Diem and American liaison officers, in which the Americans had been told about the operation the Vietnamese National Army was planning to mount against the Binh Xuyen, the Cao Dai and the Hoa Hao.

The first American military men who arrived in Saigon to advise the National Army were very discreet indeed. The same could hardly be said for the US Navy, though – the Rue Catinat positively swarmed with sailors, all wearing their distinctive white pyjama uniforms. Already the street traders and prostitutes were beginning to haggle in pidgin English. In Ngo Dinh Diem's anterooms the special envoys of the CIA were busily planning a new phase in the Indochinese war. Washington had been extremely reluctant to accept the terms of the Geneva ceasefire, and the signature of the US government was still conspicuously absent from the final documents. The American experts were most worried about the joint Vietnamese elections that were to be held in 1956, which they were determined to block – not realizing that the Marxist regime in Hanoi was not at all bothered about this formal exercise in token democracy. A stubborn rivalry was steadily growing between the French and American secret services. Washington was working towards achieving the fastest possible withdrawal of the last French troops from Vietnam. Only when that happened would Diem's government be able to demonstrate its national independence to the outside world and appear as a respectable partner for other Third World countries. The French, for their part, were hanging on stubbornly to the Cochin China they knew and loved, and trying to stir up local opposition against this stiff-necked mandarin and his US advisers. At one stage they even tried to have the province declared a neutral zone.

The so-called Third Force that was to be such a talking point during the American involvement in Vietnam was already in existence by then. One of the leading supporters of a compromise solution in Saigon was 'General' Xuan, a member of the wealthy bourgeoisie. He was a dapper old gentleman with exquisite manners – a Frenchman with yellow skin, in fact – and he did not look at all like a military man. He received me in his drawing-room, which was crammed full of Chinese paintings and mother-of-pearl and lacquer furniture. The way Xuan saw it, the most important thing was to preserve the spiritual unity of the Vietnamese people in the face of the inevitable partition of the country. He knew what the Viet Minh were really like. They weren't nearly as barbaric as they were made out, and they were nationalists first and foremost. They had already made it clear that they wanted to dissociate themselves from their old arch-enemies, the Chinese. Xuan obviously kept in close touch with the leading politicians of the Fourth Republic in Paris. Influential circles in the French government were openly toying with the idea of letting the Communist Democratic Republic of Vietnam remain within the French Union. The last French civilians left in Hanoi had received official orders to stay put, in case the new cooperation treaty with Ho Chi Minh offered fresh hopes of a peaceful French presence remaining in the North.

Back in the military staffs in Saigon, French officers held out their hands in mock despair at this unbelievably foolish and naive attitude. Reports were coming in daily from their own bases, which were currently being evacuated systematically. The war in Indochina had been anything but glorious, but now it was over the French military were making sure the withdrawal was conducted in a suitably dignified and defiant manner. They knew they were finished in the Far East. They had underestimated Diem's energy; they had imagined him incapable of proclaiming himself head of state so quickly, or of acting so ruthlessly against France's trusted allies, the sects and the river pirates. Meanwhile the French acted like jilted lovers towards the dynamic Americans who were currently installing themselves in all the Vietnamese staffs and ministries. In the months that followed a farcical and bloody power struggle was to be played out between the French and American secret services, both in Saigon and on the edge of the Plain of Reeds.

I had been back in Europe for some time when the evacuation of Hanoi was finally completed in the spring of 1955. One of the most memorable pictures of the war appeared on the front page of the Paris newspapers. It showed the last French detachment pulling out of the city, crossing the Paul Doumer bridge on the way to Gialam airport. Immediately behind them came an élite regiment of Viet Minh troops, marching in close order. The soldiers carried their rifles Russian-style, with bayonet at the ready, as if they were going into the attack. Between the two hostile units marched a solitary French captain. He carried a folded tricolour over his outstretched arms, like someone bearing aloft the holy sacraments.

Meanwhile, gathering in the wings, were the actors and puppeteers who were to take part in the new tragedy of Indochina, the one that was to unfold in North and South Vietnam.

THE SECOND INDOCHINESE WAR

The Americans

The Khmer Smile

Cambodia, Spring 1965

The full moon stood high in the sky above the towers of the temple of Angkor Wat. The huge stone monument was covered with a riot of carvings showing creatures from Hindu mythology. In the darkness you could just see their vague outlines, silhouetted against the starry sky. Nearby were the sinister, unmistakable profiles of the Naga snakes guarding the bridge between the temple's two pools. They stood erect and clearly visible in the silvery moonlight, rearing their massive heads against the night sky. The entrance to the temple was illuminated by powerful floodlights. Inside, Cambodian temple-dancers acted scenes from the Ramayana with slow movements of their long, supple fingers. The girls, living replicas of the images frozen in the stone behind them, wore glittering head-dresses and heavy brocade robes, and their bare shoulders gleamed like bronze. They wore heavy make-up, and their eyes were the only things that seemed to move in their immobile, mask-like faces.

I was sitting comfortably on the terrace of my chalet in the Auberge du Temple. I leant back in my bamboo chair and listened to the familiar sounds of the South-east Asian night filtering through the dull clang of the temple gongs. I was continually pestered by clouds of mosquitoes, for the jungle lay at my feet. I was back in Indochina again after an absence of eleven years. During that time I had been busy pursuing my journalistic career, working mainly in black Africa and the Arab world. Now I had returned and I felt a sharp stab of pleasure at finding myself once more in this crossroads of Indian and Chinese culture. My last stopover before arriving in Cambodia had been in Delhi, where I had gone to visit the tombs and palaces of the Mogul emperors. The religious history of the region turned out to be fascinating.

95

The people of the Punjab had, on the whole, managed to resist the attempts of their Muslim conquerors to convert them to Islam, and they had clung defiantly to their primitive myths and their vast pantheon of gods. But even in the Punjab much of the uninhibited sensuality of Hinduism had evaporated as it came into contact with the austere desert religion of Islam and the teachings of the one God. I realized afterwards it would have been easier to trace the religious ties that had existed between India and Cambodia for thousands of years if I had set out from the southern part of the subcontinent – the Malabar coast, possibly, or Madras or Madurai.

The mighty kingdom of the Khmer evolved against a religious background of flourishing Hinduism. The empire, which at its height extended far beyond the frontiers of present-day Cambodia into South-east Asia, reached the peak of its might and magnificence in the twelfth century. Then came a period of inexorable but inexplicable decline. The flamboyant, exuberant monuments of Khmer culture – Angkor Wat, Angkor Thom, and Bayon, to name only the most famous – were swallowed up by the jungle and eventually lay completely buried under the creepers and vegetation. The vast temple sites around Siem Reap were uncovered by French archaeologists just a few decades ago. The inhabitants of the region must have been terrified at the sight of these colossal relics of a bygone civilization, obviously so much greater than their own. They had, by that time, suppressed even the folk-memory of their remote Khmer ancestors.

The decline and fall of the Khmer kingdom was paralleled by a bitter feud between the followers of Hinduism and Buddhism. Through the surviving monuments of the age we can chart the progress of the internecine wars fought between the two religious camps. We can see, for instance, that from time to time the Hindu obsession with rebirth and the Brahman preoccupation with caste gave way to the contemplative ecstasy of the Buddhist ideal of nirvana. The release Buddhism promised from the Hindu nightmare of eternal reincarnation had, in fact, been used many times in the past to wean followers away from the sinister attractions of Shiva and Kali. Then there were periods when both sides indulged in an orgy of self-destruction, smashing sacred images in their own temples. In the end, though, it was the smiling Buddha that emerged triumphant. The Khmer people settled into a state of tranquil resignation, turning their backs forever on the giant memorials to past greatness. From that time on, the

Cambodians dutifully gathered in the shade of their wooden, shingle-roofed pagodas and bowed down before their golden statues of the wise Gautama. And every morning, without fail, they would fill the bowls of the numerous monks who passed through their villages begging for alms, aloof and dignified in their saffron robes and shaven heads.

After much toil and effort the huge and ancient temples were finally wrested from the clutches of the jungle. The sculptors and stonemasons of ancient Cambodia obviously started out by faithfully copying the traditional styles of their Indian masters, and for generations they simply went on endlessly reproducing the stereotyped images of the fabulous world of the Mahabharata and the Ramayana. The Hindu obsession with ceaseless, frenetic regeneration appears again and again in countless representations of the lingam, or phallus. In the end the Cambodian craftsmen came near to attaining something like artistic perfection, but they had to wait until they eventually broke out of the mould of imported Hindu imagery. Once they freed themselves from these foreign influences the movements of their slant-eyed temple-dancers began to come to life, and their figures took on a lithe grace and gentle charm that the Indian originals had lacked. At about the same time, their huge statues of the Buddha acquired an aura of Oriental mysticism and serenity that could never have evolved on the troubled banks of the Ganges and the Brahmaputra. The smile that played on the stone lips of these Buddhas as they gazed down on the sunken temples of Cambodia was the famous Khmer smile, rapt and enigmatic, cruel and abstracted at the same time.

The rulers of Cambodia, like the Egyptian Pharaohs, had their military exploits immortalized in sweeping stone friezes by armies of slaves. These heroic battle scenes depicted, with monotonous regularity, the struggle of the Khmer people against the Chams, who were constantly threatening to invade the country. The Chams originally came from the area we now know as the Mekong Delta. They sailed up the Mekong River in their armed galleys, ending up in the rich fishing grounds of the great inland lake of Tonle Sap. At that time the kingdom of Champa, which had also been converted to Hinduism, was involved in a feud with the Cambodian god-king. Today you would search in vain on a map of East Asia for any trace of the warlike nation of the Chams, once so feared throughout Indochina. Over the centuries their territory was gradually taken over by a new master race from the north, and their people were subjugated and assimilated. These newcomers came from what we now know as China. They advanced southwards inexorably, like a column of ants on the march, after seizing possession of Tongking and Annam. These warlike people were the ancestors of the present-day Vietnamese.

Phnom Penh, the capital of Cambodia was, for me, the most beautiful city in the whole of Asia. The French had left behind broad avenues lined with mango trees, their branches heavy with fruit. The villas and public buildings previously occupied by European civilians were a soft ochre yellow. The city got its name from the 'phnom' or hill near its centre, from where you could look out over the whole capital. The hill had a big stupa perched on its summit, and a Buddhist pagoda with gaily-coloured flags that fluttered in the breeze. Down by the river banks the gold and green roofs of the Royal Palace shimmered in the sunlight. The new town had been ambitiously planned and its streets branched out around the busy Boulevard Monivong. The university campus, built on either side of the road leading to the airport, was an attractively laid out complex of whitewashed buildings. In the evenings the city seemed to convey a strange sense of tranquillity. It descended on you gradually as you drove along in your rickshaw in the balmy evening air, passing beneath the canopy of tall trees, heading out towards the waterfront. Here nothing much had changed since the days of French colonial rule. The dark-skinned Khmer girls, with their softly curling hair, had an earthy sensuality and a carefree abandon that made them very different from the more subdued Vietnamese women.

In all its long history the kingdom of the Khmer had never once known hunger or want. Its ricefields were the most fertile in Asia and its lakes and rivers teemed with fish. The stamp of Buddhism was everywhere and it dictated the whole rhythm of life. Buddhism had instilled in this peasant race an easy-going indolence and a tremendous sense of calm, or at least that was how it appeared. To the eyes of foreign visitors, the Cambodians seemed like true children of nature, happy and carefree, forever laughing and chattering even when working in the ricefields. Their society had no sexual taboos, and the concept of original sin seemed to have completely passed Cambodia by. If ever a corner of the world approximated to my vision of an earthly paradise it was the kingdom of Cambodia under Prince Norodom Sihanouk.

The first opportunity I had to observe Prince Sihanouk was during the annual fertility celebrations outside the capital. He was ploughing the first furrow in the mud of a rice paddy, walking along behind a team of buffaloes. At that time he still had the status of the traditional Hindu god-king, although it was many years since he banished the court Brahmans from his palace in Phnom Penh. (The King of Siam, unlike Sihanouk, still kept up this ancient Hindu tradition.) Norodom Sihanouk was a living descendant of the great Khmer dynasty immortalized in the ruined temple of Angkor Wat. He had abdicated the throne and proclaimed himself head of state, but he still possessed the absolute powers of an autocratic monarch. The French in Cambodia always used to address him as Monseigneur. The peasants, on the other hand, continued to look on him as some kind of godly reincarnation, for the old Hindu beliefs died hard. Whenever Sihanouk appeared in public the people would kneel at his feet – whereupon the prince would plunge into the crowd and bow down too, smiling broadly, his hands folded in the traditional *lai* posture. He had two ambitions: first, to be an enlightened ruler, and secondly, to keep his country free from the military unrest that was rife throughout the rest of Indochina. He had succeeded up till now, but five years after the French defeat in Tongking the Vietnam war had flared into life again. The Saigon administration of the Catholic dictator, Ngo Dinh Diem, was under increasing pressure from Communist guerilla units in the South. The joint banner they were fighting under was the National Liberation Front of Vietnam, but to the people they were known simply as the Viet Cong – in other words, Communists. For the past six years this revolutionary movement had received steady support from North Vietnam. Now, in March 1965, everyone was talking about the Ho Chi Minh Trail, the maze of jungle tracks that led across the rugged mountains of Laos. The trail bypassed the South Vietnamese defence lines and enabled Communist guerilla forces to infiltrate deeper into the South. The Viet Cong were most solidly entrenched in the border region between Cambodia and South Vietnam, where the local rubber plantations and marshy terrain provided excellent cover for troops. In a comparatively short time they had managed to construct a vast network of dug-outs and underground tunnels. On the Cambodian side of the border, there was little Sihanouk could do to prevent this systematic infiltration by the Vietnamese Communists. His position was further weakened by the fact that he had considerably reduced the role of his army – no doubt out of an understandable desire for self-preservation. Much to the annoyance of his French army instructors, he had deliberately followed a policy of restricting his forces to minor duties like road-building and engineering.

Sihanouk, in fact, found himself caught in a precarious balancing act, trying to juggle with the rival claims of East and West or, more accurately, Hanoi, Peking, Moscow, Washington and Paris. His aim was to pursue a policy of neutrality and diplomatic opportunism – as he saw it his only chance of preserving his country's independence. Now Sihanouk did, it must be admitted, have a habit of giggling for no apparent reason every time he spoke, but he was a far cry from the 'political clown' his Western critics liked to label him. Rather, he was a master of political disguise. What is more, he was constantly alive to the dangers threatening his country. There was, after all, no shortage of precedents. In the nineteenth century Cambodia had been faced with a similar threat when the Siamese in the west and the Vietnamese in the east had been on the point of carving up the kingdom between them. In the end, only the establishment of a French protectorate in Vietnam had saved the country from this deliberate policy of encroachment. But no Khmer could ever allow himself to forget that up until 1700 the whole area of the Mekong Delta, including Saigon (then called Prey Nohar), had been Cambodian territory.

Sihanouk was a man with many enemies. First, there were the Americans, still obsessed with the old Dulles idea that neutrality was somehow immoral. Then there were the generals in Bangkok, constantly threatening to seize control of the provinces of Battambang and Siem Reap. Aided and abetted by the CIA, they were busily channelling aid to an underground movement known as Khmer Serei and plotting to overthrow Sihanouk. Finally, there was the Saigon government, which viewed Viet Cong infiltration of Cambodian territory as a grave threat to the security of South Vietnam. As it happened, its concern was perfectly justified. Every day columns of lorries carrying supplies and ammunition for the South Vietnamese Liberation Front would roll out of the harbour of Sihanoukville, heading along the red laterite road towards the controversial border with Vietnam. And malicious rumours circulated in Phnom Penh about Princess Monique, Sihanouk's beautiful, half-Italian wife, who was alleged to have a share in the profits from this illegal trade with the Viet Cong. Whatever the truth behind the gossip, people in the Western embassies in Phnom Penh were certainly talking openly about the existence of a Sihanouk Trail.

Monseigneur was well aware he was on a knife-edge. He had only one real friend and ally, and that was General de Gaulle, in power in France since 1958. Unfortunately France's protection was not going to be enough to save Cambodia. Sihanouk had, with good reason, forbidden American journalists to set foot inside his country. This was because they persistently misinterpreted the complicated chess-game he was playing as mere double-dealing, whereas in fact what he was doing was pursuing a policy of national survival – at any price. History had taught him one lesson and one lesson only, namely that the people of North and South Vietnam, whatever their political colouring, would always be his country's deadly enemies.

Sihanouk was a plump, energetic little man, almost always on the go. When he received visitors he would talk incessantly in his falsetto voice, fixing them with a beady gaze that somehow managed to look shifty and steely at the same time. The overall effect was anything but reassuring. Whenever his courtiers and ministers came and knelt before him, the fixed smile would harden into a grimace. Everyone feared his terrible rages.

Sihanouk was a man of many talents. He was choreographer to the Royal Ballet of Cambodia, and had a large room in his palace set aside for them to rehearse in every morning. The principal ballerina in the troupe was no less a person than his daughter, Bopha Davi. He was a keen film director too, and was active in trying to revive classical Cambodian art. He played the saxophone and accordion and even wrote tangos and pop songs. When de Gaulle visited Phnom Penh and Siem Reap in the summer of 1966 he was given a state reception fit for an eastern potentate. The celebrations in his honour included a concert with a programme of works by Rameau, Mozart – and Sihanouk. This extraordinary man even wrote plays. One of them, a one-act drama entitled *The Ideal Husband*, went down particularly well with the French in Phnom Penh. In it a king disowns his favourite wife because she likes tormenting her cat and pulling its tail. Sihanouk also wrote the leaders for the official government newspapers. At times he used to sign himself, tongue-in-cheek, as the foreign correspondent of *Le Canard Enchaîné*, the French satirical newspaper.

Under Sihanouk's rule Cambodia was, by South-east Asian standards, a fairly well-run country. He built a giant new stadium, where he staged games and festivals for the people of Phnom Penh. Sihanouk's only real failure in this constant search for new projects was in education. It was a failure that was to have dire consequences for his regime, however. The prince had founded a whole string of new faculties and endowed a large number of scholarships for Cambodian students to study abroad, particularly in Paris. What he failed to foresee, however, was that these young people would get involved in the ferment of student politics in the Latin Quarter and be influenced by Marxist ideas. In the end, ironically enough, it was the young intelligentsia of Cambodia, for whom Sihanouk personally had done so much, who were to spearhead the militant left-wing opposition to his regime.

Until now Sihanouk's main political opponents had been the so-called Khmers Viet Minh, the Cambodian allies of Ho Chi Minh. The prince had already been forced to crack down on this organization, which until 1954 had agitated for the right to set up a Communist Federation of Indochina. In the early 1960s these scattered groups of Marxist sympathizers were reinforced by a new generation of Communist cadres, who also happened to be hard-line nationalists. They stirred up a peasant revolt in Battambang province and established secret links with the Viet Cong hiding in the jungles of Ratanakiri. Henceforth they began calling themselves the Khmer Rouge. Sihanouk decided to send in the police against the Communists, and the revolt was put down with savage cruelty. Some rebels were publicly executed by firing squad. According to one story, the ringleaders were taken out into the jungle, buried up to their necks in the ground, then left to be eaten alive by red ants. The brutal treatment meted out to the rebels prompted one or two of the younger ministers in Sihanouk's government to go over to the Khmer Rouge. Among the defectors was a man called Kieu Samphan, who had spent some time as a member of Sihanouk's left-wing interim cabinet. According to Western diplomats these politicians were supposed to have been rounded up and put to death by the authorities. Imagine everyone's surprise when, some years later, the leading member of the dissidents reappeared from nowhere to take over military control of the Khmer Rouge. This same man was eventually to become the first head of state of Communist Cambodia.

In the spring of 1965 these political upheavals lay far in the future and Phnom Penh was still a haven of peace. You could enjoy excellent French cuisine in the restaurant of the Royal Hotel, and you could still watch the stewardesses from the national airline, UTA, parading the briefest of bikinis beside the swimming pool. Other regular visitors to the pool included a handful of French veterans from the first Indochina war and an impressive line-up of secret agents from all over the world. Together the old soldiers and the spies would sit and listen, spellbound, to the stories and reports of the American war coming out of Vietnam, hearing every sound, living every moment.

War, American Style

Vietnam, Spring 1965

The American way of fighting a war is quite unlike any other. To begin with, nobody seems at all interested in building fortifications or digging in – firepower is the thing. In emergencies you fall back on the air force, and if things get really bad there are always helicopters – always the inevitable chopper standing by, ready to fly out American advisers to the trouble spot. I was to have my first taste of the second Indochina war – the American one, that is – in Kontum, up in the highlands of Annam, not far from the point where Vietnam, Laos and Cambodia meet. A squad of American Special Forces troops were billeted just outside the small town, and I went to visit their camp. They had already erected prefabricated barracks for themselves and laid barbed wire all around. The Green Berets, so-called because of their headgear, were an élite troop. They had the personal backing of President Kennedy himself.

When we arrived in Kontum we were greeted by the officer in charge, a major who looked as if he was of Lebanese descent. Both he and his men seemed to have a confident, positive air about them. They were professionals to their fingertips. They knew how to fight behind enemy lines and had been specially trained in jungle warfare, sabotage and counter-insurgency. They had even been coached in dirty tricks. French observers reckoned three Special Forces men were worth an entire regular US company. The major, who had a pockmarked face, told us something about his career to date, which had been fairly eventful by all accounts. He could speak perfect Arabic and consequently had been sent on several hair-raising special missions to the Near East. From what he said, virtually all the Special Forces had been ordered into

South Vietnam to fight off the Communist threat from the North.

In Kontum the Special Forces had got together a band of loyal native troops to supplement their own fighting strength. These men were members of the local hill-tribe. The Americans used the French term for the tribe, Montagnards, but the Vietnamese living in the plains and coastal region had another name for them – Moi, or wild men. The Moi were copper-skinned, with slightly slanting eyes; they were supposed to be of Polynesian descent. They still clung to their traditional animist belief in the supernatural, except for those who had had contact with Christian missionaries. The Moi were split into several different tribes, each with its own language. But they were united in one thing at least: their common hatred of the Vietnamese, who, over the centuries, had gradually driven them from the fertile plains up into the bleak highlands. Back in 1946 I had seen Moi tribesmen roaming the forests in the hills around Dalat wearing nothing but loincloths. Now most of the men were dressed in green American fatigues, and the women had their shapely breasts covered up. I visited one of their pile villages outside Kontum. The village was dominated by a long house in the centre, with tall, Malayan-style gables. They were a simple people, completely trusting and friendly towards Europeans. Some of the village elders saluted when introducing themselves; apparently they had once been reserve troops in the French colonial army. They insisted we drink their foul-tasting beer (if beer you could call it), so we had to suck the awful stuff through straws out of wide-bottomed pitchers. There was no cheating allowed either. The Moi checked to ensure we had drunk a decent amount of the ceremonial brew.

During the day it was hot and dusty in Kontum. The men in the Special Forces unit quickly made friends with us, in the easy, open way Americans have. These professionals with their tattooed chests and arms were hardly typical of the rest of their fellow-countrymen in Vietnam. They were far tougher than the GIs we had met in and around Saigon. Most of the Special Forces had either recently emigrated to the USA or else had never quite fitted in to the traditional categories of American society. The small contingent in Kontum included a Mexican, a Finn and a full-blooded Indian, but only one black. Despite all the fuss being made of them in the American press, the Green Berets were basically just misfits. Now that the days of the backwoodsman and the lone gunfighter were over, there was no place left in America's puritanical society for outsiders like these.

The Lebanese major who, it turned out, was a Maronite Christian, gave us a straightforward if cynical run-down on America's growing involvement in South-east Asia. It had been a bad year for the South Vietnamese National Army in 1964. The American advisers had calculated that the army could destroy an entire Viet Cong battalion each month, but this had turned out to be rather optimistic. In any case the Communists had gone onto the offensive now and lately had been attacking in regimental strength. The men from the Special Forces didn't think much of the American staff officers who had been acting as military advisers to the Saigon army. What they had done, in effect, was to train the South Vietnamese to fight a replay of the Korean war. They had equipped them with a massive amount of heavy artillery and armoured personnel carriers – what for, nobody knew. 'You can just see it, can't you,' said the Finnish lieutenant, laughing, 'the North Vietnamese rolling across the 17th parallel in Russian tanks!' The men in Kontum were equally dismissive about the first US combat units who had just landed at Da Nang. The first to come ashore had been a regiment of marines. They had waded through the surf to the beach, where Vietnamese girls were waiting to hang garlands of flowers round their necks. 'We're fighting a guerilla war out here,' said one of the men. 'The marines will try and make it a rerun of Guadalcanal and Okinawa all over again.' They weren't even impressed by President Johnson ordering the bombing of strategic targets. As the Indian put it: 'You can't kill ants with a steamroller.'

Next morning the major invited us to attend a 'visual instruction report'. Local scouts had just located an enemy base near the Montagnard village in Dak Seng, a few kilometres from the border with Laos. At first they had thought it was a Viet Cong base, but it turned out that it was held by North Vietnamese regulars. A dozen helicopters were standing by on the grass at Kontum airport, which was no bigger than a football pitch. We could see Vietnamese soldiers climbing into the waiting aircraft. They were armed with M-16 automatic rifles and had on heavy American combat helmets that were far too big for them. Most wore bullet-proof waistcoats under their jackets – a little extra weight here or there seemed to make no difference to these tough little Asians. The pilots were all American.

We set off, flying low over the jungle. At one point, about half-way into the flight, the racket of the helicopters startled a herd of elephants below. As we looked down we could just glimpse a jungle track snaking through the dense undergrowth. 'You know the Ho Chi Minh Trail? Well, that's just what it looks like,' said the pilot, shouting to make himself heard above the noise of the rotor blades. Suddenly the helicopters clustered together in formation, like a swarm of hornets. Then three of them split off and made straight for a hill, which we could barely pick out from the rest of the jungle. They fired off several rockets, which exploded in a pall of black smoke. While this was happening our helicopter came to a standstill, hovering a few metres above the ground. The Vietnamese soldiers jumped out and we followed after them, running to take cover at the edge of the clearing. The noise and commotion of the firing quickly died away. The attack had taken the enemy completely by surprise. Some of the North Vietnamese had taken to their heels as soon as the shooting started. The half-charred corpses of the rest lay on the ground beside a bamboo hut. The French would never have believed you could fight a war like this, not even in their wildest dreams. A few minutes later we climbed back into our helicopters and headed for base. The South Vietnamese troops had to return to Kontum on foot. The plan was for them to try and make contact with the enemy, but they didn't seem particularly keen on the idea.

The most impressive building in Kontum was the bishop's residence. Immediately adjoining it was a seminary that looked like a French colonial army barracks. The seminary had been closed down, but the bishop, Monseigneur Seitz, had stayed on. He was a Frenchman from Alsace, bearded and down-to-earth. He still sent his priests out into the remote villages to administer the sacraments and teach catechism to the Moi tribesmen. These French missionaries knew more about the Viet Cong than all the intelligence experts working for the Special Forces put together. They were continually coming up against the guerillas as they went about their pastoral duties, and every so often one of them would be carried off by the Communists. 'I'm very well acquainted with my opposite number in the Viet Cong,' the bishop told us. 'He's the commissar in charge of the area, a real old war-horse who's been fighting underground since '46. Compared to the likes of us he's totally selfless and idealistic – you could almost say he's a saint.' The bishop said that when the French garrison pulled out in July 1954, just before the ceasefire, the Viet Cong came out of the jungle and set up a Socialist administration in Kontum for a few weeks. Then, when agreement was reached at Geneva shortly after, they withdrew across the border to the

North. 'They're back here again now, though. We've got a South Vietnamese division stationed with us, but they're very reluctant to venture outside the town. They're totally demoralized, and I can't see them being able to hold out much longer, unless the Americans start relieving them.'

No matter where you travel in the Third World, missionaries are one of the best sources of information. When it comes to giving a rational account of a situation the Catholic fathers tend to have the edge over their Protestant colleagues. This is because priests whose faith has survived intact view the world as a vale of tears, so they understand that no one on this earth can wield power and retain their innocence. Listening to Monseigneur Seitz, I was reminded of the Franciscan brothers I once met in Lashio, in northern Burma, in the spring of 1952. They had been able to give me far more detailed information about the civil disturbances going on between the local Communist factions and the local tribes, the Karen, the Shan and the Kachin, than any Western military attaché in Rangoon could. But the bishop of Kontum seemed to be made of sterner stuff than the melancholy French Salesian I also met in Burma on that occasion. I remember him sitting among the bombed-out ruins of Mandalay, telling me how disillusioned he felt with the Burmese who had been put in his charge. He said, with a note of despair in his voice; 'I thought they were like children, but now I've found out they're naughty children.' Monseigneur Seitz had no time for such pessimism. He was fond of his Montagnards, and he battled hard to save their souls from the corrupting influence of Marxism. He had the build and the faith of a medieval Crusader.

In Kontum I also met the vicar-general of the diocese, who struck me as a thoughtful, intellectual man. He started talking about the tragedy of Ngo Dinh Diem. He described the efforts this incorruptible mandarin had made to turn his country into a kind of Dollfuss republic, with a Catholic minority of barely two million people. The effect of Diem's religious policies had been to provoke a Buddhist backlash in South Vietnam. Not surprisingly, perhaps, Diem's attempts to launch a campaign to convert his people to Christianity had eventually led to armed resistance from the younger members of the Buddhist community. From there it had been a short step to forming a movement of political activists opposed to Diem's regime. Needless to say, this conversion of the Buddhist monks – who up to then had been strictly neutral – into fanatical revolutionaries did not happen overnight. Buddhism, it should be remembered, had already played a significant role in the French Indochina war. Then when Diem came to power Viet Cong agents began a deliberate campaign of Communist infiltration of the pagodas. And in a country like South Vietnam, where every practising Buddhist was expected to spend at least some time in a monastery, it had been a fairly simple matter to disguise political commissars as yogis and turn Viet Cong agents into meditating monks.

The stepping-up of America's involvement in Vietnam had brought hordes of American journalists flocking to Saigon. They had set up camp in an air-conditioned bar on the top floor of the Caravelle, a modern hotel rumoured to be owned by the Catholic Church. It did not take the Americans long to reach a unanimous verdict on the political situation in Saigon. Diem the dictator had to go, leaving the true representatives of the Vietnamese people, the Buddhists, to save the day and point the way to peace and democracy. It was up to them, and them alone, to steer a middle course between the clerical fascism of 'The Incorruptible' and the left-wing Communism of the Liberation Front.

But in coming to this decision the American reporters overlooked one or two crucial facts. First, the Buddhists were in no way representative of the Vietnamese people, whose basic religious outlook had been profoundly conditioned by Confucianism. Secondly, Buddhism was only a fringe religion in Vietnam, the last refuge of the poor and the oppressed. Thirdly, the relatively strong position of Buddhism in Cochin China was mainly due to the proximity of Cambodia, where the Theravada branch of the faith was solidly entrenched. These facts were almost certainly known to a few CIA mavericks, but nobody was interested in what they had to say. In the end a handful of monks decided that martyrdom was the only course left to them. They poured petrol over themselves and set fire to themselves in the street, where they burned like living torches. When that happened the American correspondents could contain their indignation no longer. It spilled over into the newspapers, carrying their readers in its wake. Madame Nhu, Diem's beautiful and influential sister-in-law, unwittingly added to the outcry when she flippantly remarked in an interview that she couldn't stop the Buddhist monks having a 'do-it-yourself barbecue'.

Ironically enough it was President Kennedy, the first Catholic president of the United States, who was responsible for bringing down Diem, the Catholic dictator in South Vietnam. The end came for Diem in the autumn of 1963, and his downfall was to usher in one of the more sordid chapters in the history of American diplomacy. Kennedy apparently took as gospel everything he read in the press reports of David Halberstam, the *New York Times* correspondent in Saigon. Halberstam was bitterly anti-Diem; he was also an old friend of mine from the days of the Congo and Katanga troubles, and I knew his strengths and weaknesses well. He was a witty chronicler of the smart East Coast set, but when it came to unravelling the mystery of South-east Asia he was a little out of his depth. Diem finally fell victim to a plot engineered by the Americans and carried out by the generals in the South Vietnamese army. The plot eventually led to the murder of the president, but this may simply have been due to a slip-up somewhere along the line. US liaison officers gave Diem the option of fleeing, but the president, being a man of some pride and dignity, turned down the offer and so chose death instead. Diem may have been stiff-necked and intransigent, but he was a patriot and a man of integrity. The Americans let him down, and their policy in Vietnam never recovered from the odium of that crime. Henceforth it was forever to be branded with the mark of Cain.

According to reports that had reached the vicar-general of Kontum, Diem had tried, in his last weeks in power, to strike up a dialogue with Ho Chi Minh. In this he had the support of the French. The aim was to try and prevent foreign powers from intervening in the conflict and so stave off the inevitable escalation of the war. But the feelers Diem put out to the North Vietnamese merely hastened the fatal White House decision. Once Diem was removed from the scene, the Americans were left effectively with a power vacuum, although the government was run by a military junta positively dripping with gold braid. At the head of it was General Duong Van Minh, known as Big Minh. It wasn't long before the Americans began to have doubts about him, too. Minh was a phlegmatic individual who had won his stripes in the French army. His experiences there had left him with a fierce, and somewhat surprising, loyalty to the old colonial power and General de Gaulle. This made Duong Van Minh highly suspect to Washington, and after a brief spell in power he was toppled in yet another coup, also American-inspired, and sent into exile in Bangkok. Minh's true moment of tragedy was to come on the eve of the Communist takeover in Saigon in April 1975. He was summoned out of exile to head the existing government of the Republic of South Vietnam – just in time to announce the unconditional surrender of his country to the North.

After Big Minh had been exiled from the Norodom Palace, there followed a period when a succession of Gilbert and Sullivan generals and puppet politicians passed through the former residence of the French Governor in Saigon (now rechristened the Doc Lap Palace, or Palace of Independence). The American embassy finally selected General Nguyen Khanh to head the new government. Khanh was a stout man and had a goatee beard that made him the butt of endless jokes. He was the son of an actor and hence came fairly low in terms of social prestige in the eyes of his fellow Vietnamese. The Americans found him a comfortable ally – too comfortable, unfortunately. Khanh was simply not of the calibre required to meet the demands of leadership at this critical period in South Vietnamese history.

At this point the vicar-general broke off and smiled wickedly at me from behind his thick glasses. He knew very well he had been telling tales out of school. 'Since Diem's murder you don't hear very much of the Buddhists,' he said. 'The CIA meantime have had a word with the local Viet Cong agents, and now they're smuggling their own men into the pagodas. The militant wing of the Buddhists have gone to ground in Hue, the old imperial city. It's become the last stronghold of political Buddhism in the country, and they're dug in there, waiting.'

Hue was the traditional heart of Vietnam. The Americans had not moved into the old capital of Annam yet, but already the locals were tense and hostile, waiting for this new wave of intruders to descend on them. The city of Hue itself was dominated by the grey, crumbling ramparts of the citadel, which bore the unmistakable stamp of Vauban, the great French military engineer. The grounds of the palace had been allowed to run wild and no longer retained an imperial splendour.

One evening a young German doctor who taught medicine at the university hospital in Hue took us in his Peugeot to visit the old imperial burial grounds. The mausoleums themselves were situated in the hills outside Hue, in an area that had become a virtual no-man's land. As soon as it got dark, the Viet Cong took over. The ancient burial temples were faithful replicas of older Chinese tombs. The only difference was that here everything, including the figures of elephants and mythological beasts lining the avenues, was on a smaller and more human scale. Rows of stone mandarins stood waiting to pay homage to their dead emperors, each one positioned according to rank. This place, more than any other I had seen, testified to the desperate struggle the Vietnamese had made to stave off domination by China. It was a struggle they had very nearly lost, too: the Vietnamese had already adopted Chinese script and cultural patterns by the time the first European missionaries came along and transcribed the language into the Roman alphabet. In the secluded grounds of this city of the dead, pagodas were scattered everywhere. Water-lilies and lotus flowers blossomed in square pools filled with stagnant green water. We walked further west along a muddy path until we came to a hill topped by an old French pillbox dating to the last war. The red ball of the setting sun was sinking slowly behind the black contours of the Cordillera. Over towards the west lay the border with Laos, and spread out at our feet was one of the loveliest landscapes in the whole of Asia. The broad silver ribbon of the Perfume River wound its way through the fresh green of the ricefields and the rolling forests of bamboo. Fishing boats and junks sailed up and down the river in the hazy evening light. Somewhere in the distance a tall pagoda unfurled its curved roofs against the darkening sky.

The blond German doctor was in a hurry to get back. 'Personally I'm not too worried about the Viet Cong,' he told us. 'They've known me for quite some time now, and they know I don't ask awkward questions about the political leanings of my patients. During the daytime I go out to villages well known to be full of rebel sympathizers. I can't take any risks with you, though. You're strangers here and they might think you're American.'

I later found out that the young doctor was murdered during the big Tet offensive of January 1968, along with several of his colleagues. Then, for the first time ever, Communist troops raised the yellow-starred banner of the revolution over the imperial citadel, and held out for forty days against the full might of the American war machine. At first everyone blamed the North Vietnamese for the killings, but this didn't seem very likely, since Giap's regular troops were known to be extremely well-disciplined. According to the story going the rounds later, what actually happened was that the doctors in Hue were murdered by a group of former medical students. Some did it for revenge, because they had done badly in their exams, but others acted as supporters of the Communist revolt.

Back in Hue, we got our Chinese landlord to translate the news bulletins on the radio for us. It seemed that General Khanh's military regime had decided to crack down on all neutralists and those who supported the so-called Third Force, who were mainly concentrated around the Buddhists' pagodas in Saigon. As far as we could tell, though, there was still no sign of any action being taken by the authorities in Hue. That morning we had attended a rather strange Buddhist ceremony in the town. The main effect of Diem's clerical policies and conversion programme had been to spur the younger Buddhists into active rebellion. But another unexpected side-effect had been that the Buddhists started mimicking Catholic ritual in their services of worship. Hence we found ourselves inside the main pagoda in Hue, watching the priests celebrate their rites according to the exact liturgical form of a Latin mass. The congregation had obviously been thoroughly coached beforehand, and they recited their sutras as if they were Catholic litanies. The girls in the congregation looked like a band of novitiates in their sky-blue *ao dais*. The boys were dressed as Boy Scouts, complete with Baden-Powell hats; you could hardly have told them from the English original. Before the ceremony they stood outside the entrance to the pagoda, handing out religious tracts. A year later the militant opposition of the Buddhists in Hue flared into open revolt. The object of their protest was the Saigon government and what they saw as excessive American interference in Vietnamese affairs. But it was quickly put down when General Ky ordered South Vietnamese paratroopers into Hue to crush the rebel monks.

In the Spring of 1965 three leading advocates of neutralism had been arrested in Saigon without warning and driven to the demarcation line on the 17th parallel. Waiting there was a howling mob of spectators who had been rounded up by the propaganda chiefs and deposited on the south bank of the Ben Hai River. They yelled and jeered at the three 'peacemongers' (the name coined for them by the Saigon press) as they were herded across the bridge into North Vietnam. The Communists in Hanoi had enough sense to extend a warm welcome to their reluctant visitors. Later they allowed them to travel on to Paris, where they carried on agitating for a Third Force to be set up in South Vietnam.

At that time the whole of Vietnam was caught up in a bloody civil war, and nobody would have disputed the seriousness of the conflict. But up around the demarcation line dividing the two hostile territories, near the wasp waist of this narrow coastal country, Giap, the North Vietnamese Commander-in-Chief, had been biding his time. Until now he had carefully refrained from sending his regiments into action; he wanted it to look as if the uprisings in Annam and Cochin China were the work of local freedom-fighters. Now, however, the massive intervention of the Americans in the war meant that Giap no longer had to worry about world opinion, and the whole face of the war changed irrevocably.

Night Patrol with the Marines

Vietnam, the 17th Parallel, Autumn 1966

The marines were certainly not bothered about saving on ammunition. They were positioned about half-way between the South China Sea and the border with Laos, and the jungle, which was within easy reach of the North, was already under North Vietnamese control. Our helicopter landed, making a deafening noise. The marines' mortars and howitzers were firing the contents of their barrels at the surrounding cliffs, where the North Vietnamese were sheltering in limestone caves. We were assured right away that this was only a routine exercise, their way of saying goodnight to the enemy. 'Here are the Krauts,' said the lieutenant who had met us from our helicopter, introducing our television crew to his colonel. 'We're all Krauts,' the colonel replied laughing, and pointed to the name tag on the green jacket of his uniform. His name was Hess. The marines obviously felt German descent was something to be proud of.

Everyone seemed to accept the shooting going on all around as a fact of life. The French would never have considered not digging entrenchments in an exposed rock basin like this, where we were overlooked on three sides by the enemy. But the marines obviously were not interested in constructing entrenchments, and at this stage of the war there was no need for them to dig in. Hanoi still could not match the sheer volume of material coming from the USA. At dusk I took off my camouflage jacket and exposed the white T-shirt I was wearing underneath. Only then did the corporal who was helping us erect our tent warn me: 'They've got snipers on the slopes and they're looking for a target.'

When night fell, the black smoke clouds creeping over the

northern heights along the 17th parallel turned into brilliant red funeral pyres. A battalion of marines had run into a crack North Vietnamese unit and had suffered heavy losses. The enemy positions were so close to one another that infantry action mainly consisted of throwing hand-grenades. Eventually the Americans got their long overdue air support. The hilltops in the North were pelted with napalm and went up in a great blaze of fire. Even more eerie was the sight of the 'Dragon Ship'. This was a specially designed aeroplane that fired rapid streams of bullets onto enemy positions. The jungle looked as if it were being swept with laser beams, and it was left burning furiously after the attack.

We joined up with a night patrol and stumbled along through thick undergrowth. The night was so black that each of us held on to the man in front so as not to get lost. When we started going round in a circle, we shooed a scout up a tree to get our bearings from the stars. After three hours we were all drenched in sweat and exhausted. By this time there was nothing left in our water bottles, but the Americans refilled them with muddy stream water. It was too dark to see what it was like, but they added two purifying tablets to it and within ten minutes all the germs were killed, though the liquid still had a disgusting taste. They used an evil-smelling oil to repel mosquitoes which, though it burnt the lips, at least gave effective protection. Hygiene in the tropics had made considerable progress since the French war in Indochina. On this particular night the marines had no contact with the enemy. We enjoyed the sleep of the dead under our tarpaulins.

Reinforcements arrived next morning. It should have been easy for them to reach our camp from the coast, with their cross-country vehicles, but this crack American fighting unit believed in pushing its men to the limits of physical endurance. They were subjected to merciless discipline and driven almost to breaking point. The soldiers, who had closely cropped hair, groaned under the weight of their heavy packs. They were dragging mortars, machine-guns, bazookas, and crates of ammunition. They trudged past us like robots. The officers looked like actors in a Western with their regular features and clean-cut profiles. They were a real bunch of athletes. Whether they would be suited for guerilla warfare, however, was another matter. They were probably too committed to unquestioning obedience and too contemptuous of danger to cope with this type of small-scale war. A lieutenant with a baby face showed a hefty master-sergeant and his men to their temporary quarters.

'All the fields round here are full of Viet Cong,' he said.

'Gooks,' grunted the master-sergeant.

'We'll be lucky if the Red Chinese don't join them next,' the lieutenant added.

'Chinks,' commented the master-sergeant, stoney-faced. There was a widely held belief among American officers at the time that the US engagement in Vietnam was merely a prelude to a full-scale reckoning with Mao Tse-tung's China.

It was Sunday morning. A Catholic chaplain rang the bell to summon the men to divine service. He managed to assemble a fair-sized congregation. Quite a few of the men took Communion. Just before the *Ite Missa Est* two enemy shells hit the edge of the camp and triggered off a blast of counter-fire. The marines knelt down to receive the blessing.

Victor Charlie Keeps a Low Profile

The Kim Son Valley, Autumn 1966

General William Westmoreland, the US Commander-in-Chief in Vietnam, had, so it was claimed among military staff in Saigon, found a foolproof method for fighting the guerillas. It was happily taken up by the Western press. The new formula for victory was 'search and destroy'. Nobody was interested any more in the 'clear and hold' strategy which had been mainly used until recently. Victory seemed within reach now that the First US Cavalry Division, the so-called First Cav, together with a whole armada of helicopters, had swept across central Annam in an attempt to wipe out Viet Cong hide-outs.

We had been warned of the presence of enemy guerillas in the Kim Son Valley. We arrived in our chopper to join the First Cav company, who had landed a short time before us. The GIs had already trudged through several kilometres of tall elephant grass. We walked along in single file, always placing our feet in the tracks of the man in front so as to lessen the risk of treading on a mine. We were particularly afraid of the treacherous *punji* sticks – razor-sharp bamboo spikes smeared with poison and concealed underground. We waded through two fords and went past several paddy fields. The troopers discovered a number of clay jugs filled with rice under a tangle of bamboo. They shattered the vessels and left the ants to do the rest. On the edge of a tiny settlement we came across some freshly scattered earth. The GIs dug around, holding their noses. They uncovered a mass grave containing about twelve rotting corpses.

I had been struck before by how often the soldiers of the First Cav took breaks, and how careless they were about infantry security. The helicopter was obviously such a convenient means of transport that they had quickly forgotten the basic rules of marching. Apart from one incident we destroyed very little, except for a few bamboo huts which went up in flames. 'Please don't film this,' said Captain Lewis, who came from Alabama. 'Officially, you see, we're not allowed to burn down these houses.' The captain was a handsome, genial Negro. He was in command of an almost exclusively white company, and his authority was undisputed. During the midday break he told me his story. On the day before his departure for Vietnam, when he was in a public telephone-box in Montgomery saying goodbye to his wife, he had been shot in the back by a white racist. The army had completely backed him up, giving him preferential treatment, and promoted him to company commander.

In the afternoon we reached a cone-shaped mountain which was supposed to be a command post for an irregular VC battalion. (VC, or Victor Charlie, was the abbreviation for the Viet Cong used by the Americans.) The mortars were fixed in position and we fired at random into the jungle. We had not seen a single Viet Cong the entire day. When we established radio contact with regimental headquarters an hour later, Captain Lewis announced twelve enemy dead. When I asked him where he got the figure from he answered, with a shrug of his shoulders, that it was an approximation based on the successful mortar attack. In any case fixing enemy casualty figures was a widespread practice. Every regimental commander who was interested in his personal standing or promotion had to submit the highest possible figures to the supreme command, since the body count (the calculation of enemy corpses) was one of the chief occupations of the staff in Saigon. These details were fed into computers which then determined the remaining fighting strength of Victor Charlie. 'My superiors expect me to go along with the game,' said Captain Lewis, breaking into loud laughter.

In the course of 1966 the attractive little fishing villages and sandy bays of Annam-Nhatrang, Cam Ranh and Qui Nhon, among others, were transformed into gigantic war factories, becoming drab camps of Nissen huts and barren wastes of asphalt. On the Da Nang airfield, battle and transport vehicles of every description thundered up and down from early in the morning until late at night. The US Air Force began to bomb fuel stores in the immediate vicinity of Hanoi. The endless round of take-offs and landings functioned with the technical precision of an assembly line, the whole thing organized to perfection.

The Americans were in their element here. Only a few kilometres from the naval port and the Da Nang air base, however, there was a barren, rocky headland that jutted out into the South China Sea. Despite their marvellous technical equipment, the GIs had not managed to gain full control of this hill. It was hardly surprising, then, that the Viet Cong were able time and time again to launch rocket attacks against the most powerful military base in the world.

Since the massive American intervention the city of Saigon had changed in a most unwelcome way. The streets and alleys off the Rue Tu-Do now swarmed with Americans in green battledress. But the trees were becoming stunted and withered with living under a dark petrol cloud. The cause of this was not just the exhaust fumes from endless military convoys, but the amazingly large number of motor scooters and mopeds (called Hondas for short) which congested the major roads. As a consequence of the overwhelming US presence, Saigon found itself the centre of a hectic boom in consumer spending, and the symbol of the new life was the Honda. Simultaneously, the capital had turned into one huge brothel. Shady bars with hostesses in skimpy clothes had sprung up like toadstools. Prostitution was a prestige industry. The choice ranged from luxury rooms with stereo music and mirrored walls to evil-smelling dens of squalor, where ecstasy was purchased on wooden beds separated from one another only by grimy lengths of curtain. The black GIs had their own red-light district on the other side of the river. The sight of this Sodom and Gomorrha set up by the descendants of the pious Pilgrim Fathers was enough to make any Vietnamese become anti-American, whether he was Communist or not.

Early in the morning of the national holiday, two rockets struck next to the cathedral. They had been fired from the Rungsat swamps. Despite this the grand parade took place in front of the Doc Lap Palace at the appointed hour. Saigon had learned to live with attacks. 'If the South Vietnamese could fight as well as they can parade, we would have won the war long ago,' whispered a military attaché on the platform reserved for dignitaries. Wearing elegantly tailored battledress, with brightly coloured neckerchiefs and highly polished boots, the units of the ARVN (the Army of the Republic of Vietnam) marched past the head of government, General Nguyen Cao Ky, and the US Ambassador, Henry Cabot Lodge. It was a sort of wartime fashion show. The female contingents looked very sexy in their skin-tight trousers. Montagnards from the highlands swayed on their elephants, and frogmen in rubber suits rolled past on inflatable dinghies. The parade was also meant to demonstrate that Vietnam did not stand alone. The American regiments were out in force, their silver helmets gleaming. Behind them came the South Koreans of the Tiger Division, with their fearsome Kabuki masks. The Australians filed past to the tune of 'Waltzing Matilda'. There were even a few Thais and Filipinos, and some New Zealand soldiers. The security chief, Colonel Loan, a lean Tongkingese with a receding chin and a hawk-like nose, walked tirelessly back and forth with his walky-talky. Loan's policemen inspired almost as much fear as their predecessors, the Binh Xuyen.

I had returned the day before from a tour of Cochin China. The Mekong Delta was still very unsafe, 'rotten' as the French used to say. What was really rotten, though, was the military leadership, headed by the corpulent, falsetto-voiced General Quang, whom it would be hard to beat for sheer corruptibility. A venomous quarrel had taken place in my presence between Quang and a US colonel over six feet tall, who was assigned as divisional adviser. The tall, straight-talking Americans naturally found it difficult to get along with this cunning little dwarf.

In Tay Ninh, at the foot of the Black Virgin, the Special Forces, helped by native mercenaries who belonged to the Cambodian minority, the Khmer Krom, had finished building a star-shaped encampment. The Viet Cong were particularly active near the border with Cambodia and they had a number of impregnable supply bases in the surrounding countryside. For General Westmoreland these sanctuaries represented a challenge he could not ignore. The Green Berets based at Tay Ninh were forced to acknowledge that the slopes of the Black Virgin were still swarming with VCs, in spite of the fortified American radio and observation station they had erected on its summit. The fighting strength of the Cao Dai had already been smashed by the attacks of

Ngo Dinh Diem's soldiers, and part of the sect had even gone over to the 'Liberation Front'. Only the warlike Buddhists of the Hoa Hao kept watch on the edge of the reed flats to make sure the Red commissars stayed away from their villages. They, however, were furious that their mad and bloodthirsty prophet, Ba Cut, had been captured and publicly beheaded by Diem's soldiers with the support of American agents. The only places where you could find security, order, and decency were the neat little villages where the Catholic refugees from Tongking were settled. In the shadow of their yellow and white church towers, and their statues of Virgin Mary, battle-scarred priests from the North led a strict and very moral regime. I watched a young chaplain instructing his parishioners in the art of grenade-throwing and bayonet warfare in front of a statue of the Lourdes grotto. His black soutane didn't seem to hinder him in the least.

The Manila Summit

Manila, Autumn 1966

An invitation had gone out from President Lyndon B. Johnson summoning his allies and minions to a conference in the Malacanang Palace in Manila. The old Spanish colonial residence made a magnificent setting for the meeting. The prime ministers of Australia and New Zealand, together with the Korean president, Park Chung Hee, and a Thai general from Bangkok, had all come in answer to the American summons. South Vietnam sent two representatives: the head of government, Nguyen Cao Ky, and his political opponent, General Nguyen Van Thieu. Ferdinand Marcos of the Philippines played the part of official host with his usual tact and flair. For the duration of the conference, politicians as well as military men wore the traditional Filipino dress of a white lace shirt over dark trousers. The shaded walk-ways in the palace grounds were lined with almond-eyed girls, who wore their Spanish colonial costume with provocative grace.

The conference itself did not last very long. President Johnson informed his allies, in camera, that the USA was to step up its war effort in Vietnam in order to ensure an American victory. This would involve increasing the strength of the US ground forces to 500,000 men. Apparently General Westmoreland had decided he could no longer rely on the ARVN units; in future the GIs would need to have personal control of all offensive operations, and the South Vietnamese would be assigned a purely defensive role in the war. Ky and Thieu had to accept this decision with as much grace as they could muster. Air Vice-Marshal Ky, who came from Tongking, suggested that the war on the ground should be carried to the enemy in North Vietnam, but Johnson brushed the idea aside. The Americans argued there was too great a risk of 'intervention' by a Chinese force, along the lines of what had happened in Korea. The determination of the US president, and the huge commitment of American manpower, were certainly impressive. The world press, who had flocked to Manila in droves, duly took note and prophesied that the days of the Viet Cong were numbered.

The Manila summit wound up with an informal banquet. The official guests sat at a long table, with Johnson and Marcos in the centre. The banqueting hall, with its heavy Spanish furniture, was lit by torches for the occasion. A Filipino dance band played discreetly in the background. The American president had already consumed more than his fair share of alcohol. He had the powerful build of a Texan cowboy, and when he stood and raised his glass for a toast he towered over his Asian partners. Johnson had flung himself into the Vietnam venture. He had gambled on the prestige of the USA as a world power and had laid his own political career on the line. However it was actually Kennedy, not Johnson, who had mainly been behind the bold US intervention in Vietnam. The American journalists who flew in with Johnson on Air Force One admitted the president was a pretty smart operator in the field of domestic politics, but claimed he was completely out of his depth when it came to understanding international diplomacy. Because of this, Johnson always turned to Kennedy's former advisers and ministers for guidance on his Vietnam strategy. Whenever a decision was taken to step up US involvement, or escalate the war, certain names always cropped up – names like Robert McNamara, McGeorge Bundy, Walt Rostow and Dean Rusk. They were 'the best and the brightest', to quote David Halberstam's ironic description of them. In the end their pseudo-scientific analyses and predictions would bring Lyndon Johnson to the brink of catastrophe.

That evening I kept a close eye on the men and women at the top table. The Philippines was a highly sophisticated and cosmopolitan part of the world. The civilizations of Asia and Spain had lived side by side here for centuries before the Americans came, but fifty years of US occupation had added that final gloss in the form of 'the American way of life'. Against this background of Old World sophistication, Johnson's rough-diamond manner had an appealing spontaneity and freshness about it. The president had brought his wife, Lady Bird, along with him to the summit. She looked like a bird, too, with her beaky nose and magpie eyes, but she radiated that uniquely disarming brand of American friendliness. The hostess for the evening, Imelda Marcos, was in quite a different class. She was dazzlingly beautiful and held herself like a queen. Over the years the former Miss Philippines had put on a little weight, admittedly, but the extra kilos suited her. There was a lot of talk locally about the enormous influence she had over her husband. The anti-government press in Manila was still very aggressive at that time, and it was always attacking her for having increased the wealth of the Marcos clan to staggering proportions. Like so many other Asian women in positions of power, she had personality, brains and boundless energy. The natural grace and sheer presence of this *grande dame* captivated the American president. Ten years later, even the ageing Mao Tse-tung was to succumb to her charm; at one of his last official appearances, he was seen to kiss the hand of the First Lady of the Philippines.

President Marcos also came over as extremely personable. He knew how to get on with the Americans, having fought on their side in World War II, and had been awarded their highest military honour for valour. Although head of state, Marcos still had something of the rakish gang-leader about him. This was not entirely coincidental, either, for it was common knowledge in the Philippines that he had gunned down one of his father's political opponents during his early career as a gangster. That evening his guests round the table politely refrained from mentioning the problems he was having at home with political opposition in Parliament and student unrest on the streets. They also carefully avoided the topic of the scattered forces of the New People's Army which were holding out in the mountains of Luzon. These rebels had recently sent envoys into the south of the archipelago, which was already a hotbed of Muslim unrest.

The prime ministers of Australia and New Zealand looked like senior officials on the White House staff. Premier Harold Holt of

Australia was bright red in the face from the combined effects of alcohol and the heat. His high colour contrasted startlingly with the ivory pallor of the Asians. The band struck up a waltz, and Lyndon Johnson led off the dancing with Imelda Marcos. He held her tightly to him, and seemed to be having difficulty keeping his balance. Nguyen Cao Ky than asked Lady Bird to dance. Ky had been trained as a pilot by the French in Morocco in the early 1950s; and had earned a reputation for being something of a whiz-kid. It was Henry Cabot Lodge, the American ambassador to Vietnam, who made the fatal error of elevating Ky to the position of premier. Now, as he glided across the parquet with the wife of the American president, Ky looked just like a gigolo with his slicked-down hair, his little Adolphe Menjou beard and his flattened nose. He was not the sort of person who commanded respect in Asian society. His first marriage to a Frenchwoman had ended in divorce, and immediately afterwards he had married the most attractive air hostess in Air Vietnam, which confirmed his reputation as a playboy. His American backers had virtually given up all hope of him ever shaping up as a politician, or showing any real initiative as head of government.

Ky was in high spirits that evening, enjoying his big moment. His ebullient mood was not shared by the other Vietnamese representative, General Nguyen Van Thieu, who looked diffident and ill at ease. Thieu was Ky's main political rival and he presided over a kind of parallel regime in Saigon that had the full backing of the other generals. He originally came from a family of humble fisherfolk in south Annam, but despite his poor background his manner and bearing had all the dignity of a mandarin in uniform. It was not hard to predict which man would emerge the victor in the power struggle going on.

At the far end of the table sat a still, lonely figure, President Park Chung Hee of South Korea. He might have been a bronze statue for all the signs of life he showed. The drunken high spirits and noisy heartiness of the gathering, plus the bluff Australian and American mateyness of it all, had succeeded in driving President Park inside his shell. He sat there sulking, making no attempt to hide his contempt for the whole proceedings. He refused all invitations to dance and hardly touched his food. The skin was stretched taut over the prominent bones of his tough soldier's skull. His eyes were half-shut and he looked as if he could have been asleep.

The son of poor Korean peasants, Park had worked his way to

the top, first as a teacher and later as a second lieutenant in the Japanese army. Towards the end of the war, he began his inexorable rise up the ladder of the South Korean military hierarchy. After the coup in 1961, the military junta turned to Park Chung Hee. They wanted him as leader because they thought he would be content to stay in the background and act as a stop-gap. As it turned out, they gravely misjudged their man. Park, after all, had inherited the traditional Confucian belief in authority. He had also been through a tough school in the Japanese army and had had a ruthless sense of discipline drummed into him. As soon as he was installed as head of the South Korean government, Park proceeded to take over the reins of power for himself. At the Manila summit he was nicknamed the 'Stony-faced Guest', but he could afford not to worry about his image. At that very moment two crack divisions of South Korean troops were fighting in the Qui Nhon sector of central Annam. And once the soldiers of the Land of the Silent Morning set foot in a place, the grass never grew there again. The South Koreans were feared in Vietnam as the Huns must have been in ancient Rome; it was no accident that the two peoples were thought to be distantly related. Any prisoners they took were finished off with a brisk karate chop. The Viet Cong in the Qui Nhon sector hardly dared venture out of their hiding-places.

Compared to the ruthless efficiency of the South Koreans, the contingent of Thai troops and the handful of Filipinos sent to Vietnam seemed something of a joke. New Zealand had sent only a token force, but the Australian troops were acquitting themselves well in the jungle war and had managed to hold their own in the sector between Xuan Loc and Vung Tau.

A member of Johnson's staff leaned over and told him that a mob of students and young people were besieging the hotel where the American delegation was staying. They were chanting slogans and calling for an end to the Vietnam war and the evacuation of US bases in the Philippines. By this time it was well after midnight, so Lyndon Johnson gave the signal for everyone to rise from the table. He was obviously feeling very affable. He got into his armoured limousine and began speaking the traditional Filipino greeting, '*Mabuhai*', over the loudspeaker. His slurred voice echoed through the silent grounds of the Malacanang Palace, which was shrouded in darkness. As the car drove off Imelda Marcos stood waving goodbye from the stairs, an inscrutable smile on her lovely face.

Remembrance of Things Past

Laos, Autumn 1966

'Down there is where the Plain of Jars begins,' said the pilot, pointing to a huge trough in the ground with hills all around it. He told us it wasn't really advisable to fly over the plain these days. It was one of the key strategic positions in northern Laos and it had fallen into North Vietnamese hands. Recently they had brought up some Russian anti-aircraft guns. 'Only last week they shot down a civilian plane over Sepone,' said the pilot, changing course and turning his Cessna towards the north-west.

The pilot's name was Pierre Mounier, and at one time he had been a sergeant in the French Air Force. Together with another veteran of the first Indochina war he now ran a tiny airline in Vientiane. Mounier seemed to have carried every sort of contraband in his plane, opium included. We had chartered the Cessna from him at what seemed a ridiculously cheap price, to transport our TV crew. We had the distinct impression we were his first 'straight' commission in a long time; we were probably providing him with an official alibi to keep the authorities off his back. Mounier turned out to be a steady, dependable sort of character. He lived with a Laotian woman and he knew the country like the back of his hand.

We touched down on a flat stretch of grass in the middle of the jungle. The clearing had sturdy corrugated iron huts all around it, bristling with tall aerials. The moment we got out onto the landing strip we were surrounded by Asian soldiers. I thought I recognized the racial type and they turned out, in fact, to be Meo. During the first Indochina war these hill tribesmen had fought on the side of the French. Then the North Vietnamese, together with one or two token units of the Pathet Lao, the Laotian Communists, marched across the 1954 demarcation line and took the Plain of Jars. After that the Meo had decided to put themselves in the hands of the Americans. However the Meo troops seemed to have changed quite a bit since those early days. The main difference was that they were all actually in uniform for once, and they had swapped their old flintlock rifles for spanking new M-16 automatic rifles. They were being handsomely paid for their services by the Americans. An airline called Air America regularly flew in supplies of food and ammunition to the mountain outposts.

Air America was supposed to be a private commercial outfit but, in fact, was part of the CIA's highly efficient operations' network in Laos.

I noticed the Meo women still dressed in their picturesque traditional costume. The heavy silver rings they wore round their necks and ankles were status symbols, traditional signs of wealth. 'The Meo have never had it so good,' said Mounier. 'Since they started fighting for the Americans they've had everything they could possibly want. Every Meo tribesman is issued with a pair of rifles to keep under his palliasse, and they can go out and fight to their heart's content.' This command post was the local headquarters for Meo resistance in the area and it was run by a small group of American civilians. In charge was an athletic-looking man in a Hawaiian shirt who spoke fluent Laotian. He introduced himself, with typical American casualness, as John. He told us he was working for a relief organization whose job was to get food supplies through to the hill tribes in the area. But he knew we weren't taken in by his story. The other members of the team living in this secret hideaway were a radio operator, a few professional soldiers – Special Forces men, by the look of their crew-cuts – and three American women. One of the women taught the local Meo children, the second supervised the distribution of food, and the third ran the hospital. Her only patients were a couple of Meo tribesmen who had been severely wounded in the fighting and were now peacefully dozing their way towards death or recovery. The teacher had the toughest job of all. As soon as the Meo boys turned twelve they would put on green fatigues, grab one of the M-16s that were lying around and follow their fathers into war.

'I've got one more outpost to inspect,' John announced. 'But your plane won't be able to land there, I'm afraid.' I climbed up after him into a tiny light aircraft and we circled up over the black mountain ravines into a solid wall of mist. The horizon was completely invisible, even though it was the dry season. We must have climbed to a height of 2000 metres before the plane headed for a 'defensive village' which turned out to be just a collection of wretched mud huts. Then I caught sight of the landing strip, which was laid out like a ski-jump. When the plane came in to land, it touched down with a jolt and was gradually brought to a halt by the gradient. When we took off again the plane had to taxi down the steep slope until it gathered momentum, then it launched itself into the void like a ski-jumper. The whole thing was fairly hazardous, to say the least.

'We're right on the edge of the Plain of Jars. That means we're completely surrounded by Communist Pathet Lao and North Vietnamese,' said John with a grin. 'The Meo are the only tribe I know that could possibly survive the kind of cat-and-mouse game going on up here. We can't give them very much air support because the terrain is so rough and hilly.' On the outskirts of the village I came across the inevitable poppy fields. The Meo still seemed to be harvesting and selling their opium, despite the war. A persistent rumour in Laos claimed that Air America was owned by a big drug ring. The demand for drugs among the GIs in Vietnam was heavy, not to say insatiable. The use of heroin, in particular, among American troops had already reached epidemic proportions. We tackled John on the subject but he refused to be drawn. All he would say was: 'The Meo have to live somehow, and you can't grow rice at this height.'

Everyone in Laos seemed to think the war was one big adventure. According to Mounier, nobody took it seriously. For one thing the Laotians were far too easy-going and peace-loving to be any good as soldiers. But then they didn't really have to be effective fighters; there were plenty of other people willing to take care of that. One side had the CIA experts with their Meo tribesmen, while the other had North Vietnamese intervention regiments. The Communists recruited guerillas for the Pathet Lao among the Kha tribesmen up in the mountains. For centuries the Kha had been exploited as slaves by the Laotians in the Mekong valley. Now they were eager to side with the Hanoi commissars, who promised them greater equality and improved living conditions in the new Socialist Laos of the future.

It would have been difficult to find a more absurd situation than the political set-up in Laos at that time. The Communist revolutionaries in the country were led by no less a person than Prince Souphanouvong. The prince had a square head and a droopy moustache and he looked just like an Indochinese samurai. With the help of the Russians, members of his movement had dug out a warren of caves in the hillsides of Sam Neua and Vieng Xai. The caves provided a safe refuge from US Air Force bombardments and they had even been used as schools and repair shops. Souphanouvong was greatly respected by supporters and opponents alike. It was only when the Laotian Communists seized power in 1975 that people eventually realized the Red Prince had been merely a front man for the Hanoi military. The real leader of the Pathet Lao turned out to be a half-Vietnamese party worker whom nobody had even heard of before. His name was Kaysone Phomvihane, and his aim was to turn his country into a satellite state of North Vietnam.

While all this was going on the prime minister of Laos, Souvanna Phouma, continued to rule the country from Vientiane. Souvanna Phouma was a prince, like his half-brother and Communist rival, Souphanouvong. He was a portly aristocrat, a highly cultivated man with exquisite manners. He had originally been appointed to head the government because of his neutralist stance. He looked on France as his second home after Laos. The French had taken charge of the training of the Royal Laotian army after the 1954 ceasefire. Since then their military position in Laos had grown steadily weaker, particularly after the small contingent of neutralist forces, led by the gallant Colonel Kong Le, were defeated in the battle for the Plain of Jars. After the collapse of the troops, the 200 French army instructors in Laos stayed on, though with a much reduced role. They invited us to an official reception in their camp in Vientiane to commemorate the 1918 armistice. We were welcomed by the brigadier in charge who, like the rest of the French officers, wore white dress uniform. The guests included a sprinkling of Laotians, among them Prince Souvanna Phouma. It was a very nostalgic occasion.

The original settlement guaranteeing the neutrality of Laos had been negotiated between Kennedy and Khrushchev, but the whole thing collapsed as soon as serious unrest broke out again in Vietnam. Souvanna Phouma tried hard to persevere with his Third Force policy but was unsuccessful. Particularly in Vientiane and the southern province of Champassak, which had a strong conservative feudal tradition, the aristocratic warlords were constantly plotting to overthrow his government. The situation was complicated by the fact that these warlords were in league with the CIA and its various confederates on the opposite bank of the Mekong. At the same time Communist opposition in Laos was growing more and more aggressive and intransigent in its demands. Hence Souvanna Phouma found himself under attack on two fronts at once. He was left with no choice but to throw in his lot with the Americans. He hoped, by so doing, to outwit his right-wing opponents, who were led by Prince Boun Oum. But further complications arose when trouble broke out with China. In the north of Laos, Mao's envoys had turned the province of Phong Saly (bordering on Yunnan) into what was, in effect, a client state. What is more, the Chinese refused to allow any Vietnamese into this northernmost province. Eventually top-level negotiations took place in which the Vientiane government agreed to appoint the People's Republic of China to construct a system of all-weather roads linking Yunnan with Dien Bien Phu and the old imperial city of Luang Prabang. In the long term this would mean the establishment of a strategic road link between China and Thailand. American fighter pilots in Laos received strict instructions to avoid the airspace over areas where Mao's engineers were working.

There was an old legend about the bronze drums of Laos that everyone in the embassies of Vientiane always enjoyed relating. These famous bronze drums are regarded as some of the finest examples of Laotian craftsmanship in existence. The circular tops of the drums are decorated with the signs of the zodiac. Around the rims are motifs of tiny copulating frogs, arranged in groups of three, and the welding joint is worked with a design of miniature elephants. According to the legend, a crafty Laotian prince once used these temple drums to trick an enemy centuries ago. The Chinese had invaded Laos from the north with a vast army. The Laotians were hopelessly outnumbered, so the prince gave orders for the temple drums to be fetched from the pagoda and set up under the numerous waterfalls of the mountains of Laos. As the water cascaded onto the drums it created such a terrible booming noise that the troops of the Chinese emperor were tricked into thinking that a mighty Laotian army was advancing on them. Panic-stricken, the Sons of Heaven turned and fled from the Land of a Million Elephants.

All the many facets and contrasts of Laos were mirrored in its capital, Vientiane. It was a sleepy and rather unprepossessing city. It had a wide main avenue with a hideous grey triumphal arch at the far end. The arch was to have been erected in honour of the men who had been killed in the Laotian war, but somehow the colossal memorial was never completed, although the building costs spiralled to nearly ten times the original estimate. It appeared that the money disappeared into the pockets of the Chinese construction firm and corrupt local bureaucrats.

Not far from the colourful bustle of the central market was the heavily guarded compound of the American embassy, screened off from public view behind high white walls. The US ambassador in Vientiane also acted as unofficial commander-in-chief of the American forces in Laos. He was in charge of all missions carried out by the US Air Force and personally selected the targets of their bombing raids. The CIA was all-powerful in Laos, and was doing quite a good job technically. Hordes of adventure-seekers and cowboys had arrived in South-east Asia from the USA in answer to the call of Air America. They flew on hair-raising missions, went in for all kinds of shady deals and generally played at being James Bond. After dark they would raise hell in the streets of the sedate capital and add to the notorious reputation of its seedier nightclubs. Their arrival brought a whole army of Siamese prostitutes over the Mekong border into Laos. The girls divided their time between Vientiane and the little Thai town of Udorn, where there was a huge American air base. They had been followed into Laos by a swarm of transvestites who flew in from Bangkok to service the troops. They looked so incredibly seductive and feminine – the surgeon's knife had worked wonders – that the drunken mercenaries of Air America often didn't discover the true sex of the 'girls' they picked up until it was too late.

About 300 metres from the American embassy a pair of odd-looking soldiers stood guard outside a secluded villa. They had peasant faces and wore green bonnets with blue and red cockades. Their uniforms were too big for them and they carried Chinese AK-47 rifles. Their job was to guard the official residence of the Pathet Lao delegation in the heart of the Laotian capital. The Pathet Lao had about thirty soldiers permanently detailed to guard their special envoy, a man called Loth Petrasy. It must have been deadly boring for the troops as they were forbidden to leave the immediate vicinity of the villa. To while away the time they played volleyball and grew vegetables in the garden. Loth Petrasy himself was always extremely affable. Every time I visited Laos I would go to see him and we would talk over a cup of tea. A small Aeroflot plane was the only link between this bizarre legation and the Communist authorities in Sam Neua; it also flew in the odd replacement to relieve the guards. The Aeroflot pilots were just as dubious as their colleagues in Air America.

The Laotians were a naturally happy, carefree people. The tolerance preached by the Buddha had left its imprint on the national character. In the midst of the war the people of Vientiane went on celebrating their religious festivals, seemingly oblivious to the plight of their country. Meanwhile, up in the mountains, the CIA and the North Vietnamese carried on waging their mini-war to gain control of the key positions in this the second Indochina conflict. At the same time the US air force continued in its efforts to put the Ho Chi Minh Trail out of action, dropping hundreds of tonnes of explosives on it and putting to use the very latest electronic hardware.

That afternoon the entire government, led by Prince Souvanna Phouma, had walked in solemn procession to the whitewashed monastery of Tat-Luang, to the east of the capital. The ministers all wore the official court costume of white jacket and black knee-breeches. Monks in saffron-yellow robes accepted their tribute with quiet dignity. The Laotian girls in the procession bent their lovely moon-faces in respectful homage. Their magnificent black hair, which fell to below their knees when loose, had been gathered up. At night the procession went from one pagoda to the next, everyone carrying a torch to light the way. A lot of laughing and joking went on during the proceedings, and the golden smile of the Buddha was mirrored on the happy faces of his followers.

Next morning King Savang Vatthana made his way in royal procession to the main pagoda in the centre of the city. The king was an imposing, self-willed man who was greatly respected by his people. He hated leaving his sumptuous palace in Luang Prabang, even though the Communist guerillas were now within twenty kilometres of the old imperial city. The king was accompanied by a magnificent retinue. The heavy temple gongs were carried by Kha tribesmen clad in bright red. The palace guards were armed with halberds, like the Swiss guards in the Vatican. The king could never bring himself to stay for long in wicked, cosmopolitan Vientiane. After a few days he would start longing to be back in the drowsy peace of the palace grounds in Luang Prabang, where the only sounds to disturb the evening stillness were the beating of gongs and the monotonous praying of the monks. Savang Vatthana had one weakness, and that was an almost comical passion for the works of Marcel Proust. According to some of the French in Laos this eccentric monarch could recite whole chapters of *A la Recherche du Temps Perdu* by heart. In fact 'remembrance of things past' would have made a fitting title for the history of this delightful South-east Asian kingdom, which was being slowly destroyed in the contemptible game of power politics going on between America and the USSR.

We were able to cover quite a large area of Laotian territory in our chartered plane. One place we visited was Vang Vieng, where the tall cliffs rose up like green sugar-loaves, shutting out the sky. Vang Vieng was where the last remaining band of neutralists were holding out against the enemy. They were led by a solitary French major who seemed to have no illusions about the futility of his task. Later, as we flew over the mountains of Thakek, we decided to head east and find out whether the American plan to place a cordon sanitaire right across Laos was, in fact, feasible. But when we eventually got to the area, we could see the idea was completely impracticable. Between Thakek on the Mekong River and the village of Sepone on the Vietnam border lay a mountainous landscape of deeply fissured rock. This terrain was the last place on earth to try and build a line of interconnecting defences. We flew on to the northern fort of Ban Huei Sai, only a stone's throw from China and Burma. This was where the opium smugglers used to meet, right on the edge of the Golden Triangle. In the end we were unable to land because the Mekong River, fed by melting snow from the Himalayas, had burst its banks and flooded the landing strip.

We decided to cut across country instead, flying low over the Boloven plateau in the far south of the country. We landed near the isolated garrison of Atopeu, where we were greeted by a fat colonel from the Royal Laotian Army. The colonel took us to visit his easternmost checkpoint, two kilometres from the pile village of Atopeu. Directly beyond it lay no-man's land. The colonel was fairly sure the first North Vietnamese outposts were hidden just around the next bend in the jungle track. The intelligence services in Saigon had reported that the area immediately around Atopeu was an assembly point on the Ho Chi Minh Trail. The colonel showed us his official map and explained how the Viet Cong had recently enlarged their strategic road link.

'We can hear the convoys of lorries going past at night – in fact we can actually see the light from their dipped headlights in the distance. Sometimes it's just like the Champs Elysées out there,' he said with a grin. He was obviously exaggerating, but he was very proud of the fact that he had once attended a training course in France. I asked him whether he thought he could hold out with his 200 troops if the worst came to the worst and Atopeu was attacked. This made the colonel roar with laughter. 'With luck we might manage to fight our way out across the plateau to Pakse, on the Mekong. But it'd take us all our time just to do that. We're like sitting ducks here. The situation's hopeless.' Evidently the days when the Laotians could frighten off a powerful enemy with the noise of a few bronze drums were well and truly gone.

'Destroyed in Order to be Saved'

Vietnam, Autumn 1967

The US Army spokesmen in Saigon kept on saying that the war was 'as good as over'. Every day the briefing officers would report the destruction of hundred of 'structures', or oil and ammunition depots, on either side of the 17th parallel. If you questioned them more closely you learned that a 'structure' often meant nothing more than a bamboo hut in enemy territory. Details of the body count were painstakingly centralized and fed into an elaborate computer system. From this it was calculated that the enemy's 'main force' had been essentially destroyed, and that the 'irregulars' were holding on by the skin of their teeth. But up in Con Thien, at the point where North and South Vietnam meet, nobody took much notice of these victory bulletins.

The zone around the demarcation line was now a hotly-contested battle front. The weather was cold and windy, and the grey clouds hung low in the sky. The rain poured down, drenching the treeless countryside until it looked as if it was slowly disappearing under a sea of mud. I had joined up with a column of marines on their way to the front. The carcasses of three buffalo hit by mortar fire lay rotting at the side of the slippery laterite road, filling the air with the sickly sweet stench of decay. The marines were weighed down with gear. They were soaked to the skin and covered in mud from head to foot. Their dark silhouettes against the lowering sky reminded me of old pictures of Verdun in World War I.

In the northern sector of the Vietnam war you didn't hear much about the search and destroy missions, the bold new formula for winning the war. The B-52s of the US Air Force had blanket-bombed the North Vietnamese bottleneck, the narrow coastal strip between the Ben Hai River and the town of Vinh. It had been left looking like a lunar landscape. General Curtis Le May had threatened to 'bomb the Communists back into the Stone Age'. Yet despite all this, General Giap had managed to extend his network of emplacements and dug-outs right up to the American lines. Recently he had actually brought heavy artillery up to the front, though goodness only knows how he did it. Now the Viet Cong had started shelling the US fire bases at irregular intervals. The cursing marines were forced to dig tunnels and ditches into the clay soil. 'This enemy fire is a terrible nuisance,' said the major who showed me round Con Thien. 'The rats are the worst thing, though. We've got to live with them in the mud. Sometimes they even attack my men.' In the distance I could hear the rolling thunder of artillery fire and exploding bombs. The enemy were nowhere to be seen, but they must have been dug in behind the ridges of brown earth. 'We've put down barbed wire and minefields,' said the major, 'but they're still infiltrating our positions.' He wiped the rain from his face. 'Goddammit, we're fighting an army of *moles!*'

This was the time of year when Saigon basked in the warm, dry rays of the November sun. It was the season for *la bonne société saigonnaise* to meet by the swimming pool in the Cercle Sportif. This exclusive club preserved something of the mood of the old colonial days. It was also a marvellous place to swap news and gossip. Among the regulars at the Cercle Sportif were the German and Dutch military attachés. The Dutchman was a colonial officer who had done long service in Malaysia and was nobody's fool. The German was a lieutenant-colonel who had a reputation for being something of a killjoy among the rest of the embassy staff. While the other German diplomatic representatives were sending back the usual favourable reports on the American position, full of reassuring noises about the 'stabilization of the situation' and the 'inevitability' of victory, the military attaché would be wallowing in gloomy prediction and tales of woe. The other group you met in the Cercle Sportif were the French plantation managers. They were mainly young officers who had resigned from the army after the Algerian debacle. Every week they had to haggle with the local Viet Cong commissars, pay them taxes and settle any queries about their employees. Only then were they allowed to carry on with the job of tending the rubber trees on their plantations and exporting the raw latex. The wealthy socialites of Cochin China frolicked about on the tennis courts of the Cercle Sportif and generally felt quite at home. There were a number of American regulars, of course, but it was always the done thing to speak French.

One evening I was invited to dine with the French consul general, a gruff Corsican by the name of Tomasini. As a young man he had fought bravely for the Resistance in Savoy, and he had also served in the Maquis under Vercors. Although his hair was now grey he still loved to take risks. We had known each other since the days of the Katanga troubles, when he had been consul general in Elisabethville. At the time he had shown enormous concern for the welfare of the French troops fighting in the province, and at one stage he had been severely wounded in an attempt on his life. I was the sole guest at table that evening in the old-fashioned villa on the Rue Hai Ba Trung. Over the years Tomasini's predecessors had collected a veritable museum of rare East Asian objects, and these were on display around the room.

After the boy had left, Tomasini took a thick envelope out of the safe and showed it to me. 'What you see here is a message from the Viet Cong,' he said. 'Several weeks ago one of our plantation owners, a man in his sixties called Jean Dufour, disappeared without trace. He'd spent his whole life in Indochina and he insisted on staying on in his plantation out on the old colonial road to Dalat. We advised him to leave, but it made no difference. The Viet Cong must have seized him during the night and taken him to one of their hide-outs. Since then we've tried to contact Dufour several times, but without success. Then yesterday morning I had a visit from an envoy of the Liberation Front – very mysterious he was, too. He was Vietnamese, extremely well-mannered, middle-aged, I'd guess. I'm pretty sure he must have gone to one of our schools at some time. When we were alone he said he had some very distressing news for me. M. Dufour had unfortunately died in captivity. The National Liberation Front had regrettably been forced to take him prisoner after he had ignored the express instructions of the revolutionary authorities not to clear a piece of ground. If he had been allowed to carry on it would have meant jeopardizing the security of guerilla forces in the area. While in captivity Dufour had become gravely ill. Every effort was made to save his life, but he died before he could be taken to Saigon and released. The envoy said he was charged, on behalf of the National Liberation Front, to hand over to the French consul general all the personal effects Dufour had on him when he was abducted, and all the money that had been confiscated from him. He said the costs of Dufour's medical treatment had been deducted from the original sum, but there was a detailed bill in the yellow envelope. Furthermore, the Liberation Front wished to extend its heartfelt condolences to the relatives of M. Dufour for the tragic loss they had suffered. Perhaps it would be some consolation for them to know that before he passed away Dufour had been informed of the goals of the Vietnamese revolution and made a spontaneous declaration of support for these objectives.' Tomasini shook his head. 'Isn't it comforting to know that poor old Dufour was given the last rites of the Viet Cong before he went to meet Karl Marx.'

I told Tomasini about my experiences of the past few weeks. I had finally got somewhere with my attempts to arrange an interview with a representative of the Viet Cong. I had first tried to set up a meeting through a Saigon lawyer, Madame Ngo Ba Thanh. Madame Thanh was a well-known neutral and had spent a lengthy period in a dank Saigon jail for her beliefs. She had finally been released after a US human rights organization put pressure on the authorities. Madame Thanh was a dynamic and courageous woman who had earned herself an international reputation as a jurist. When I approached her for help she said she was being too closely watched to be able to do anything for me. However she told me her political views remained as unshakeable as ever. She was convinced that if the Third Force in Vietnam joined forces with the Buddhist Nationalists they would have a real chance of ending the war and paving the way for a democratic future. At the time she spoke to me Madame Thanh had no idea that when the Communists took over in Saigon she would be forbidden to take part in any political activity and would be placed under house arrest.

My secret rendezvous with the Viet Cong was eventually organized through a Saigon button manufacturer who occasionally allowed his workshops to be used for printing anti-government leaflets. The meeting was to take place in a restaurant-cum-dance hall on the main Bien Hoa road. The man I was to speak to would be carrying a raincoat over his arm. I was frankly puzzled by the choice of venue. When I arrived at the place I no sooner stepped inside the door than a crowd of extremely pert and pretty hostesses came forward to greet me. The restaurant was a favourite haunt of senior officials and government ministers, who used to go there to relax. It was run by a charming woman who also happened to be the mistress of the head of the Saigon secret police. She led me straight to a secluded table out in the garden. I waited a short while and then three Vietnamese in civilian clothes came up to my table. One was carrying a raincoat over his arm. They introduced themselves and I tried hard to memorize their names, even though I knew they were probably fictitious. The eldest of the three told me he was an ex-trade union official who had been active among the Saigon dockers in the days of French rule. His story certainly had a ring of truth. The second man was a typical Vietnamese intellectual, with thick pebble glasses. As the evening went on he gradually emerged as spokesman on matters of ideology. The third Vietnamese was a powerfully built, taciturn individual who looked as if he had undergone some form of military training. We ordered ourselves a large Chinese meal that took in most parts of the menu and then we were left alone.

All in all I didn't learn anything new or sensational from my cloak-and-dagger meeting with the Viet Cong. I already knew the slogans and catchphrases of the Liberation Front's propaganda machine – only too well, in fact. What did surprise me, though, was the confidence these men had, considering they were living on a knife-edge. There they were, calmly going about their business, just like Daniel in the lion's den. What really interested me, I said, were the future objectives of the Liberation Front. The young ideological spokesman answered on behalf of the three of them. He said that foreign journalists should beware of being misled by the proclamations of victory coming from the American imperialists and their Saigon puppets. The people of Vietnam were waiting for their historic moment, the moment when the whole nation would rise up in revolt. The revolutionary forces of Vietnam would soon show the rest of the world what they could do.

Throughout the meal the Viet Cong envoys helped themselves repeatedly to the wine and rice liquor on the table. Gradually the tension eased and the mood became more relaxed. The two younger ones remained on their guard, but the trade unionist became quite expansive and told me all about his twenty years as a secret activist. He was very much the jovial, fatherly type, and I was sorry to hear later that he had been captured and tortured during Operation Phoenix, when the police cracked down on local Communists. I never knew what became of the other two, and to this day I have no idea whether they were killed during the New Year uprising they spoke about so freely.

Reports were coming in to Saigon of heavy fighting up around the US base at Dak To, near that sinister corner of Indochina where Vietnam, Cambodia and Laos meet. The Americans were under heavy attack from North Vietnamese regulars in the area. Down at the Cercle Sportif reactions to the news were mixed. Most of the regulars interpreted the news as a clear indication that the Communists were desperately trying to keep the battle alive now they had lost the war in the plains of Annam and Cochin China. As they saw it, the fact that the North Vietnamese had shifted the main thrust of their attack to this remote border region simply proved how weak their position really was. The Dutch colonel, on the other hand, viewed things quite differently. He strongly suspected that this latest move by Hanoi could be a major diversionary tactic. He was worried in case the North Vietnamese were planning a totally different strategy for the next phase of the war.

The following day I flew to Dak To in a Hercules transport. I had left Saigon in such a hurry that the only cameraman I had been able to get hold of was a Frenchman who was severely handicapped. His name was Auguste Lecoq and he had lost a leg during the siege of Dien Bien Phu. When we landed at Dak To we stood on the metal grid of the landing strip and surveyed the wooded hills that surrounded us on all sides. Lecoq looked distinctly unhappy. 'This place reminds me of the time I lost my leg,' he said. 'I was standing on the runway at Dien Bien Phu when the first Viet Minh shells came over, and that's when they got me.' He had little to worry about in Dak To, however. The Americans had total superiority in the air and their bombers flattened everything in their path.

The actual trouble spot lay in the hills in dense jungle a few kilometres south-west of Dak To. A battalion of the 172nd US Airborne Brigade had been ordered to search out enemy forces in the foothills around the Ho Chi Minh Trail. The troops had walked straight into a North Vietnamese ambush on the slopes of Hill 875 and it looked as if they might be totally wiped out. Reinforcements had been rushed to the area but they had suffered heavy losses as well. We decided to try and get a closer look at the fighting. First of all a helicopter flew us to a sector outpost, where we stopped to take ammunition on board. Lecoq seemed to have no difficulty getting up into the helicopter, despite his amputated leg. We eventually took off from the artillery base and headed towards the sound of fighting.

The Americans were in desperate trouble. From the air we could see where the F-100 fighter bombers had managed to blast a clearing in the jungle so the hard-pressed paratroopers could form a temporary hedgehog defence. Their bombing must have been incredibly accurate. Suddenly we felt our helicopter fall through the air like a lift going down a shaft. We descended steeply and came to a halt just above the jungle clearing. The GIs were using fallen tree trunks for cover. They were digging foxholes like men whose lives depended on it. All around us was the deafening roar and whine of firing. A short way off fighter planes screamed overhead, diving to bomb the unseen enemy below. The North

Vietnamese hide-outs were barely 300 metres from the US emplacements. Our helicopter hovered above the rutted ground as I helped Lecoq jump out. Those paratroopers still on their feet were plastered in mud from head to toe. They had wrapped the bodies of their dead in green plastic bags. Now they hurriedly bundled these grisly parcels aboard the lurching helicopter, like so many mailbags. As soon as maximum loading point was reached the chopper took off again. The next helicopter was already hovering overhead, waiting to come in to land. The American casualties had been unusually high so they concentrated on getting the wounded flown out. The eyes of the men who were left were staring and glazed. All you could read in them was total exhaustion and the agonizing fear of death. Their uniforms hung in tatters on their bodies. The bullet-proof waistcoats were the only things that had stood up to the ravages of the undergrowth. Darkness fell and our teeth chattered with cold. All through the night the F-100s circled over Hill 875 making an unholy, ear-splitting din. The perimeter was lit up like daylight. The napalm had set entire hillsides ablaze and the jungle burned and crackled around us.

In the grey light of dawn the hill looked as if it had been almost completely stripped of vegetation by the raging battle. The paratroopers went into the attack again, this time with heavy covering fire. They ducked their heads and ran towards the charred and smoking hill. Three times they were fired on by enemy mortars, and one or two men hit the ground. At last they reached their objective, and found themselves confronted by empty, smoked-out entrances to foxholes and underground tunnels that looked as if they'd been dug for dwarfs. The GIs trained flame-throwers on the holes and hurled explosive charges inside. They then reassembled and stood waiting for a helicopter squadron to take them back to Dak To.

The sky above the highlands of Annam had returned to its original pale blue. The fighter planes left vapour trails behind them, silver threads unwinding against a soft azure hue. The GIs stared out, unseeing, over the unending green of the jungle, completely and utterly drained. They had finally wrested Hill 875 from the clutches of the enemy – but now what? Out there before them lay a hundred more hills just like it, still waiting to be conquered. 'Do we really have to take them all?' asked a sergeant as he handed us a can of Coke.

When we got back to Dak To the paratroopers held a service for the dead. It was a strange, strange ceremony. The Stars and

Stripes were lowered to half-mast, and the men stood motionless as the chaplain read from the Bible. The boots of the dead men were carefully arranged on the ground. They had been polished till they shone, and now they sat neatly laid out beside one another in a ghostly semi-circle, like symbols in some peculiar rite. I thought of one of the old Westerns about the Indian wars, *They Died with their Boots On*. The title had a new meaning for me now.

Two months later news of the big New Year offensive reached me in Europe. It was the time of the Buddhist Tet festival marking the beginning of the Year of the Monkey, and the Viet Cong had taken advantage of the holiday mood to launch a major attack on all American bases in South Vietnam. The Americans were caught completely by surprise. The new US Embassy in Saigon, which had recently been reinforced and looked more like a fortress than an official residence, was attacked by a Viet Cong suicide squad. Practically every town and village in the Mekong Delta fell into rebel hands at some stage, and the fighting was heavy. Ben Tre had to be 'destroyed in order to be saved': those were the official spokesman's actual words. The old imperial city of Hue was occupied by North Vietnamese units who had marched over the border from Laos. They raised the Viet Cong flag over the citadel and held out for nearly forty days against the furious counter-attacks of US marines.

In the end, however, the Tet offensive lost momentum. The Communists had expected the entire population of South Vietnam to rise up against the Americans in a mass revolt. Instead, the vast majority remained completely passive. The Viet Cong had banked on mass desertions by South Vietnamese troops, but in the end not a single unit of the national army went over to the Communists. From a purely military standpoint the 1968 Tet offensive was a complete fiasco and a disastrous blow to Hanoi's hopes. The combat units of the National Liberation Front of South Vietnam, which had taken so long to build up, were now entirely wiped out. All the political commissars, agents and activists who had come out of hiding during the offensive were systematically rounded up over the following months in a massive police operation. Most commentators in the Western press hailed the Tet offensive as a victory for the USA.

In reality, the significance of the Tet offensive was quite different. The real consequence of this tragic prelude to the Year of the Monkey was that the balance of the war was tipped in favour of the North Vietnamese. Back in the United States all the pent up indignation at the 'dirty war' in Vietnam had gradually built up into a storm of protest, with students and intellectuals in the van. Veterans and women's groups marched in protest to the White House. The US Army had won outright military victory in its New Year counter-offensive but the long-term political victory went to Vo Nguyen Giap, the North Vietnamese commander-in-chief. Giap's tireless troops had ultimately succeeded in de-moralizing their mighty American foe. More importantly, the US generals failed to foresee the effect their rout of the Communists would have on President Johnson. It was the Tet victory, ironically, that convinced Johnson it was time to pull out of the war, and led to the announcement that air strikes over North Vietnam would be suspended, and American troop strength in South Vietnam systematically reduced. Washington declared itself ready to open negotiations on a ceasefire with Hanoi. And the president announced that he would not stand for nomination in the forthcoming presidential elections.

Ready for the Revolution

Cambodia, Spring 1970

The French priest was white with anger and despair. 'Just look at what the new Cambodian government has done,' he said, pointing to the crowd of Vietnamese who had come to seek refuge in his church. Their faces bore the marks of their recent ordeal. The refugees were mostly women and children. 'They shot all the men of military age because they claimed they were Communists,' continued the priest. 'The terrible thing is, every one of these people is Catholic. There's not a single Viet Cong sympathizer among them. If the powers-that-be in Phnomh Penh carry on much longer with this reign of terror they're going to end up driving all the Vietnamese in the countryside straight into the arms of the Khmer Rouge.' Despite the throng of people inside the church a terrible stillness hung over everything. The women sat sobbing silently to themselves. The wounded, some horribly maimed and lacerated, hardly uttered a sound. Even the babies were quiet, clinging to their mothers without so much as a whimper. During the night most of the women had been raped by troops.

The entrance to the church was guarded by heavily-armed Cambodian soldiers. Their uniforms were filthy and their discipline was not up to much, either. Their faces looked sullen and hostile, somehow un-Asian. 'You know who they remind me of?' asked Horst, the German photographer with me. Horst and I had worked together years ago in central Africa and now we had met up again in Phnom Penh. 'They remind me of those black troops from the old Belgian Force Publique in Leopoldville, the ones who were rioting and mutinous.' Overnight, it seemed, idyllic Cambodia had turned into an Asian Congo. The troops of Lon Nol, the new Cambodian head of state, were hunting down members of the Catholic Vietnamese minority in Cambodia. These were the first victims in a terrible series of massacres.

All the celebrating and rejoicing was over now for the people of Phnom Penh. In March Prince Sihanouk had set off on an extended foreign tour, ignoring the warnings of his advisers to remain in the capital. Their fears turned out to be justified, for during his absence Sihanouk was deposed by a military coup. He had gone abroad to try and get Moscow and Peking to put pressure on Hanoi. In recent years the North Vietnamese and the Viet Cong had gradually been building up their network of 'sanc-tuaries' in the border area between Cambodia and South Vietnam, until eventually they had a whole chain of inviolable bases from which they could direct their military operations inside Cochin China. Sihanouk weighed up the situation and concluded, quite correctly as it turned out, that there was a serious risk of the USA overreacting to this encroachment by the North Vietnamese. Unfortunately, however, he completely misjudged the political situation inside his own country. He made the fatal mistake of banking on the continued loyalty of his army, a poorly-equipped force of 35,000 men led by their commander-in-chief, General Lon Nol. Sihanouk, overstaying his time abroad, brushed aside Lon Nol's urgent appeals to him to return home immediately, with fatal results. Of course, had it not been for the intervention of the CIA and the Americans there would never have been any coup in Phnom Penh. US intelligence agents kept telling the Cam-bodian military that a new pro-Western government in Phnom Penh would give their divisions the shot in the arm they needed to drive the Viet Cong out of Cambodia for ever. And pro-US agents of the underground movement known as Khmer Serei – the Free

Khmer – handed out substantial bribes to remove any lingering doubts the Cambodian officer corps might have had.

The first weeks of the new regime seemed more like a public holiday than a military uprising. The whole population of Phnom Penh seemed to be out on the streets. Ironically enough, the students and schoolchildren who had benefited so much from Sihanouk's enlightened and benevolent monarchy now displayed the most fervent republicanism. The students staged an elaborate spectacle before a baying mob in the stadium in Phnom Penh. In the play an actor dressed as Sihanouk was hunted down by a group of student revolutionaries, who then proceeded to arm themselves with wooden rifles and win a series of glorious victories over numbers of Viet Cong in black pyjamas and Vietnamese straw hats. The guest of honour at this popular celebration was the usurper himself, Lon Nol, who had since appointed himself marshal. Now, as he sat there watching from the royal box, his swarthy face looked grave. There was no look of triumph on it, only the uneasy air of a man who had once been regarded as the most loyal of officers and who had been forced to betray his master by the sheer pressure of events.

Every time I met Lon Nol in the course of the next five years he had the look of a man who was suffering severe pangs of conscience. As time went on he tried to assume the role of an Asian warlord, but even then he never seemed quite at ease. He was finally left half-crippled by a stroke that reduced him to a pathetic pawn in the complex chess-game of the great Indochina conflict. Even before this, however, he had tended to leave his fate, and his future strategy, in the hands of his court astrologers. Try as they might, his American advisers could do nothing to influence this headstrong, deeply superstitious man. Lon Nol, the Cambodian Wallenstein, finally created his own esoteric and somewhat mystical brand of nationalism. He claimed he had read in the stars that he would one day be called on to lead the Khmer kingdom to a new era of glory. He would triumph over his foreign enemies and crush all the bloodsuckers and parasites – the Vietnamese, the Siamese, the Chinese. Lon Nol was rumoured to have Chinese blood in his veins but fortunately, perhaps, it didn't show. As far as he was concerned he was an authentic representative of the dark-skinned Khmer-Mon people whose civilization – before it was destroyed by the fair-skinned conquerors from the north – had been the greatest South-east Asia had ever known. Lon Nol always insisted on being addressed as the Great Dark One during his astrological deliberations.

The rejoicing that marked the first weeks of the revolution did not last long. Soon the great mass of the people, particularly in the rural areas, began to yearn for their fallen prince. They wondered how the kingdom could survive and prosper without the blessing of its god-king. Meanwhile Sihanouk had settled in Peking, where he set up a government-in-exile. Chou En-lai, the Chinese premier, welcomed the exiled prince and showered him with honours. The North Vietnamese, acting on behalf of Sihanouk's government-in-exile, advanced deep into Cambodia and seized control of the provinces east of the Mekong. Then they declared their support for the small band of Communist guerillas in the country, later to become known as the Khmer Rouge. It was a name that would one day spread fear and terror throughout the whole of Cambodia.

The war was over almost as soon as it had begun for Lon Nol and his regime. His soldiers were holding out in the little town of Siem Reap, but already the blood-red flag of the Khmer Rouge was fluttering above the temples of Angkor Wat. The Americans wasted no time in acting. They advanced about twenty kilometres inside Cambodian territory in division strength, their objective being to destroy the Viet Cong sanctuaries in the border zone. Their main target was the headquarters of the Liberation Front. But when the US Army entered Cambodia they found the bird had flown: all the Viet Cong hide-outs in the area had been abandoned. Clearly the intelligence services hadn't done their homework.

From the American point of view, then, the Cambodia campaign turned out to be a complete fiasco. It could be argued that it forced the Vietnamese Communists to abandon temporarily their positions around the rubber plantations of Snoul, Krek and Mimot. It also forced them to pull out of the 'Parrot's Beak' and 'the Fishhook', the twin prongs of Cambodian territory jutting out into Vietnam. But from now on the Viet Cong had the whole of the western sector of Cambodia to operate in. The élite troops in the South Vietnamese army couldn't do a thing to stop them, either; they were trapped on their side of the border. Given the circumstances, it cannot have come as much of a surprise when a flotilla of gunboats sailed up the Mekong from Saigon and dropped anchor in Phnom Penh. What, in fact, was happening was that President Nixon, acting on the advice of Henry Kissinger, was destroying the last bastion of national independence and neutrality in Indochina – Sihanouk's Cambodia. He was pitching the country headlong into war. Worse still, it was a war that America herself was in the process of pulling out of. It was an unforgivable error of judgement. Nixon abandoned the land of the Khmer to a steady but inexorable takeover by the Communists.

Early one Sunday we made the one-and-a-half-hour journey by hired car from Phnom Penh to Sihanoukville, recently renamed Kompong Som. On the way we passed several columns of military vehicles. At the top of the Pich-Nil Pass, where Sihanouk used to have his summer residence, the once-elegant villas had been gutted by fire. Our Chinese driver told us the Khmer Rouge set up road blockades at night round the area. In Kompong Som itself the harbour was dead, empty of ships. The station, built with aid from West Germany, now stood deserted. We booked in at the luxury hotel down by the beach and found we were the only guests. The waiters bowed respectfully. The sea shone like crystal and the sand was silvery white beneath the palm trees. When we got back to the capital we discovered we had been bitten all over by sand fleas.

This was to be our one and only major outing by car; the Communists were closing in on the capital from all sides now. The war in Cambodia was more vicious and cruel than the conflict in Vietnam. In the first weeks of fighting as many as a dozen Western journalists were killed. They probably had the misfortune to bump into a gang of Khmer Rouge at a bend in the road. It would all have been over very quickly: there would be no questions asked, no mercy shown. The ones who were shot straight away could count themselves lucky. The Cambodian Communists, with their caps, their spotted scarves and their AK-47 rifles, killed like robots. They were a savage, bloodthirsty lot – even their Vietnamese allies felt uneasy with them. A kind of frenzy was sweeping through the land of the Khmer. The pagodas, with their golden, serenely smiling Buddhas, began to look more and more like oases of peace and sanity. Cambodia was at the mercy of a murdering army of zombies.

The little town of Neak Luong, which had a regular ferry service across the Mekong, was strategically important in the war. The town was only seventy kilometres from the capital along Route 1, the old colonial road that used to link Saigon and Phnom Penh. It was here we caught up with the Cambodian army, who looked a fairly ill-assorted bunch. The reserves had been called up at the last minute, then bundled into gaudily-painted buses and thrown into the path of the advancing North Vietnamese and Khmcr Rouge forces. The Vietnamese settlements along Route 1 were now charred ruins. Driving along the embankment that looked down onto the Tonle Sap River, we sighted a river-boat belonging to the Cambodian navy. We watched through binoculars as the sailors tossed handcuffed Vietnamese civilians into the yellow water, then opened fire on them. And yet, provided of course they didn't shoot you straight away, Lon Nol's troops could be thoroughly friendly and obliging if you caught them in the right mood. Most had brought their families into the actual combat zone. There were always women and children up near the front line, going about their business seemingly oblivious to the danger all around. In this part of the world Mother Courage wore a sarong. Sometimes we would be scared by a sudden loud noise from a clump of bamboo and dive for cover. The women and children always found this terribly funny. There were twelve-year-old boys here carrying M-16 rifles that had been originally sent from Saigon for the Cambodian troops. The women seemed to spend most of their time preparing meals for the men and suckling their babies. These peaceful scenes of family life right in the very jaws of death were about the only sign left of the famous Khmer smile.

On the west bank of the Mekong, just across from Neak Luong, the peasants sold rice and black pigs to the troops. The main market on the far bank had been hurriedly cleared away by the Chinese stallholders and shopkeepers. On the opposite side of the river you were in no-man's land. We had a young Chinese driver with us, and his initiative, intelligence and general tidiness made a refreshing change after the slapdash Cambodians. Now that we were driving through enemy territory he was constantly alert and on the look-out for danger. We found ourselves anxiously scanning the trees and jungle beyond the dry paddies. There was no other traffic on the road, and no sounds of firing. But in this war silence was always a bad sign, your first warning of real danger. We were making for a hamlet called Svay Rieng, which we knew was encircled by Communist guerillas. I was all for turning back when suddenly we caught sight of the last line of outposts of the Lon Nol army. As usual the troops were being billeted in a pagoda. The men were pleased to see us and showed no sign of hostility.

The captain in charge of the company spoke halting French. He used the American expression 'VC' for the Viet Cong. He said the enemy weren't far away, just behind the sugar-palms to the east.

He reckoned the road to Neak Luong would be risky and advised us to head for home right away. If the worst came to the worst the men would try and fight their way back to the Mekong River since they didn't know the area all that well. But if we were caught out there after dark we wouldn't stand a chance. Our Chinese driver raced back to town, doing 100 km/h. The next morning he told us the pagoda we had visited had, in fact, been overrun by Communist guerillas after dark. The garrison had not held out for very long. There were now no Lon Nol units on the west bank of the Mekong across from Neak Luong.

A few weeks was all it took for Phnom Penh to slide into a state of squalor and neglect. Rubbish began to pile up in the streets. Government departments barricaded themselves behind sand-bags and barbed wire, and close guard was mounted at all the bridges. Yet in spite of the siege you could still buy more or less anything you wanted in the big round covered market. There seemed to be no problem about getting supplies through. Later it transpired that the Khmer Rouge were letting all kinds of provisions into the besieged capital, on the understanding that Lon Nol's army would supply them with mortars and ammunition in exchange. The US military advisers in Phnom Penh were driven to despair by their Cambodian allies. What could you do with troops who sold off part of their arsenal to the enemy? It was tantamount to suicide, but the Cambodians didn't seem at all worried. And officers were entering whole battalions of non-existent troops in the record books so they could claim pay for them. But for the intervention of the US Air Force the war in Cambodia would have gone in favour of the Communists far sooner than it did. As soon as it got dark in the evenings the streets in the centre of town emptied rapidly. The curfew tended to be rather haphazardly enforced and the patrols were trigger-happy. The last civilians to disappear indoors were always the prostitutes. You could hear their shrill laughter ringing through the deserted streets long after it got dark.

As war correspondents we were automatically issued with passes that enabled us to move around the city after the curfew came in force. All the same it was safer to leave the light on in the car as you drove round at night so you could immediately be recognized as a European visitor. One evening I drove with Ian Manoch, a freelance journalist, to a silent, wooden-built house overlooking a pond, just off the Boulevard Monorom. As I got out of the car I could hear frogs croaking at the moon. Ian was working for a number of English journals and newspapers. The first time we had met was in Guinea, in Sekou Touré's Revolutionary People's Republic. Ian was a redheaded giant of a Scot, heavily built and rather overweight. He suffered badly from the heat and the tropical humidity. He wore a Chinese amulet round his neck that disappeared among the sweat-soaked fair hair on his chest. He was constantly wiping perspiration from his brow.

The door to the house, an opium den, was eventually opened by a toothless old Chinese woman. She greeted the Scotsman like an old friend, then led us into a tiny wooden cell completely bare of furniture. We settled ourselves as comfortably as we could on the straw matting on the floor. Two Cambodian girls rolled the black opium into pellets and melted them, then handed us the pipes.

I was feeling completely shattered after the awful journey from Neak Luong, utterly drained by all the tensions of the day. It wasn't long, though, before I could feel myself slowly unwinding, and a sense of peace gradually began to overtake me. In between pipes the girls massaged us, sitting astride our backs and chests and kneading us gently with their feet. We lay almost stark naked in the dim red glow of the oil lamp. I had forgotten all about the sticky, sultry heat and the mosquito bites. Despite the close physical contact we did not feel at all sexually aroused by the Cambodian girls. They say the gentle god of opium is a brother of Death. Another thing he most definitely is, is an enemy of Eros. I let myself drift, quite happy to stay silent, but the fumes of the opium gave Manoch the urge to talk. He told me a long story about the book he was planning to write on the war between the secret services in Africa and Asia. This was the book his publisher was waiting for him to produce, the big one that was going to make his name as a writer. I remembered him going on to me about exactly the same book ten years before in Conakry. We had drunk a bottle of whisky between us that evening, and we sat there listening to the sounds of the tropical West African night. Outside in a nearby courtyard, an official of the Unity Party of Guinea was hammering home to a small group of people the slogans of Sekou Touré. 'Honour, Glory, Revolution!' he roared, and the cry was taken up by the audience. Lying in the opium den in Phnom Penh, many thousands of kilometres away, I suddenly thought I heard that same chorus again: Honour, Glory, Revolution. The land of the Khmer was about to do what black Guinea had done and take on board a rag-bag of half-baked European ideologies that would bring ruin and destruction on its head. I caught myself murmuring, like a prayer, another slogan from Guinea (it was a way of silencing Ian, after all). The catchword was 'Ready for the Revolution'. African past and South-east Asian present began to get confused in my mind. It then occurred to me that the whole of the Third World had fallen under the spell of the same phoney ideologies, and I felt vastly, and childishly, amused.

Dispersal and Flight

Hue, Easter 1972

The Filipinos had their own unique way of celebrating Good Friday. In Luzon we watched the Passion being acted out in a small town on the south side of the island. The penitents, all male of course, had pressed crowns of thorns onto their temples, and trickles of blood ran down their foreheads. We saw dozens of flagellants lashing their naked backs with whips until angry red weals appeared through the skin. Others were dressed as Roman legionaries with tin helmets and spears. Their job was to whip the actor impersonating Christ through the narrow streets and then tie him to a cross. Every Easter there was always some crank willing to be actually nailed to the cross. We decided, however, that we could probably give this particular spectacle a miss. All round us loudspeakers were blaring out penitential hymns and chants, though oddly enough the most popular songs this Easter Week seemed to come from *Jesus Christ, Superstar* – a great hit at the time. On this island archipelago with its Spanish and American influences, Seville and Hollywood had come together in a bizarre union. Some of the more devout members of the crowd joined in the flogging. I stared, fascinated, as an old woman beat away at the blood-stained back of a young man lying stretched out in the dust; her stick came down again and again with deliberate, methodical strokes. Just then Ben, our driver, called me over. Ben was a little man, almost ridiculously tiny in fact, and a broad knife scar on his cheek gave his fierce Malayan face a slightly rakish appearance. We had a sneaking suspicion that Ben was a member of the highly-organized Manila underworld – not that that necessarily made him any less trustworthy. The other members of the camera team called him Mack the Knife.

Ben had been listening to the car radio while waiting for us. 'The North Vietnamese launched a big offensive yesterday,' he said. 'They reckon they've already broken through the South Vietnamese lines.' We turned up the volume and listened. Ben had heard right, General Giap had struck again, and had taken the enemy completely by surprise. He had attacked in the very place no-one thought he would – the narrow demarcation line along the 17th parallel. Since President Johnson had reduced American strength in Vietnam to 50,000 GIs, the South Vietnamese had been left to fight the war on the ground on their own. The 17th parallel was usually considered to be the forgotten sector of the war, so the South Vietnamese had stationed their weakest division, the 3rd, up there. It was mainly made up of petty criminals and deserters who had been caught on the run. On the Thursday before Easter, Giap's assault troops suddenly appeared out of nowhere and began blitzing the 3rd with artillery fire. They started charging towards the South Vietnamese positions in Soviet T-52 and T-54 tanks. There was nothing for it but to retreat. The US Air Force were prevented from intervening by low-lying cloud. American military advisers were promptly evacuated from the encircled bases around Dong Ha and Cam Lo. This destroyed the morale of the Saigonese army. Reports were already coming in that the provincial capital, Quang Tri, had fallen.

Meanwhile another column of North Vietnamese tanks had sped south from the Cambodian border along Route 13 and captured the district capital of Loc Ninh, just north of Saigon. Things were not going quite so well for the North Vietnamese around An Loc, however. Giap's troops were relatively inexperienced when it came to mobile warfare, and they had made the mistake of sending their tanks forward without sufficient infantry support. To make matters worse, their advance had run into South Vietnamese paratroopers who put up fierce resistance using armour-piercing weapons. As a result of their efforts, the offensive had been brought to a standstill twenty kilometres south of An Loc.

A few days later – the time it took us to get a visa and plane tickets in Manila – we flew into the rainswept airstrip at Phu Bay, south of Hue. It was freezing cold and the whole place looked grey and depressing. We climbed into a rattling old bus and set off for the old imperial city. On the way we passed abandoned US army camps and bases surrounded by high, barbed-wire fences. The

Americans hadn't been gone long, but already the barracks looked dilapidated and run-down. Only one hotel in Hue was still open. It was down by the Perfume River and was already bursting at the seams with pressmen from all over the world. As we drew up outside we saw a solitary white man standing by the main door. He was wearing a GI combat helmet, his face was unshaven and tinged with yellow. His clothes were soaking wet and sticking to his body, and his steel-rimmed glasses had misted up in the damp air. I would have known that face anywhere. I walked towards him and called out his name, and we fell into one another's arms.

I first met Dietrich Schanz in the Congo. He had been travelling round Africa in a Volkswagen van with his Russian wife. He had already crossed the Sahara and half the continent by the time he arrived in the hell-hole of Leopoldville. Dietrich had set out from Bonn full of liberal ideas and staunchly opposed to colonialism, but the events in the Congo were to shatter a good many of his illusions. The incident that finally set the seal on his disenchantment with the Third World happened one day when his car was stopped in the Boulevard Albert by a drunken soldier from the Force Publique. In barely comprehensible French the soldier asked the bearded Dietrich whether he was a missionary. When Dietrich replied that he wasn't, the Congolese soldier slapped him in the face. The drunken lawman then told Dietrich that only missionaries wore beards, and that anyone who dressed up as a clergyman was automatically suspected of being a spy. Much later, after Patrice Lumumba had been murdered and Moise Tshombe kidnapped, and Mobutu had begun his glorious reign in Kinshasa (the new name for Leopoldville), Dietrich had gone to work as a correspondent in Hong Kong. Since then he had been travelling non-stop throughout South-east Asia. He had had enough of blacks, he said, though he wasn't too keen on Asians either. He found the Hong Kong Chinese too cold and calculating – too brazen, as he put it. The Thai were, in his own words, 'a race of gigglers', and there was a certain amount of truth in what he said. As for the Vietnamese, the ones in the south were too easy-going, and the ones in the north were all fanatics. It was only when he was transferred to Tehran several years later that he began to miss the East Asians, and possibly the Africans as well.

In the world of journalism, which has its fair share of pompous fools, half-educated morons and incurable drunks, Dietrich Schanz stood out as an honourable and refreshing exception to the rule. He still had a child-like enthusiasm for things and he never lost his spirit of adventure – an essential quality for a journalist going into a trouble spot. Whenever fighting broke out you knew that Dietrich would be on the first plane in. It didn't seem to bother him that as a freelancer he risked his neck for a mere pittance while other more established East Asian correspondents sat in their air-conditioned hotel rooms composing their eye-witness reports from the front. He had managed to retain a sense of humour, too. Basically he was more interested in living life to the full than in making a name for himself. He was a kind of Don Quixote of journalism.

Dietrich advised us to visit the market on the other side of the iron bridge and buy ourselves some mattresses (the beds had disappeared from our hotel rooms), raincoats, steel helmets and bullet-proof waistcoats. If we were lucky, we might be able to get hold of a taxi to take us to the front. He had just got back from a trip to the front lines at Dong Ha. He had been on the far bank of the Cua-Viet River when, without warning, a fleet of B-52s had appeared out of the sky and blanket-bombed the whole area with a hail of explosives. The ground had heaved beneath his feet, just like an earthquake. In a blind panic he had jumped into a crater full of water, much to the amusement of some South Vietnamese soldiers. They were quite used to the earth-shattering roar of the bombers.

Next morning we drove north along Route 1 in the direction of Quang Tri. This old colonial road was nicknamed 'the dreary road' by the French, and was later immortalized by Bernard Fall in his book *Hell in a Very Small Place*. We had hired an old Citroën for the journey, the type that you always used to see in French gangster films before the war. This particular model had been nicknamed 'Queen of the Road' in its day, because of its excellent road-holding. However our Queen of the Road was in a pretty bad way. The rain came in the roof and the springs stuck out of the torn upholstery. One or two people tried to tell us it was made out of the front and rear ends of two different cars that had been welded together by an enterprising Vietnamese mechanic, but we refused to believe them. When we told Nho, our driver, where we wanted him to take us he shook his head disapprovingly. 'C'est très mauvais, Monsieur,' was his only comment. However it didn't seem to deter him unduly, for he promptly bundled his ten-year-old son into the front seat and headed north with a crashing of gears.

The North Vietnamese had advanced from the west along Route 1, the vital defence link between Hue and Quang Tri, the provincial capital. They were now about four kilometres from Quang Tri. The surrounding countryside was sodden with rain. The distant thunder of artillery wafted towards us on the westerly wind. Somewhere out there in the mist lay the South Vietnamese position called 'Bastogne', where heavy fighting had been going on. Bastogne was the last position blocking the exit to the A Shau Valley, where the North Vietnamese 324B Division was reported to be waiting to pounce. South Vietnamese marines fanned out on both sides of the road, which ran parallel to the Saigon–Hanoi railway. They were combing villages and bamboo thickets in search of enemy troops who had managed to sneak through their lines. The marines were an élite troop, the backbone of Saigon's strategic reserve. They had been flown north at short notice as soon as the fighting got heavy. These little yellow men in their mottled camouflage uniforms were real pros. There was no trace of fear or mutiny in their faces. They simply got on with the job of building a defensive position within sight of the tarmac road. Every now and then they would glance up at the sky to see if the cloud had lifted; when it cleared the US fighter-bombers could come in.

In Quang Tri all the shops were closed and barricaded. The streets were thronged with refugees carrying bundles of belongings or small children on their backs. They stood there in the pouring rain waiting for food to be distributed, unbelievably calm and composed. Easily the most miserable-looking were the Montagnards, the Moi hill-tribesmen. They belonged to the Bru people and had originally inhabited the region around the US combat base at Khe Sanh. Since 1968, however, they had had to flee their homes on at least three separate occasions. Above the citadel in Quang Tri fluttered the Stars and Stripes; it was the most northerly American flag in Vietnam. The US advisers to the South Vietnamese 3rd Division were stationed here in a snug little command post fortified by hundreds and hundreds of sandbags. Unlike the military staffs back in Saigon, who always painted a rosy picture of the American position, the military advisers in Quang Tri looked to the future with foreboding. They insisted we wear bullet-proof waistcoats, or 'flakjackets', before we went further north. American uniforms used to be regulation dress for anyone wanting to enter the combat zone; but now no correspondent wore American uniform any more. Lately the press corps had taken to wearing blue or yellow shirts instead. They made you an easy target, but at least they singled you out as a non-combatant. The Americans told us the South Vietnamese were now refusing to go on raiding parties to recover US pilots shot down behind enemy lines. A perfectly normal reaction, perhaps, in an army which didn't value the life of a white soldier any more highly than that of an Asian.

Pontoons lay piled up outside the command post. The army had to be on the look-out at all times for enemy saboteurs trying to blow up the bridges on Route 7, a vital road link. Two hours before our arrival a squad of North Vietnamese sappers had managed to get as far as the outskirts of Quang Tri, but luckily they were spotted by a South Vietnamese reconnaissance patrol and shot – barely 100 metres from the first pillars of one of the bridges. Now there were two dozen bodies lying on the ground like blood-stained dolls. Their green pith helmets with the red star lay scattered round about. Some of the wounded had terrible, gaping holes in their heads. They were shot at point-blank range to put them out of their agony.

As soon as Nho laid eyes on the dead troops he refused to drive our big black hearse of a Citroën any further. He was quite right to feel worried: from here on the only traffic you saw going north were armoured vehicles heading for Dong Ha as fast as they could travel. By this time the sound of gunfire was continuous. We found an ambulance driver who agreed to take us to Dong Ha. He dropped us off at a fork on the southern edge of the town. Route 1 now looked ominously empty. Dong Ha fell to the North Vietnamese three days later.

We had to make our way back to Quang Tri on foot as no transport was available. Just 500 metres from the road we came across a column of seven North Vietnamese tanks that had been stopped by the bazookas of the Saigon marines. They had been charging south like a herd of wild buffalo and hadn't bothered to take even safety precautions. It was the first evidence of Hanoi's switch to conventional mobile warfare along Soviet lines. As we were on the point of throwing our heavy flakjackets into a ditch, a jeep stopped and gave us a lift back to base. When we got back to Quang Tri, Nho was waiting for us in his Citroën.

We arrived in Hue just as it was getting dark. The outlines of the black walls of the imperial citadel were obscured by the drizzling rain. A crowd had gathered outside the main entrance to the citadel. They stood there soaked to the skin, pushing and jostling

one another. Two captured enemy tanks were on display outside
the gate. They had been abandoned by the North Vietnamese at
Dong Ha because of lack of fuel, and had been towed back to Hue
as trophies of war. One was a Russian-built T-54, the other a
Chinese vehicle. Both looked confusingly alike. One of the
American military advisers climbed inside a turret hatch to take a
closer look. As a rule the American military still in Hue kept as low
a profile as possible. Relations with the Vietnamese, particularly
the ARVN units, had worsened, especially now that the Saigon
army was beginning to feel it had been abandoned by its powerful
ally. Tens of thousands of refugees had already poured into the
city, and now they were camping out in the mud in terrible
conditions. The only people who could afford a plane ticket were
the really wealthy citizens of Hue. Every seat on every flight out of
the city had been booked several times over. The sums being paid
as bribes were staggering. Since the Tet offensive, when bands of
Hanoi troops had rampaged through the city killing large numbers
of civilians, everyone in Hue had been terrified of the
Communists.

In a nearby sidestreet an inquisitive crowd stood clustered like a
swarm of flies round the bodies of three Viet Cong guerillas. Early
that morning the guerillas had tried to storm the prison. Now they
were dead, and their corpses had been left out in the rain to rot as a
warning to others. The young South Vietnamese militiamen gazed
down at the bodies, apparently unmoved. And yet these men could
have been their brothers.

The dining-room of the hotel had been hastily moved to the first
floor. Cold, damp air came whistling in through every crack and
crevice. The correspondents were trying to warm themselves up
with whisky from the local PX stores. The atmosphere was
decidedly gloomy. I caught sight of Claude Rouget sitting among a
little knot of South Vietnamese staff officers. Rouget had been a
soldier in Vietnam but now he was back in his capacity as special
correspondent for *Le Figaro*. He never stopped thinking of himself
as an officer, though. Seeing him today, with his shock of white
hair, you would have taken him for a sensitive, highly-strung
intellectual. Yet this was the man who, in the spring of 1954,
volunteered to be parachuted into the jungle stronghold of Dien
Bien Phu, then encircled by the enemy and certain to fall. Before
that he had served as aide to General Navarre, the French
Commander-in-Chief. After the fall of Dien Bien Phu he had
spent several months being 're-educated' by the Viet Minh, and

the experience had undoubtedly left its mark on him. During the Algeria war, for instance, Rouget was one of the band of young French officers who played around with pseudo-revolutionary methods of psychological warfare. He was rumoured to have been involved in the generals' coup against de Gaulle. At Dien Bien Phu he had had a fairly low opinion of France's nationalist Vietnamese allies, like most of his colleagues. Today, however, all that was forgotten. Now that Hue was in a really desperate plight, all the old loyalties of his colonial days flickered into life again. Rouget sat swapping reminiscences with the Vietnamese colonels, asking after old friends, and cursing the Yankees.

A few days later Nho drove us south along Route 1, to Da Nang. Since the road was a vital strategic link between the northern front and the American supply and air base at Da Nang, you might have expected it to be under constant attack by the Viet Cong. But the enemy made no attempt to stop the lorries carrying supplies in and out of Da Nang, not even on the hairpin bends going up to the Col des Nuages. As we approached the base we passed lorries driving through the billowing mist with dipped headlights. They were military convoys a hundred vehicles long, carrying ammunition to the front. Fearing an ambush, the drivers stuck close to the lorry in front. It was a miracle there wasn't an accident every time one of them braked. The rain had not let up all day. Through the mist we could just pick out the ghostly silhouettes of the South Vietnamese watchtowers. In conditions like this war became totally unreal. Then, abruptly, the cloud lifted. We rounded a bend in the road and saw, through the bamboo branches, the bay of Da Nang stretched out before us. Like figures in a landscape in a Chinese watercolour, the junks stood out black against the pale, calm sea.

A fortnight later we were back in the northern sector. The weather had changed suddenly, and now the sun beat down mercilessly out of a cloudless sky. The mud of the rainy season had dried to a fine dust that penetrated into every nook and cranny and swirled up behind the trucks in red-brown clouds. No-one was allowed to travel beyond Quang Tri now. The provincial capital had been completely surrounded by North Vietnamese troops. The front extended as far as the My Chanh River, where South Vietnamese marines had dug in in old concrete bunkers left over from the French war. The marines watched impassively as the rolling thunder of the US bombers broke over the heads of the enemy, barely 200 metres away. As they sat watching they calmly scooped their rice ration into their mouths with chopsticks.

The first refugees to come out of Quang Tri were civilians. Weary and exhausted, they trailed across the Bailey bridge spanning the My Chanh River. Some had ox-carts piled high with household equipment and children. The old men and women limped on sore feet, using their bamboo sticks as crutches. The wounded tried to support each other as they walked along. The inhabitants of Quang Tri had managed to get through the minefields and artillery barrages to the south of the town. Now they were heading for safety – or so they thought.

Major Price, American adviser to the South Vietnamese marines, had been acting as artillery observer until now. His job had been to direct the fire of the US 7th Fleet onto Communist outposts and note where the rockets of the Cobra helicopters fell. He stood up now, stroked his sandy moustache and put on his helmet and flakjacket. He had just received a message over the crackling radio-telephone, a message he was extremely reluctant to pass on to us. Early that morning the commander of the South Vietnamese 3rd Division had lost his nerve. He had abandoned his command post at Quang Tri and flown out by helicopter. His US advisers were not long in following suit, though they had to leave on foot. Now the men who had been left behind had panicked. The South Vietnamese Rangers – a crack unit of the Saigon army – had commandeered all the available lorries and headed off south. The North Vietnamese had let them go. They were quickly followed by the remnants of the 3rd Division, terrified out of their wits. The stronghold at Quang Tri had been taken without a fight. It was a bad omen for the future. The North Vietnamese could have turned this debacle into a bloodbath with some well-aimed fire, but they held off. Possibly they were hoping the sight of panic-stricken deserters would create a shock wave that would throw the entire defence system of central Annam into chaos.

Around noon the first bunch of fleeing soldiers started arriving at the My Chanh bridge. All in all it was a pretty unedifying spectacle. Some were drunk and kept firing wildly into the air. The line of lorries and army vehicles roared on south as if the devil himself were at their heels. Some deserters tried to hide their shame and embarrassment by fooling around and chasing dogs and chickens. On our way back to Hue, our Citroën was stopped by three grim-faced soldiers who fired their M-16 rifles into the air until we pulled up. All three squeezed into the front beside the driver, and we drove off again. We gave them cigarettes to try and calm them, and the further we got from the front the friendlier they became. When we reached the outskirts of Hue they excused themselves, very formally, for their bad manners, thanked us for the lift, and stood waving goodbye until we disappeared from view. It wasn't really so surprising; they belonged, after all, to a very civilized race.

As we expected the imperial city was in the grip of the collective hysteria defeat always brings in its wake. Two-thirds of the population flowed out along the 'dreary road' in a swaying mass, pushing carts and carrying bundles, battling their way towards the harbour at Da Nang. There was something eerie about the sight of this mass of humanity, sweating and groaning under their loads, moving south in virtual silence. They were like wounded animals, mute and undemonstrative. Even in despair they retained their dignity. That night in Hue the red glow of artillery fire lit up the dark sky over the river. Then shots rang out. Marauding troops had started looting and burning the market, irate because the local shopkeepers refused to hand over their stocks of alcohol. The military police were trying to control the mob – hence the sound of shooting. We could hear the dull explosions of underwater mines going off down by the river. They were supposed to stop the North Vietnamese frogmen blowing up the one vital bridge across the Perfume River.

We would never have got a seat on the heavily-booked Air Vietnam plane to Saigon if it hadn't been for Tran Van Tin, our Chinese escort and interpreter. Perks like this could be bought for a supplement of US $100 and nobody knew this better than Tin. He was small, like all Vietnamese, with a pale skin that hinted at Chinese blood in his ancestry. He couldn't see a thing without his glasses. He had worked for both German TV networks for over ten years and in that time had become a byword for dependable, efficient service. There was no permit, no visa, no customs clearance on earth that Tin couldn't arrange at a moment's notice. On top of everything else he was a wizard at languages. He was fluent in French, Chinese and English, and he had taught himself to speak amazingly good German. Tin looked younger than his years. Nobody knew much about his past, and there were conflicting stories about his early life. According to one version he had been an orphan in Hue before a colonel in the Foreign Legion adopted him during the French war. Another version claimed he had only been a regimental mascot. He must have had a family at some stage because from time to time he spoke about his poor old mother and a brother who had been a policeman and been shot by the Communists. Tin was a meticulous individual, and his fussing and flapping tried the patience of many a correspondent. After some years of working full-time for the German networks he had managed to acquire two old but completely roadworthy de luxe American limousines, plus a whole horde of drivers, camera-assistants and porters. These he variously introduced as his uncles, nephews or grandsons, and he paid a pittance for their services. His keen business sense was allied to a certain talent for survival. It was rumoured, for instance, that Tin had once been a supporter of Ngo Dinh Diem, the Catholic dictator, but he had experienced a sudden and timely change of heart prior to Diem's demise.

I had always had a delightfully uncomplicated relationship with Tin. Occasionally he would say to me, 'You know, you're just like a father to me' – a remark I always took with a pinch of salt. But in all the years we worked together Tin never once went behind my back or let me down. This highly unusual production manager was, like so many of his countrymen, a political dreamer. He had written a 300-page essay formulating his views on the best way to rid South Vietnam of corruption and moral degeneracy and build a successful anti-Communist state. Of course before any of this could happen a great many 'undesirable elements' would have to be 'ruthlessly eradicated'.

Anyhow, Tin managed to get us on the plane to Saigon, despite the thousands of other would-be passengers queuing up for tickets. He was, you could tell, enormously pleased with himself at having proved once again how indispensable he was. When our plane stopped over in Da Nang one of the passengers, a beautiful Vietnamese woman, exchanged a few words with an air force officer, then collapsed into hysterical sobbing. I asked the Vietnamese steward what had happened. He burst into high-pitched Oriental laughter, then said: 'Her husband's a pilot in the Vietnamese Air Force and she's just been told he's been shot down.' The steward's laughter had been a polite way of covering his own reactions of sympathy and dismay. But he realized, just in time, it might be misinterpreted by Europeans or Americans, so he quickly set his face in a suitably solemn expression.

The Vietnamization of the Coffins

Saigon, Spring 1972

On Sundays the Botanical Gardens in Saigon were an oasis of peace and respectability. This was where the young daughters of the bourgeoisie came to show off their very best *ao dai*. Not that they flirted with strange men – they were on the look-out for suitors with serious intentions. Families would line up in front of the backdrop of palm trees for a group photograph, and endless snapshots were taken of the children as they perched on the stone dragon of the ancestral temple. One five-year-old boy was dressed up as a South Vietnamese paratrooper, complete with toy sub-machine gun. Afterwards most of the people who had been strolling through the gardens went putt-putting back on their Hondas towards Le Loi Boulevard in the centre of town. On the way they would pass the hideous war memorial erected by Marshal Ky that stood, like a threat, right in front of the Parliament Building – which had been an Opera House during the days of French rule. Out of a ghastly black and green mass are sculpted two larger-than-life-sized Vietnamese soldiers, to whom the local journalists gave an obscene nickname. Following close on one another's heels, with bayonets fixed, these soldiers storm endlessly up to the doors of the South Vietnamese People's Mission.

In the main square nearby, the usual Sunday crowd gathered to look at the weapons captured from the North Vietnamese during the Easter offensive. Even the two armoured vehicles taken at Hue, recognizable by their markings, were transported to Saigon by sea as evidence of the successful resistance the soldiers of the South had shown against General Giap's divisions. In fact, to the inhabitants of Saigon the vehicles must have seemed more like harbingers of doom than the symbols of victory they were intended to be. There, too, the children were the ones who enjoyed themselves most. They got South Vietnamese soldiers to lift them into the gunner's seat of the four-barrelled anti-aircraft gun, and once up there they cranked away enthusiastically and swivelled the barrels from side to side.

A few days before, President Nguyen Van Thieu, having finally established himself as the strong man of South Vietnam by ousting his rival, Ky, laid aside his general's uniform and donned the official dress of an Annamite mandarin. During a Confucian festival in honour of the ancestral spirits he paid homage to Huong Vuong, the mythical forefather of the Vietnamese people, who, legend has it, founded the nation 4000 years ago far away in the north. With the stiff gait of the professional soldier, Thieu walked up to the ancestral altar, flanked by officiants wearing scarlet robes and tall black caps in the style of the Chinese court. He was escorted by youths dressed in blue who traced geometric patterns with their feet, making little skipping movements as they went.

The president was a man of humble origins, of a family of fishermen in south Annam. On this occasion, however, he had an air of stern dignity. His constant companion, his wife, was a Catholic of middle-class background who was reputed to have a good head for business. It was partly as a result of her influence, and partly in order to further his former career as a lieutenant in the French army of the Far East, that Nguyen Van Thieu became converted to Catholicism during the dictatorship of Ngo Dinh Diem. His conversion, however, did not stop him from playing a prominent role in the generals' coup against Diem. The president never failed to attend high mass on Sundays in Saigon's Catholic church; he was also frequently seen in the pagodas of the Buddhist faction loyal to the government. And yet Thieu was neither a puppet of the Americans nor an unscrupulous opportunist. Beneath the neatly parted hair, in which the first white strands were beginning to appear, the forbidding, mask-like, extremely yellow face had an intense expression which betrayed, quite simply, an overwhelming lack of confidence. Thieu was a man of the people, but he lacked charisma. This stiff, unapproachable mandarin in uniform led South Vietnam into its darkest hours.

The South Vietnamese army, after showing initial signs of collapsing under the Communist onslaught, managed to hold together after a fashion. In order to frustrate Hanoi's plans, the Americans wielded the big stick of their air force and assembled eight aircraft carriers in the South China Sea. After Quang Tri was captured by the North Vietnamese the city was reduced to a ghostly pile of rubble – a kind of Hiroshima of conventional warfare; then the ruins were recaptured by South Vietnamese marines. At the time, it was reckoned that in some provinces of North Vietnam an average of three American bombs fell on every square metre of ground. While President Nixon was bluffing the enemy into signing an agreement with Washington to guarantee the safety of shipping on the high seas, he had the ports of

Tongking bombed – an action which Moscow, incidentally, did nothing to prevent. Henry Kissinger, who would have liked to appear as a modern-day Metternich, instead found himself cast in the awkward role of Dr Strangelove 'who learned to love the bomb'.

In stepping up their bombing campaign the Nixon-Kissinger team was, in fact, creating the conditions supposedly necessary before negotiations with Hanoi to end the Vietnam conflict could be opened. Once again, a major operation by the North Vietnamese – the Easter offensive of 1972 – started by achieving some modest successes, and then fizzled out. From a strictly military viewpoint, the Easter offensive was a failure. Its effect, however, was to show the world that the fortunes of the South Vietnamese depended on American air support. Since Johnson's retirement from the presidential race, the withdrawal of American ground troops had gone ahead in such an organized fashion that by the spring of 1972 only 50,000 GIs out of the original 550,000 were left in South Vietnam – and these were mainly in supply and administration services. The rate of withdrawal of American troops was being speeded up as a result of pressures from an anti-war campaign in the USA that had by now reached fever pitch.

Meanwhile, divisions of North Vietnamese regulars were infiltrating deeper into South Vietnam across the poorly-defended borders of Laos and Cambodia. Hanoi may already have had about 130,000 regular troops in the hills and jungles south of the 17th parallel. President Thieu was anxious to force their withdrawal before entering into definite negotiations over a ceasefire, but the Hanoi politburo refused to budge on this issue. They categorically denied the presence of their military forces in the South and forced the American envoys (who for reasons of domestic policy were being pushed into a complete and speedy disengagement from Indochina) to turn a blind eye to the situation. The sacrificial victims of this policy were General Thieu and his army. The Vietnam ceasefire which Henry Kissinger was to hammer out over the coming months in negotiations with Le Duc Tho, the Hanoi representative, was nothing more than a smokescreen. (The principal negotiators of final settlement of January 1973 were later to be awarded the Nobel Peace Prize by a misguided Scandinavian jury.) Thus the Americans procured themselves an alibi, while at the same time delivering the South Vietnamese to their tragic fate. A further political charge to be made against the Americans, in Thieu's eyes, was the fact that they were prepared to sit down at the negotiating table with the National Liberation Front of South Vietnam. This amalgam of different groupings, which was clearly dominated by the Communists, proceeded to set up a rival government in Cam Lo, a small town lying directly to the south of the old Demilitarized Zone. It was presided over by Nguyen Huu To, a lawyer from the Cochin Chinese bourgeoisie who was still listed as a French citizen in the Saigon consular records.

Meanwhile, in the war cemetery at Bien Hoa, the heated debate going on in nearby Saigon over the success or failure of the Vietnamization of the war seemed academic. Here the Vietnamization programme had been put into practice; what the cynics called the 'Vietnamization of the coffins' had been successfully implemented. At the hill cemetery of Bien Hoa, whose summit was toppled by a tall pagoda, South Vietnamese soldiers killed during the previous week arrived from all directions in an endless funeral procession. There seemed to be more enthusiasm there for digging graves than for building trenches and field fortifications at the front.

Whether Catholic or Buddhist, rich or poor, alone or surrounded by lamenting relatives with their white headbands of mourning, the dead had in common their yellow skin and the yellow flag of South Vietnam, with its three blood-red stripes, draped over each coffin. The current practice in the Anglo-Saxon press was to belittle the military achievements of the South, but these graves testified to the courage and stoical endurance shown on the South Vietnamese side.

In the giant US fire base in Bien Hoa, right next to this South Vietnamese Golgotha, the evacuation of the last remaining GIs continued inexorably (the election promises of the American president had to be kept). When the soldiers from the New World first arrived here they had garlands of flowers hung round their necks by young South Vietnamese girls. Now they were leaving in an atmosphere almost of shame. Surly military policemen had Alsatian dogs sniff over the luggage of the returning soldiers in search of drugs. The use of heroin among Americans in Indochina had reached alarming proportions, and now it was feared the epidemic would spread to the United States. The army, demoralized, was pulling out of Vietnam. A few soldiers tried to impress the crowd of press photographers by popping one last champagne cork and giving the V-for-victory sign before they boarded the transport plane for Guam. It was grotesque. A good many people said that whores and drugs had been the ruin of this army, but it was a gross exaggeration. Yet it brought to mind the remark made by General von Mackensen in World War I; after his lightning conquest of Romania he declared: 'I marched into Bucharest with an army of soldiers, but I shall leave with a herd of swine.'

Some GIs wore badges on their shirts that said: 'I'm not scared of Hell any more – I've been through it in Vietnam.' In most cases this was an empty boast. On average one in twenty American soldiers, at most, actually had contact with the enemy. Every soldier wounded in action was transported by helicopter, without delay, to operating theatres equipped with the very latest equipment. Compared with this, the conditions the French had had to fight in during their war in Indochina were appalling. In their day, being slightly wounded out in the rice paddies often meant death due to gangrene and lack of mobility. In the bars on Tu-Do Street where the Americans in their green uniforms and the bar girls seldom let up, protest songs were heard increasingly often on the jukebox. One was called 'Bring them home'. It went: 'Our boys are going to live, we'll show the Vietnamese, everything will work out O.K.'

Near the 'iron triangle', where the Viet Cong, reinforced by North Vietnamese regulars, regained the initiative, a rearguard of the famous 1st Cavalry Division held out in firebase Melanie. Seven years ago, when American involvement in Vietnam got off to such a promising start, GIs dug themselves in in star-shaped strongholds like Melanie as if Vietnam was all about fighting another Indian war and living out a twentieth-century Western. But for the last remaining helicopter troopers in firebase Melanie, whose forefathers, on horseback, fought the Indians at the bloody battle of Little Big Horn, all that remained of those great expectations of victory was a sour taste in the mouth. The Soldier Blue of the Indian wars had been replaced by the Soldier Green of Vietnam. Hollywood film producers suddenly discovered that a gruesome parallel could be drawn between the extermination of the Indian tribes by the bluecoats in the nineteenth century and the massacre carried out at My Lai by the distraught greenjackets of the chubby Lieutenant Calley. The outposts of the 1st Cavalry Division had become cemetery keepers for the abandoned giant bases around Saigon. They guarded the remains of a vast army that had vanished into thin air. Mountains of scrap metal – the excrement of war – piled up on rubbish dumps that stretched into the distance, kilometre after kilometre. On the wreckage of one tank I made out a clumsily-written inscription: 'Give Peace a chance!'

When American engineers were ordered to extend Route 13, they called it The Road to Peace. It was a sick joke since Route 13 led in a straight line north from Saigon to An Loc, which had been christened the Verdun of Vietnam. Since the start of the Easter offensive, An Loc had been surrounded and under continual attack from the North Vietnamese. General Thieu's paratroopers stood firm against the assault that suddenly erupted from over the Cambodian border supported by Russian and Chinese tanks. Further south, units of élite North Vietnamese troops advancing along Route 13 got within 70 kilometres of Saigon. They were stopped only after hard fighting. A massive amount of material was expended, and three divisions were sent into action.

After travelling through rubber plantations and bustling villages we eventually reached South Vietnamese divisional quarters at Lai Khe, where a few days previously the ammunition dump had been blown up by enemy rockets. Before long the sound of fighting increased and the place started to swarm with soldiers. On the outskirts of the small town of Chon Tanh we came near to the front line. American advisers looked worried because the counter-offensive by the 21st ARVN Division, brought up from the delta, had failed to make any headway. Relations between the Americans and the South Vietnamese officers were strained.

Punishment squads of South Vietnamese deserters were busy building dug-outs, piling up sandbags which gave, at best, a minimum of protection against bomb fragments. Like the Americans, the South Vietnamese always started from the premise that they had total superiority in the air and assumed, falsely, that the enemy had no firepower worth mentioning. A few North Vietnamese positions were captured on both sides of the asphalt strip; their underground shelters, each for one or two men, were built like mole-tunnels. Yet what could Giap's assault troops do to escape the napalm and the shock waves of the bombs but scramble underground as fast and as deep as they could go? The stench of corpses hung over the ravaged plain. A wounded North Vietnamese prisoner squatted beside a forward artillery emplacement. His feet were chained together and his expression was entirely blank.

The Road to Peace was lined with debris on either side. Communist rockets and grenades did not strike all that often, but when they did they generally landed on target. In the combat zone between the two hostile armies all hell had broken loose. US fighter-bombers circled overhead then plummeted like hawks before releasing their load of napalm and explosives. How did the North Vietnamese infantry manage to endure and survive this appalling hail of metal for weeks on end? A small group of journalists had followed the South Vietnamese advance party as far as the front line. It included one or two with nostalgic memories of the French war. The South Vietnamese never used infantry to overcome enemy resistance. Instead they waited until the enemy had been worn down and crushed by air and artillery bombardment. This tactic cut no ice with Hanoi's seasoned troops on Route 13.

The North Vietnamese front line was dug in right where the napalm bombs sent up black puffs of smoke and fountains of mud rose high in the air. They were careful not to give away their position by returning fire. In the afternoon, advance guards of the ARVN tried to push north a few hundred metres in the direction of An Loc with the aid of armoured personnel carriers but they got bogged down and had to request renewed artillery support. While all this was going on the encircled stronghold of An Loc was clearly visible through binoculars about 12 kilometres away on the far side of a dip in the landscape. You could even make out the breached white walls of the old prefecture. It seemed incredible that, with the colossal reserves of men and equipment the army of the South had at its disposal, it could not dislodge those few hundred North Vietnamese. 'You want to give them a kick up the backside to force them to go into attack,' said a German reporter. He used to be an officer in a Panzer division and his American colleagues called him the Galloping Major.

Late in the evening we were sitting over glasses of Pernod on the terrace of the Continental Hotel when Edith Piaf's defiant song *Non, je ne regrette rien* came over the music system. In 1962 it had become the theme song of the French paratroopers when they were forced by de Gaulle to surrender Algeria following their final abortive coup. 'No, I regret nothing,' she sang. Rouget, a veteran of Dien Bien Phu, sat down at our table and said: 'The Americans will never be able to sing that when they finally get away from this place.' The last line of the song goes: '*Je me fous du passé*' – 'I don't give a damn about the past.'

Secret Agents and Opium Smugglers

The Golden Triangle, Summer 1973

The students in Bangkok had taken to the streets. They had hung black ribbons over the ugly statue of democracy as a sign of mourning. The young people of Thailand, or rather the sons and daughters of the Thai bourgeoisie, were demanding, among other things, a new constitution and the right for other political parties to exist. What they wanted, in a word, was democracy. In the face of their demands the military junta of Marshals Kittikachorn and Prapass was beginning to look rather shaky. The students stopped short of asking for the monarchy to be abolished; the person of King Bumiphol of Thailand was evidently still regarded as sacred. At the end of their rally the royal anthem boomed out over the crowd and the students turned and bowed towards the royal palace. The intelligence services of the Western powers were not fooled by this display of loyalty, however. Behind all the unrest in the colleges they thought they could detect the familiar hand of professional Marxist agitators, skilled in subversion. Until now the Communist guerillas had concentrated their recruiting drive on the peasants of the forgotten north-eastern provinces. Their next target would be the students and intellectuals in the towns, whose support was so vital to the revolutionary cause.

Was the Domino Theory, that favourite bogey of the West, becoming a reality after all? Was the great political convulsion in Indochina about to spread to the whole of South-east Asia? There would inevitably be political fallout following the American climb-down in Vietnam: that was only to be expected. The Asians, in particular, were under no illusions about the ceasefire signed in Paris at the end of January. Western commentators might welcome it enthusiastically, hailing it as a brilliant piece of statesmanship by Henry Kissinger, but the Asians knew better. They knew, for instance, that when President Thieu agreed, under pressure, to the North Vietnamese divisions staying outside the gates of Hue and Saigon, he was signing his government's death warrant. Henceforth South Vietnam was doomed: it was simply a question of when the final blow would fall.

We were anxious to find out what was really going on in the

Golden Triangle, that mysterious, magical-sounding region at the intersection of Thailand, Burma and Laos. By a lucky coincidence it just so happened that a young journalist on the Bangkok *Nation* was hoping to make a name for himself by doing an exposé on the opium trade in Burma. The reporter, whose name was Chula, came from a highly respectable Siamese family who were proud of their connections at court. Chula, however, always went around in jeans and with his hair hanging down his back in a long mane. He liked to think he was as radical as the Paris students of May '68. He had a girlfriend, a very determined young lady from an equally respectable background, who was no doubt a major factor in his conversion to left-wing ideas.

The obvious place to start our trip would have been Chieng Rai or the border crossing at Mei Sai, but Chula steered clear of these. They were already becoming tourist traps, with busloads of visitors busily taking snapshots of the pipe-smoking, bare-breasted Hakka women. We travelled instead to the remote trading centre of Mae Hong Son, where whole caravans of smugglers were arriving daily from across the Burmese border 15 kilometres away, bringing with them a never-ending supply of fake Buddhas for the antique dealers in Bangkok. We had to wait around for a few days while Chula tried to get in touch with his contacts. To help while away the time I climbed the hill to the local pagoda with the pair of huge white stone lions outside it; in fact, I did it no less than four times. In the evenings I would sit by the peaceful lotus pool, staring at the reflections in the water of the rich gold robes of the monks.

In Mae Hong Son we came across a very untypical wooden Thai house which appeared to be occupied by a group of young whites. At first we thought we had stumbled on a hippie commune. The place reeked of hashish, the men looked as if they had just stepped out of the cast of 'Hair', and the girls wore long Indian dresses or the traditional sarong. They were more than just hippies, however. The leader, a would-be Hemingway type, was a geology professor from Missouri. The ascetic-looking individual sitting beside him claimed to be an archaeologist, while the third member of the group, a monkish-looking youth with short hair and thick glasses who went by the name of John, turned out to be one of the leading ethnologists in his field. He said he was a specialist in this particular corner of South-east Asia; apparently the patchwork of different races and mountain tribes made it a kind of living museum for ethnologists.

I introduced our camera team to the group, who were polite but guarded. A voluptuous blonde South African girl called Mandy more than made up for the American girls' lack of erotic interest. She sat stroking the neck of a pretty young man who looked Italian-American and was the only one who seemed to lack professional qualifications. We produced a bottle of whisky, and the Hemingway type introduced himself as Andrew. Two easy-going Thai servant girls seemed to belong to the commune; they probably took care of his sexual needs.

Chula, who came with us to the commune, looked distinctly unhappy all the time he was there. As he left he whispered to me that the place was, in fact, a CIA listening-post. I had to admit I had never met such a colourful collection of 'spooks'. The group had offered us hash and alcohol, probably to try and find out what we were really after, and gradually, as the drugs began to take effect, the 'honourable schoolboys' became more communicative. They told us their studies mainly centred on the racial minorities in Burma who had been in open rebellion against the Rangoon government since the end of World War II.

There couldn't have been anyone in the whole of South-east Asia who hadn't heard of the Karen. The Karen, who were mainly Christian, controlled most of the border-crossing points between Thailand and Burma with the help of their 'Liberation Army'. They also controlled the extensive smuggling ring that operated between Bangkok and Rangoon. They levied a duty of four per cent on the goods that flowed out of the consumer paradise of Thailand into Burma. Burma itself was a ready market, having been reduced to a state of comparative poverty by an absurd experiment in socialism. From the opposite side of the border the Karen organized the caravans of elephants transporting Burma's rare ores, particularly antimony and tungsten, to Siam. Western intelligence showed little interest in the Karen rebels for they had become a stabilizing force in the chaos of Burmese politics. The fake hippies of Mae Hong Son (who had all spoken excellent Thai) were far more interested in what was happening in the north of Burma, in the mysterious Shan states. Here the struggle for political autonomy was being fought out between a welter of racial minorities – the Shan, the Lahu, the Meo, the Yao, the Kachin and the Lolo, to name but a few. In most cases, though, the fight for independence was simply a front for bitter vendettas between rival bands of common robbers. What was really at stake in all this apparent political turmoil was a lucrative commercial prize, namely the trade in opium throughout the Golden Triangle. Opium production was a highly sophisticated industry, and there were even specialist laboratories hidden deep in the jungle that processed heroin.

John seemed very pessimistic about things. He pointed to a book, recently published, entitled *Heroin Politics in South-east Asia*. He had written it himself, and I was surprised to see him described on the inside cover as a US intelligence agent. According to him the whole situation in this part of the world had changed quite radically. His father had been a Methodist missionary in the southern Chinese province of Yunnan. He had worked among the warlike Lahu people who had worshipped him as a white god. John himself had grown up among the children of the tribe and so it had seemed an obvious move for him to go and work among the branch of the Lahu living in northern Burma and who had recently got caught up in the general political upheaval. Andrew then asked us if we intended visiting the Chinese Kuomintang units. I was careful not to tell him what our real plans were.

Andrew had, in fact, hit the nail on the head. The real reason we had come north was because we wanted to make contact with the remnants of Chiang Kai-shek's troops who had been stranded in Burma. In 1950, fleeing before Mao Tse-tung's divisions, they had crossed into northern Burma from Yunnan. Most had settled in the Shan states and were living there to this day. In the spring of 1952, I almost succeeded in tracking down this ghost army, but at the last minute I was arrested by the Burmese security police and escorted back to Rangoon. All kinds of memories of that trip came flooding back to me now. I remembered my short drive along the winding, legendary Burma Road, at one time the lifeline of the Chinese defence forces before Rangoon fell to the Japanese. Now it was the only existing supply link the Americans had to Chungking. The driver who took me to Lashio, in the far north of Burma, came from Arakan, where the people were half Bengali. Throughout the journey he kept insisting he was a Muslim and therefore an 'honourable man'.

Lashio had been abandoned by the British years ago, and the only Europeans left in the town were six Italian friars. The priests were worried about the threat from the nearby border with China, for Peking was still thought to have territorial designs on South-east Asia. Their other main cause of anxiety was an agent from the US secret service who had fled to Lashio from Yunnan, where he had been manning a lone radio station. The American had turned up, terror-stricken, on their doorstep and asked them to hide him. The Italians had dressed him up in a brown habit and prayed to God he would leave soon for Rangoon. The priests ran a mission school for the local Kachin where the newly-baptized tribesmen were taught to say their Latin mass. The converts took a keen interest in the new arrival and asked to receive communion from him. The prior managed to save the situation by telling a judicious white lie. He said the new father was so devout he celebrated mass in the small hours of the morning. The Kachin were a simple people and they accepted his story quite happily.

I had been in a tea-room in Lashio one day when three ordinary-looking, poker-faced Chinese came over to my table and asked me, in reasonably good English, what weapons I had for sale. When I later told the Franciscans about this they said I had probably been talking to members of the Triad, a Chinese secret society with networks all over Europe, Asia and America. They begged me not to et foot outside the mission in future. However I did manage to persuade them to let me ride north with one of their number, a priest from Piedmont. He was travelling with a mule train and told me he wanted to trace some of his converts who were scattered about the countryside. My reason for going was to try and meet up with General Mi Li's infamous Kuomintang troops. We eventually got as far as the little village of Kutkai, where old Chinese women with crippled feet sat by their spinning wheels laying strips of indigo cloth out in the sun to dry. Then two armed plain-clothes policemen appeared and announced they were secret police employed by the central government. The next thing I knew they had bundled me onto the first plane south.

Now, twenty years later, I wanted to forget that earlier fiasco. It was barely light when we set out from Mae Hong Son. We drove north in the jeep for about 40 kilometres then changed onto a gravel road leading to a pile village. When we got to the end of it we found eight sinister-looking men waiting. Their ringleader was a man called Cheng who had a face that would have graced any Kung Fu film. Cheng was bad-tempered and sullen but – as we later found out – basically dependable. He rounded up ten horses for us out of nowhere, all of them sorry-looking beasts. Klaus, our assistant cameraman, was given a one-eyed mount which we promptly christened 'Moshe Dayan'. The camera crew had brought along pillows from the hotel to soften the impact of the rock-hard saddles. We rode for a few kilometres through ricefields and flat countryside, then gradually the ground began to rise steeply and we found ourselves climbing wooded hillsides. In the end we had to dismount; we covered most of the rest of the journey on foot. Cheng had brought along some mules. We didn't know what they were carrying, and we didn't ask.

Around midday, just as we arrived puffing and panting at the top of a particularly steep jungle path, the monsoon broke. The rain pelted down and the ground turned into a treacherous quagmire beneath our feet. We had to drag the horses after us. Whenever we came to a downhill slope the horses would sit down in the mud and slide past us effortlessly with what looked like an expression of malicious glee on their faces. Then we would have to clamber down after them, slithering and stumbling. After what seemed like an eternity we finally came to a plateau and the sun's rays began to pierce through the clouds. Later in the afternoon we met a caravan of horses and mules driven by a band of heavily-armed Asians. It was impossible to tell what nationality they were. They looked us over with deep suspicion, rifles at the ready, then rode on without so much as a 'hello'. We would have given anything to know what was hidden under the tarpaulins of their animals. When you were in the Golden Triangle, however, it was best not to ask questions.

Eventually we arrived at the village where we were to spend the night, a Meo settlement called Ban Na Plak. Some of the women sat embroidering or grinding millet; the rest were returning from the opium fields. Children ran around naked, despite the intense cold. Although they didn't have a stitch of clothing on their backs, they all wore a broad silver band round their dirty necks. The men got out their musical instruments to celebrate our arrival. They were pipes made of bamboo cane and they produced a high-pitched, screeching noise. The men held them between their legs like phallic symbols, swaying rhythmically from side to side as they played.

We continued riding north for the whole of the next morning. Then Cheng suddenly stopped and pointed to the shallow stream we had just waded through. 'That's the border with Burma,' he said. We were now inside Shan territory. We got soaked three more times by torrential monsoon rains before we came in sight of a tumbledown camp on the slopes of a red laterite hill. We had finally reached our destination. This was Ban Meo, where a detachment of Kuomintang troops was stationed. The mud huts had a line of shelter trenches and bamboo fencing around them. We approached and stood in the shade, waiting. For a full fifteen minutes nothing stirred. Then five men in shabby green uniforms came down the hill towards us. Somehow they had heard we were coming. Although they looked like brigands they invited us to take tea with them in a courteous enough manner. Chula had difficulty translating what they said, but we managed to establish that eighty Kuomintang soldiers were living with their families in Ban Meo. They were a fairly ramshackle outfit, too. Back in 1950 the Li Mi Army had moved into northern Burma, hoping to use it as a base that would enable them, one day, to reconquer mainland China with the help of Taiwan and America. However, their plans had gone awry. The units had gradually drifted away and the men merged with the local people. As the years went by the veterans of the Kuomintang grew older. In time they married women from the local hill-tribes and settled down. Every so often an emissary would fly in from Taipeh and pass on a few empty words of encouragement. At first the Peking government had condemned the 'imperialist plot' being hatched between the Americans and the 'Taiwan bandits' in northern Burma. But the People's Liberation Army soon realized the scattered remnants of the Kuomintang divisions presented no real threat to them – in fact they believed they might even be useful to them one day.

The Burmese forces had launched a number of operations against the leftovers of the Li Mi Army, always with a great deal of ostentatious display. The Kuomintang troops were, after all, armed and potentially dangerous, and on several occasions in the past had been known to turn to marauding. The truth was, however, that Rangoon was basically not that interested in eliminating them, and all its sorties against them were really just for show, a way of staving off action by China. The Kuomintang rapidly became absorbed into the general anarchy and sinister goings-on around the Golden Triangle. It slowly began to dawn on the generals in Bangkok that these Chinese refugees could be very useful to them, particularly as the Thai army had not been trained to fight in the mountains and jungles of the north. As it was, they had difficulty getting anyone to fight in the area and even the much overrated Border Patrol Police were reluctant to venture into such inhospitable terrain. So it was that the Kuomintang finally came to be regarded as an ideal means of defending the northern frontier of Thailand against bandits and Communist infiltrators. They ended up controlling a whole string of bases along the border, and this meant they could ensure that the opium and heroin trade stayed in the hands of the Thai authorities. For in this idyllic, anarchic land of bandits, smugglers and cut-throats, drugs were the prime reason for the outbreak of fighting.

We were brought tea by young Chinese children who had been born in exile in Burma. They were the new generation of Kuomintang, but there were still veterans around like the old man in the threadbare grey uniform and soft hat who hobbled over and introduced himself as Colonel Lao Bo of the Chinese Nationalist Army. He must have been seriously ill because there seemed to be nothing left on him but skin and bone. His nephew, Major Lao Li, a burly man in a white shirt, did all the talking. Later Chula was to write a series of articles on the strange goings-on along the Burma-Thailand border in which he portrayed Lao Li as a key figure in the South-east Asian opium trade. Lao Li certainly seemed to be the recognized leader of the base at Ban Meo. The Chinese had retired to a nearby hut to discuss whether they should allow us to film the camp. While they were talking things over, Chula explained that the Kuomintang were used as a kind of cordon sanitaire by certain military authorities. At the same time they also had direct, and very discreet, links with the powerful Chinese business community in Bangkok. Because the Kuomintang troops were far superior in experience and training to the other bands in the area, they were able to keep the drug trade firmly under central control and fight off any challenges from rival smugglers. From time to time the authorities would publicly burn quantities of confiscated opium in Bangkok and other major provincial cities. These elaborately stage-managed scenes were simply a cover for the government's own interests. According to Chula, the Thai generals were heavily implicated in the drugs trade and the whole operation went on under their direct supervision.

It turned out that one of the Chinese troops, Lieutenant Fang, spoke passable English. Fang, who was twenty-three, was responsible for operating the radio equipment at the base. After several fruitless attempts to get through, he finally managed to contact a secret command post in northern Thailand. We heard the voice of General Li issue strict instructions to the troops. There was to be no filming in Ban Meo, and that was final. However we were to be hospitably treated and then escorted safely back across the border. Fang, having passed on the message, proceeded to chat quite openly and freely to us. He had a roguish, very engaging look about him. He complained about the bad pay and the isolation of this remote outpost. The walls of his radio booth were plastered with pictures of Asian pin-ups; he told us he dreamt all the time about the girls back in Bangkok. We described to him an encounter we had had with a band of Burmese guerillas near the border west of Mei Sai. They had worn a military insignia on their sleeves that looked like a tiger's head with the rather grand-sounding name Free Shan State Army underneath. Fang told us they were just run-of-the-mill robbers. They had done a deal with the Burmese authorities whereby they would keep down rival bands in return for complete control of the opium trade in the Keng-tung sector. However, President Ne Win's commissioners had recently tried to revoke the concession, and the robbers had taken to the jungle proclaiming themselves to be Shan 'freedom-fighters'.

Fang went on: 'Peking only has to lift a finger and the whole Union of Burma, which really exists only on paper, would collapse overnight.' According to him the only other military force in the area worth taking seriously was the Burmese Communist Party, which owed allegiance to Peking. The Kuomintang soldiers were careful to avoid coming into contact with this highly disciplined body of fighting men. The Burmese Communists recruited most of their troops from the hill-tribes in the area. Their main centre of activity was the Wa states, a narrow strip of land along the border with Yunnan. The Communists not only maintained law and order and social justice in the area, they even helped the poor hill peasants bring in the harvest. Political differences apart, you could tell Lieutenant Fang felt a genuine admiration for the colossus of Red China, his homeland across the border.

Our fake American hippies in Mae Hong Son already knew all about our trip by the time we got back. Chula warned us against getting too friendly with them. 'The Thai authorities will break up the group soon,' he said. 'The days of close cooperation between the CIA and the Thai government are over. And you never know, one of the Americans might be a member of the Anti-Narcotics Brigade in disguise.'

We had a nightmare drive from Mae Hong Son to the peaceful Mekong port of Chieng Saen, on the border with Laos. I unwisely decided to travel in a Landrover driven by an American called Sam, a recent arrival to the commune. Sam was a wiry young man who made no secret of his passion for intelligence work. As we drove along the winding road he seemed determined to break every speed record in existence. His speciality was chasing stray dogs and running them over. Once he had to pull up sharply with a screech of brakes to avoid running over a naked brown child he had mistaken for a dog in the fading evening light. Despite his murderous streak, Sam claimed to be a Buddhist. He told me he was married to the daughter of a Thai general; from the description he gave of her she sounded a fairly tough customer. Every time we passed a pagoda or an altar Sam would get out of the Landrover, bow down before the 'Phi', and light a joss-stick. He particularly enjoyed letting off jumping jacks as an offering to a street spirit who was supposed to watch over travellers. Sam assured me with a mischievous grin that the spirit was particularly fond of fireworks.

At Chiang Saen we boarded a river craft and drifted south, carried along by the waters of the Mekong. I was enormously relieved to see the back of Sam, what with his frenetic driving and his dabbling in spirits. Our roofed canoe kept close to the Laotian bank. We sailed past whole villages of people splashing about happily in the shallows. The river flowed with majestic calm. We passed working elephants hauling great tree-trunks to remote sawmills. At one point we sailed through the area where the Kuomintang tried to extend their opium monopoly in the late 1950s. The paratroopers in the Royal Laotian Army, guided by their French advisers, had managed to rally themselves and chase the Chinese back across the river into Thailand. It was a historic moment for the Laotian army – their first and last military victory.

The fort at Ban Huei Sai reminded me of the citadel in Tay Ninh. When we arrived we tried to get hold of the Laotian commander, but he was nowhere to be found. A truce had been called in Laos between the right-wing government forces and the Communist Pathet Lao. The unaccustomed peace had rapidly led to a collapse of discipline among the pro-US troops. We were warned by a lieutenant in the Laotian army, who we disturbed in the middle of his siesta, not to continue our journey east. There was a risk we might bump into engineers from the Chinese People's Liberation Army, working just 7 kilometres away. Peking was pressing ahead with its programme for building a system of all-weather roads linking Yunnan and Thailand. This would provide a basic communications network that could cope with all eventualities, from commercial traffic to military invasion.

In the royal city of Luang Prabang we found John Everingham waiting for us. John was a young Australian with blond hair and an angelic face. He looked almost delicate but was definitely no weakling. He had to work hard to make a living as a freelance journalist. He lived with a Laotian girl and spoke the language reasonably fluently. His command of Laotian came in useful when he was captured by the Pathet Lao once when he was on a lone expedition. The Communists held him prisoner for a few weeks then turned him loose. Seemingly they parted on amicable terms.

Now John had agreed to take us into Communist territory. The ceasefire in Laos had been signed almost simultaneously with the Vietnam Accords in Paris, and by this time the fighting in the country had more or less come to a halt. (The situation in Vietnam was quite different, of course.) The peace-loving nature of the Laotians had soon reasserted itself, and people were already beginning to talk about weddings and Buddhist festivals in towns and villages that, until recently, had been in the very heart of the combat zone. Yesterday's enemies became brothers once again and resolved their differences. In fact, had it not been for the implacable North Vietnamese waiting in the wings with their allies, the Communist Party of Laos, this South-east Asian buffer state might have had hopes of a happy outcome to its long years of political unrest.

The Communist villages we were to visit lay downriver from Luang Prabang. Behind us the pagodas of the city vanished into the dark and lowering monsoon clouds. The yellow waters of the Mekong were in spate, and we were carried swiftly south. The pilot of our narrow motorboat kept having to steer out of the way of floating branches and tree-trunks. The banks on both sides of the river were overgrown with dense jungle, and we saw only the occasional tiny hamlet or narrow strip of rice paddy. We lay flat in the bottom of the boat and covered our faces with our pith helmets, so nobody could spot we were Europeans.

We rounded a bend in the river and came upon a colourful scene. Just ahead of us was a Laotian pile village, built close to the bank. Naked children played under a waterfall while one or two bare-shouldered women were washing their sarongs. A group of about six Buddhist monks in saffron robes were just stepping into a canoe. When they caught sight of us everyone stopped dead and stared in astonishment at our European faces. John told the boatman to heave-to. The village was called Pak Howe. The Pathet Lao had captured it a few hours before the ceasefire came into force, so it had escaped the American bombing. Pak Howe lay on the west bank of the Mekong, just inside Sayaburi province. It had been a last-minute conquest for the guerillas, but a useful one. It would make an important support base for rebel groups operating in neighbouring Thailand.

We panted up the path from the river bank, lugging our camera equipment. We were met first by a group of Yao, dressed in their traditional exotic black costume. Next a soldier appeared from out of nowhere and stood in front of us. Just then we caught sight of Pathet Lao troops in a long hut. They approached us gingerly, looking inquisitive but friendly, and invited us to sit down at a bamboo table outside the hut. The Communist Laotians were more or less as we had imagined them. They wore Chinese-style caps and green uniforms with baggy trousers. Everything was spotlessly clean and neat. They showed us their weapons, Chinese AK-47 automatic rifles. Two of the soldiers carried transistor radios on a strap over their shoulders.

While John translated for us somebody went to fetch an officer. He was probably the company commander but there were no insignias to indicate his rank. He carried a pistol instead of a rifle and he had a map-case hanging from his belt. The officer sat down at the table, examined our papers, then explained to us, very politely, that he could not give us permission to film without written instructions from his superior officer. But he could assure us we would not be arrested, and we would be allowed to continue on our way. He wished us a safe journey, then said: 'People always say we're like wild animals, but as you can see it's not true.' If nothing else, our brief contact with the Pathet Lao had indeed shown us they were not a wild mob of snipers, but a disciplined and well-equipped fighting unit. The soldiers seemed to have up-to-date information on the closing stages of the peace negotiations between the pro-Western government in Vientiane and the Communist-controlled Patriotic Front, or Neo Lao Haksat. We even had a brief discussion about the possible date when the two political factions in Laos would reach agreement in coalition talks. This agreement, which had involved both sides in protracted negotiations, was meant to come into force simultaneously with the establishment of garrisons of Pathet Lao troops in Vientiane and Luang Prabang.

The officer, who reminded me in many ways of a young, idealistic priest, waved aside the small gifts we had brought – cartons of cigarettes and tins of Ovaltine. His soldiers were unable to accept any presents. So we handed our gifts over to the village elder and the children of Pak Howe instead. The ethnic mix in the small band of Communists was striking. The officer in charge had the typical features and colouring of a Laotian from the Mekong Plain. His dark-skinned troops, however, looked almost dwarflike in comparison. Most of them belonged to the Kha, a hill-tribe which had been renamed the Lao Theung, or Mountain Lao, as part of a new policy of national integration.

When we arrived in Vientiane we found our American intelligence staff busily clearing out their offices and dismantling electronic equipment. Prime Minister Souvanna Phouma took the unprecedented step of inviting all the foreign journalists in the city to his attractive villa on the Mekong, where he tried to convince them that the basic good nature of the Laotian people would ultimately win out over the present political upheavals. 'If only people would leave us alone,' he said, 'we would manage to find a solution to our problems.' The unfortunate thing was that Laos was not going to be left alone. Even as he spoke, Hanoi's envoys were strengthening their position inside the country. No-one was more aware of this than Souvanna Phouma himself, who was currently about to appoint his half-brother, the 'Red Prince', vice-premier of Laos.

We said goodbye to John Everingham in the Constellation Hotel, always a useful place for picking up news and gossip. That was not the last we were to hear of him, though. Five years later John's name cropped up again in a press agency report – and his photo appeared in several Far Eastern papers. When the Communists finally took over in Laos he was deported from Vientiane and forced to leave behind his Laotian wife. Nothing daunted, John swam across the Mekong one night and carried the girl (who, to cap it all, couldn't swim) across the river to freedom on an air cushion.

We managed to talk one of the few remaining Air America pilots into flying us to the secret CIA headquarters at Long Cheng. We had to pay him well for his trouble, of course. During the war we had never managed to obtain an authorization to visit Long Cheng, which also happened to be the main centre of Meo resistance in the area. Our plane had to circle twice over the Nam Ngum reservoir because a sudden tremendous cloudburst had blanketed the dangerous jungle ridges ahead of us in a thick, warm mist. Below us blackened tree stumps rose out of the water like stakes waiting to impale their victims. On our third approach we managed to make a safe landing in Long Cheng. The landing strip was deserted, apart from a few Green Berets who had just flown in. Otherwise a wall of bunkers was the only sign that this base had once been a key position in the Vietnam war. A Meo major drove us in a jeep to a nearby hill to show us the burnt-out wreckage of two North Vietnamese T-54 tanks. The Meo knew it was only a matter of time before the Americans pulled out and left them to fight the full might of Hanoi entirely on their own. They knew, too, they were condemned to certain defeat and annihilation. Their commander, General Vang Pao, was just about to fly to the USA, taking his war-chest with him. He later settled there and bought a ranch in Montana. There were, of course, some Meo fighting on the side of the Pathet Lao, but there was no possibility of the two hostile camps ever being reconciled. The worst ordeals still lay ahead for this stubborn, shy yet fearless people, who had initially been driven into South-east Asia by the later Manchu emperors.

Groups of Thai mercenaries were wandering aimlessly about in the muddy village street in Long Cheng. The Chinese shop-keepers, on the other hand, were hurriedly gathering up their things so as to get across the Mekong into Siam before it was too late. At the height of the conflict the CIA had hired as many as 17,000 mercenaries from neighbouring Thailand. Most had returned home by this time, leaving an ugly reputation among the people of Laos in their wake. The mercenaries' elaborate uniforms were covered in tigers' heads and silver buttons, and the men went about with black stetsons on their heads. They were obviously playing at being Thai cowboys.

The Pathet Lao divisions advancing on Vientiane from the north and east were getting close now, and the usual wave of revolutionary puritanism was threatening to engulf the capital. Down at the Mekong Bar, however, they were making a gallant last-ditch stand. Inside, go-go dancers gyrated in the red glare of spotlights, while unemployed officers of the Royal Laotian Army and Chinese businessmen stood around the edge of the dance floor, drinking crate after crate of beer. The bar hostesses were doing their best to lay aside a few extra kips before the arrival of the new era of moral stringency. In an adjoining room a crowd of Asians and Americans ogled a naked Laotian woman, no longer in the first flush of youth, who was performing an obscene routine with a packet of lighted cigarettes. Among the crowd of spectators I noticed the piercing blue gaze of the Galloping Major, who must have been in Vientiane on business.

The Lane Xang hotel had been taken over by a group of American women aged between about twenty-five and forty. They all looked very respectable and wore a mysterious badge bearing the letters MIA. We spent a long time trying to guess what the

initials stood for. At first we thought it must be some kind of
Christian name. Then we decided it was probably an auxiliary
medical corps. Finally we went and asked. Apparently MIA stood
for 'missing in action'. The American women were the wives of
US pilots who had been shot down over the jungles of Laos and
North Vietnam and had disappeared without trace. They had
come to Vientiane to try and find out what had happened to their
husbands. If they managed to get positive confirmation that they
had been killed, then they could always put in a claim for a widow's
pension. One or two of the MIAs sought consolation in the arms of
the Air America pilots still hanging on in Vientiane. The men,
some of whom had just arrived in Laos, had probably grown tired
of the plentiful supply of Asian women and wanted to feel a
familiar bit of home beneath them once again.

Pol Pot at the Gates

Cambodia, August 1973

At dawn on 15 August the last American B-52 fighter-bombers
swooped into the base at Utapao in southern Thailand after the
final bombing raid over Cambodia. President Nixon had at last
given in to pressure from the Senate and agreed to suspend the air
strikes against Cambodia. The pilots of the B-52s were mobbed by
pressmen wanting some quotes, but all they would say was they'd
'done a good job'. What this meant, in fact, was that they had
destroyed virtually every pagoda in the area where the Khmer
Rouge were active. Entire villages in the rebel zone now lay totally
devastated. Yet despite the intensity of the bombing, the impact of
the air strikes on the military strength of the Communists was
practically nil.

The whole population of Phnom Penh had been expecting an
immediate all-out offensive by the Khmer Rouge. The attack
never came. Instead, to everyone's surprise, the rebels relaxed
their stranglehold on the capital. Route 5, which ran through the
fertile rice-growing province of Battambang, was suddenly open
to traffic again. River convoys arriving in Phnom Penh from
Saigon were allowed to travel up the Mekong with relatively little

harassment. The port of Kompong Som began working again, and Route 1, which was under Khmer Rouge control up to about 5 kilometres from the city gates, became passable once more. (We drove along it to the Mekong port of Neak Luong, strategically situated on a bend in the river, which had recently had the misfortune to be accidentally flattened by the US Air Force on one of its last bombing raids.) Inside the Western embassies and intelligence agencies in the capital, people were baffled by this sudden change of tactic by the Khmer Rouge. But the Communists were not stupid, and they knew they stood to benefit as much from having the transport system functioning again as Lon Nol's troops. Meanwhile the North Vietnamese divisions were taking advantage of the lull in the fighting to prepare for their final major assault on those areas in South Vietnam where they already had a foothold. At this stage they were badly in need of reinforcements, both of men and equipment, and so it suited them very well to have the traffic load on the Ho Chi Minh Trail eased by an increase in the flow of arms deliveries via Cambodia.

The Americans, of course, were heavily involved in all this. The mercenaries working for the CIA and Air America had stepped up the number of transport missions to the government troops. By this time nearly all the provincial capitals were encircled and had to be supplied by air. One morning, at the crack of dawn, we flew to Kompong Cham in a plane garishly painted to look like a monster bird whose bows opened up like an enormous beak to take in cargo. Kompong Cham lay about 120 kilometres north-east of Phnom Penh on the banks of the Mekong. The area round here was under particularly heavy pressure from the enemy. We unloaded our cargo of ammunition, sacks of rice, and tinned milk. Then we drove from the airport, which was protected by a rather haphazard system of dug-outs, into the centre of town. Most people seemed to have abandoned their homes and fled. We managed to find a Chinese restaurant that was still in business and ordered noodle soup for breakfast. The restaurant owner had no illusions about the outcome of the war and had sent his family to Thailand for safety. In the market place we filmed two propaganda posters. One showed a frenzied Viet Cong soldier setting fire to a pagoda and killing Buddhist monks. The other depicted the divine intervention of the Buddha, who with one magical gesture had managed to destroy a barrage of tanks advancing on his lotus throne. The tanks bore North Vietnamese and Russian insignia and were manned by terrifying demons.

The river was the only place in Kompong Cham where we saw any signs of activity. Small flotillas of canoes and motorboats were arriving from across the Mekong. The Khmer Rouge had just gained control of the far bank, only 700 metres away. On the near side of the river were the vast rubber plantations previously owned by French colonials. Some were still working, despite the effects of the war and decolonialization. The latex, or raw rubber, was unloaded from river craft as huge, slippery, evil-smelling lumps and transported to the airport by lorry. Once there it was flown to the harbour at Kompong Som by American planes. The US Air Force thereby contributed indirectly to the funds of the Cambodian Revolutionary Army. The coolies groaned under the weight of the heavy balls of rubber as they heaved them up the steep river bank.

While in the restaurant we got talking with a lean, sad-faced Frenchman. He was obviously in bad physical shape but was immaculately turned out and had a smart silk scarf round his neck. Despite his misfortunes, he had managed to preserve a sense of humour. The Frenchman was one of the many rubber experts who had refused to be driven off their plantations, even when the Communist guerillas took over the area. At first the enemy troops had tolerated them to some extent because they were vital to the survival of the latex industry. But that was in the days when the North Vietnamese were in control. With the rise of the Khmer Rouge, life in the 'liberated' regions of Mimot, Krek and Snoul had become unbearable.

'It's been absolute hell,' the Frenchman said. 'At the start of the Cambodian war there were only 1000 Khmer Rouge at the very most, and all the fighting was in the hands of the North Vietnamese and the Viet Cong. The Vietnamese tend to be suspicious and bureaucratic, it's true, but at least you could always rub along with them. You always knew you were safe with them, that was the main thing. Then gradually the Khmer Rouge started taking over things, and before anyone knew what had happened they had grabbed all the real power for themselves. Their commissars were absolute fiends. Nobody knew who they were, but they had the power of life or death over you and they used it just as it suited them. It's not surprising people always go on about the "stone-age Communism" of the Khmer Rouge. The thing I remember most is the reign of terror. They spared nobody in the massacres – monks, intellectuals, even bourgeois opponents of Lon Nol. They killed them all. And the terrible thing was, they used children and teenagers to carry out these crimes.

'I had one especially painful thing happen to me. When there was all the heavy fighting in the summer of 1970, I took in a five-year-old orphan girl to live with me. I fed her and provided a roof over her head for two years. Then the Khmer Rouge organized a big anti-imperialist demonstration and I was put on public display – it was pretty low-key stuff by Khmer Rouge standards. I had to stand there while all the "revolutionary children" filed past me and spat and cursed at me. There was one who really behaved badly and kept on pulling my beard and spitting in my face. It was the little orphan girl I'd been so good to. It's unimaginable, the hell that's going on over there. The Vietnamese Communists have completely lost control of the Cambodian Reds and their faceless leaders. You can tell even they're horrified by what's going on. The Khmer Rouge and the Vietnamese won't be comrades for much longer, I bet.'

The town of Kompong Cham is named after the old Hindu kingdom of Champa, now part of modern Annam. The Cham fought a series of bold campaigns against the old empire of Angkor but their kingdom was destroyed and taken over by the Vietnamese. Very few traces of the Cham people survive. There are probably about 80,000 of them left in Cambodia. They are impossible to pick out on the basis of ethnic type or language but they do have a distinguishing feature. At some stage in their history they became converted to Islam, possibly out of a strange compulsion to preserve their separate identity. These Cambodian Muslims, who still go by the name of Chams, settled around Phnom Penh and built their villages and mosques along the arterial road leading north-west out of the capital.

I visited the imam of a humble mosque made of metal. When I greeted him with a quotation from the Koran the old man was nearly reduced to tears. He took me into his Koran class and introduced me to his pupils, about fifty boys and a handful of girls. The girls sat at the back of the room and wore headscarves. He got the children to recite some passages for me, then proudly presented me with a booklet dedicated to the Cham minority. The Cambodian Muslims were staunch opponents of Communism. They had even set up an independent militia commanded by a man called General Karim. Now that the Americans had withdrawn from Vietnam the officers in Lon Nol's army were being trained in Thailand. Perhaps out of a sense of religious obligation, Indonesia gave support to the tiny Cham community by flying its officers out to Djakarta for military training.

A strange air of unreality hung over Phnom Penh. A few weeks previously a squad of North Vietnamese sappers had got as far as the town centre and blown up the graceful arches of the bridge over the Tonle Sap. Afterwards they commandeered the armoured vehicles parked in the big sports stadium and drove through the streets of the sleeping city, firing wildly at anything that moved. By the following morning Lon Nol's troops had finally got the situation under control. They put the bodies of the suicide squad on public display, like so much meat on a butcher's slab. In March a rebel pilot in the Cambodian Air Force had tried to bomb the heavily-guarded residence of Marshal Lon Nol. Luckily he missed his target by about 200 metres. Since that incident Lon Nol had tended to shut himself off from the outside world more and more. Latterly he had had several members of the royal family put in prison. He was gradually delegating more power and influence to his favourite brother, the notorious Lon Non, whose corruptness – even by Cambodian standards – was scandalous. The US ambassador tried to relegate Lon Non to a subordinate role where he could do less damage, but it was no use. Eventually it got to the stage that the Marshal had his court astrologers thrown into prison because their horoscopes failed to live up to his aspirations. Père Ubu now reigned in Phnom Penh.

Outside the Royal Palace we stopped to watch a Buddhist funeral procession. The coffins of three senior Cambodian officials were being carried on gun carriages to be cremated. The officials had been caught in an ambush on the road to Neak Luong – the same road we ourselves had travelled along so many times. A military band played a funeral march in a tango rhythm and every so often the sound of a French bugle would blare out, incongruously. But the monks in their saffron-yellow robes lent an air of authenticity to the whole proceedings. The mourners seemed calm and composed. Here death was thought of as something natural, a simple process of moving on to a new incarnation. Soon we saw the smoke from the funeral pyre rising above the waters of the Tonle Sap, where the wrecks of sunken ships stuck their rusting snouts up into the grey monsoon sky. The smell of incense blotted out the sweet stench of corpses. An old man in a black suit drew me to one side and said: 'We must have sinned very badly in a previous life to be so harshly punished today.'

The West German chargé d'affaires in Phnom Penh, Marshal von Bieberstein, was famous for his hospitality among the diplomats and journalists in the capital. Before the Khmer Rouge finally tightened their blockade around the city, he made sure he had enough excellent wine sent out to him from his home in Baden to withstand the siege. I spent many an evening with him and other guests on the terrace of the German residence, discussing the future of Cambodia. Whenever the conversation turned to the prospects of Prince Sihanouk, opinions tended to divide sharply. In the early autumn of 1972, I had paid a personal call on the deposed head of state. Sihanouk was still the same restless, mercurial figure I remembered from earlier interviews. At the time he was living in exile in the diplomatic district in Peking. The main door and anteroom leading to his private chambers were guarded by soldiers from the Chinese People's Liberation Army, dressed in green uniforms. The prince enjoyed the personal friendship and protection of Chou En-lai. However the emissaries of the Khmer Rouge had the backing of the radical left-wing group that was later to become famous as the Gang of Four. Sihanouk's political activities were kept in check by a high-ranking watchdog called Ieng Sary, who kept the prince under constant supervision. Ieng Sary, who had risen from the ranks of the Cambodian Communists, was later to become foreign minister under the bloodthirsty regime of Pol Pot.

During the whole of our interview Monseigneur never once made any mention of his own predicament. He told me his main goal was the continued independence and survival of his country; ideologies had become irrelevant to him. It was up to the people to decide whether there was still a place for him in the new Cambodia. 'I've seen a world smashed into smithereens – my world,' he said, then gave a shrill, nervous laugh. All the time his eyes remained fixed on my face, gazing sadly at me.

On the terrace of the German chargé d'affaires, we sat enjoying our white wine and arguing fiercely in the dying rays of the sun. The point at issue was whether or not Norodom Sihanouk had paid a visit to the so-called 'liberated' regions of Cambodia. I myself had seen a film of this journey, shot by a Chinese camera crew, before I left Paris. There was no possible doubt about its authenticity. It showed Sihanouk, together with his wife, Princess Monique, dressed in the black pyjama uniform of the Khmer Rouge and wearing the traditional *karma* tied round their heads. (The karma was the black-and-white cloth worn round the neck in the region to give protection against the sun. The local peasants used it as a cummerbund or scarf, or sometimes even a blanket.)

The head of state (Sihanouk had retained the title while in exile) accepted the homage of a unit of black-clad guerillas, who hid from US reconnaissance planes under the hevea trees of a rubber plantation. The prince visited Buddhist pagodas where he folded his hands together and bowed to the shaven-headed monks. He was filmed on a visit to the temple city of Angkor Wat, and stood in front of a memorial to the days when Cambodia was a powerful nation. The scene enhanced Sihanouk's authority.

But the high point of the film was when the prince came face to face with his old enemy, Kieu Samphan. The Lon Nol regime had officially declared Samphan dead, but at the time of the film he was regarded – wrongly, it turned out – as a key figure in the Khmer Rouge. When he was a student he had received a doctorate from the Sorbonne for his thesis on land redistribution in Cambodia. He had served for a short time as a minister in Sihanouk's government but had then been dismissed by the autocratic prince. He was supposed to have been killed by the royal gendarmerie in the purge that followed but he had evidently surfaced again. Now the prince and the commissar faced one another in the jungle of Ratanakiri, and they embraced like long-lost friends. The pictures in the film were genuine enough, but all the friendliness and scenes of mutual tolerance it showed were false and contrived. For one thing, it was well known that at that time the monks were having a particularly hard time of it under the Khmer Rouge.

When you visited the West Germans you were always given white wine from Baden. When you visited the East Germans, on the other hand, you were served with Radeberg beer. East Germany had just sent out a dynamic new press attaché to Phnom Penh. One day I found his visiting-card in my pigeon-hole at the hotel Monorom together with an invitation to dinner. Herr K was an energetic forty-year-old with short blond hair. He spoke with a Berlin accent but unlike so many of the other East Berlin envoys his manner was relaxed and even casual. He must have been in a highly trusted position to have been allowed to seek out my company so freely. That evening it was stiflingly hot in the town centre, and the excellent Chinese restaurant K had invited me to unfortunately had no air-conditioning. Dense clouds of mosquitoes buzzed around the lights as we ate. At nearby tables sat rich Chinese businessmen from Phnom Penh, who had made their fortune out of the war. They drank each other's health, amid much belching, and as their alcohol intake increased so the volume of noise they made steadily rose.

After the meal we made a flying visit to the press attaché's house where the inevitable Radeberg beer was served with typical Saxon cheer by a hearty blonde woman. K then asked me to accompany him on a tour of the local night-clubs. I was rather taken aback to hear a suggestion like this coming from an Eastern European diplomat. Eventually, however, we found ourselves perched at a bar surrounded by a crowd of heavily made-up prostitutes, drunken Cambodian officers and American mercenaries. We learned that shots had been fired that afternoon in a gambling club next door when a Cambodian officer had insisted on being paid a bigger share of the winnings. When he failed to get what he wanted he flew into a rage and produced a gun, fatally wounding a visiting Scandinavian. The owner of the club had shown great presence of mind by diving for cover behind the bar.

After our third round of Scotch, K finally came to the point. He drew a very detailed picture of the current situation in Indochina. The Easter offensive of 1972 had been launched without the support, or even the approval, of the Soviet Union, he said. Hanoi was going ahead with its policy of reunification at any price. As the Russians saw it, Giap must be crazy to concentrate on tank warfare and let the guerilla war slide. The North Vietnamese simply couldn't handle the logistics of a conventional, Russian-style war. I asked K why it was that the Soviet Union and her allies had kept on their diplomatic representatives in Phnom Penh when Lon Nol took over; surely their sympathics must lie with the Khmer Rouge? It seemed the Eastern bloc wanted to keep a close eye on events in Phnom Penh; they wanted to keep a foot in the door. Things would have to come to a showdown at some stage, because the Khmer Rouge was gradually being taken over by disruptive and highly volatile elements. This meant the Warsaw Pact countries had to maintain a presence in Phnom Penh, if only to safeguard the interests of their Vietnamese allies. The Cambodians seemed to be deviating more and more from the party line, and Hanoi was growing increasingly concerned. If the Chinese wanted to stay out of things, that was their business.

That night as I went back to my hotel, the implications of what K had been trying to tell me had still not sunk in. The hotel lift was out of order, so I wearily climbed the four flights of stairs to my room, my head pounding. I could hear the metallic sound of exploding shells coming from the direction of Pochentong airport. I prayed that my Air Vietnam flight would take off for Saigon on time the following afternoon.

Prisoner of the Viet Cong

South Vietnam, August 1973

It was an awesome sight. We were standing in front of a huge arch that towered above the devastated plain like the entrance to the gates of Hell. The top beam contained Vietnamese writing, obviously some kind of Communist slogan. We got our guides to translate for us, and apparently it said something about liberation, socialism and the reunification of Vietnam. The red and blue flag of the Viet Cong with its central yellow star fluttered from one of the side posts; a dove of peace made out of tin clattered in the wind. Beneath the arch was a low mud wall about 50 centimetres high that formed a barricade across Route 13. We found out later it had anti-tank mines hidden inside.

Up until then we had had a fairly uneventful trip. I had decided to drive north from Saigon to try and find exactly where the ceasefire line – or more accurately, the new front line – cut across Route 13, the scene of heavy fighting the previous year. I had asked around in Saigon but nobody knew. Forty kilometres outside the capital we had had to drive in a big loop round the South Vietnamese divisional command post at Lai Khe. Normally all unauthorized persons were stopped and turned back here, but we managed to get past the checkpoint without being spotted. Further on we saw a group of Vietnamese civilians on heavily-laden Honda scooters waiting at a road block while government troops checked their papers. The soldiers waved us through without stopping us because, we were told later on, they thought we were members of the International Control Commission. We passed one or two sandbagged bunkers by the roadside, still with the flag of South Vietnam flying above them, and we also passed a watchtower. Then there was nothing. We were completely alone, surrounded by utter devastation. On both sides of the badly-damaged tarmac road the detritus of war piled up: rusting tanks, wrecked lorries, bombed-out dug-outs and gun emplacements. The trail of destruction left by the holocaust was already hidden by tall grass. Leaden-grey monsoon clouds hung low in the sky. There was something oppressive about this hostile, deserted landscape.

I was standing with Jean-Louis Arnaud, Saigon correspondent for AFP, the French news agency. I had met him at a cocktail party the previous evening and persuaded him to join me on this tour of inspection. He laid a warning hand on my shoulder. 'Don't forget I've got an appointment with Mérillon, the French ambassador, at 4 o'clock,' he said. I told him not to worry, we had to send off our film by 5pm at the latest. We were no more than 50 or 60 kilometres from Saigon and it was not yet midday.

Then out of the blue, we came upon this arch. It was clearly a kind of boundary marking the beginning of Viet Cong territory. There was no official demarcation line between the North and South Vietnamese forces, and shooting was still going on despite the Paris ceasefire agreement. The Viet Cong emplacements were cunningly arranged so as to link up with one another and they were dotted all over the Communist-controlled sectors. People had described the lay-out of these positions in terms of spots on a leopard's coat, but it was actually more like ink stains on a blotter with the edges gradually spreading into one another. I told both of our drivers to turn round at the arch so we could set out for home immediately. But before we headed back I wanted to do a quick on-the-spot commentary in front of these symbols of the Vietnamese revolution. As we were setting up the tripod for the film camera we heard a rustling noise in the tall clumps of grass around us. Then a ring of about twenty soldiers in green uniforms appeared and began closing in on us, moving silently through the long grass, with automatic rifles at the ready. There was no mistaking who they were – the round green jungle hats, the AK-47s, the baggy trousers, the Ho Chi Minh sandals: they were either Viet Cong guerillas or North Vietnamese regulars, and we were their prisoners.

The men stood round us in a circle, not uttering a word. They all looked very young and had open, peasant faces. I walked up to the nearest one and shook him firmly by the hand. This was a trick I had learned in the Congo. Those had been difficult times, but the age-old gesture of understanding had never failed to calm down mutinous black soldiers and inspire some sort of trust. Then, of course, there was the added advantage that an armed man is unable to use his gun and shake hands at the same time, and the Africans tended to shoot first and ask questions later. But it didn't look as if we would have any worries on that score with the Viet Cong as the men seemed to be well disciplined and under control.

Calmly and without fuss, the guerillas ordered us to take cover in the ditch by the side of the road. Evidently they were expecting harassing fire from the South Vietnamese. They got our clumsy big limousines to drive round the arch and head north. Two hundred metres further on we stopped, and the cars were camouflaged with foliage. Then we were driven to a wooden barracks that was a kind of official checkpoint. Our camera equipment was confiscated, despite vigorous protests. Our cameraman was issued with a receipt bearing the official stamp of the Liberation Front. Communication was difficult, and we had no idea which one of them was meant to be the officer on duty: the Viet Cong had no insignia to indicate rank. I had told the others to speak nothing but French to our guards; on no account should they try English. Thanh, our interpreter, looked thoroughly dejected. He was the nephew of Tran Van Tin, our Vietnamese contact. Thus far he had avoided being called up for the South Vietnamese Army by a bit of string-pulling and a lot of help from his uncle. He was obviously in a rather awkward position now, and he stood there looking pale and anxious, hardly daring to say a word. The guerillas didn't seem particularly interested in our passports. Jean-Louis Arnaud had a French identity card, but they weren't impressed by that. They told Thanh they thought our status as journalists was extremely suspect, and they had no way of guaranteeing we weren't CIA agents. We sat down on a bench and waited. The looks the young Communist soldiers gave us seemed more curious than hostile. We could tell which were the more senior officers by the guarded, distant manner they adopted towards us.

As we were sitting there we heard a sudden commotion out on the road. The columns of Hondas we had passed earlier on at the checkpoint at Lai Khe were now queuing up in front of the Viet Cong arch. Here, right in the middle of the uneasy no-man's land between the two front lines, a trickle of regular border traffic was still going back and forth. Shortly before the official ceasefire the nearby town of Chon Tanh had been surrounded by the North Vietnamese, but they had never managed to capture it. The two sides had eventually come to an arrangement whereby the people of Chon Tanh were allowed to travel south to Lai Khe every morning to buy food, then travel back again in the afternoon.

Towards evening a rather gruff young political officer turned up, accompanied by six armed men. He inspected us without saying a word. Through our interpreter he told us we would be taken to a hide-out in the jungle 7 kilometres north-west of the border control. We were escorted there by guards carrying AK-47 rifles. The commissar had a hand-grenade. The terrain we marched through had been completely devastated by the B-52 air strikes. The bombs had left huge craters which had filled up with rainwater; most of them already had a fringe of pale green grass growing round the edge. Over in the west the evening sun disappeared behind an eerie-looking bank of black cloud with tropical suddenness. None of us had any baggage. We hadn't thought to bring anything else with us on our day's outing. We hadn't so much as a toothbrush or an anti-malaria pill between us, let alone a change of shirt. Arnaud and the rest of the crew were wearing light shoes or sandals. I wore boots, because I knew from my first trip to Indochina how important it was to have strong and waterproof footwear when you went into the ricefields.

As the light began to fade we plunged into a thicket where the air was rank with rotting vegetation. After a short time we came without warning on a few bamboo huts and a dug-out. It was a tiny Viet Cong base, protected by a row of barbed wire and a fence of bamboo stakes. We were handed over to a solemn-looking officer, obviously some sort of captain. He got Thanh to translate a warning. 'Don't try to escape,' he told us. 'We've laid mines right round the camp and you will almost certainly tread on one.' The soldiers, who wore round green jungle hats and green uniforms, watched us like hawks but were always perfectly well-behaved. Before our drivers were segregated from us later on that evening, they managed to whisper to us that the accents of the young soldiers indicated they were definitely North Vietnamese. We knew then that we must be with a regular unit from the North. I pretended to be suffering from diarrhoea so I could scout around and see what the possibilities of escaping were.

After a while the captain called me into his hut. By this time darkness had fallen and the soldiers were sitting round singing doleful songs. The captain said he was worried about my physical condition. He suggested I rub Tiger Balm on my stomach. He explained that was the only medicine they had, and he gave me a tiny jar of the ointment. (The East Asians believe Tiger Balm has almost magical properties.) I told him it would be more helpful if he gave my friends something to eat and found them a bed for the night. We had all been left sitting perched uncomfortably on a wooden bench while the soldiers were busy hanging up green plastic hammocks, obviously getting ready to turn in for the night. The captain must have taken what I said to heart, because we were brought some rice and hot water plus a few stalks of some unidentifiable green vegetable. The soldiers were given the same meagre helping of food as we were. The captain then showed us to a big plank bed.

So far my colleagues had taken the whole episode amazingly well. Josef Kaufmann, the cameraman, was mainly worried about his equipment, he was afraid the damp might get to it. He kept trying to convince the guards, in broken French, that they could be held responsible for any damage to it. Klaus Pattberg, a humorous, easy-going man who originally came from Cologne, was already trying to work out the best way for us to keep in reasonable physical and mental shape during the days or weeks that lay ahead. He drew up a programme of exercises that evening, and the next day he started trying to make a crude form of ludo and halma for us to play. Dieter Hofrath, our sound engineer who came from Rhinehessen, was a giant of a man who towered above our Vietnamese captors. He reacted to the uncertainty of the situation with his usual stolid calm. He said, half-jokingly: 'Ah well, this is probably what it was like at first with the Maltese.' The 'Maltese' were a group of German men and women who had been working for the Knights of St John and had gone on a Sunday outing into the hills around Da Nang and been kidnapped by the Viet Cong. Although they were fairly young and inexperienced they had been forced to march through the jungle all the way to Hanoi. The journey took several weeks and very few survived the terrible physical hardships they suffered *en route*. I reckoned this was the greatest danger we might have to face, too. I was confident the North Vietnamese would not mistreat us or kill us – I had known them too long to think they would try anything like that. But if they were to make us march north over many kilometres of jungle and mountain – and even if they gave us some of their precious food rations – the risk of us dying from illness or sheer exhaustion would be high. As for Jean-Louis, he was positively enjoying the adventure in his typical French way. You could tell his intellectual curiosity was vastly stimulated by the whole thing. Every so often, though, he would look worried and sit twirling his long handlebar moustache, which he had grown to remind him of the time he spent as a correspondent in Delhi, when everyone still felt nostalgic for the days of the British Raj.

We were woken next morning by the noise of hens clucking and sentries shouting. During the night our guards had been in radio contact with the headquarters of the revolutionary forces in Loc Ninh. A young nurse with a Red Cross armband had been sent to check up on our physical condition. She told each of us to take a quinine tablet with the cup of hot water we were regularly given to drink instead of tea. (Later we discovered that most of the North Vietnamese losses in the war were actually due to malaria.) That morning we were lucky: our rice soup contained a tiny piece of meat. The captain told us we would be kept prisoner for at least a few more days. As we had neither soap, shaving gear nor towel he would provide us with all the basic essentials required. The daily procession of Hondas to Lai Khe was due to start in about three hours, and he said he would send Thanh, our interpreter, along with them. All we had to do was make him out a list of the things we needed and give him some money to buy them. In the afternoon Thanh would travel back with the scooters returning to Chon Tanh.

I got out a visiting card to write down the shopping list, but instead of putting down what we needed I wrote on the back in English: 'We are prisoners of the Viet Cong near Road 13. Please notify immediately German Embassy in Saigon for release. Help!' I whispered the message I had written to Jean-Louis, who thought the last word was particularly funny. 'You've been seeing too many Beatles films,' he said. I impressed upon Thanh the need to go to Saigon immediately and alert the French and German embassies. I warned him to be careful of the South Vietnamese police, and said that under no circumstances should he come back to the Viet Cong camp. I felt quite pleased at having beaten the professional conspirators of the North Vietnamese underground at their own game.

Towards midday we were transferred to a new hide-out. We now found ourselves in a large camp in the middle of the jungle. It seemed to be a relief camp behind the front lines for one of the North Vietnamese battalions. The personnel in the camp alternated every week. The actual front itself was no more than 5 kilometres away, and at night we could hear artillery fire in the distance. The enemy were experts at camouflage, and I was sure no-one could have spotted our camp from the air. The huts were made of foliage and branches and led to a series of underground caves where we could take cover in the event of a mortar attack. We were taken to our roofed-over trenches and hung up our green nylon hammocks and mosquito nets. The captain said that the food provided in the revolutionary army was fairly basic. Nevertheless they would do the best they could for us. He assured us the water we were given had been boiled and was completely germ-free. I told him we could make do with very little food. We liked rice, and so long as we could mix some *nuoc mam* in with it we would be perfectly satisfied. (*Nuoc mam* was the sauce made of rotten fish which the local peasants traditionally ate with their rice.) The captain looked rather embarrassed when I said this. '*Nuoc mam* is a luxury for us,' he said. 'We just use salt water to season our rice.'

We were forbidden to move outside the immediate vicinity of the three huts we had been allocated, two to each hut. The guard detailed to keep a watch on us never took his eye off us for a second. Fortunately they gave us a transistor radio to help pass the time. A young soldier from Tongking told one of our drivers that he and his comrades were regular listeners to the BBC World Service. As he put it: 'The BBC doesn't lie.' By this time we were feeling very low. After all the excitement of the previous day a terrible feeling of anti-climax had set in. In the afternoon we were visited by a gaunt, austere-looking officer. He told us with a note of stern reproach in his voice that Thanh had gone running to the 'puppets' in Saigon to report what had happened instead of doing the shopping and coming straight back to camp. We protested our innocence, naturally, but they were not convinced. From then on they kept us strictly segregated from our two Vietnamese drivers, who seemed a great deal more anxious about the situation then we were, and made sure we had no means of communicating with them.

In the early evening Josef Kaufmann managed to get the BBC on our radio, and after a while we heard him let out a whoop of joy. The newsreader had just announced that a German television crew and a French AFP correspondent had been taken prisoner by the Viet Cong. A representative of the Liberation Front had said the prisoners were in good health. So Saigon did, in fact, know about our disappearance. We offered up a silent prayer of thanks to Thanh who, although we did not know it at the time, had been grabbed by the South Vietnamese military police in Lai Khe and was at that very moment languishing in a damp prison-cell, half-frightened out of his wits.

In the afternoons we could hear people shouting and a ball being thrown around – the North Vietnamese enjoyed volleyball in their off-duty hours. At night the troops would sit together and sing revolutionary songs. One of them, in particular, stuck in our minds, mainly because of its monotonously repetitive chorus. Even we could understand what it meant without too much difficulty: 'Vietnam, Ho Chi Minh! Vietnam, Ho Chi Minh!

Vietnam, Ho Chi Minh!' Most of the time our captors seemed to take hardly any notice of us at all. They brought us food and quinine tablets at regular intervals, but they were obviously hanging on, waiting for further instructions from headquarters at Loc Ninh. Meanwhile we kept on insisting we were innocent journalists whose sole wish was to get back to our hotel in Saigon. Now, however, all our pleas were met with stony-faced silence. By our third day in captivity the outlook didn't seem to be too promising.

On the morning of our third day two soldiers took us outside the camp to a huge B-52 bomb crater filled with clear rainwater. We stripped off our sweat-stained clothing and bathed thankfully while the guards stood watch, AK-47s at the ready. Then, in the sultry noonday heat, while everyone was taking their siesta, things suddenly took a turn for the better. We heard an unfamiliar sound coming out of the jungle – the putt-putting of an engine. Then a mud-caked Honda drew up outside our hut. The driver, a man of about fifty, had on a green uniform but he looked more like a civilian than a soldier. He came straight over to us, shook our hands and welcomed us to the 'liberated zones' on behalf of the 'National Liberation Front of Vietnam'. He spoke fluent, almost elegant French with a heavy Vietnamese accent. 'My apologies for taking so long,' he said, introducing himself as Commissar Huyn Ba Tang. 'The roads between Loc Ninh and the camp are virtually impassable in the rainy season. However I have good news for you. Our liaison officers in Saigon have clearly established that you are, in fact, journalists. That means you are no longer our prisoners, so from now on you should consider yourselves our guests. As soon as you want to return to Saigon just let us know and we'll send you back promptly. If you should wish to film the liberated zone and make a report on us, then please feel free to do so.' He pointed to a column of soldiers, who appeared out of the bush and handed over all our camera equipment neatly wrapped up in protective nylon covers. Even the batteries for the cameras were charged and ready for use. This sudden change in our fortunes seemed almost too good to be true. The guards who had glared at us suspiciously only that morning now became smiling and friendly. Nothing was too much trouble. We were even served watery tea in an empty grenade case. 'You'll have to do without a lot of things you've been used to,' said Huyn Ba Tang with a shy smile, 'but we'll do our best to make you feel comfortable here.'

We all took instantly to this quiet little man. He later told us he had been a political activist for over twenty years. First he had fought against the French, then Diem, then finally the Americans and President Thieu. He had had a few narrow escapes in his time. Twice he had been caught in B-52 bombing raids, but had survived. He must have had nine lives. Commissar Huyn Ba Tang was definitely the odd man out among the comrades – somehow his face just didn't quite fit. His background was unusual in itself. His father had worked as an official in the French administration in Saigon. Yet for all his years of loyal service to the cause, Huyn Ba Tang had received precious little reward in terms of rank or honours. We noticed it was the hardened 'professionals' from the North, the party workers and the technical experts, who now made all the running in the guerilla army. Huyn Ba Tang, on the other hand, was a dedicated idealist, a man with a simple vision of the truth. He was, in short, too good to live. Dieter Hofrath hit on the nickname we gave him: Father Albert. He really did have something of the monk or the clergyman about him, and he reminded me of a remark by Bishop Seitz in Kontum, who described one of his Viet Cong opponents as a 'saint'.

After that we were allowed to wander round the camp with our cameras and tape-recorders exactly as we pleased. The soldiers were open and friendly, and smiled at us. In the main they were burly peasant lads between eighteen and twenty-eight. They showed us the camp kitchen, which had a tunnel 100 metres long for drawing away smoke from the fire and preventing enemy reconnaissance planes from learning of its exact location. The field hospital was completely hidden under a screen of foliage and green netting and was built in such a way that it could be dismantled in two hours flat. Power for the lights above the operating table was provided by a bicycle. There was no back-up system or auxiliary power unit here; in an emergency they just had to rely on muscle-power. In many ways this jungle hide-out reminded me of a scout camp. The soldiers always had some job to do to keep them busy – they were never allowed to be idle. And yet, however spartan an existence they were leading in these camouflaged huts and underground tunnels, when you compared it to the hell they had just been through, when they had to hide from the bombs and the napalm in cramped foxholes and burrows, their present conditions must have seemed idyllic. After all they had gone through, what difference did it make if the shells came in a few metres closer one night?

By the end Jean-Louis and the guerillas got to be on very good terms with one another. Some of the old chemistry was obviously still working between Arnaud, so typical of the old colonial types, and the peasants' sons from Tongking. For the vast majority of the Communist troops did belong to the North, and they made no secret of the fact. Most came from the densely populated Red River Delta, and their eyes lit up when I told them I knew towns like Hanoi, Haiphong, Nam Dinh, and Tanh Hoa from my experiences in the first Indochinese war. Here in the camp, barely two hours drive from Saigon, Giap's army always set their watches to Hanoi time, which was an hour behind South Vietnamese time. The only portraits they had on the walls were of Ho Chi Minh. And though they flew the official blue and red flag of the Viet Cong, their real emblem was the blood-red banner with the yellow star, the symbol of Ho Chi Minh's People's Revolt. One name never mentioned was Nguyen Huu Tho, the Cochin Chinese lawyer who led the South Vietnamese National Liberation Front. Tho had invited the diplomats and representatives of the Eastern bloc countries to a meeting in his headquarters at Cam Lo on the 17th parallel. Hanoi had long since abandoned the pretence of a separate North and South Vietnam. Here, barely seventy kilometres from Saigon, the reunification of Vietnam was being treated as a reality and not simply a dream.

The guerillas, still known as Bo Doi in the international press, were constantly on the look-out for danger. They sent patrols out day and night, even though they were only in a relief camp. When the men went out they were skilfully camouflaged with leaves and branches. The effect of their disguise was somehow comical, and they reminded Jean-Louis of Papageno in *The Magic Flute*. In their spare time the soldiers either played volleyball or wrote essays on the revolutionary war under the watchful eye of their political commissar. They had to describe their wartime experiences in the most high-flown patriotic language, of course. In one of the other bamboo huts regular art classes were held when the Bo Doi would sit sketching a picture of a heroic soldier battling against imperialism. The results were depressingly unoriginal, all done in the most boring Identikit Socialist Realist style.

We were invited to film the ideological training courses every soldier had to attend for about two hours daily. These classes took the form of sessions of self-criticism followed by earnest resolutions to do better in future. The men would then recite the ten commandments of the revolutionary soldier and discuss their implications. Rather to my surprise, I found myself thinking of the intellectual atmosphere of a seminary. The ideological commitment of the troops was almost religious in intensity. The classes did more than teach the men their political catechism. They used the practice of Biblical exegesis to explore and affirm the doctrine of Marxism-Leninism. It struck me as being very much in the spirit of St Ignatius of Loyola, but I refrained from saying so to Father Albert.

We decided we ought to familiarize ourselves with the ten commandments of the Bo Doi. The first article of faith called for the reunification of Vietnam. Then came obedience to one's superiors, participation in the struggle of the proletariat, and cooperation in raising productivity and disseminating propaganda. Military secrets should never be revealed, even under torture. The revolutionary soldier had to love his comrades as he loved himself. He had a duty to look after his weapons and to help the Vietnamese people. Above all he must never steal from the people. And, of course, it was his duty to criticize the faults of his comrades, and himself in particular.

When it got dark in the evenings we would go and sit with the soldiers, stumbling blindly through the vegetable patches they had planted, hoping to find some relief from the mosquitoes in the smoke of the camp-fire. Communication was far from easy, since Father Albert left us to our own devices at such times and our drivers were still kept apart from us in a separate hut. The North Vietnamese troops were very sober and clean-living. Some had been fighting as guerillas for seven years continuously. Many had lost their best friends in the war. They didn't wear military insignia in the field, though back in Hanoi the officer corps strutted around with wide, Russian-style epaulettes. Quite a number of the men in this élite unit had won decorations for valour, and they took pride in wearing them. They explained that the postal service between the camp and their families in Tongking was very infrequent, and they were lucky if they got a postcard once every six months. Many hadn't seen their girlfriends or fiancées for several years. Out of their breast pockets they would take yellowing photos of smiling girls with broad peasant faces – photos they had carried on them through all the mud and the napalm.

A number of these youthful veterans had seen some of the worst of the action during the Tet offensive and had been in the thick of the fighting around Khe Sanh, Tay Ninh, Kontum, and Route 13 as well. We asked them what they would do when they were eventually demobbed. The answer was always the same: 'We'll do whatever the Party asks of us.' Of course there were things they would have liked to do, private ambitions they secretly cherished. Quite a few would have liked to become teachers or engineers. Some wanted to go down the mines, while others simply wanted to go back to the land and be peasants. Again and again we would end up discussing their favourite topic of conversation – the girls they had left behind. We asked them how much longer they thought they would have to wear the green uniform of the revolutionary soldier. Again, the verdict was unanimous: 'Until Vietnam is one country again and we have carried out the task handed down to us by Ho Chi Minh.' The words were empty rhetoric, learned parrot-fashion, almost inhuman in a way. And yet, coming from these young men, they had real sincerity and spontaneity. Those were stirring, uneasy moments for us.

In the evening they would all join in singing patriotic battle-songs till the early hours of the morning. The songs were all about courage, patriotism and sustaining morale: 'Don't just think of your own life when you're fighting imperialism.' The chorus of one song went: 'Our Fatherland may be split in two, but from the Mekong to the mountains in the North, we are all one nation.' One evening as we sat listening to them, Father Albert came up and asked one of the young Bo Doi to give us a song called 'Letter to a friend in Washington'. Apparently it was a declaration of solidarity and friendship addressed to the Americans. It ended with the words: 'Justice will unite us, and one day we shall sing our songs together in Hanoi and Washington.' We used to walk back to our bunkers afterwards feeling saddened at all this naive innocence and enthusiasm.

The South Vietnamese guns had started up again about 8 kilometres away. The weather was clammy and hot. Undeterred by the sporadic firing, Father Albert would painstakingly check that there were no gaps in the mosquito nets draped over our hammocks. That man had a Franciscan's eye for detail. He would even come in while we were asleep just to make sure we hadn't thrown off our covers and made ourselves vulnerable to insect bites.

The following morning he introduced two new escorts to us. The older of the two, Major Tac, was a fatherly-looking North Vietnamese who had been assigned to look after us by the authorities in Loc Ninh. His companion, Lieutenant Trung, looked a rather nasty piece of work, however. I guessed he was a member of the North Vietnamese secret service. We were told he had spent some time in Cuba and the Soviet Union and had been trained in intelligence and counter-intelligence in the Caribbean. He had also done a crash course in American English in one of Castro's training schools for secret agents. Looking at Lieutenant Trung, I got the uneasy feeling he had probably had a lot of experience interrogating captured American GIs. He certainly wouldn't have been my first choice for a jailer. He spoke American with an exaggerated nasal accent and finished every sentence with 'OK'. The way he treated us was like some awful American Express courier. Whenever he got too bossy we would call him back into line and he would apologize rather sulkily. We used to tell him he ought to try and acquire a civilized English accent.

The North Vietnamese had invited us to tour part of the 'liberated zones' and make a film of the area. Before we left they sent along an army tailor to take our measurements, for despite all our careful washing the clothes we had on were stiff with dirt and sweat. We eventually set off in a convoy which included a Russian Zil lorry and a Chinese jeep. We drove for about thirty kilometres in the direction of An Loc. The vehicles trundled slowly through the desolate landscape. The place we were making for was the village of Minh Hoa, which had previously been the home of the coolies working on the French rubber plantations. Our guides were anxious that we should show the civilian as well as the military side of the revolution. So we then went west in the direction of the Cambodian border, heading for one of those rare parts of the country where people were supposedly living a more or less normal existence under Communist rule.

The Easter offensive of 1972 had caught the locals in these parts so completely unawares that the North Vietnamese had overrun them without any trouble. At the time of our arrest, the Communists already controlled substantial areas of South Vietnam. But only five per cent of the population – roughly one million people – lived in these remote and inhospitable 'liberated zones'. Since the ceasefire agreement, which had effectively ratified the presence of 150,000 North Vietnamese regulars south of the 17th parallel, Hanoi had lost no time in extending its military infrastructure in the region. But the long years of fighting had reduced the main Viet Cong force in South Vietnam to about 50,000 men. After we got back to Saigon the Western military attachés assured us we had been in the sector occupied by the 7th or 9th Division of the North Vietnamese Army, yet we had seen comparatively little sign of troops in the area.

On our way to the 'liberated zones' we met our first civilians. They seemed to have been hit by the war far more badly than the soldiers. The bridges in the area had all been destroyed by bombs and had been replaced by makeshift gangways or concrete fords. We didn't see a single car. But we did pass several soldiers and peasants pushing heavily-laden bicycles. I remembered that during the battle of Dien Bien Phu the Viet Minh had managed to transport up to 500 kilograms on each machine. As we drove on now we could see lightning flashing and storm clouds gathering in the grey monsoon sky.

Our arrival in Minh Hoa caused something of a sensation among the 800 people of the village. Ours were the first white faces they had seen since the revolutionary army had marched into the area. Before the fighting started they had worked on the nearby rubber plantation, but now they looked as if they had fallen on hard times. There were plenty of signs that the northern troops were in charge here, and loudspeakers kept booming out battle-songs and rousing speeches through the deserted main street of the village. We were officially welcomed by the local party and army officials in a bamboo hut specially erected for the occasion. We gave them a friendly smile and introduced ourselves, one by one, to the reception committee. Major Quoc was in charge of propaganda while Major Hoang was commander of the battalion stationed in Minh Hoa. His smile froze somewhat when he learned we came from West Germany. Captain Thien was a reporter working on the army newspaper. Their cameraman, Lieutenant Diet, and our own camera crew hit it off right from the start.

Trung, our Cuba-trained escort, introduced us in his grating American voice to the civilians on the local revolutionary committee. We were particularly impressed by Madame Nam, a formidable and energetic lady who obviously had a will of iron. 'We should like to welcome you here as friends from Europe,' said Major Quoc, winding up his brief speech of welcome. We clapped politely when he had finished, and then it was my turn to say a few words in English. My speech was recorded and (so I later found out) broadcast over the Liberation Front radio station that same evening. I spoke about the admiration we in the West felt for the Vietnamese guerillas and freedom-fighters, and said I hoped the country would be restored to peace and prosperity again after the devastation of the war. I added that as Germans and members of a nation that had been divided against its will, we felt a profound sympathy for the Vietnamese demands for reunification. When I finished we all clapped again and smiled at one another. The sentence about reunification was apparently omitted from the broadcast that evening, probably out of deference to their East German allies.

In the afternoon the tailor brought us our new outfits. The blue and green drill fabric reminded me of the summer uniforms worn by Bulgarian policemen. When we pulled on the trousers and jackets and saw ourselves, we nearly collapsed with laughter. The waist was either so narrow you couldn't fasten the trousers or else so wide that it ballooned out in front. It was impossible to get your arms into the sleeves without splitting the back seam, and the cut of the trouser legs made it impossible to even move. Nevertheless we were so touched by the thoughtful gesture we decided to wear the ridiculous-looking outfits as pyjamas when we climbed into our hammocks that night.

Next morning we watched a political gathering in Minh Hoa. We were told that every family in the village had sent along at least one representative. The leader of the revolutionary committee was a long-standing underground fighter with a broad, chubby face. He called for an increase in farm production and said the people should aim to build up the economy 'using their own strength'. (Our interpreter translated this as 'self-reliance'.) There was also some discussion of the preparations for the coming national holiday on 2 September, the anniversary of the declaration of Vietnamese independence by Ho Chi Minh. The mood of the meeting seemed tense and subdued. At the close everybody gave the customary three cheers, but their faces remained blank. A white-haired old man stood up and spoke in a flat voice about the unanimous desire of the village to take part in the Socialist reconstruction of their country. We saw no signs of revolutionary fervour among the listeners.

The first time we heard any laughter during our trip was on the outskirts of the rubber plantation. Women and girls from the village were cutting slits in the trunks of the rubber trees and checking the level of the latex in the wooden bowls placed below the incisions to collect the milky sap. The French plantation owners had apparently managed to escape to Saigon in time. Now the Liberation Front officials had no idea what to do with the poor rubber harvest, particularly as there was no demand for exports. The young southern women giggled as they watched the revolutionary troops struggling to plant vegetables and manioc in the barren laterite soil, and their hilarity unsettled the troops.

The children of the village were assembled in the big shed used as the local school and waiting for us to come and film them. They were a bright, happy bunch and seemed to find it easier than the adults to adapt to the Socialist demands of their new life. We got someone to translate the words of one of their songs: 'Last night we dreamed about Uncle Ho Chi Minh, nice old Uncle Ho with his long beard and his white hair. We love Uncle Ho, and if we work hard at our lessons then Uncle Ho will let us wear the red scarf of the Young Pioneers.'

Apart from the children, the Communists saw the young women in the 'liberated zones' as potentially the most useful disseminators of the revolutionary gospel. Young women workers were taught to read and write in special adult education classes. The main theme of these lessons, apart from crash courses in Marxism, was the glorification of the idea of Vietnamese nationhood. The teacher would tell them the mythical story of the creation of the Vietnamese people, and the young women would copy it down in their notebooks. This was the way they were taught the legend of King Hung and Queen Au-Cho, and how back in the mists of time they had fifty sons and fifty daughters who sprang forth out of a hundred eggs, like Cadmus and the dragon's teeth. These sons and daughters were their ancestors, the very first Vietnamese.

Towards evening our guides seemed to get a little restless and edgy; some ceremony or other was about to take place. By this time we had spent a whole week with the Viet Cong, and our unplanned excursion was drawing to an end. We had already used up our last few feet of film and the batteries, which had resisted the heat and the moisture amazingly well, were beginning to run out too. Major Tac and Lieutenant Trung brought us an unusually large meal that evening: chicken soup with pieces of meat in it, rice, tinned sardines from Morocco, and a loaf of bread. (The bread was crawling with maggots.) Then, much to our amazement, Trung suddenly produced two bottles of vodka. The vodka came from Hanoi and was distilled from rice, and the Vietnamese brand name had an inscription in Cyrillic script alongside. We had already changed into our night clothes by this time, but the two officers quickly cleared the table and wiped away the crumbs. It never ceased to amaze us how the officers in the Liberation Army would carry out the humblest tasks without batting an eyelid; they would even set to and help to hump our camera equipment around.

The alcohol lifted our spirits dramatically. During the past weeks all we had had to drink was tepid boiled water or occasionally, as a special treat, bitter tea that kept us awake all night. Now Tac was peering into the darkness, straining to hear something. The glow-worms out in the jungle had started up their nightly dance, and the steady rumble of gunfire could be heard again in the distance. Suddenly we heard the noise of an engine and a jeep appeared out of the darkness. Two senior officers of the guerilla army climbed out of the jeep and walked over to our hut.

We never did find out what their rank was. They could have been colonels and one was almost certainly a high-ranking political commissar. Both seemed very self-confident. They introduced themselves as Hung and Tung, but these were almost certainly pseudonyms, for in the South Vietnamese underground an agent's true identity was always kept a closely-guarded secret. Tung looked remarkably like General Giap, the North Vietnamese Commander-in-Chief, while Hung reminded me a little of Pham Van Dong, the ascetic-looking prime minister of the Hanoi government. We had hopes of having a high-powered political discussion with them, but we were to be disappointed. Even high-ranking Bo Doi like these were subject to the all-embracing regulations about secrecy. They never once spoke about the administrative structure of the provisional government in the 'liberated zones' – for good reasons, as we later found out. However both Hung and Tung were very willing to talk about themselves and their careers. One had been an underground activist for twenty-seven years (he was now forty-seven), while the younger one had been involved in the revolutionary struggle for twenty years. Both seemed to have emerged from these terrible times relatively unscathed. Their voices were surprisingly soft, and they never once stopped smiling. They said the worst was behind them now they no longer had to live under the ground, day and night, like rats. And yet they had both suffered much hardship during the war. It was years, for instance, since they had seen their families in the South Vietnamese towns of Camau and Can Tho. Hung had no idea what had become of his two daughters. Tung had lost a son in the war, and another had been badly wounded. He said: 'It is a dignity and a glory to lose a son in the struggle.' The two men vanished into the night as suddenly as they appeared. They went back to where they really belonged – the past twenty years, the darkness, and the jungle.

We returned to our original camp near Route 13 and got ready to go back across the frontier. We met up with Father Albert again, still smiling his shy and kindly smile. We wondered what would happen to the film we had taken when we reached Saigon; the authorities would almost certainly confiscate it. We asked if we could send the film back to western Europe via Loc Ninh, Hanoi, Peking and Moscow. The guerillas seemed to find the idea highly amusing. 'Don't worry, we'll find a way to get your pictures to you in Saigon,' said Father Albert confidently. 'But you'll have to think of a way of smuggling them out of South Vietnam. As soon as you're safely back in Saigon, we'll send a messenger round to see you.'

It was still dark when we set out to walk the seven kilometres from the camp to Route 13. We were accompanied by an escort of heavily-armed guards, but this time they were there to protect us, not to prevent us escaping. The day dawned grey and pale. Eventually we came to the massive Viet Cong arch across Route 13 and we hid in the undergrowth by the roadside. By some miracle of timing our two limousines were there waiting for us, together with our two drivers whom we hadn't seen for seven days. Both men looked fit and well-fed; the cars still had bits of old twigs and branches sticking to them. Overhead South Vietnamese helicopters clattered northwards in the morning haze on their way to drop supplies to the besieged garrison at An Loc. Captain Tac suddenly leapt out of the undergrowth onto the tarmac. He pointed his rifle at the procession of scooters arriving from Chon Tanh, punctual as ever. Father Albert rushed up to us, looking nervously around him. 'The Hondas will cover you when you pass the Saigon troops,' he whispered. 'If you are the only ones on the road, you might well be shot at. Try and squeeze in between them.' Father Albert and I embraced like old friends, then I hugged Captain Tac. It was a genuinely emotional moment. I said goodbye to interpreter Trung and shook his hand. He would probably have been embarrassed by a warmer gesture of approval from a class enemy like myself.

Tac threw open the car doors for us and told our drivers to step on it. We drove round the mud wall that ran underneath the arch, carefully avoiding the concealed anti-tank mines, then bumped and heaved our way through a ditch towards the South Vietnamese outposts. We had Hondas on both sides of us now, and their drivers stared across at us in astonishment. We had barely gone a kilometre beyond the border when we were stopped by a party of South Vietnamese soldiers who yelled at us to pull over. They were wearing American combat helmets and bulletproof vests and carried M-16 rifles. When the drivers didn't immediately slow down they fired a couple of shots into the air. We stopped the cars and three soldiers squeezed in beside us. They seemed very agitated, and they kept their rifles trained on us for a while. Gradually, however, the tension eased and they began to relax. By this time we had acquired an escort of jeeps driven by South Vietnamese military police. We continued in convoy like this until we came to a regimental camp flying the South Vietnamese flag, and our car turned into the entrance. A paratroop major in a smartly tailored uniform was waiting to greet us. He was pencil slim and wore a pale blue silk scarf in the neck of his camouflage jacket. 'You're very welcome here, despite everything,' was his first remark. 'You're probably all fed up eating rats – I imagine that's the best the Communists could do for you in the way of food.' He handed us each a bottle of ice-cold Coca-Cola. All that week as we had sat sipping our tepid water in the camp we had dreamed of the moment we would taste our first Coke. In the end we had practically developed a craving for it, though normally it wasn't a drink any of us particularly cared for. At last the long-awaited moment had arrived. We threw back our heads and gulped it down, but somehow the drink tasted flat and stale.

Jean-Louis Arnaud invited all of us round to his place one evening to celebrate our safe return to Saigon. He had a rented apartment in the Rue Tu Do which was directly above the flat where I had met up with 'Pasha' Ponchardier in 1951. Jean-Louis was looked after by two elderly Vietnamese sisters, simple old peasant women who cooked him marvellous meals and were generally very proper and ladylike. Whenever I called round to see him before he got home from work at night, one of the sisters would always sit down beside me and have a chat. It was only after the North Vietnamese captured the city that Jean-Louis found out that the husband of one of the women had lived in Hanoi since 1954 and was high up in the Communist Party hierarchy.

All sorts of people had been invited to the party: journalists, American PR men, diplomats and members of the International Control Commission. Then there was the usual crowd of old hands from the French days, of course. Jean-Louis, like the rest of us, had had several anxious days upon his release by the Viet Cong. After our escapade in the 'liberated zone' the Saigon police suspected us of working for the Viet Cong. For four hours we were detained in police headquarters in Saigon and interrogated, but the attempts by counter-intelligence to frighten us were not very impressive. When the security officer ordered red wine and sandwiches to be brought in, as in a Simenon story, we knew we were in the clear. The French and German embassies lost no time in coming to our aid. There were, inevitably, a lot of disgruntled press colleagues who tried to make out that our trip inside VC territory was, in fact, a put-up job, but that didn't bother us. On the other hand we were very worried about what had happened to our two drivers, to say nothing of Thanh, the interpreter we had sent back to Lai Khe on the first day of our imprisonment. All three seemed to have vanished off the face of the earth. We were fairly sure they were stuck inside some police cell somewhere in the capital. It took several days of unrelenting effort to get them freed. During that time we made endless appeals to the South Vietnamese authorities on their behalf, but to no avail. In the end we asked our embassies to intervene, and even – in desperation – called in the CIA. Eventually, however, they were released and they returned to work smiling broadly, apparently none the worse for wear.

It was raining that evening in Saigon so I looked from my hotel window at the tarts being dropped off outside the bars in Tu Do Street by their brothers or pimps. It was nearly time for the city's night-life to start up again. The girls hoisted up their mini-skirts and put plastic bags over their heads to keep their make-up and false eyelashes dry. I gazed in fascination at the hustle and bustle. After my time with the Viet Cong, I still felt a bit like a visitor from another planet in the midst of this den of iniquity. It was hard to believe that barely seventy kilometres from this pleasure-seeking, extravagant, happy-go-lucky metropolis of three million inhabitants, an army of dedicated puritans sat waiting in the jungle – almost champing at the bit – eager for the day when they could finally destroy the tinsel glitter of Saigon's twin industries, sin and consumerism.

My thoughts were interrupted by the sound of a familiar voice 'I was hoping to find you here,' speaking in a heavy east European accent. It was Laszlo, a Hungarian friend from my Paris days. We hadn't seen one another for ages and were delighted to meet again. Laszlo used to send us documentaries he had made on the Communist-controlled areas of Laos (Eastern bloc journalists could, of course, come and go as they pleased inside Communist territory). I asked him if he was reporting for Hungarian television, and he laughed. 'I'm a member of the International

Ceasefire Commission, would you believe. And what's more, I've got full diplomatic privileges.' The Poles and Hungarians represented the Socialist countries on the committee. 'While I'm here,' he added, glancing round quickly to make sure nobody was listening, 'I'd like a word with you in private.'

We went over to the hotel window. On the pavement below we saw two particularly eye-catching examples of Saigon night-life strolling by. 'What's the official attitude of the representatives of the Socialist world towards morality?' I asked Laszlo, who I knew was no puritan. 'Our colonel is one of those fatherly, understand-ing types,' he replied. 'When we first arrived in Saigon he called us all together and said: "Comrades, I know the temptations here are too great to resist, and I don't expect you to even try. Just remember when you go to bed with one of these lovely Vietnamese girls that she's helping to feed her family. And that makes her a very respectable person." ' I had to admit that Hungarian Communism seemed to take a refreshingly liberal attitude on morals.

'I hear you're waiting for a package,' said Laszlo. He had heard about the arrangements I had made with the Viet Cong and he knew how impatient I was to get hold of the film. 'We'll make sure you get your film all right,' he said. Since the ceasefire agreements the National Liberation Front had set up their own enclave at Tan-Son-Nhut airport just outside Saigon. Inside this enclave, which had the apt nickname of Camp David, North Vietnamese liaison staff enjoyed rights of political immunity. Viet Cong envoys held regular press conferences there for Western corre-spondents. 'Just go along to the next press briefing at Camp David,' Laszlo advised me. 'Colonel Phuong Nam, the press officer, is waiting for you to contact him, but he won't hand anything over to you. The whole point of the exercise is to confuse South Vietnamese intelligence. I'll deliver the film to you myself as soon as it's flown in from Loc Ninh.'

Everything happened just as Laszlo said it would. I went to the airport and was given an unusually cordial reception by Colonel Phuong Nam. I met him outside his hut at the airport, where the press used to roll up daily in a grey bus provided by the Saigon government. The colonel made no mention of a package when I spoke to him. Tin, my Vietnamese colleague, who had recently worked hard to get his nephew Thanh released from prison, went with me to Camp David. After the communiqué had been read out, Tin asked the press officer for the Liberation Front what would happen to someone like him, a collaborator with the Thieu regime, when the Communists took over Saigon. 'We'll give you some good books to read and hope you see the error of your ways,' replied the Viet Cong colonel, smiling.

Three days later in the Atabea restaurant Laszlo gave me the signal. 'The package has arrived safely,' he said. 'I'll be at the West German embassy in the Rue Vo Tanh at eleven o'clock tomorrow morning. Make sure you're there a couple of hours earlier, to give the person tailing you time to cool off and lose interest. The rest is up to you.'

The German ambassador in Saigon was a typical gentleman of the old school with a reputation for being extremely right-wing. Yet when I asked him to send on the film of the Viet Cong zones to Bonn by diplomatic courier, he agreed without a moment's hesitation. So at eleven o'clock sharp, a stately black limousine flying the blue pennant of the control commission pulled up outside the courtyard of the German embassy. I had already told the doorman, Arno Knöchel, an ex-legionnaire, to open the car door immediately; I didn't want any hanging about. Laszlo got out of the car and was shown into the ambassador's office, where I was sitting having tea. He was carrying a big black briefcase, which he casually put down in a corner of the room. The ambassador and Laszlo exchanged pleasantries for about fifteen minutes, then Laszlo took his leave and was shown the way out. The limousine drove off. I opened the case and there were the rolls of film and tape we had taken during our time with the Viet Cong. The briefcase was dispatched to Bonn by courier and arrived there safely a few days later.

Troubled Dreams in Bali

Bali, March 1975

The crashing of the gongs and cymbals of the gamelan orchestra reverberated in my head like the clanging of a blacksmith's anvil. I was in Bali, laid low with another attack of fever. Through the red mist in my eyes I could dimly picture the Hindu temple girls performing next door – figures out of the Ramayana executing stately, measured movements in front of a cardboard temple. They were dancing for the tourists in the soulless atmosphere of a modern, package-tour hotel. Surroundings like these destroyed all the mystery of the Hindu world, torn between the forces of light and darkness, between gods with beatific smiles and Trantrist demons with grotesque masks. The tourists saw none of this, however: all they were being offered was packaged exoticism. My fever was probably caused by a tropical virus picked up on a recent trip to New Guinea. Now I was lying back in a chair in the hotel garden, swallowing the pills the Indonesian doctor had prescribed for me and wiping the cold sweat from my neck and forehead.

As I listened to the orchestra I was reminded of an odd historical coincidence: the two great Hindu dynasties of the Shirivijaya and the Madjapahit, both seafaring Malay peoples, had flourished at the same time as the Khmer empire of Angkor. My mind went back to the performances held every night in Siem Reap outside the Auberge du Temple, and the Balinese dancers and their Cambodian sisters seemed to fuse into one graceful image. But it was ten years since I had stayed in Cambodia – ten years that had seen the world of Sihanouk, the prince worshipped by his peasant subjects as the reincarnation of Krishna, ousted by the nightmare universe of Kali, the Hindu goddess of revenge. This was the hell that had spawned the Khmer Rouge, the murdering fiends who now stood on the altar of their victims' bodies, howling for vengeance.

I had heard from the hotel doctor that Marshal Lon Nol had recently arrived on Bali. The Cambodian head of state had eventually given in to pressure from the Americans and abandoned his country in its darkest hour. Since his recent stroke, Lon Nol, the man who used to call himself the 'Great Dark One', had been reduced to a pathetic figure, hobbling on crutches. President Suharto of Indonesia, who for historical and cultural reasons felt a certain affinity with the Khmer republic, had offered Lon Nol a temporary refuge in Bali, the last remaining Hindu island in Muslim Indonesia. For a moment I considered getting in touch with Lon Nol, but felt too ill to even try.

Towards the end of January I had paid a farewell visit to the Cambodian capital. I could hardly believe the change that had taken place in Phnom Penh; it was just like walking through a mortuary. We had flown from Bangkok in an Air Cambodge plane. When it got to Pochentong it practically had to nose-dive to avoid the artillery fire of the besieging Khmer Rouge. By now the enemy had the city in a stranglehold. It was cut off on all sides and was slowly being throttled to death. The end couldn't be far off. The Khmer Rouge had seized control of Neak Luong and had effectively prevented any river traffic reaching Phnom Penh along the Mekong. Down in the harbour the cargo boats lay idle. They had high fences of wire netting around them, which were meant to trap enemy rockets and detonate them before they could do any serious damage. All the schools and hospitals in the city were filled to overflowing with the wounded and dying, who lay groaning among pools of blood in the corridors and stairways. International relief organizations had set up food kitchens in the half-finished shell of a massive concrete hotel, one of Sihanouk's pet projects. There were thousands of refugees thronging round, waiting for their daily hand-out of rice. The swimming-pool stank of urine and excrement, but there were naked brown children splashing around in it just the same.

The battle front was out along Route 5, two kilometres past the Cham mosque whose tin dome shone silver in the sunlight. The Cambodian Muslims had come here by ox-cart in their hundreds, fleeing from the Khmer Rouge, and had set up camp around their place of worship. The Cham knew that the beleaguered remnants of their people had embarked upon a new era in their tragic history; they also knew it might well be the last. They stood facing the *mihrab*, chanting the Islamic prayers for the dead in faultless classical Arabic. Meanwhile, back in the palace at Phnom Penh, the rehearsals of the Royal Ballet had ended – for once and for all. But in the gardens on the bank of the Tonle Sap the grey-haired old fortune-tellers were being deluged with customers. We thought the Cambodians wanted to know what fate had in store for them when the Red guerilla army eventually took over the city, but apparently we were wrong. 'They're only the same old things – is their fiancée being faithful to them, are they going to be lucky in love, is their wife going to give them lots of children,' said Yung, our young Chinese driver.

It was from Yung I finally managed to find out what had happened to Fillioux, a French AFP correspondent who had gone missing. Fillioux, after much persistent effort, had persuaded the Khmer Rouge and the Cambodian revolutionary government to allow him to film in the 'liberated zones'. He had gone to Cambodia via southern Laos but had only got as far as the border province of Mondulkiri when he was stopped by a mob of black-pyjamaed guerillas and accused of being a spy. They searched him and found a map with his route marked out in red. That was enough: without giving him a chance to prove his innocence, they clubbed him to death with bamboo sticks.

The American State Department had sent to Phnom Penh one of its top experts, John Gunther Dean, to try and sort out the chaos caused by the Lon Nol regime. Dean (born in Berlin with a different name) was said to have a talent for hammering out compromise solutions. He had, for instance, played a major role in negotiating the Laos peace proposals, and even though critics of the settlement claimed it made a seizure of power by the Communist Pathet Lao virtually inevitable, it did at least bring an end to the bloodshed. In Phnom Penh, however, there was no time for any delicate balancing-acts. All along Henry Kissinger had stubbornly refused to back Sihanouk – in fact he had shown himself so hostile to the prince anyone would have thought he had a personal grudge against him. This meant that Ambassador Dean was left to try and play off the professional politicians against the gangsters. The three men he had to reckon with were Prince Sirik Matak, Sihanouk's crafty political opponent; General Lon Non, the delinquent 'little brother' of the Cambodian head of state; and Prime Minister Long Boret, one of the few politicians in the country to command any respect among foreign observers. One other distinguished figure in the jungle of Cambodian politics, former prime minister General In Tam, had retired in a gesture of Buddhist renunciation. Dean's main objective was to persuade Lon Nol to leave the country. Sitting in his embassy in Phnom Penh, which now looked more than ever like a fortified command post, the American proconsul did his best to contain his frustration and exasperation.

By the end of March, however, John Gunther Dean had succeeded in persuading Lon Nol to go into exile. It was to be his last diplomatic coup. Seventeen days later Phnom Penh fell to the barbaric hordes of the Red Anabaptists. And so the 'Stone-Age Communists' acting in the name of Karl Marx and claiming to liberate mankind, took over Cambodia and plunged it headlong into an abyss of unspeakable horror.

The Malayan waiter standing beside me cleared his throat and touched me gently on the arm. I emerged from a fevered sleep to find myself alone under the palm trees, looking up at enormous stars. The tourists had all gone to bed, the orchestra was silent, the dancers had vanished into the night. The gentle gaze of the waiter conjured up a memory of the time in Djakarta in 1954 when I sat next to Aidit, the Indonesian Communist leader. He was later butchered in the mass killings of 1965, along with thousands of like-minded followers. I got up and shook myself to try and clear my befuddled brain, then dragged myself upstairs to my room. The crudely painted wooden masks on the wall looked malevolent, almost frightening, as I put out the light.

In bed that night a host of images kept beating at my brain. Some incidents from our recent three-month trip filming in Australia came back to me with amazing clarity. I had a sudden flashback to the time I spent in the little town of Derby in the Northern Territories. I was sitting at the feet of the old shaman, Baronga. He was naked apart from a loincloth and had greyish-black skin and shaggy, matted hair. He could have been Neanderthal man sitting there with his broad, flat nose, his powerful jaw, his heavy brows and sloping forehead. Baronga picked up a twig and drew a mark in the sand – the spiral, the sacred emblem of the 'Dream World', the sign of endless regeneration, the constant renewal of life. He explained to me in surprisingly good English the pantheistic, cyclical beliefs of the aborigines. 'Life for us is like the waves of the sea. As long as you have an anchor – you know what an anchor is? – you are safe, because you will always return to the same place. We believe that men used to live beside the big sea. Then the great flood came and swept them away. They drowned, but straight away they were changed into rocks and living, moving creatures. We call these rocks and trees and animals Wungur. They are our people, our family.'

The women stood apart from us, keeping a respectful distance. They were wearing shabby cotton dresses and were horribly, pathetically ugly. They stood staring at us with sad expressions, like dumb beasts. They looked like characters out of some ridiculous science-fiction film. Steve, our sound engineer, spoke the thoughts that none of us dared to utter: 'If you're looking for the missing link, that's it in front of you.'

In the mission stations and reservations around Derby, Broome and Beagle Bay you either had to have a strong religious faith or a great deal of human conceit not to believe in the Theory of Evolution. I reflected that Darwinism represented a far more fundamental challenge to Christianity than Marxism: instead of redemption in an afterlife, Marxism merely promised salvation in a utopia this side of the grave.

Another face that kept surfacing in my delirium that night was

Suharto, the 'smiling general' of Indonesia. One image, in particular, stood out clearly. He was officially opening a village on central Sumatra as part of the resettlement programme known as Transmigrasi. The programme was meant to relieve the serious overcrowding problem on the island of Java, where about eighty million people lived herded together, in places at fourteen hundred to the square kilometre. The new settlers, who came from central and east Java, had the unenviable task of trying to cultivate land that was a farmer's nightmare. Naked tree-trunks rose into the sky out of the black, marshy ground. Clouds of buzzing mosquitoes hovered over dark brown pools of water. During this trip we ended up spending an evening strolling through the Chinese district of Jambi. The shadowy outlines of the shops of the Sons of Heaven swam before my eyes once more. The shops belonging to Chinese who did not have Indonesian citizenship had the letters 'WNA-JINA' – 'Chinese foreigner' – written above the entrance, like a mark. The problem of Indonesia's four million Chinese foreign nationals, and their relationship with Red China, was one of Suharto's biggest headaches, and one he still had to find a solution to.

The scene shifted and I was staring, in horrifying close-up, at a slaughtered pig I once saw at a wedding ceremony in the wild highlands of New Guinea. The giant, coal-black Melanesians with their Semitic profiles and Assyrian beards seemed more interested in the dead pig than the primitively decked-out bride with the bare, pointed breasts. In New Guinea pigs were valued not only as dowry but as a traditional peace-offering between warring clans. The day before we had witnessed a fight between two half-naked groups of tribal warriors. All the time the men kept up a plaintive and oddly tuneful singing. Apparently these clashes were never very violent, even though they concerned such things as territorial rights, women, cattle or questions of honour. All that would happen would be that each warrior would try to hit his opponent in the calf with his spear.

Nearby I saw the powerful tusks of about fifty wild boars stacked on top of one another against a tree, like an offering in a temple. In many of the mountain valleys a pig was actually worth more than a woman, and it was quite common for piglets to be suckled by the women of the tribe. This was because the pig had a mystique that had been handed down in tribal legends; for the people of New Guinea it was somehow human. The Australian authorities, and particularly the missionaries, had begun to keep a close eye on the New Guinean tribesmen to make sure they didn't revert to cannibalism. As a result the tribesmen had been forced to use the pig as a substitute for human beings in their ritual feasts. As I looked on, a headman with a magnificent feather head-dress imperiously handed me a piece of solid pig fat. At that moment I woke up, retching.

The boy had pushed a telegram under the door. It had been sent from Jakarta, where the camera team were filming. It said that the previous day the Vietnamese town of Da Nang, home of the biggest military air base in the whole of South-east Asia, had surrendered to the North Vietnamese without a struggle. First in Cambodia, and now in Vietnam, events had taken a disastrous turn for the worse. A spasm of shivering took me. A couple of months ago, at the beginning of January, my editors had suggested I make a detour to Saigon. Since I couldn't get hold of a German crew at such short notice I had to take a Vietnamese team with me, rounded up at the last minute by the indefatigable Tin.

I arrived in Saigon just before the North Vietnamese launched their last major offensive on the city. What they had done, though, was to attack and overrun the town of Phuoc Long, near the Cambodian border. Phuoc Long was only a miserable dump on the edge of the jungle, but it was the first provincial capital the North Vietnamese had managed to capture. The fall of Phuoc Long was a bad omen for President Thieu, who was desperately trying to rally the people of Saigon into a new spirit of patriotic resistance. But it was a comparatively minor threat compared to the long-term strategic implications of the completion of the all-weather road linking the main centres of Tongking with the South Vietnamese province of Tay Ninh. The North Vietnamese coolies and pioneer squads had somehow managed to build this stretch of road through impossible terrain despite terrible physical hardships. The opening of the new road meant that arms and reinforcements could now get from Tongking to Cochin China in only fourteen to eighteen days instead of four months. One immediate consequence was that the troop strength of the North Vietnamese forces south of the 17th parallel was reckoned to have increased to 200,000 since the turn of the year. With all these ominous developments I arrived in Tay Ninh with Tin and the Vietnamese crew feeling understandably tense and on edge. I visted the Cao Dai cathedral in the main town. The only people in the congregation were half a dozen leading members of the sect, clad in their blue and red robes. I tried to speak to them but they just carried on bowing before the mystical eye of Cao Dai, swathed in clouds of incense, and ignored me completely.

By then most of the population had abandoned Tay Ninh. Every so often the North Vietnamese would suddenly begin shelling the deserted market-place, then they would stop just as abruptly. When I gave our driver instructions to go as close as possible to the Black Virgin he protested vigorously, but eventually, after much arguing and haggling, he agreed. We drove towards the Cambodian border and suddenly there it stood, a sinister black pyramid of a mountain looming out of the jungle. The Communists had recently seized the Black Virgin and now had control over the strategically vital 'Fish-hook' sector. It seemed an ill omen. Thirty years ago the Black Virgin had witnessed my baptism of fire when I first arrived in Indochina at the start of the French war.

Many more confused memories haunted my dreams that night in Bali. I saw green stalks in a ricefield that became transported into a delicate, tremulous web. Then the web became a suffocating net, threatening to entangle me in its folds. Then another terrifying image came into view and I saw bloated corpses floating in a lotus pool. When I woke up next morning the crisis was past, and two days later I was sitting on a plane, flying home to Europe.

In Frankfurt Jörg Wimmelmann arranged to meet me. 'You must know why I got in touch with you here,' he said. As it happened I had a pretty shrewd idea. 'The office wants you to fly to Vietnam as soon as possible. It's all happening out there now – Da Nang has fallen, and the North Vietnamese are advancing down the coast towards Saigon.' Four days later I had landed in Saigon. Tran Van Tin was waiting for me at the airport, looking very dapper in a safari suit. 'It's nearly all over,' he said with a grim smile as he steered me through customs and passport control.

The Last Days of Saigon

Saigon, April 1975

Saigon never looked so Asian as it did during those last days before
the fall of the city. As soon as you turned off Tu Do Street and the
flower market, you suddenly found you were the only white
person among a sea of yellow faces. The people of Saigon reacted
to the crisis by hiding behind a mask of indifference. They didn't
want foreigners to see what they were going through, and it was
only when they thought you weren't watching that they allowed
the worry and fear to show. Then there was Canh, my driver. In all
the years I had known him I had never seen him drive so carelessly
or absent-mindedly through the traffic jams in the centre of town.
When I told him off for not concentrating, he suddenly blurted out
all his fear and anxiety. 'You know, Monsieur, in 1954 I left Hanoi
and fled to the South to escape the Communists, and now they've
caught up with me again.' The lady in charge of the telegraph
office, a serious-looking Annamite with her hair drawn back in a
severe bun, took me to one side and asked: 'Is it true that the North
Vietnamese are going to kill all the civil servants working for the
Saigon government?' She said there were rumours going around
that when the North Vietnamese captured Da Nang they picked a
hundred people off the street and shot them, obviously to
intimidate the rest of the population. That was what she'd been
told, anyway. Sometimes you got the feeling the enemy were
deliberately spreading scare stories to cause panic and confusion.

The people of Saigon just wanted to be left alone to nurse their
grief and anxieties in private. For the Vietnamese a whole chapter
in their history, 200 years of collaboration with the West, was
ending on a sour note. They felt bitterly disillusioned by their
recent partnership with the USA. The fickle, frivolous town of
Saigon, Pearl of the Far East, knew it would have to give up many
things: its luxury, its corruption, its hectic bustle, its amazing zest
for living. Soon life in the capital would be as dull and prim and
proper as it was in Hanoi. There had probably been a similar
atmosphere in Shanghai in 1949, when Mao Tse-tung's troops
marched into the Sodom and Gomorrah on the banks of the
Hwang Pu River. The arrival of the soldiers from Hsuchow must
have been like an invasion from another planet.

The photographs that came out of Saigon at that time, showing people staring up at the camera with eyes filled with horror and dread, tell only half the story. The fact remains that the South Vietnamese accepted their fate with a dignity I have never seen the like of, before or since. It showed in the faces of the refugees, whose apparent resignation concealed a driving energy and a fierce will to live. It showed in the conduct of the government troops, who knew as surely as any foreign correspondent that the war was lost, that the day would soon come when they would have to answer before North Vietnamese people's tribunals. And yet, knowing all this, the troops remained exceedingly calm and collected, even in the thick of the fighting at the front. They maintained their dignity right up to the end, in classic Oriental fashion. During those last days this country showed its greatness in defeat, as it got ready to join with the proletarian Sparta in the North, the land of iron discipline and self-control. How on earth could Americans be expected to make anything of a people and a country like this? How could they ever hope to understand Vietnam, when they insisted on dividing it up into 'good guys' and 'bad guys' in their military briefings?

Every day the queues of petitioners outside the American Embassy grew longer. With luck they might get away on the last planes out of the city. These were the little people, the small-fry collaboration always catches in its net – respectable Saigon citizens, terrified out of their wits; GI brides; clerks employed by the countless US agencies. The real profiteers and sharks, the ones who got fat on the proceeds of ten years of American involvement, had planned a safe getaway long ago. They were the real manipulators, the men who pulled the strings behind the scenes, the big operators who ran the black market, the heroin trade, the prostitution racket. They even managed to fix themselves up with American partners who transferred whole chains of Vietnamese brothels to Manila and Bangkok, and it later turned out, Florida and New Mexico, too. The prostitutes were evacuated without legal passports or papers, which meant, of course, that they would be vulnerable to all kinds of blackmail and extortion later on. As for the rest, the decent, honest army officers and civil servants employed by the Saigon government (and there were more of them than the Western press cared to admit), they were all left behind simply because they could not stoop to trading their self-respect for a plane ticket out of the country.

The French Embassy in Saigon was right next door to the American Embassy. The French diplomatic staff had received a directive from the Elysée Palace ordering everyone to stay put, and extra security personnel had been flown in. There were about 10,000 French citizens in the Saigon area, at least eighty per cent of them of Vietnamese extraction. The embassy had organized assembly points for them in the event of a speedy evacuation. In Ambassador Mérillon's study the mood was defiant, harking back to the days of Fort Chabrol. It was as if the French were determined to set an example to the Americans, to show them how a nation with a historic tradition conducted itself in moments of crisis. The Americans, unlike the French, had never known what it was like to lose a war. Perhaps now they would find out. A Washington correspondent summed it up neatly: 'The French lost the war in Vietnam in 1954, at Dien Bien Phu. They were defeated, but it was an honourable defeat. Now we're pulling out of Vietnam, only this time it's called Watergate.' When I went to see Mérillon the little, wiry Frenchman struck a suitably defiant pose, blinked at me, and declaimed, in the best French rhetorical manner: 'I shall remain here on the orders of my head of state. I shall wrap myself in the folds of the tricolor and await the inevitable without flinching.' Over at the German Embassy the mood did not reflect quite the same degree of stern resolve. The only member of staff prepared to stick it out was Arno Knöchel, the janitor. Arno had served in the Foreign Legion and had a number of dependents in Vietnam. After the diplomatic staff were evacuated he went and hoisted a black, red and gold pennant over the entrance to the building. He literally showed the flag.

The defeat of the South hit the government of President Nguyen Van Thieu with hurricane force. In mid-March North Vietnamese tanks and artillery attacked the town of Ban Me Thuot, in the highlands of Annam. The army of the South made a rather half-hearted stand for about four hours. Then General Giap's troops won the day, and from then on there was no holding them. The strongholds of Kontum and Pleiku, which had been built to protect South Vietnam on its vulnerable border with Laos, fell without a struggle. Saigon then decided to carry out a drastic realignment of the front, but it was too late. The whole of Sector 1, which included Quang Tri, Hue and Da Nang, had been more or less left in limbo now that the North Vietnamese had broken through to the plain, so the Saigon generals were forced to order the withdrawal of their élite troops from the narrow northern coastal strip. The plan was for these forces to form a new front line around Nhatrang behind which they could defend the capital, together with the vital hinterland extending to Tay Ninh in the west and the fertile Mekong Delta in the south.

Unfortunately for the Saigon strategists an orderly retreat is one of the most difficult military operations to carry out. To be successful it requires two things: flawless logistical preparation and a high level of troop morale. Both of these vital pre-conditions were lacking. In Hue and Da Nang panic broke out among the troops. The garrison in the old imperial city descended on the harbour at Da Nang like a pack of hounds in full cry. Surprisingly, the veteran troops of the South Vietnamese marines acted shamefully. In their haste to get away they pushed past the long lines of fleeing civilians, sending them flying into the gutter. Where their path was blocked, they simply shot their way through until they got to the harbour and the waiting ships. On board the transport ships and cargo boats that sailed out of Da Nang, crowded with passengers, terrible scenes of looting and violence took place. The marines stripped the civilian refugees of their money and jewellery and raped the women and girls. Those who lacked valuables to hand over were simply thrown overboard.

Meanwhile in North Vietnam Vo Nguyen Giap had been replaced by a new chief of staff, Van Tien Dung, who ordered the North Vietnamese tank columns to make a blitzkrieg assault on the South Vietnamese lines. The infantry had difficulty keeping up with the motorized columns, which sped down the coast meeting very little resistance on the way. The coastal towns of Annam, where the Americans had left behind huge military bases crammed full of equipment, hoisted the white flag without a shot being fired. Nobody tried to hold out long enough to negotiate proper terms of surrender. The Army of the Republic of Vietnam, the ARVN, quietly disintegrated. The North Vietnamese, on the other hand, were riding the crest of a wave. For thirty years they had been fighting an exhausting guerilla campaign involving tremendous sacrifices and physical hardships. Now, suddenly, they were discovering the exhilaration of a mobile war, the thrill of advancing on the enemy in a victorious sweep, carrying all before them. Since the phoney ceasefire had come into operation, the Russians and the Chinese had stepped up their deliveries of equipment and hardware to the North. Thanks to their efforts, the army advancing on the South was mechanized to the hilt. The barefoot guerilla bands had been transformed into a Russian-style armour-plated juggernaut. Even the different stages of the march south were divided up according to Soviet army regulations. The North Vietnamese were taking no chances. The command to go onto the offensive was given only when they outnumbered the enemy three to one. It took just a month for the northern front to shift from the devastated provincial capital of Quang Tri, on the 17th parallel, to the outskirts of Saigon.

Barely eighty kilometres outside the capital two regiments of Catholic paratroopers had dug in in the little town of Xuan Loc in a desperate, last-ditch stand. It was the first resistance the North Vietnamese encountered since the fall of Ban Me Thuot; they had gained, incredibly, more than 1000 kilometres of territory in the course of this one unique campaign. In no time at all Xuan Loc was encircled. General Dung could easily have sent in his assault troops to capture Saigon at once, but he was leaving nothing to chance. Instead of going into the attack, he began assembling more troops in preparation for the final death-blow.

Press coverage of the last days of the war made monotonous reading. The only fighting taking place centred on Route 1, which went east to Xuan Loc. If you drove out past the abandoned, dilapidated US base at Long Binh, then on past the air base at Bien Hoa, after another sixty kilometres you eventually came to the front. After the Geneva ceasefire agreement in 1954 about 300,000 Catholic refugees had fled to Bien Hoa from the North. They had settled in the area and eventually achieved a reasonable standard of living after much hard work and effort. They surrounded themselves with the trappings of their religion – simple concrete churches, altars to the Virgin Mary, imitation Lourdes grottoes. Now these people, who for fifteen years had been the mainstay of the Vietnamese struggle against the inexorable advance of Communism, were once more fleeing before the North Vietnamese divisions. As in 1954, it was the nuns and priests who organized the evacuation. But this time there was a major difference: they had no safe refuge to go to. All they could look forward to was a long day's trek that would take them to the overcrowded suburbs of a doomed city.

The South Vietnamese army had managed to assemble a few batteries and were firing sporadically at the invisible enemy along Route 1. There were no proper lines of defence that we could see; the conditions needed for a serious campaign of resistance were simply not there. We drove along Route 1 until the road suddenly became completely empty – a sure sign that the enemy lay just around the corner. The government troops we met seemed friendly enough, despite the gravity of the situation; some even joked and laughed with us. We were wearing black, red and gold badges with Bao Chi Duc (German press) on them. We did not want to be mistaken for Americans at the front, what with the crowds of refugees.

The soldiers warned us to take care because the North Vietnamese were just over the next ridge. I got the driver to turn the car round and we walked the last few hundred metres to the observation posts. Nothing stirred in the empty fields. But about 300 metres ahead of us the road was blocked by a low bank of earth, probably hiding anti-tank mines. It reminded me of the time we were captured by Viet Cong in the summer of 1973 when we found a similar bank of earth under the arch leading to the 'liberated zones'.

The foreign troops, had left Saigon by this time. Even the US military advisers had packed up and gone. Following coded instructions received over American radio, they had been driven to Tan-Son-Nhut airport and flown out of the country, as if they were being deported. The only white mercenary force left in the city was the press corps. They reacted predictably to the signs of impending disaster, one of their major worries being the threatened wave of militant puritanism, about to descend on Saigon and purge it of its evil ways. Their main target had been the large stock of alcohol left behind by the German legation. The curfew came into force at eight o'clock every evening, which meant you had to dash from the telex office or studio into one of the French restaurants near the flower market. Once you were safely inside you ordered yourself a *steak au poivre*, which always had to be *bleu* or *saigant* because you were in such a hurry. You would curse because there were no strawberries from Dalat on the menu, knowing full well that Dalat had been taken over by the Communists weeks ago. But it was all part of the game. One of the last acts of the Thieu regime had been to ban alcohol; so your wine was now served in cups, like coffee.

At eight o'clock everyone would meet in the Continental. This big old barn of a place, in the very heart of Saigon, still had a slightly musty air about it. Nothing much seemed to have changed since the old colonial days: most of the waiters and 'boys' had worked there for at least thirty years. The most recent owner of the Continental was a son of the Franchinis, an old-established Eurasian family in Saigon. He had been generally popular and respected among the French correspondents, and had a reputation as both a connoisseur of Oriental art and a fascinating conversationalist. He and his wife had got out of Saigon in time and had gone to live in Hong Kong. He had left the hotel in the care of the regular staff, mostly little old men, wrinkled and hard of hearing. It took them all their time to write down an order correctly. They spent most of the day sleeping on their mats in the corridors. They would smile gratefully at regular guests every time a piastre note was slipped into their hand. Every evening they would go back and forwards with little tripping steps, fetching ice and soda for the noisy crowd of journalists who had commandeered the alcohol left in the German Embassy. Everyone would drink late into the night, telling their favourite stories over and over again: episodes from the Tet offensive of 1968 and the spring offensive of 1972, tales about President Diem and President Thieu, stories of monks and generals and small-time crooks. The conversation always got back to women and smut in the end, though. In Rilke's *Cornet* he calls it 'Songs of Love and Death'. In our cocked-up colonial war we sang of blood and sex.

There were some young Vietnamese girls in the bar, sitting beside the reporters and looking like exotic blooms. The more glasses of alcohol the Europeans knocked back the more beautiful the girls became. They themselves hardly touched a drop. On the wall was a publicity poster left over from the days when Saigon was still trying to attract tourists. It showed an attractive Asian girl wearing the national dress, the *ao dai*. She was standing seductively among flowers, a slightly blurred vision of loveliness done out in pretty pastel shades. The words at the bottom of the poster beckoned: 'Follow me to Saigon!'

So journalists ended up being the last clients of the Saigon bar girls, standing in as father confessors before the day of judgement. In the last hours before the fall of the city, the girls poured out their hearts to us. One of them was resigned and philosophical about it all. 'When the Viet Cong take over I'll go and plant rice for them – what's wrong with that? I come from a peasant family anyway.' Another one claimed she would never be able to give up wearing nice clothes and having a good time. She couldn't bear the thought of the humiliation she would have to go through; all that was left for her was to throw herself in the Saigon River. The third one was defiant: 'When the people in Saigon were doing well for themselves and were able to buy more or less anything they fancied, I wanted a share of it all as well. So now when the people have to work hard and go without, it's only fair I should go without too.' Most of the girls came from large extended families and maintained close ties with them. Some had sacrificed their youth and good looks to help provide for their families; they felt depressed at the thought of how they were going to manage in future, without the extra money coming in.

The prostitutes you saw flitting about the Rue Tu Do were, in their own way, simply following in the footsteps of the two legendary Hai Ba Trung sisters. According to the old Vietnamese story, these women defied their Chinese conquerors by choosing to take their own lives rather than suffer defeat. The legend is a good illustration of how tough and resilient the Vietnamese are underneath it all. And that applies particularly to Vietnamese women. They are not like Siamese women, for example, who are basically good-natured and uncomplicated, true creatures of instinct. The Vietnamese woman, like her Chinese sister, is essentially cerebral. When she throws herself away, it is either a calculated act or an act of despair – sometimes both, but never the result of thoughtlessness or caprice. That evening I sat in the Continental watching a girl called Minh. She looked respectable enough, even demure, as she stood there motionless like a doll with her heavily made-up feline eyes. She reminded me of a quotation from Graham Greene's novel, *The Quiet American*: 'She's no child. She's tougher than you'll ever be. Do you know the kind of polish that doesn't take scratches? That's Phuong.'

Right up until the very end there were always crowds round the terrace of the Continental – beggars, cripples, shoeshine boys, prostitutes of both sexes, souvenir-sellers. As the police force gradually disbanded they grew progressively more bold. One exception was the local bookseller, who continued to be a model of decorum right up to the last. He always had a marvellous collection of books on sale about Indochina. On top of the pile lay *The Quiet American*. I saw one of my German colleagues leafing through it, and I told him to buy it. I think it is probably the best book ever written about Vietnam. The action of the novel takes place between 1951 and 1952, and its setting is the terrace of the Continental. The main theme is the three-cornered relationship between Fowler, an ageing English journalist, Pyle, a young American secret agent, and Phuong, a Vietnamese girl. Fowler has been living with Phuong for two years when Pyle, the quiet American of the title, suddenly appears on the scene. He falls in love with Phuong and promises her marriage and security. She just has to say the word and he will make an honest woman of her. In the end the abandoned Englishman tips off the Viet Minh, who lure his rival into an ambush and kill him. The first time I read this book, many years ago now, the story struck me as being heavily symbolic. Greene had, in fact, anticipated with uncanny accuracy the direction things would take in Indochina. The character of Phuong stood for Vietnam: the ageing, Francophile Englishman symbolized France, the colonial power: while with his portrait of the young, naive, thoughtless Pyle, Greene seemed to prophesy, with bleak lucidity, the American invasion of Vietnam.

Much has been written about the satisfaction the French were meant to have felt at America's discomfiture in Vietnam. The French were undoubtedly better informed than the Americans; they had closer links with the country, and they very quickly recognized the USA could never win the war. In addition to all this there was a tension almost amounting to jealousy between the older, experienced, jilted lover, and the young, wealthy rival from the New World – naive, brutal and yet somehow impotent. The French army was never quite the same after its defeat at Dien Bien Phu. It never really got over Indochina. It suffered forever after from what the novelist Jean Larteguy, a former paratroop officer, called the 'yellow sickness'.

In the early evening we took another quick scout along Route 1 in the direction of Xuan Loc. The North Vietnamese were now installed on both sides of the road. In the neighbouring town of Tu Duc the local Communist propaganda unit had actually come out into the open and told the local people there would be a truce until 1 May. If, however, President Thieu had not stepped down by then the battle for Saigon would begin, and after that it would be a case of every man for himself. Back in Saigon, too, everyone was waiting for the president to resign. He had been due to make a speech at the big Confucian festival in honour of Huong Vuong, the mythical founding father of the Vietnamese people. However, he had cried off at the last minute and decided instead to appear on television at eight o'clock that evening, just when the curfew was beginning.

Nguyen Van Thieu, the insignificant little man with the poker face who had been so unjustly blackened by the Western press, showed his true stature during the final hours of his government. 'The United States have not kept faith,' he said, barely controlling his anger. 'They have acted badly. They are inhuman. They are not to be trusted. They are irresponsible. I would never have believed a man like Henry Kissinger capable of abandoning our people to the terrible fate that lies in store for us.' Thus Thieu finally spoke out against his treacherous American ally and in doing so proved that he was more than a mere puppet. In his final moment of bitter defeat, Thieu took his place among the tragic successors of Ngo Dinh Diem. But among the superstitious inhabitants of Saigon Thieu's fall had been a foregone conclusion since the last Vietnamese New Year's festival. I picked up this astrological titbit from Minh, the Vietnamese girl. According to her, the head of state was born under the sign of the Mouse, which meant the Year of the Cat would be crucial for him. She pointed out that Ngo Dinh Diem, also a 'Mouse', was toppled and murdered in 1963, another Year of the Cat. If Thieu was lucky enough to escape with his life this time round, it would probably be due to the astrological influence of his wife, who was born under the sign of the Horse.

At midnight we broke the curfew and drove through the deserted streets in a car with a special CD number-plate. Police patrols were busy cordoning off crossroads with barbed-wire barricades. At Tan-Son-Nhut airport the evacuation of civilians was going ahead round the clock under American supervision and in an atmosphere of uneasy tension. The local police had been joined on the streets by suspicious-looking figures in black pyjamas. These were the volunteer militia and they were the last remaining reserve forces the government had at its disposal. These troops were undisciplined and unreliable; they had already started looting and rioting in the city. The sooner the North Vietnamese took control of Saigon now the better it would be for its people. That night we ended up in the Viking bar of the Palace Hotel. We were the only ones in the place apart from a few American stragglers. The other reporters had been waiting all day for news of Thieu's resignation, like vultures hovering over a dying animal. Now they were laughing loudly and fooling around with the waitresses. It was all too much to stomach.

The North Vietnamese victory was handed to them on a plate. It came far sooner than the politburo in Hanoi had expected. The original objective of the highland offensive had clearly not been the capture of Saigon: General Dung would have been quite happy to rest on his laurels after his spectacular successes in the Hue area. But the dramatic and unexpected collapse of the South suddenly set things in motion. While the North Vietnamese were

hastily assembling their strategic reserves in star-shaped forma-
tions to spearhead an attack on Saigon, they also moved the bulk of
their anti-aircraft defence from Tongking to the South. Hanoi was
still expecting the US Air Force to make a last-minute intervention to give their South Vietnamese allies a breathing space.
But President Gerald Ford, who had taken over from Nixon after
the Watergate affair, had other things on his mind.

The rapid advance of the North Vietnamese army thwarted the
plans for compromise solutions and transitional arrangements
drawn up by the French. Mérillon, always quick to spot an
opening, had urged the Quai d'Orsay to act as mediator between
the two sides. The main priority was to find a successor to Thieu
whom Hanoi would be prepared to sit down with at the negotiating table. The ceasefire agreement of 1973 had made provision for
a Council of National Reconciliation as an interim solution to the
crisis. It was a brilliant idea, logical and apparently feasible, like
so many other schemes put forward by the French diplomatic
corps. Unfortunately it did not accord with the harsh realities of
the situation, or the grim determination of the Communists.

For two days all eyes were fixed expectantly on General Duong
Van Minh. But Big Minh no longer believed in his role as
Vietnam's saviour. In a crisis like this the blessing of Paris was
virtually worthless. He knew only too well that his eleventh-hour
attempt at a neutralist intervention was doomed to fail, as it had
failed twelve years ago when he had been instrumental in bringing
down Ngo Dinh Diem. His political ambitions had collapsed then
too.

The well-meaning, long-suffering general invited the press to
interview him in his villa, situated next to the cathedral in a shady,
tree-lined avenue. 'I know I shall shortly be called on to lead the
government of my country – or rather what's left of it,' he said.
'The very thought is a nightmare, believe me.' Looking at this
awkward, rather clumsy man you could see how much he regretted
being dragged away from his quiet life by the vagaries of politics.
He would have been far happier to have been left in peace to grow
his orchids. Who knows, for a brief moment he may have toyed
with the idea of becoming a Vietnamese Marshal Pétain. But it was
not to be. The only role left to him now was the humiliating office
of a Vietnamese Admiral Dönitz. Because of the efficiency of the
North Vietnamese army all he could now do was surrender
unconditionally. Yet nobody at that press conference had any idea
that a few days later, on 30 April, North Vietnamese T-54 tanks

would go thundering past the deserted American embassy, smash through the iron railings of the Doc Lap Palace and complete the destruction of the Republic of South Vietnam. Before the North Vietnamese political commissars finally dismissed him, Duong Van Minh, the twenty-four-hour president, murmured to a foreign correspondent: 'The best side won.'

The ten days preceding the fall of Saigon went by in an atmosphere of frenzied excitement. The Americans had already issued details of their evacuation plan to all the Western foreign nationals still left in Saigon. On D-Day the following coded message was to be relayed over the US radio station in Saigon: 'The temperature has reached 105° Fahrenheit.' We would then hear Bing Crosby sing 'I'm Dreaming of a White Christmas'. This would be the signal for everyone to dash to the waiting helicopters and be flown out to the waiting US 7th Fleet. I had decided not to be a part of this undignified scramble for safety. Thirty years ago I had arrived in this country like a conquistador discovering the New World. I didn't want to have to sneak out of it by the back door like some kind of pariah, escorted by the American marines.

So, together with a few colleagues, I decided to stay on and wait for the North Vietnamese to take over. It was a calculated risk, one I was prepared to take. Then a cable came from head office telling me my special programme on Vietnam was due to go out on 2 May. That meant we would have to work flat out to get the editing done in time, so on 26 April, without more ado, we flew back to Europe.

Indochina, *Mon Amour*

On the flight home, 26 April 1975

The Air France jumbo jet climbed into the air in a steep, spiralling curve. On the ground below we could see North Vietnamese advance guards dotted round the outskirts of the suburbs of Saigon. The pilot had to watch out for them, and for the Soviet SAM rockets that had been moved into position along Route 13. I found out later my plane was the last commercial flight out of Saigon. Nobody on board had any idea that the fall of the capital was just three days away, but all of us sensed we were leaving for good. Even if we did return some day everything would have changed: the city on the banks of the Saigon River, the country of South Vietnam, the whole of Indochina itself. It would all be alien and unfamiliar. The cameramen, whom I would never had thought capable of such emotion, were clearly moved as they gazed down at the familiar landscape. Below us the flooded ricefields and the broad arteries of the Mekong Delta shone golden and bloody in the last rays of the sun, like the colours, indeed, of the South Vietnamese Republic that was disappearing forever into the limbo of history. The steward served champagne. We had managed to escape the tragedy but there was no sense of relief. The prevalent feeling was of grief and pain – like the end of an affair. They should have played 'Autumn Leaves', but instead we had to listen to a French pop song.

The drive to the airport at Tan-Son-Nhut had not been quite as bad as we expected. It was only when we got to the last security checkpoints that we came across long queues of people and vehicles. There was no panic, and the policemen were trying to be as helpful as possible. The huge throng of refugees trying desperately to push their way to the departure lounge were neither noisy nor violent. On many of the faces was a look of deep resignation that told more about Saigon's likely future than hysteria or rage. Nobody bothered to look at the huge, unfinished memorial inside the airport whose foundation stone had been laid two years ago by President Thieu in honour of Vietnam's 'victorious' American allies. When we passed through customs and passport control there was no panic or jostling there, either. Ironically, our flight was not even fully booked, so we were able to take 250 kilos of excess baggage without any problem.

Most of the passengers were Vietnamese who possessed French citizenship. Everyone was calm and composed. Quite a few of the Vietnamese clearly belonged to the cream of Saigon society. They chatted to one another, apparently relaxed and at ease. It was as if they were taking a page out of their French history books and trying to imitate the nobles of the *ancien régime* who danced minuets before they went to the scaffold. 'How can they sit there and be so unaffected by what's happening to their country?' asked a German welfare worker. He hadn't understood a thing.

Half an hour before we set out for the airport Minh had rung me at the hotel. She said goodbye politely and wished me *'bon voyage'*. She didn't mention the worry and fear she must have been feeling. I promised to take the first plane back to Saigon as soon as the film was finished, if it was possible. The faithful Tin, who had worked for us all those years, came as far as the foot of the boarding ramp. 'Do you think I should try and escape in a helicopter?' he asked. I didn't know what to respond. 'You have to decide that for yourself,' was all I could say. 'You have to make the choice between living in a foreign land and being oppressed in your own country.' But I promised we would give him all the help he needed if he ever turned up in the West. Tin, who was usually so excitable and tense, now stood beside the aeroplane, apparently unmoved, and made a formal little bow of farewell.

We all hoped the Vietnamese who stayed on in Saigon would survive this ordeal as they had survived so many others in the past. If they spent long enough living and working with the North Vietnamese they might end up passing some of their gentler, softer ways onto the northerners. In times of crisis like this Asians possessed a degree of adaptability that Westerners found totally baffling. And it wasn't just opportunism, either: it was more to do with inner strength, a tenacious will to live. In the end the South Vietnamese would go along with the whole business of revolutionary Socialism, just as the political commissars knew they would. Little by little – starting with the children and teenagers – they would become trapped by their own pretence, prisoners of the very role they were acting out, until eventually they would be imperceptibly absorbed into the new revolutionary order.

The jumbo jet stopped over at Bangkok. I stayed on the plane as I didn't think I could face the sight of happy, carefree Asians that day. Why, I wondered, did I feel this overpowering sense of personal loss? After all, I had spent five years as a correspondent in Africa and had lived through the shock of decolonization in the Congo. Yet when I left black Africa all I experienced was a sense of relief; I felt as if I had had enough and simply couldn't take any more. Then again, I spent many years reporting on the Arab world, and during my time in the Lebanon hills I studied the language and religion in an effort to learn something about the country. But I felt on familiar ground there, or at least in a culture that had obvious points of contact with my own. The unique, almost painful attraction of Vietnam lay in its contradictions, in the way it managed to be hard and unapproachable and yet seductive and exotic and provocative, all at the same time. Vietnam had a feminine mystery all its own. People have often said to me that the quasi-colonial situation we found ourselves in must have made life in the Far East so comfortable that we couldn't help but feel nostalgia for it. And yet I feel exactly the opposite to be true. The fascination of this part of the world is all about the uncluttered, unadorned simplicity of its life-style, the often flawless natural beauty of its people. The cultivated European arriving in Indochina must have seemed almost barbaric in comparison.

The alcohol we had been steadily downing since the start of the flight gradually took effect, and we began to get a bit maudlin. The French tea-planter sitting next to me kept talking about Vietnam as if it was a sweetheart who had reluctantly given him up to become a nun and follow strict orders. He obviously felt that if he returned he would be able to see her only through the iron railings of the convent; even then he probably wouldn't recognize the face behind the veil. Like him, I had the feeling I was not only turning my back on the memories of my youth, I was leaving behind a whole part of my adult life – a whole way of life, in fact. Perhaps I was being too sentimental about my thirty years in Vietnam. After all, how much was memory and how much imagination? Yet on that flight my thoughts were all about Indochina, *mon amour*.

THE THIRD INDOCHINESE WAR

The Chinese

Re-education and Realignment

Ho Chi Minh City, August 1976

It will always be a mystery to me why Hanoi's information service suddenly invited me back to Vietnam to film a report, fifteen months after the capture of Saigon. I can only suppose the ministries and security services in Communist countries are so persuaded by their own propaganda and their own ideology that they cannot conceive how shocking and cynical their methods seem to someone brought up in the West. We are simply not used to seeing political facts being so ruthlessly manipulated and tailored to fit the party line. That, anyway, is the only explanation I can think of for the fact that on our first day back in Saigon we were asked to film, of all things, the human flotsam and jetsam washed up on the beaches of the new, reunified, Socialist Vietnam by the collapse of capitalism and imperialism.

The first stop on our tour of inspection was a prostitutes' home. We were driven out to the suburb of Tu Duc where the authorities had taken over an old training school for Catholic nuns. The school was fenced in with barbed wire and armed guards stood at the entrance. The authorities had herded together 600 girls with the aim of knocking immorality out of them by dint of hard, useful labour. The girls sat weaving baskets and mats. Those who were illiterate were taught reading and writing by female supervisors. The girls knitted baby clothes for the Socialist community shops and did some planting and weeding in the garden. Apart from the stern-faced party matrons who ran the centre we saw a few Catholic nuns gliding silently about. In front of the crude propaganda posters promising a happy, virtuous future stood a solitary statue of St Joseph. In his hand he held a lily, the symbol of chastity.

A pleasant-faced Vietnamese supervisor gave us a few statistics.

235

The American occupation and the Thieu regime had left 500,000 prostitutes in their wake, 200,000 in Saigon itself. After a six-month course here the girls would be rehabilitated and sent out to live and work in the New Economic Zones. Most of the prostitutes in Tu Duc were poor-looking things, plain and unattractive, victims of a brutal world of men and armies. They sat working away, timid and well-behaved, stealing inquisitive glances at our camera equipment and giggling every now and then. The prettier, bolder ones sneaked sidelong coquettish glances at us when they thought the supervisors weren't looking. The more up-market members of the profession, the *poules de luxe* as they used to be called, were noticeably absent from these strictly-run hostels of the Good Red Shepherd. Either they had managed to escape from Saigon in time or they had got themselves fixed up with new protectors and clients among the North Vietnamese commissars, already notorious for the discrepancy between their public pronouncements and private morality. Looking at the caged birds of Tu Duc, it was difficult to feel anything but sorry for them. At the end of the day they had to assemble in a tiled hall and clap their hands in time to a revolutionary song with an all-too-familiar chorus: 'Vietnam, Ho Chi Minh! . . . Vietnam, Ho Chi Minh!'

The next place on our list was a centre for drug addicts. Formerly a Catholic boarding school, it had been transformed into a kind of fortified prison. We were told the corrupt regime of President Thieu had produced 100,000 drug addicts, 20,000 of them in Saigon itself. Most patients seemed to come from middle-class backgrounds, but they included a fair number of war-wounded who had initially taken heroin in an attempt to relieve their pain or despair. The atmosphere was tense and harrowing. A doctor explained that they used Eastern and Western medicine to wean their patients from the drugs. They had obtained good results with acupuncture, and they found 'music and movement' exercises to be very helpful. The inmates of this institution (we were probably only allowed to see the milder cases) sat staring listlessly in front of them every time there was a break between exercises, which seemed to be based on some form of T'ai-Chi. Once they were cured they would be sent off to work in the new pioneer zones, like the prostitutes. Most would probably die out there. At the end of our visit the patients sat round in a circle, singing and clapping in time to the inevitable chorus of 'Vietnam, Ho Chi Minh! . . . Vietnam, Ho Chi Minh!'

Our third port of call on the road to rehabilitation was the orphanage at Diuc Quang, just south of Cholon. This time we found ourselves in a Buddhist institution dating from the time of the American war. A huge statue of Buddha still stood in the courtyard, but it was draped in red banners bearing revolutionary Marxist slogans. About 300 orphans aged between six and seventeen lived there. The Buddhist monks had been driven away and replaced by teachers from the old Communist underground with proven track records. The children included a fair sprinkling of the cigarette-sellers, shoeshine boys and pickpockets I used to see crowding the terrace of the Continental in Saigon. They were being raised in the strict discipline of the Socialist state, not that there was really much to object to in that. We came across a handful of the sad by-products of the foreign occupation – half-a-dozen Eurasian children with wispy blond hair and slanting blue eyes. We also saw two dark-skinned girls with curly hair and thick lips who had obviously been fathered by black American GIs. The place was run as strictly as an army camp. At the end of our visit the children lined up at the foot of the Buddha statue and applauded us. As we took our leave a familiar chorus rang out across the courtyard in shrill unison: 'Vietnam, Ho Chi Minh! . . . Vietnam, Ho Chi Minh!'

Arno Knöchel was waiting for me in a Volkswagen outside the Majestic Hotel. 'Get in quick! We'll drive straight to the German embassy, then it'll take the people tailing you a while to find out where you've gone. I've arranged a get-together with Madame Tin.' We went haring off in the direction of the Rue Vo Tanh and the German embassy. Arno, the ex-legionnaire, had stayed behind to look after the building. He was guarding it with his life; it had become his own little kingdom and he had refused to budge from the place even when the Communists took over the capital. 'How's your friend Tin getting on?' Knöchel wanted to know. 'It's a long story,' I said with a rueful smile.

On 29 April 1975, three days after I left South Vietnam, Tran Van Tin, my long-standing Vietnamese friend and colleague, escaped from Saigon on one of the last American helicopters to leave the city. He spent some time in a refugee camp in Guam then reached the United States, where a German broadcaster had managed to get him a temporary residence permit. Between us we organized his flight to Germany, where I found him a job in television. Unfortunately, however, Tin had left his wife and children in Vietnam. The only relative who had managed to get away in the helicopter with him was his young nephew Thanh, who was with us the time we were captured by the Viet Cong. He had since flown out to join his uncle in Wiesbaden. Thanh, who was a bachelor, quickly put down roots in Germany, but Tin seemed to sink into a state of despair. It was quite obvious what the trouble was: he could not get over the fact that he had left his next-of-kin behind in Vietnam. We decided to transfer him to our Paris studio, where there would be plenty of other Vietnamese for him to talk to, and where he could set about acquiring French nationality. But the change made not the slightest bit of difference. Tin's separation from his wife and children meant, for him, disgrace. He would have to retrieve his honour. So he launched himself into the fight to save his family with the kind of grim determination you only ever find in a Vietnamese. Before I left for Saigon he gave me a letter to take to his wife, together with a few hundred dollars in cash.

It was raining heavily as I arrived at the German embassy, and I could only hope the police spies had got fed up watching for me and gone home. Knöchel had started keeping geese in the forecourt because the last time the building was broken into the guard dogs hadn't even barked. But the geese could be relied on to warn of any intruders: they had been kept for exactly the same purpose in classical times, and had once saved the Roman Capitol from being attacked by the Gauls. Madame Tin was waiting for me inside, dressed in a simple *ao dai*. She was wearing dark glasses, but I could see that her eyes were red and puffy from crying. When I handed her the letter and the money she burst into tears. She had brought along her daughter, a neat, well-behaved girl who followed our conversation with a grave expression. 'I want to join my husband,' sobbed Madame Tin. 'I want him back again. We're being hounded all the time by the Communists. Every day I have to face the thought I might be sent into the jungle with my three children. Hundreds of thousands of people have been taken prisoner or gone missing. Everyone from a middle-class background is being sent to the clearing zones. Most of them become ill and a lot of them die. If I can't join Tin then I'll kill myself and the children.'

Arno Knöchel stood listening to her, a look of consternation on his face. He knew that hers was just one case among thousands. The worst thing about the repression going on was that it was so unpredictable, so totally random. Soldiers who had been conscripted into Thieu's army quite against their will had been kept prisoner for over a year in the so-called re-education camps. Quite a few had been released afterwards, but by then they had been reduced to physical wrecks. Time and time again I heard people say that the worst thing about the revolutionary authorities was not their maliciousness or their vindictiveness, but the totally haphazard way they went about things.

I asked Madame Tin if her husband would have been better off staying in Vietnam instead of fleeing to the West. She stopped crying and let out a horrified shriek. 'Oh no, they would have killed him if he'd stayed behind!' She gave me a letter for Tin and I promised to do all I could from the Paris end. I told her the main thing was for her to be patient and have faith. They were empty words, and I knew it. Knöchel steered her out through a side-door into the street, trying to attract as little attention as possible. The rain was still teeming down when she left.

Luckily, however, this family drama was to have a happy ending barely three months after I returned from South-east Asia. When I first got back to Paris and saw Tran Van Tin again, the man was so depressed he seemed practically on the verge of hysteria. He couldn't sleep, he was no good at his job any more, and he was using up all his energy making countless petitions to every French and Vietnamese government body he could think of. I gave him the same advice I had given his wife and told him to be patient. The immigration authorities in Ho Chi Minh City were in such a chaotic state that it would take at least a year before his application was even considered. In the meantime we could help speed things up a bit by handing out a few bribes in the right quarters. (Those paragons of virtue, the northern revolutionaries, had succumbed to the corrupt ways of the South amazingly quickly.) But Tin brushed aside my arguments. 'I'm going to go the whole hog,' he said. 'I'm going to try and create an enormous scandal. I know what the Communists and the Vietnamese are like, and I know how to get round them. All I need is one chance.'

He had managed to find his adoptive father at last, and the mysterious gentleman turned out to be a retired colonel in the Foreign Legion. The colonel, who was blessed with an impressive-sounding aristocratic surname, would do all he could to help. He said he had a large number of useful contacts and claimed he was distantly related to Madame Giscard d'Estaing. He started off by getting Tin his French citizenship in an incredibly short time. Now Tin could start on his long, lonely battle with the Vietnamese diplomatic envoys in Paris. How he even managed to get near the ambassador of the Socialistic Republic of Vietnam in the first place I shall never know. The fact remains, however, that he pestered His Excellency to death, even phoning him up late at night. He managed to wring a promise out of him that Prime Minister Pham Van Dong himself would personally look into the matter. Tin then stood for hours in the pouring rain outside the building in the Rue Le Verrier, holding a large placard spelling out his grievance. When nothing seemed to be working and his wife still hadn't received an exit permit, he tried one last desperate tack. He threatened to set fire to himself outside the Vietnamese embassy. He issued an ultimatum to the envoys, and invited reporters and photographers to view the spectacle. The German television networks decided not to film the burning and the French felt the same way.

But Tran Van Tin would not admit defeat. Via the South Korean embassy he contacted an official camera team from Seoul. He knew President Park Chung Hee would not pass up such a golden opportunity of denouncing the inhumanity of the Vietnamese Communists. Tin had gone past the point of no return; he was determined to go through with it. Things were just reaching a climax when he phoned me up at home late one night. He was so excited he could hardly stammer out the news. He had just received an official communication from Vietnam informing him that his wife and three children would be arriving in Paris the day after next on an Air France flight. So everything turned out happily for Tin in the end, and his dream came true at last on the tarmac at Charles de Gaulle airport. Today Tin is running an organization in Paris dedicated to the establishment of human rights in Vietnam.

We were back again on Route 13, the old Road to Peace. The monsoon clouds were hanging low in the dark sky, just as I remembered them. It was a nice gesture on the part of the authorities to allow us to revisit the area where we had been held prisoner in the summer of 1973, exactly three years before. We saw hardly any signs of the debris of wrecked tanks and rusting weapons we had noticed then. The mutilated landscape was now covered with grass as tall as a man which completely hid the scars of battle. The Vietnamese called this reed-like plant-cover 'American grass'. The tarmac surface had also been repaired – a sure sign that Route 13, which led to the Cambodian border in the north, had become strategically important again. We made a wide detour to avoid the army base at Lai Khe. On the day of the surrender the South Vietnamese divisional commander at the camp had ordered his men to fall in and stand to attention. Then, as the South Vietnamese flag was lowered for the last time, he fired a bullet into his brain.

Everyone in our Volkswagen van was feeling a bit on edge, mainly because of the new escorts and supervisors assigned to us in Saigon. There was one North Vietnamese in particular, a young man by the name of Map, who made no attempt to conceal his hostility. His bulging frog's eyes never left us for a second. We learnt later he had reported to Hanoi that we were secret agents working for the West who were harbouring subversive plans. The militant woman journalist from the revolutionary committee in Ho Chi Minh City also got on our nerves, constantly haranguing us with propaganda. Luckily our guides from Hanoi, Madame Tu and Mr Hong, who had been asked to show us round by Vietnamese television, were completely different. They were always friendly and eager to help, but once we got to the South they had to take a back seat. Revolutionary vigilance was the order of the day in South Vietnam – which meant that everywhere we went we were followed by suspicious, furtive eyes. Fortunately, however, we met up with Colonel Phuong Nam in Ho Chi Minh City. During the closing stages of the war he had been press officer at Camp David, the North Vietnamese diplomatic enclave at Saigon Airport. Judging by the size of his Citroën, he was now well up in the Party ranks. But not even Colonel Phuong Nam could allay the suspicions of the security service. The fact that the Vietnamese State Police had been trained in East Germany did not make things easier for us.

The place we were heading for was the provincial capital of An Loc, once a vital strategic position and now reduced to a pile of rubble. Map kept assuring us that it was 'a Vietnamese Stalingrad', though he failed to mention that the heroic defenders of An Loc had been South Vietnamese paratroopers. All that was left of the main shopping street were some charred and blackened walls. The few people left were living in makeshift shacks or straw huts. In the market, villagers from the local hill-tribes were selling piles of fruit and manioc they had grown in clearings in the jungle. They included several Cambodians, but they were mostly from the tribe of primitive jungle-dwellers known to the Vietnamese as the Moi or 'wild men', who were related to the Montagnards of the highlands of Annam.

The Moi had dark-brown skin and curly hair; they looked coarse and big-boned beside the slender Annamites. They tended to run around half-naked most of the time, and they wore thick necklets as ornaments. You often saw them carrying heavy baskets on their backs, too. I asked our guide the names of the various branches of this primitive people, and he told me they were called the Punong, the Chauman and the Stieng. The last name rang a bell with me. I remembered how in his book *La Voie Royale*, André Malraux tells of an encounter between Claude, his hero, and some Stieng tribesmen. He then goes on to describe the sense of primeval shock aroused by these survivors of the Stone Age. The Stieng I saw in An Loc looked perfectly harmless as they crowded round the overloaded, clapped-out old bus that arrived from Loc Ninh, rattling and groaning.

Everywhere you looked soldiers and policemen stood with rifles at the ready. Suddenly we heard shooting. A handful of armed men ran along the red laterite road towards a barrier, firing their rifles and shouting at the top of their voices. The civilians standing around dived for cover. The incident lasted only two minutes, but the officials in our party looked extremely embarrassed. The frog-eyed Map, who would come out with any lie, no matter how absurd, to conceal awkward facts, explained that the soldiers had been chasing warthogs. But the captain who had welcomed us to An Loc clearly thought this was a bit far-fetched. 'A prisoner has just escaped from jail and run into the woods,' he said tersely. 'He has been recaptured.'

We were taken out onto the concrete platform of the South Vietnamese command post. We looked out upon a rolling landscape that stretched in an unbroken sweep from Loc Ninh to Cambodia. We caught sight of a tank graveyard with a dozen armour-plated monsters lying rusting in the damp air. Their tracks were broken and their turret hatches forced open, and their sides had been torn by bazooka fire. They were Russian T-54s. Map refused to allow us to film them, despite our protests. Even the good-natured captain shrugged his shoulders and mumbled: 'If they weren't ours it'd be all right, but since they are . . .'

On our return to Ho Chi Minh City we stopped off at the village of Tan Khai, a pioneer settlement in a New Economic Zone. In the spring of 1972 we had stood in exactly the same spot and watched as the South Vietnamese counter-offensive collapsed in the face of sporadic firing by a few North Vietnamese troops. Here, too, the bomb craters were overgrown with 'American grass', but there were still a few mines concealed in the ground and some of the newly-arrived settlers had been killed by them. The chairman of the local revolutionary committee (they always had to get 'revolutionary' in somewhere) explained the principle behind the new villages. About 5800 people, or 1100 families, had been transplanted from Saigon to this bleak, infertile, mine-ridden region. None of the settlers had come here of their own accord; they had simply been bundled onto a lorry – under threat of losing their food ration – and dumped outside a row of huts which literally consisted of four posts and a straw roof. The townspeople, none of whom had ever worked the land before, had to get on with the task of irrigating the thin laterite soil, clearing the under-growth, and building themselves accommodation as best they knew how. Of course there was nothing wrong, in principle, with relocating one and a half million people from the hopelessly overcrowded metropolis on the banks of the Saigon River. And the policy of reclaiming hitherto unused land in various parts of South Vietnam undoubtedly had its merits. But the way this massive operation was carried out seemed criminally disorganized and chaotic.

The new settlers seemed desperately short of everything: a basic knowledge of farming skills, implements, fertilizers, seed, the lot. In theory, during the first six months of their compulsory deportation they should have received sixteen kilos of rice per person per month, together with half a kilo of salt. But this was rarely adhered to. After a while malaria set in, and medicines were in short supply. There must have been cholera in Tan Khai, because large signs told the people what precautions to take to prevent an epidemic. The chairman showed us the local sick-bay. The only patients were an asthmatic old man and a pregnant woman. However, if nothing else, our visit to Tan Khai and the film we took had one good result: the local people, who included 600 Chinese and six Cham, were treated to an unusually generous handout of rice that day.

Three kilometres south of Tan Khai the fields on both sides of the road swarmed with black-clad youngsters most of them busy digging. The young men and women seemed to be housed in big sheds that looked much more solid than the ramshackle huts of the new settlers. It was late afternoon and those who had completed their daily quota were playing football or volleyball. These young people came from the 8th district in Saigon. They were, we were told, volunteers. They included quite a number of the sons and

243

daughters of the bourgeoisie who, said Map, were trying to 'purge' themselves of the corrupt habits of their class by working on the land. The fact was, however, that they, like the settlers, had been sent there under duress and would be required to serve a period of three years forced labour to help towards the 'reconstruction' of the area. At the end of the three years an appropriate body would decide, on the basis of their results and the strength of their revolutionary commitment, which career they should pursue.

Compared to the atmosphere in the village or in the New Economic Zone the mood in this 'volunteer' camp was almost cheerful. The youngsters received eighteen kilos of rice and four dong (approximately 60p) per month. They looked healthy and well fed and had bright, intelligent faces. They watched us filming with a look of evident disapproval. They thought we were an eastern European TV crew, because several times I heard them muttering 'Lien Xo', Vietnamese for the Soviet Union. It had been bad enough being constantly mistaken for Americans during the second Indochinese war, but being confused with the Russians now seemed ten times worse. At any rate, the attitude of the 'volunteer labour force' of the 8th District was clearly one of defiant, determined opposition to the coercive methods of the new Socialist regime. Eventually Hanoi's commissars would have to step in and break the passive resistance of the mutinous young South Vietnamese by drafting them into the armed forces.

In the village of Chon Tanh we pulled up beside an equestrian statue that had been badly damaged in the fighting. Our guides told us they could not, after all, allow us to travel on to Tay Ninh and interview the Cao Dai. It wasn't, of course, that they were having any problems with the sect. The land owned by the Cao Dai clergy had been expropriated and all that was left was a kind of Vatican State about 100 hectares square. Their political influence was now 'negligible' and it was not a convenient time for them to be seeing visitors from abroad. Map, watching my reaction out of the corner of his eye, asked me if I intended visiting the Hoa Hao. It was no secret to anyone that this militant band of Buddhists was fighting a desperate, last-ditch campaign against the North Vietnamese around the edge of the Plain of Reeds. In the end I had to be content with seeing the Black Virgin from a distance. As I gazed across its sombre face, flashes of lightning rent the grey, stormy sky and we heard the rumble of thunder, like the sound of clashing armies.

During the summer of 1976 the Vietnamese High Command had started moving divisions up to the Cambodian border. By this time even the hard-headed Hanoi Communists were disturbed by the confused reports coming out of the land of the Khmer. North Vietnam had clearly lost any influence it might once have had over its former protégé. After much difficulty Vietnamese journalists were smuggled into the ghost town of Phnom Penh. They were horrified by what they saw. The Khmer Rouge seemed to be in the grip of revolutionary frenzy. They were not only wreaking havoc among their old enemies from the Lon Nol days: anyone who had not actively supported them in the past was now considered suspect and stood in danger of being killed. The opening line of the new national anthem of 'Democratic Kampuchea' was 'Blood frees us from slavery'.

Now rivers of blood were flowing throughout the land of the Khmer. Having massacred pro-American troops the Khmer Rouge set about systematically killing the intelligentsia, teachers and students, even though most had actively opposed Prince Sihanouk and Lon Nol. At the head of this terrible regime was the secret central command known as Ankar. Its members were unknown and its murderous decrees were irrevocable. Horrified observers spoke about the 'Stone-Age Communism' being practised in Cambodia. The Khmer Rouge had abolished money. The entire population was being forced to toil around the clock, planting rice, clearing jungle, digging ditches. It was as if the mad ideologists who had seized power were striving to recreate the slave society of the great medieval empire of Angkor under a pseudo-Marxist banner. All they were doing, however, was bringing misery, despair and economic disaster to the country. The pagodas were desecrated and the monks were set to work. Killings were authorized on the slightest pretext. Religion and astrology were banned, as were dancing and all forms of pleasure. Under the puritanical eye of the Red commissars sexual acts were limited to the reproductive chore. There were no re-education centres. Anyone suspected of opposing the regime was swiftly put to death. Books were burned. The few factories that had been started up with Chinese help were quickly shut down. The fishing fleet was handed over to a group of fanatical loyalists from the interior. None had so much as seen the sea before, and they were surprised to find it tasted salty. Hospitals were closed down and doctors put to work in the ricefields. The death toll during the period of American intervention and the civil war had been estimated at 500,000. It took just a few months of 'peace' under the Khmer Rouge to double that figure.

The few diplomats accredited to Phnom Penh were not allowed to venture more than 200 metres outside their embassy without a special permit from the authorities. In addition to this, they had to eat at least some of their meals in the collective 'people's kitchens'. Since there was no longer any official Cambodian currency, petrol or cigarettes had to be paid for in American dollars. The only foreigners to enjoy any privileges were the technical experts and advisers from Peking. But as the Vietnamese noted with a certain pleasure, even they were unable to prevent the massacre of Chinese nationals in what amounted to a veritable pogrom. There were reports of murderous power-struggles and lethal in-fighting going on in the sinister ruling body. Pol Pot, leader of the regime, was the only government representative who met the visitors from Hanoi. He admitted that 80 per cent of the population were suffering from malaria and malnutrition.

The time we spent with Madame Tu, our interpreter, was one of the high spots in our depressing tour of Saigon. She was a typical North Vietnamese, the daughter of a family of intellectuals who had supported the revolution from its earliest days. She had grown up in the rebel area of Tongking around Tay Nguyen during the first Indochinese war. Later she spent some years in East Germany studying electronics. She was cheerful and good-natured and, like so many other Vietnamese women I met, had a seemingly inexhaustible supply of energy. Her husband worked as an engineer, and her pretty little daughter wore the red neckerchief of the Young Pioneers. While in Saigon Madame Tu visited the family of one of her uncles. Unlike her father, he had supported the middle-class Nationalists during the first war and had moved to the South after the defeat of the French. She returned from her visit looking thoroughly depressed and dejected.

Later that evening, however, as we sat on benches watching a performance by the Hanoi state circus, her eyes sparkled with laughter and she seemed quite her old self again. The acts themselves were fairly ordinary and dragged on interminably in the traditional Soviet manner. The animal turns were the funniest. In one of them an elephant kicked a football towards a chimpanzee dressed up as a goalkeeper. The chimp was fairly fast on his feet and seemed to be taking it very seriously indeed. At one point the enormous elephant kicked the ball with regal disdain and the chimp pounced on it desperately. You could see the goalkeeper's fear all over his little face. A group of monks beside us in the front row shook with laughter. For an instant we almost forgot that the big top was surrounded by armed Bo Doi. Even though it was right in the middle of town the authorities seemed to regard it as a vulnerable target. It was even surrounded by a barbed-wire fence. Every member of the audience had had his identity papers checked before being allowed inside. The revolutionary authorities were obviously taking no chances. It was nearly a year and a half since the North Vietnamese had walked into Saigon but they clearly didn't feel the city was yet safe.

The circus provided a pleasant change from the political children's party we had filmed three days before. The grounds of the Doc Lap Palace, formerly the official residence of President Thieu, had been decked out like a fairground for the occasion. The red and blue flags of the South Vietnam Liberation Front had been taken down, and the bright red flags of the victorious Hanoi troops were everywhere. Loudspeakers blared out military marches and revolutionary songs. Banners hailed the reunification of Vietnam, which had just been decided in a recent 'ballot'. Apparently the official proclamation was due any day now. Over everything towered the ever-present portrait of Ho Chi Minh in pastel shades of pink and blue. The old man with the scraggy beard was portrayed, as ever, with a kindly, fatherly smile. Uncle Ho had become a cult object, the idol of his own triumphant ideology, the victim of a style of revolutionary kitsch inspired by the mediocre offerings of Soviet Realism, the Sacred Heart motifs of traditional Catholicism and the bizarre gallery of Taoist saints. Bernard Henri Levy, the *nouveau philosophe*, would one day coin a phrase for this Marxist pseudo-religiosity – 'atheistic theocracy'. If he had visited Vietnam he would have found ample evidence to back up his theories.

The most off-putting thing of all about this party were the attempts of the political commissars and Can Bo to indoctrinate the Saigon children in the liturgy of the new faith. The party officials even had the cheek to wear the red neckerchief of the Young Pioneers, despite the fact that they were going grey. They smiled all the time, looking almost as benign as their ubiquitous prophet. Every so often the children, most of whose families were languishing in rehabilitation camps, would play up and refuse to cooperate. It didn't seem to deter the organizers. In fact nothing would have deterred these self-righteous, self-appointed missionaries of world revolution. They were the new, successful Cao Daists of dialectical materialism; they had simply substituted Karl Marx's beard for Victor Hugo's beard. What they would really have liked to do would have been to turn the whole of South Vietnam into one gigantic kindergarten, dedicated to singing the eternal praise and glory of Uncle Ho. These teachers were the Asian priests of Marxism. Before we left the choir performed the inevitable litany: 'Vietnam, Ho Chi Minh! . . . Vietnam, Ho Chi Minh!'

Early next day we went for a stroll through Cholon, Saigon's Chinatown. Socialism didn't seem to be making much headway among the Sons of Heaven, who were always far better at selling and organizing than the Vietnamese. During French colonial rule the Chinese had monopolized the rice trade in the country. But in the eyes of the North Vietnamese they were still a race of incorrigible 'parasites' and 'bourgeois capitalists' and *compradores*. More alarmingly, however, the Chinese were also regarded as unacceptable foreigners and a potential security risk. When the revolutionary army marched into Saigon, the crafty shopkeepers of Cholon had run up the flag of Mao Tse-tung's People's Army. But it hadn't done them much good – in fact, it had made things worse. During the fighting the old Chinese-Vietnamese enmity had been smoothed over, uneasily, by talk about 'proletarian internationalism'. Now, however, that rather fragile alliance had broken. Cholon was still full of bustle, but the Chinese knew that the authorities had decided to nationalize all trade and business. The shop-owners still sat behind their wooden abacuses looking as inscrutable as ever, but the armed Vietnamese security troops in the town were distinctly threatening. Everyone knew the blow had to fall sooner or later. The supply of goods in the shops was gradually running out, more and more families were being sent to the wilderness of the Pioneer Zones. Those who had made a small fortune speculating in rice were being detained in cells and being interrogated by police night and day.

Things were looking bad for the Chinese in Cholon, and the moment they realized we were foreigners from the West they took us aside and poured out their worries and fears. I entered a shop and bought a tiny lacquer painting, the shop-owner offered me some tea. 'The old regime wasn't particularly kind to us, Monsieur,' he said. 'But what's happening to us today is criminal. The only thing left for us is to emigrate, but where can we go?

They're always going on about social justice, but just look at this new lot of profiteers from the North. They claim to despise the consumer society, and then they grab all the goods they can. They either requisition our property or simply take it from under our noses. Before, there were rich people and poor people in South Vietnam, but now there are only poor people. Take these two statistics, for instance. At the end of the war there were only 30,000 TV sets in North Vietnam, and two million in the South. That means there must have been two million South Vietnamese families – and that's ten million people at least – who weren't doing too badly for themselves.'

Our next trip was to give us a glimpse inside Vietnam's very own Gulag Archipelago. The authorities in Ho Chi Minh City suggested we might like to film the land reclamation going on in the bleak wastes of the Plain of Reeds. The plain was bordered on one side by the fertile ricefields of the Mekong Delta, and on the other by the Cambodian plantation belt. The Plain had always been difficult to police and in the past had been a traditional refuge for guerillas of all types. During the rainy season this expanse of marshland became a vast lake. In the dry season it turned into a greenish-black mass of slimy mud and rotting vegetation. During the American war it had been declared a 'free-fire zone', which meant that troops inside the area were allowed to shoot at anything that moved.

We were scheduled to spend the night in the provincial capital, My Tho, which lay on the northern edge of the Mekong Delta. After dark we went for a stroll through the streets of the town. It was pitch black, and we had only the red glow of an oil lamp to see by. An escort of heavily-armed troops accompanied us, as there was a constant threat of assassination and armed resistance in the area. The revolutionary authorities in My Tho had brought along two former Saigon army officers for us to talk to, but the interview didn't go well. Both men had a cowed, frightened look in their eyes. They were obviously afraid of saying too much. We couldn't even get them to give us an approximate figure for the number of suspects and opponents of the regime being held in detention. So we were never able to disprove our theory that several hundred thousand political prisoners were languishing in re-education camps. We knew there was no way that anyone who had supported or worked for the former American-backed regime – particularly the CIA – could escape the clutches of the political commissars. It was said that when the Americans quit Saigon, they remembered to take the results of their test-drillings for oil around the coast, but they left complete lists of all their Vietnamese allies and collaborators lying around for the Communists to find.

We drove on from My Tho, leaving behind the rich green of the ricefields, the teeming, throbbing life of the canals, the pretty villages with their bamboo plants growing all about. We reached the edge of the Plain of Reeds and the air became filled with clouds of mosquitoes and the stench of decaying vegetation. Our arrival in the little village of Phuoc Tay caused chaos and confusion. We seemed to have stumbled on a small unit of former Viet Cong guerillas wearing yellow khaki police uniforms instead of the usual green army dress. Their function seemed to be purely military, judging by the weapons they were carrying. The original plan had been that we should visit a sector where a regiment of Vietnamese regulars was stationed. According to the official story we were given, the troops had been sent there as part of the Socialist programme for the reconstruction of the economy. They were supposed to be digging ditches so the plain could be eventually reclaimed for agricultural use.

Nobody in the village seemed to have expected us; either the message hadn't got through or else someone had got the day wrong. The police officer in charge of the unit, a surly-looking individual who kept giving us dirty looks, went into a huddle with his men to try and sort something out, and after much deliberation the soldiers took up picks and shovels and began digging in the mud, purely for the benefit of our cameras. The smart khaki uniforms the men had on were quite unsuitable for this kind of work and they were soon covered in mud and muck. We filmed a few not very interesting shots of them at work, then the policemen put down their tools and took up their AK-47s again. I was impressed by the men's faces, which looked hard, almost cruel, in a way. The years of hell they had spent fighting a guerilla war in this godforsaken swamp had certainly left their mark. Even the fanatically loyal Map was somewhat chastened by the sight of these grim-faced veterans of the revolutionary struggle.

We wanted to film a shot of the surrounding landscape and then pack up and go home. From our vantage-point on the roof of our van we spotted an ant-like swarm of people in the distance, beavering away in the mud. Looking through our camera we saw what looked like a crowd of men busily digging some kind of trench or canal. They wore tattered army fatigues and were so plastered in mud that they looked more like part of the countryside than human beings. They moved about in the slime like crabs, closely watched by heavily-armed guards. Our embarrassed guides immediately launched into a long-winded explanation, saying that the men were local peasants who had volunteered for collective work. We got permission to have a closer look at these rather unusual 'peasants'. The men (there were no women around) dug up the mud with crude shovels then cleared it away. There were one or two old wheelbarrows but most men had to make do with shovelling the earth into two baskets, which they then carried over their shoulders on the end of a long, swaying bamboo pole. The men, who were all between twenty and forty, looked exhausted and half-starved. The paid hardly any attention to us but simply carried on with their digging; presumably they had a hefty quota of work to get through each day. They didn't look at all like typical peasants and Madame Tu let slip that they were former troops of the South Vietnamese army. We realized then that we had stumbled on a labour camp. Most of the inmates must have been former officers. We stood and watched the 'marsh soldiers' of the new Socialist Vietnam, slaving and toiling and suffering before our very eyes. We were quite speechless.

We hadn't been filming long when the police officer came along and signalled for us to stop.

On the way back to Phuoc Tay we were driving over a wooden bridge when we caught a clear view of the camp. It had all the classic features of a concentration camp: barbed-wire fencing, floodlights, watchtowers with machine-gun posts. Inside the compound were a few miserable reed huts. One or two ragged figures were shuffling about, others were lying motionless on the ground, probably half-dead with malaria.

We were anxious to get out of Ho Chi Minh City as fast as we could. During the night we received several phone calls from strangers wanting us to take messages and letters to relatives in Europe, but we said no to all of them. We had to be wary of Communist traps. Going through passport control and customs at Tan Son Nhut airport was a long, drawn-out business. Every passenger had to have his identity papers checked. Communist Party officials had no problem getting clearance for the numerous goods they were taking back North with them. Transistor radios, sewing machines, TV sets, cameras – you name it, they had it; every imaginable consumer durable ever to emerge from the festering pit of capitalism.

The best seats aboard the Ilyushin plane had been reserved for a delegation from East Timor made up of representatives of Fretilin, the Timor Liberation Front. Their features were a mixture of Malayan and Melanesian, and they wore black and red insignias and old-fashioned commissar's caps. The Fretilin rebels had tried to set up a Marxist state on the island, but the government in Djakarta had anticipated their move. The army was sent in to Dilli, the capital, and the guerillas were driven into the mountains. Hanoi had now decided to take the rebel movement on the distant Sunda Islands under its wing. The delegates from Timor had been warmly welcomed in Vietnam and had been escorted everywhere by high-ranking members of the military. The dark-skinned Indonesian Communists, who until two years ago had been Catholic priests or seminarists, were clearly enjoying being part of the great Asian revolution. Before the plane took off the party were festooned with garlands of flowers in a final gesture of goodwill.

Our plane stopped over in Da Nang, the town which had once reverberated to the roar of the monstrous hardware of the American war machine. Now there was only silence and desolation. The green-uniformed Bo Doi looked tiny against this vast panorama of concrete and corrugated iron. America had left behind a graveyard of military technology in Da Nang. I wondered how much longer the airstrips and bunkers would remain unused. Rumours were circulating that Russia was interested in the former base. Whether the bay at Da Nang could cope with the needs of modern naval warfare, particularly submarine warfare, was a question being vigorously debated among Western military experts. There were good historical reasons why the Russians had doubts about taking over this natural harbour. In the days when the French ruled Indochina, Da Nang had been called Tourane, and it was in Tourane in 1905 that the tsar's fleet had taken on coal for the last time before sailing north to meet the Japanese. The Russian fleet was later sunk in Tshshima Strait by the insignificant little navy from the Land of the Rising Sun.

The Sparta on the Banks
of the Red River

Hanoi, August 1976

How on earth could a victory like this ever have happened? How could this divided country, robbed of its richest provinces, survive thirty years of war – and not only survive, but win? How did North Vietnam, this impoverished, undernourished dwarf, manage to take on the spectacular might of the American army and beat it? Every time you walked through the streets of Saigon these questions would recur time and again. There was no easy answer. When you looked around you in Hanoi everything was dilapidated, worn out and run down. Since the French pulled out in 1954 the city centre hadn't changed at all. The trams, which had been taken off the road by some French provincial city and shipped to the Far East during the Third Republic, still ran around the Little Lake on buckled rails. The character of the city was still dominated by its colonial architecture, and there was little sign of modern innovation. The Chinese quarter was still the same seething mass of humanity. The shady avenues around the citadel were still a monument to the late flowering of colonial town planning. But the buildings were neglected and badly maintained, gently crumbling in the monsoon rains. Very little care had been lavished on Hanoi in recent years. The French department stores, the Indian bazaars, the Chinese backstreets with their air of secret camaraderie, had all been replaced by the drab emporiums of state-run commerce. The choice of goods was meagre, and the articles themselves were expensive and of poor quality. The people in the street looked thin and long-suffering; their yellow skin resembled old parchment. The children were the only ones who had rosy cheeks and laughed.

There were long queues of bicycles, and Chinese-built lorries would barge their way through them constantly tooting their horns. Every now and then a high-ranking party man would drive past in a black Volga. As in the Soviet Union, the cars of Communist dignitaries all had white curtains to shield the occupants from public gaze. The only area where buildings had been restored to something like their former splendour was in the old public administration district, which dated back to the time of the French. The Socialist Republic of Vietnam had its official ministries there and it was also the site of the Ho Chi Minh mausoleum. The Russians had also set up shop in this exclusive district. Theirs was a massive, sprawling complex rather like the Forbidden City in Peking.

A newcomer to Hanoi would look in vain for traces of American bombing. The capital was spared by the US Air Force – except one street, the Rue Thu Kien. This was completely flattened in December 1972 when a B-52, presumably damaged by anti-aircraft fire, released its bombs over the city, leaving a trail of destruction in its wake. Earlier in the war the French embassy received a direct hit. The accuracy of the bombing was regarded as highly suspect at the time, and to this day the diplomats in the Quai D'Orsay are not convinced it was entirely accidental. Other than that, the visitor looking for signs of rubble or devastation had to leave the city and cross the old Paul Doumer bridge over the Red River, where the traffic was even more chaotic than in the days of the French. It was probably part of a tacit Soviet-American understanding that the US bombing campaign, which damaged nearly every province in North Vietnam, should stop just short of the gates of the capital.

August in Tongking was always unbearably hot and humid. The air was so clammy you could feel it sticking to your skin. Judging by the mood of the people in Hanoi, the initial reaction of euphoria at the victory of the North had given way to a feeling of anti-climax and resignation. But at least there was the consolation of knowing that young men were no longer dying in the South. Daily life was no easier, however, and the problem of food supplies was, if anything, more acute than before. Long queues were everywhere. Kerosene, used for lighting as well as cooking, was in particularly short supply. The grandiose claims of the propaganda posters, some of which stretched the width of a house, were the only evidence of the new affluence and dynamic progress Socialism was meant to bring. But though the North Vietnamese hadn't achieved the utopia promised in the posters, nevertheless they had fought for, and won, the reunification of their country, and it was enough. The patriotism of these people, starving and on the verge of exhaustion, may sometimes have been maddening, but it was always impressive.

On the outskirts of the capital the Hanoi of tomorrow was slowly taking shape. The districts built by the French were to be pulled down and the town centre was to be transferred to the banks of the

Red River. The Chinese quarter would also fall victim to the demolition sound very soon. But the modern concrete blocks the regime was so proud of, the rectangular barracks in which the new Socialist citizens of tomorrow were to be raised, were taking a long time to rise from the ground. The new Vietnamese architecture was woefully uninspiring – the kindest comparison you could make would be with Novosibirsk. What was worse, building standards on new projects were deplorable. The tower-blocks going up in Hanoi were like the 'instant slums' familiar to all visitors to Eastern Europe. What the authorities were building were drab, dismal termite colonies, not housing schemes for human beings to live in. There was no space to enjoy life, no room to develop as an individual. Even the East German architects called in to advise their Communist allies were driven to distraction by the regime's attitude.

One of them described his experiences in the town of Vinh, which had been totally flattened during the war. Against all reason, and regardless of cost, the Communist officials there were determined to build ten-storey blocks of flats – skyscrapers by Vietnamese standards. The East German architects put forward all sorts of counter-arguments but the Vietnamese administrators were unshakeable. Then one of the architects had a flash of inspiration. He remembered that no Vietnamese working man liked to be parted from his bike. It was his most treasured possession, his pride and joy. He even hung it up above his bed at night so that it wouldn't be stolen (despite the stern moral climate of revolutionary Vietnam, bicycle thefts were common). How, the architect asked, were people living in ten-storey tower-blocks to get their bicycles up to the top floors – especially if the lifts were out of order. His objection really hit home, and so the people of Vinh were spared another act of administrative folly.

It was the same all over Hanoi – on the building sites where new housing schemes were going up; down by the banks of the Red River, where they were reinforcing the dykes to prevent flooding; at every road works and construction site in the city, it was always the women you saw doing the bulk of the work. It was the women who carried the heaviest loads, the women who refused to let the drudgery of it all get them down. In this part of the country, which had been under Communist rule for twenty years, equality for Vietnamese women meant that they got the hardest and dirtiest jobs to do. Of course in the upper echelons of the party and the army and the state, women officials often had an important say in the running of things. What is more, they invariably won respect for their unswerving loyalty to the party line. In some cases, however, women were worse off under Marxism. The truth is that the double standard underlying the regime's official stance found its way into every sphere of life.

A classic example of this was the unsightly grey building on the Little Lake, with its windows covered in whitener to keep out prying eyes. Behind those windows lay a whole world of special rations, hard-to-come-by consumer goods, and imported articles from the 'liberated' South, all reserved exclusively for privileged members of the regime and foreigners resident in North Vietnam. The ordinary party member could barely afford to look at this exclusive shop, never mind buy anything there. Western diplomats turned their noses up at the selection of goods, which by their standards was pretty unexciting. For the Russians, though, it was a shopper's paradise, and they would regularly empty the shelves. The Soviets and their badly dressed wives quickly inherited the mantle of the 'ugly Americans' in the new Vietnam. They were extremely unpopular among the North Vietnamese, though the People's Army maintained close links with their comrades-at-arms in the far north.

Generally speaking, however, the atmosphere in Hanoi was less depressing than in Saigon. The years of uninterrupted fighting had given the people a strong sense of unity. The Tongkingese were a tough race; they had never really had it easy, and they tended to be slightly contemptuous of the hedonism of their fellow-Vietnamese in the South. But the real motivating force behind this people was national pride. A kind of South-east Asian Sparta had sprung up on the banks of the Red River. The Marxist ideology that had been drummed into them for the past twenty years had fired their revolutionary zeal like a promise of salvation. The North Vietnamese had willingly put up with material hardships during the war as long as their tiny, drab little country continued to chalk up military victories in the name of the revolution.

The harsh regime in Hanoi that ruthlessly suppressed the peasant revolt in 1954–56 was well known for its austerity and puritanism. In fact it was only after the conquest of the South that corruption became part of the Northern way of life. It even penetrated the fossilized hierarchy of Lao Dong, the Workers' Party, which was soon to proclaim itself the Communist Party of Vietnam. The politburo naturally deplored this disgraceful state of affairs. They regularly criticized the growing corruption, the red tape, the arrogance and incompetence of party officials, but their warnings seemed to fall on deaf ears. The North Vietnamese had won a great victory by dint of superhuman effort, but now they were beginning to run out of steam. They simply did not have enough strength left to carry out the enormous task of reconstruction. As a result agriculture was stagnating; industrial projects were getting bogged down in administrative detail. Everywhere work was being botched and bungled, and the smallest sign of effort or initiative was singled out for lavish praise. New ideas foundered on endless security checks and a blinkered mania for planning. Foreign experts from East and West despaired at the technical and economic ignorance of a people whose fighting skills had compelled the admiration of the world. The Vietnamese had opted for the Moscow brand of Socialism and adopted Soviet methods of running industry and agriculture. Now they were suffering.

The North Vietnamese Army stood out like a beacon in the midst of gloom. It was a state within a state, noted for its efficiency and exemplary discipline. When the civil authorities were unable to restore the vital rail link between Hanoi and Saigon, the engineers in the People's Army leapt into the breach. Then shipping in Haiphong practically came to a halt because everything was in total chaos. Valuable imports were left on the quayside, rotting in the monsoon rain. Ships had to wait ten weeks before they could be unloaded. The green-uniformed troops had to be called in here as well. Lately the authorities had not even been able to get the rice harvest in without the help of the Bo Doi.

General Vo Nguyen Giap, the Commander-in-Chief, had been one of the most powerful men in the politburo since the early days of the revolution. After the army's victory he had become a key figure in the government. Even in the early days, Giap, together with the Secretary-General, Le Duan, had been a committed supporter of the Russian line and an outspoken critic of close cooperation with China. Now, with both the party organization and civilian administration beginning to break down, Vietnam found itself heading inexorably towards a kind of military regime. During the war Hanoi had always managed to avoid enforcing compulsory military service. It had been left to village communities and workers' groups, guided by political commissars, to choose who should be conscripted for the army and have the honour of fighting for the Socialist fatherland. Ironically, just a year and a half after the defeat of the South, the authorities had to introduce a three-year spell of military service for all young Vietnamese. What the leadership wanted was a cheap, energetic and inexhaustible supply of labour to help rebuild agriculture. The main object of the exercise, however, was to bring into line all those wayward young men in the South who still hankered after the delights of Western society and subject them to the iron discipline of the Marxist state. This permanent mobilization would be a useful protection for the Socialist republic against China, the old enemy in the north. The blooms of Sino-Vietnamese friendship had soon withered on the stem.

You never went far in Hanoi without seeing something that touched or moved you. One evening, for example, we were invited to a concert given by war-wounded troops in the old French opera house. Two blind soldiers opened the proceedings with a violin duet, their eyes hidden behind dark glasses and their scarred faces quite without expression. The hall was packed with shabbily dressed people, mainly relatives of the disabled. The opera house itself was in an appalling state of repair. It was difficult to believe that the cream of the French colonial establishment had once sat in this same building and applauded the Comédie Française. On this very stage actors had declaimed the solemn lines of Corneille and presented the elegant badinage of Marivaux, complete with rustling silk and powdered wigs. Now the stage was occupied by the victorious peasant soldiers of the Asian revolution leaning on their crutches and white sticks. The stucco was crumbling from the walls, the red velvet upholstery was torn, and only a few bulbs remained in the chandeliers. You could still just make out the date 1911 above the stage, the year the theatre opened, when the Governor General of Hanoi had dedicated this temple of Gallic culture to the peoples of Indochina.

The blind violinists were followed by several choirs, one of which was made up of three women with amputated legs. They came on in their green uniforms, bowed briefly to the audience then presented songs they had written themselves. The opening line of one of them went, 'Our strength is not exhausted'. One ballad in particular drew warm applause. It was called 'Four Brothers in a Tank'. After that a soloist was led forward, but before he began his melancholy guitar-piece the compère announced that his instrument had been donated by American 'fighters for peace'. At the end all the wounded and crippled performers came on stage for the finale, and a mighty chorus of voices sent the inevitable refrain ringing through the dilapidated auditorium: Vietnam, Ho Chi Minh . . .' The eyes of the care-worn, undernourished audience shone with a mixture of emotion and zeal.

The day before, party and state had held a service to commemorate those who had fallen in the war. The guard of honour, smartly turned out in their white uniforms, wide epaulettes and stiff caps, presented arms. All the famous names of the Vietnamese revolution were assembled for the ceremony at the war memorial. Walking with agonizing slowness they climbed the steps to the urn where the flame of remembrance burned brightly. The pace was set by the ninety-year-old president, Ton Duc Thang, who had to be supported by colleagues on either side. The Hanoi troika filed past in the front row: Prime Minister Pham Van Dong, austere and pensive; General Vo Nguyen Giap, still full of energy despite rumours of ill-health; then finally the Secretary-General of the party, Le Duan, with his smooth, committee-man's face. The President of the National Assembly, Truong Chinh, followed in the second row. After the peasant revolt in 1954 he had been responsible for brutally suppressing the kulaks, and he was suspected in some quarters of trying to bring Vietnamese Communism into line with Peking. Further back were the leaders of the Paris negotiations, Le Duc Tho and Xuan Thuy. Most of these men were getting on in years. They were the old guard in more senses than one, used to the taste of power and determined to hang on to it. Seeing them lined up there, a startling fact came home to me: the youth of Vietnam had been led into war, and ultimate victory, by a gerontocracy. These professional revol-utionaries had grown up with Stalinism, and it showed. The French ambassador in Hanoi, a left-wing Socialist, had been secretly sympathetic to the social upheaval in Indochina. But lately even he had begun to despair of the senile ideologists running Vietnam, who had, he felt, raised Marxism to the status of a religion.

The uniforms and drill of the ceremony had a distinctly Russian flavour. It was details such as this that told outsiders that Socialist Vietnam had decided to adopt a pro-Soviet line, and hence was on an inevitable collision course with Peking. Until recently the leaders of the Lao Dong Party, in particular Prime Minister Pham Van Dong, had carefully preserved amicable relations with the two Communist superpowers, intent on ensuring that each was treated in like manner. So determined was Vietnam to remain impartial that when the party newspaper, *Nhan Dan,* published an article 1475 words long on the Russian Revolution, another contribution appeared next day devoted to the Long March – also 1475 words long. Again, when Soviet and Chinese guests were invited to official functions, there always had to be the same number of each present, and they had to be of equivalent rank. And at special receptions the rule was that equal quantities of vodka and mao tai should always be served. Now, however, people had begun to notice that this scrupulous impartiality seemed to have gone by the board.

The Enemy from the North

The northern border of Vietnam, August 1976

Anti-Chinese feeling in Vietnam was growing stronger with each day that passed. Every time we drove across the rusty old Doumer bridge Hong would curse the Chinese for not fulfilling their promise to build a new stone bridge over the Red River. Then Madame Tu kept quoting us yet another version of the old Vietnamese proverb: 'When you have fought off the enemy from the south, a more dangerous enemy will threaten you from the north.' That weekend we drove along the northern coast of Tongking heading for the Bay of Halong. On the way we passed hundreds of military cemeteries, each with a white pagoda and red star in the centre. I also had my first glimpse of the sinister-looking chain of bunkers built by General de Lattre de Tassigny to defend the delta area in the first Indochinese war. As we drove past we saw men with pick-axes and pneumatic drills laboriously dismantling this Vietnamese Maginot Line. Of greater significance, though, were the Vietnamese military convoys we passed; some were carrying artillery and they were heading north towards the Chinese provinces of Kwangsi and Kwangtung.

This time I could sit back and enjoy the Bay of Halong as a tourist. I went sailing round the broad curve of the bay with its remarkable cliffs and swam in the lukewarm waters of the South China Sea. We stayed in an old hotel dating from French colonial days; and most of the guests were Soviet holiday-makers from

Vladivostok. As the evening wore on they would start singing mournful songs before drowning their melancholy in vodka. Much more important were the large numbers of Russian and Cuban cargo boats anchored in the bay. They were unloading machine parts for the mines of Hongay and taking on coal for the Far Eastern provinces of the USSR. The Bay of Halong provided an ideal base for camouflaged Soviet radar observation vessels to keep an eye on the Chinese coast.

Our guide conceded that incidents along the Vietnamese border with China were steadily increasing. Boundary markers had been shifted, and Chinese border patrols were reported to have entered Vietnamese territory. There had even been skirmishes between border guards and militiamen. They had gone for one another with sticks and ended up shooting at one another. The Chinese were waging a non-stop propaganda war across the border with loudhailers. And yet it was only comparatively recently that Peking had issued such pronouncements as: 'China and Vietnam are as closely united in fighting off imperialism as the lips and teeth'. During the recent war nearly 24 per cent of Vietnam's equipment and supplies had come from China. All that seemed to be forgotten now. The traditional enmity between the two countries had proved stronger than their common ideological goal.

On the way to Haiphong we had to wait for the ferry at the Bach Dang River. Hong, our colleague from Vietnamese television, who had been an officer at the front only two years before, gave us a quick history lesson to while away the time. 'There's an interesting story connected with this river,' he said. 'The Chinese were twice defeated in battle here when they tried to conquer the Vietnamese centuries ago. In the year 938 a ruler of the Tang dynasty tried to annex Vietnam to China and was driven back here by Ngo Quyen, one of our heroes. Then in 1288 the really big battle took place, when Kublai Khan sent his Mongol armies south to conquer Vietnam. The commander of the Vietnamese army, Tran Hung Dao, got his men to ram pointed stakes into the shallow river bed. It was high tide when Kublai Khan's huge invasion force came rowing up the river in junks and anchored here. But during the night the tide went out, and the Chinese ships were punctured by the stakes. At that moment Tran Hung Dao sounded his horns and launched his counter-attack. The Chinese army was defeated, despite the fact it heavily outnumbered the Vietnamese. That's how the great Kublai Khan failed in his bid for world domination, all because of the heroism of the

Vietnamese.' Hong took us past the moorings to a big stone wall with a colourful mural of the battle on it. There in bold, primitive images were the Chinese junks burning and sinking and Kublai Khan's warriors drowning in the river, weighed down by heavy armour. And there, in all its glory, was the victorious army of Vietnamese peasants and fishermen, with Tran Hung Dao standing in the foreground, his arm raised in triumph.

Nobody in the Western embassies in Hanoi could quite agree on how serious the deterioration of the relationship between Vietnam and China really was. This was one time, however, when the Eastern bloc representatives had a far better idea than anyone else about what was going on behind the scenes. The correspondent for the East Berlin news agency invited me round for coffee one day. Günter Wagner was very different from the mysterious K I had met in Phnom Penh. At the Wagners you were served weak coffee and home-made cakes. 'I wouldn't have asked you to come here if I didn't happen to know you were a friend of the Vietnamese people,' was the first thing Wagner said to me. We quickly fell to talking about politics, and the conversation never really moved on from there. Günter Wagner and his wife, who also worked as a journalist, made no secret of their personal commitment to Communism.

Günter turned out to be very knowledgeable about the growing tension between Peking and Hanoi. 'You must have noticed how hard it is to get hold of petrol here, even for official business,' he said. 'That's because the Chinese have stopped their deliveries of oil to Vietnam.' He went over to a drawer and took out a map of South China. 'This is the real potential flashpoint, the Paracel and Spratly Islands. In the old colonial days these tiny islands – they're scattered over hundreds of kilometres – belonged to French Indochina, in theory anyway. First, the Saigon government stationed a few marines on them to establish its right of sovereignty. Then, during the last stage of the second Indochinese war Mao Tse-tung's troops landed on the Paracel Islands and expelled the Vietnamese. The situation on Spratly is even more complicated. It's further south than the Paracels. Hanoi's tiny navy got there first and beat Mao Tse-tung's troops to it, but then one or two of the smaller islands were secretly occupied by the Taiwan Nationalists and a token force of Filipinos. The next thing that happened was that mainland China laid claim to Spratly and all the territorial waters around it. Now because the islands are scattered over such a wide area, the territorial waters stretch as far south as Borneo and right up to Luzon in the Philippines in the east. So these sandbanks everyone's been fighting over are very important strategically. Whoever owns them can control the entire shipping traffic of South-east Asia. Plus there's always been a rumour that there are rich off-shore oil deposits around Paracel and Spratly, just waiting to be exploited.' The Wagners obviously supported the East Asian policies of the Soviet Union, and they made no attempt to conceal their satisfaction as they outlined the inevitable, not to say tragic, hardening of attitudes between Vietnam and China.

Madame Tu and Hong were waiting anxiously for me at the hotel. We were meant to be leaving for Thai Nguyen, capital of the northern province of Bac Thai. There was to be an official reception for us in the evening. The schedule worked out for our filming was always kept a closely-guarded secret, and we were only ever told what was happening right at the last minute. As I dashed upstairs to my room I passed a group of Cuban technical experts. The hotel was a present from Fidel Castro to the people of Vietnam to congratulate them on their victory over the American 'imperialists'. The modern fittings and furniture looked Scandinavian or Japanese, though. The rooms looked out over the Great Lake. The late afternoon sun had turned the muddy water gold and the water lilies and lotus flowers were silhouetted against its surface. Old men were rowing fishing boats through the water with leisurely, unhurried movements. The Great Lake was teeming with carp but there were also swarms of rats in the muddy shores of the lake, and from what we could see they had taken up residence in the Thong Nhat Hotel as well. We had got used to these rodents wandering through the building, quite uninhibited, and generally making a thorough nuisance of themselves. In the dining-room the previous day a drunken Russian had been loudly applauded by all the other foreigners when he threw a beer bottle at a particularly large specimen.

The driver of our mini-van drove like a man possessed. All the way from Hanoi to Thai Nguyen he tooted his horn non-stop, overtaking huge columns of lorries carrying ammunition north. He told us he had spent three years as a driver on the Ho Chi Minh Trail, but he didn't seem to have heard of gear-changes, for one thing, and the van had to struggle along in top the whole time. If this veteran of the Ho Chi Minh Trail was anything to go by, the North Vietnamese forces must have lost more equipment from inadequate maintenance and mechanical breakdown than from the

263

entire American bombing campaign. We reached hilly country just as the sun was beginning to set. Stretched out behind us lay the delta, the strategic triangle that had been a French stronghold during the first Indochinese war.

Just outside Thai Nguyen we saw an enormous industrial complex through the tangle of bamboo growing by the roadside. Its buildings were floodlit in the gathering dusk. Our guides made no mention of it, but we knew this to be the giant Thai Nguyen steelworks, once the showpiece of North Vietnam's economic recovery. At one time every foreign delegation visiting the country had been automatically taken round this monument to Socialist economic progress. The steelworks was tangible proof that the Vietnamese, following the true path of Communism, had successfully made the leap from peasant people to industrial nation. The US Air Force had razed this miracle of modern Socialist technology to the ground, and the rebuilding was rumoured to be running up against massive technical problems. Because of this the Thai Nguyen complex had become taboo. Nobody wanted to admit that the incompetence of the rival Russian and Chinese engineers had been as damaging as the original bombing. The East German engineers eventually brought in to advise on the rebuilding project were appalled to learn that vital, expensive machine parts had been left sitting on the quayside at Haiphong for months, rusting away.

General Chu Van Tan was waiting to greet us at the top of the steps leading up to the guest house. He was wearing full dress uniform, complete with wide gold epaulettes and heavily embroidered cap. His chest was covered in medals, in the style of a Soviet marshal at a military parade. He didn't seem at all put out by our late arrival, and he greeted us with a gruff warmth such as we hadn't encountered previously. Chu Can Tan was sixty-six. He was a founding father of the revolution, which was remarkable in itself as he belonged to one of the country's ethnic minorities, the Tay. He wasn't particularly well educated – as a boy he had gone to the local village school, but early in his career he had come into conflict with the French colonial authorities and Vietnamese mandarins. He was probably waging his own private war against the tyranny of Annamite landowners, like a kind of Tongking Robin Hood, when he came into contact with the early Communist agitators, an unknown revolutionary called Ho Chi Minh and his two followers, Pham Van Dong and Vo Nguyen Giap. In 1941 he put his small band of guerillas at their disposal. His militia was almost entirely made up of hill-tribesmen who had banded together to protect themselves against interference and exploitation. It seemed an obvious step to join the tiny group of Vietnamese intellectuals and revolutionaries who were not only fighting for the victory of the proletariat but, equally importantly, for the rights of all oppressed minorities. The time was right, too: France had just been defeated in Europe, the Japanese had marched into Indochina, the Kuomintang Chinese were sending a modest trickle of support to the rebels, and the American secret service, the OSS, had just put up its first aerial in Yunnan, helped by the Flying Tigers of General Chennault.

Overnight, and quite unexpectedly, Chu Van Tan the guerilla leader became a political force to be reckoned with. The Vietnamese began calling him the Grey Tiger because of his courage and skill as a soldier. From 1941 onwards he was a key figure in the Communist movement, valued for his loyalty and military know-how. In September 1945 he was at Ho Chi Minh's side when independence was declared in Hanoi: the former warlord had become an outstanding party man.

When Chu Van Tan shook hands with us that evening in Thai Nguyen, the propaganda chief for the province introduced him as political commander of the military division of Viet Bac, Vice-President of the National Assembly, member of the central committee of the Lao Dong Party, and President of the Committee for National Minorities. The general was stocky and powerfully-built for an Asian but he moved more like an ageing elephant than a tiger. He had an open face, plump and good-natured. He reminded me of a Vietnamese Hindenburg, and then he made me think of the grey-haired Marshal Buddeny, whom I had once seen in the Kremlin. The Grey Tiger would have looked quite at home in a line-up of veterans of Mao Tse-tung's Long March. In any case, he seemed a striking and very engaging personality. He had that air of cheerful straightforwardness that often makes elderly military men so easy to get along with. Had he been alive a century ago he would probably have fought for the Tongking river pirates. Later that evening as we sat at table I asked him what the standards of hygiene were like during the long years of guerilla warfare. The general let out a characteristic peal of laughter. 'If you mean malaria,' he replied with a chuckle, 'up in the mountains we all caught it in our mother's womb.'

That evening the ballet troupes of the Vietnamese People's Army gave a folk dance concert in a school for young political cadres. The costumes were brand new and not very accurate versions of the real thing. Not one of the dancers belonged to an ethnic minority. They sang the revolutionary hymn, 'Victory is Ours', which was written by Ho Chi Minh to mark the 1968 Tet offensive. Then some of the performers, dressed as Meo warriors, did a dance called 'New Joy'. There was something not quite right about the whole occasion, though. We questioned the provincial representative and he said that the original song-and-dance troupes, which had included a broad cross-section of nationalities, had been disbanded. Hanoi had taken a liberal line towards ethnic minorities at first, but since 1975 it had followed a policy of ethnic integration. The independent territory of Viet Bac, for example, which was largely populated by Tay and Nung, had originally been five distinct provinces. In time, however, they had been abolished in accordance with the policy of centralization. The same thing had happened to the independent territory of Tay Bac in the far north-west, which was inhabited by Thai and Meo tribesmen. Its three provinces suffered a similar fate, and the area included Lai Chau, the old capital of the Thai Federation, which I had travelled to on horseback in 1951.

Despite all our questions, we were never really given a satisfactory explanation for this administrative clamp-down. It seemed that Hanoi was deeply suspicious of the mighty Chinese superpower on its doorstep. The 'centralists' looked upon any form of individualism as highly suspect, particularly as there were also large numbers of the racially distinct hill-tribes of Viet Bac and Tay Bac living in southern China. The Tay effectively controlled a vast territory in the southern Chinese province of Kwangsi, where they were known as the Chuang.

The revolutionary museum stayed open late specially for us that evening. During the first Indochinese war the Viet Bac region had been the stronghold of Viet Minh resistance against the French, and as early as 1939 the Communist Party of Indochina had organized cells in the area. In 1943 Ho Chi Minh set up his headquarters in a cave in Pac Bo in the wild, mountainous region of Cao Bang. Working in collaboration with Chu Van Tan he successfully mobilized the local hill-tribes against the Vietnamese mandarins and landlords until it grew into a full-blown, broad-based revolutionary movement. This marked the beginning of the great liberation struggle, which was not only directed against the ruling colonial power but also against the Japanese forces that moved into Indochina with the consent of the Vichy regime.

The museum in Thai Nguyen had painstakingly reconstructed a model of Ho Chi Minh's first humble command post. Before coming to Pac Bo, Uncle Ho had been present at the founding of the French Communist Party in Tours in 1920 and had later worked his way through the Comintern school in Moscow. He gave revolutionary names to geographical features round his primitive headquarters. Hence the mountain where his cave was situated became known as Karl-Marx Mountain. The river where he used to bathe every morning was named after Lenin. The museum also had a series of yellowing photographs recording the different stages of the Communist revolution in Indochina. Two in particular were fascinating. One was taken in 1945 and showed the current Defence Minister, Vo Nguyen Giap, inspecting his little army. The guerillas were uniformed and armed like bandits and wore dappled camouflage dress. But it was Giap, the Commander-in-Chief, who wore the most original outfit. He was casually dressed, with a heavy revolver in his belt and a black homburg on his head. The second photo showed Ho Chi Minh in 1950 at the besieged French border garrison of Cao Bang. This wasn't the familiar, avuncular figure of the posters, the slightly senile popular hero who liked patting little children on the head and letting them tug his beard. The gaunt, spare figure standing on the outcrop of rock was obviously a man in his prime, a man at the height of his physical powers. His pith helmet was pushed back off his forehead and he stood surveying the enemy stronghold in the valley below with the cool, calculating gaze of a commander, the epitome of iron will and intense energy.

Madame Tu had made another discovery. She was standing in front of a photo taken in 1950 showing some French prisoners who had run into a Viet Minh ambush between Cao Bang and Lang Son. She burst out laughing. I went up to see what had amused her. The French captain in the picture was my exact double. 'That's you, isn't it?' asked Madame Tu with a little giggle. I explained that I hadn't been in East Asia then, and that it must be a much older double of me. She pretended that I had failed to convince her and for the rest of the day she kept looking at me with a mischievous twinkle in her eye.

We left the museum and drove down the deserted main street of Thai Nguyen. I caught a last glimpse of the tall entrance to the building. A huge white statue of Ho Chi Minh was set against a red background and lit up by floodlights. I remembered being told that he was no longer to be called Uncle Ho but was to be given the

267

official title of Chairman. Next day we had hoped to be allowed to make the pilgrimage to Pac Bo, but the authorities refused us permission. From what I could gather from the whispering going on among our guides, Pac Bo was thought to be too near the Chinese border for safety, and anyway the Vietnamese were building fortifications which they didn't want us to film. To make up for this General Chu Van Tan offered to show us round his old resistance headquarters in Tan Trao. We drove north-east for about two hours through a craggy, gnarled landscape of rocks and cliffs. The horizon was obscured by tall sugar-loaf mountains whose steep sides were overgrown with jungle. The ricefields became sparser and smaller. Tan Trao had originally been a Yao hamlet before the Grey Tiger moved in with his guerillas. Then in 1945 Ho Chi Minh set up his headquarters in this remote, inaccessible mountain valley. He went into hiding there, too, after General Leclerc's expeditionary force drove the Viet Minh out of the Red River Delta. In 1947 French paratroopers tried to make a surprise attack on Tan Trao in order to capture the rebels, but the operation failed.

Visibly proud and moved, Chu Van Tan showed us round the scenes of his past exploits. He had donned the light field uniform of the Vietnamese army and wore a green pith helmet. We stopped to rest under two huge old trees. In their day their branches must have provided shade for all sorts of people, from the early rebel bands of hill-tribesmen to the first assembly of Communist delegates in Vietnam. Finally Chu Van Tan took us to a simple bamboo hut standing beside a clear-running stream. It was from here that Ho Chi Minh had directed his campaign against the French between 1946 and 1954. It looked just like a hermit's hut. Chu Van Tan and the other Vietnamese went inside, stepping cautiously and with reverence as in a cathedral. 'This is where Ho Chi Minh's rice was cooked,' said the general. 'Every evening Uncle Ho would sit outside this kitchen and look out over the countryside. This is the plank bed he used to sleep on. He always received visitors outside, in the open air. He was very tidy and methodical, particularly about work. In the morning he would do exercises and then bathe in the stream.' The Communists of Vietnam looked on the area round Tan Trao as a kind of shrine, a place for political meditation and reflection. It had much the same significance in Vietnam as the caves in the cliffs at Yenan did in Mao's China.

The general had told us we could film anything we wanted on

the way back to Thai Nguyen. But just as we were getting ready to film one particularly picturesque scene, the surly security men in our party began to object. The scene we were interested in was one of the classic motifs in Vietnamese lacquer painting. Not far from the road a group of peasants were following their buffaloes behind the plough, casting long black shadows on the golden waters of the flooded ricefields. The security men had been following our discussion with Chu Van Tan with evident suspicion. Now they claimed the peasants 'weren't properly dressed', and so we couldn't take any pictures of them. Our protests were to no avail and we realized that the Grey Tiger's word was no longer law in Viet Bac.

We came to a junction with a big sign in Chinese which said that the all-weather road we were crossing had been built by Chinese engineers from the People's Liberation Army during the last Indochina war. At the side of the road was a cluster of miserable mud huts and a group of women wearing the distinctive costume of the Meo standing outside. This village community had initially settled near the Chinese border, just above Cao Bang but had been forcibly evacuated by the Vietnamese authorities. The Meo looked listless and apathetic in these strange surroundings, and they showed little enthusiasm as they went about planting manioc. The Vietnamese clearly distrusted this minority group and feared an alliance with their powerful Chinese neighbour. Once again, it seemed to me, the trials and tribulations of the Meo – this tough, intractable people scattered throughout the highlands of South-east Asia – were a warning of gathering storm clouds, an ominous sign of the new phase of confrontation Vietnam was to enter upon.

On the way home arguments broke out among the party officials in our escort. We asked Hong what the matter was. 'Things are a bit awkward at the moment,' he said, obviously embarrassed. 'Some of the comrades here are members of the Tay people, and they're feeling particularly sensitive at the moment. Every so often they have disagreements with the comrades from Hanoi.' When we finally left Vietnam we had no idea that barely six months later the genial General Chu Van Tan would fall out of favour with the regime. The official story put out by Hanoi was that the Grey Tiger had been found guilty of ruling his domain like a 'king' and a 'war-lord'. The real cause of his downfall, though, was his independent spirit, a trait he had inherited from his people, the Tay. Another reason may have been his desire to avoid the storm that he knew was slowly but inexorably brewing with China.

Scorpions in a Bottle

Hanoi, August 1976

The Ho Chi Minh Mausoleum in Hanoi was a gift from the Soviet Union. It was Cubist in style and was built along the lines of Lenin's Mausoleum in the Red Square. It was bigger, though, and in the Hanoi light the marble walls of the tomb looked more grey than white. The body of Uncle Ho lay encased in a crystal coffin looking like a wax doll, the cheeks brushed gently with make-up. Long queues of people formed outside the tomb every day. There were signs that the 'atheistic theocracy' of the Communist authorities had allowed the cult of the sacred relic to flourish here, too. Inside the freezing cold building I gazed past the statue-like figures of the soldiers guarding Vietnam's national hero and was reminded of the museum in Tshang Tcha in the southern Chinese province of Hunan, the birthplace of Chairman Mao. The most amazing exhibits in the museum were the mummified bodies of a 4000-year-old couple. Humanity had come a long way since those superstitious days; it had dispensed with religion, for one thing, and draped itself in the red flag of dialectical materialism. Even so, it apparently had not yet learned to come to terms with the awful mystery of its own mortality. In Communist Hanoi the authorities had built a shrine to the dead prophet of the Vietnamese renaissance; they had turned him into a pharaoh and made him an immortal symbol of the Vietnamese people. I half-expected to see the words 'Death, where is thy sting?' chiselled into the grey marble: they would have made a fitting inscription. The relief guard marched past the queue of waiting worshippers with goose-stepping, robot-like movements. The faces of the pilgrims expressed reverence and deep emotion.

Two weeks previously a delegation from Thailand, led by the Foreign Minister, Bhichai Rattakun, had filed past the body of Ho Chi Minh and laid a wreath on his tomb. The Vietnamese army in Laos had recently reached the Mekong River on the Thai border, much to the alarm of Bangkok, which could no longer count on American aid. Since then the Siamese, who had spent two centuries playing their enemies off against each other, had been making determined efforts to normalize relations with Hanoi.

In the international guest-house in Hanoi, another relic of French colonial rule, both sides had duly signed a protocol and drunk a toast. The Vietnamese Foreign Minister, Nguyen Dui Trinh, a little man and a reputed hard-liner, stood below the stuccoed walls of the banqueting hall, looking grim-faced and slightly sinister in his badly cut suit. He gave his official address in Vietnamese, speaking in a low growl, then handed over to his Siamese opposite number. Bhichai Rattakun, looking dapper and professorial, replied in English, which made the few foreigners present sit up and take notice. In addition to his diplomatic advisers, the Siamese foreign minister had brought along a couple of security officials. They were wearing brightly-coloured Hawaiian shirts and looked suspiciously like gangsters. Bhichai Rattakun congratulated the Vietnamese on their victory, and went on to describe the Mekong River between Indochina and Thailand as the new 'peace frontier' of South-east Asia. Earlier he had pledged his government to halt the setting up of foreign bases in Thailand and to show tolerance towards the 60,000 Vietnamese refugees who had been living in the north-eastern provinces since the end of World War II.

The two ministers had even discussed the Communist guerillas that were threatening Thailand from the border with Laos. Throughout all these talks one thing was never in doubt, however. No matter how often the Vietnamese declared their intention to respect the sovereignty of foreign states, they would never renege on their support for the Communist revolutionaries in Thailand. The two delegations eventually made a rather lukewarm non-aggression pact in which they agreed not to use force in the event of an open dispute between Thailand and Vietnam. Yet despite all the protestations of friendship, you could practically feel the hostility in the air. Despite all the toasts and expressions of goodwill, you could sense you were in the presence of irreconcilable enemies. Now that white imperialism had been driven out of South-east Asia and the sub-continent had been left to its own devices, the independent states were eyeing each other, ready to pounce, like scorpions in a bottle.

The diplomats and journalists present at the talks had been invited along to the former palace of the French governor general first thing that morning. Despite the early hour, the sky was grey and the humidity almost unbearable. The diplomatic corps turned up wearing short-sleeved tropical shirts. Inside the great hall a bust of Ho Chi Minh occupied pride of place. Prime Minister Pham Van Dong, who was due to fly to a conference of non-aligned nations immediately after the reception, arrived punctual to the minute. He walked up to the centre of the hall, followed by his retinue of venerable old men from the central committee and one or two younger party officials. The day had barely started and already his baggy tropical suit looked creased and crumpled. He surveyed the foreigners present in the hall with a beady eye. He had a monk's face, stern and austere. I noticed a certain resemblance to Le Huu Tu, the fighting bishop, who made such a powerful impression on me when I saw him leading his Catholic militia in 1951. Pham Van Dong had a smile like St Francis of Assisi, but when he got annoyed or worked up he bore an uncomfortable resemblance to Savonarola, the Florentine religious fanatic. This morning he was evidently feeling in fine fettle, and he almost seemed to be in high spirits.

He turned to Madame Binh, who had represented the Viet Cong at the Paris peace talks. After the war, she had served as minister of education for a time and was now sole representative of the South Vietnamese Liberation Front and held an important post in Hanoi. 'I'm feeling a bit nervous at the thought of this big international gathering,' said the prime minister coyly. 'I'd feel a lot happier if you were coming with me to Colombo. You're more used to moving in diplomatic circles than I am.' At this the rows of party officials and diplomats dutifully laughed and clapped. A smile spread across the face of Madame Binh, softening her rather aristocratic features. Pham Van Dong went down the row of guests and shook hands with each one. When he came to me, he fixed me with an intense gaze: 'Whether you believe it or not,' he said, gripping my hand firmly, 'we are a non-aligned country.'

When he got to the conference, which was held in the Buddhist stronghold of Sri Lanka, Pham Van Dong would no doubt stress the toleration being shown to the Buddhist community in Socialist Vietnam. By way of demonstration we were invited to look round Hanoi's Quan Su pagoda where a large crowd would celebrate the Buddhist festival of the dead that evening. Most of the congregation were old. They bowed down before the golden statue of the Buddha, lit joss-sticks, and gave small gifts to the monks. The scene took me back to the monastery of Zagorsk, just north of Moscow, where the officially atheist Soviet Union artificially preserved a remnant of the Russian Orthodox Church. We were told there were forty young monks receiving religious instruction in Hanoi. The authorities also mentioned a 'Buddhist Union' they were intending to set up to cover the whole country.

It was difficult not to read an ulterior motive into all this, particularly as the Communist commissars had successfully managed to smuggle their agents into the pagodas of Saigon and Hue once before. It would be only too easy for them to exploit this religious movement for subversive political ends in the staunchly Buddhist countries of South-east Asia. In this respect the Hanoi politburo was far shrewder than the bloodthirsty fanatics in Phnom Penh. The Khmer Rouge had mindlessly set about destroying Buddhist monasteries in Cambodia and killing most of the monks. Those lucky enough to escape death were rounded up and treated more or less as slave labour. In Cambodia, Laos, Thailand and Burma the main form of Buddhism practised was the strict Hinayana or Theravada branch, otherwise known as the Lesser Vehicle. The Vietnamese, however, had adopted the more liberal Mahayana form, also called the Greater Vehicle. The latter school dispensed with the rather rigid rules of Buddhism and tended, if anything, towards a kind of all-embracing faith. In ancient China the Buddhism of the Greater Vehicle had coexisted with Confucian ethics and the more fanciful teachings of Taoism. More surprisingly still, this religion of non-violence and tolerance had managed to find acceptance in Japan alongside Bushido, the warlike feudal code of the Samurai. All the signs now pointed to the Vietnamese Communists taking a pragmatic attitude and reaching some sort of agreement with the Mahayana Buddhists – for as long as it was worth their while, of course. The commissars would no doubt humour the yogis in the interests of furthering their grand revolutionary design, until such time as they could safely lay aside the mask of religious tolerance.

With Vietnam's Catholic population, on the other hand, the Communist officials found they were up against a brick wall, or more accurately perhaps, the rock of Peter. For twenty years Hanoi had subjected the Christian population of North Vietnam to constant harassment in a deliberate attempt to force them to renounce their faith. All their efforts had proved unsuccessful. The number of Catholics in Tongking and northern Annam remained at 1.2 million – the same number as were members of the Communist Party. But, in fairness to the Vietnamese Marxists, their campaign against the Church of Rome was nowhere near as rigorous or brutal as the action taken against Chinese Catholics by Mao Tse-tung's regime. We were given permission to film the service on the Feast of the Assumption in St Joseph's Cathedral in Hanoi. In front of the massive neo-Gothic entrance a statue of the Virgin Mary stood, looking out over the circular courtyard. Our guides assured us the cathedral was always packed with thousands of believers on Christmas Eve.

After the Viet Minh took over in 1954, Church and State in Vietnam came to an odd sort of compromise. The authorities allowed four Catholic churches to remain open in Hanoi itself. There were to be three masses every week in the cathedral, and on Sundays there would be a morning and an evening service. Since 1973 a handful of novitiates had been trained for the priesthood. Catechism could be taught to children in church for an hour on Sundays.

Nevertheless it felt distinctly odd to be standing in Hanoi, scene of the victorious Marxist revolution, listening to the church bells ringing out in celebration of the Virgin Mary's ascent to heaven. That August evening the cathedral was packed as row upon row of worshippers knelt in prayer. In front of the altar and side-pillars, pink and blue plaster saints gazed down on the congregation; the statues of the Sacred Heart and the Virgin of Fatima smiled sweetly. The uninspiring hymn tunes had originally been introduced by French missionaries; they sounded worse, if anything, when sung in the shrill Vietnamese manner.

Nevertheless I felt strangely moved by the sight of this poorly dressed, undernourished congregation. For one thing, it wasn't just made up of old women: there were men, women and children of all ages there. When they prayed their faces took on a solemn expression, a look of total submission. The men appeared devout and defiant at the same time, while the faces of the women bore the traces of recent suffering. They could almost have been standing at the foot of the Cross on some Asian Calvary. The nuns still wore their severe black head-dresses. The younger sisters prayed with radiant expressions, while the older ones gazed up at the altar like Egyptian mummies with their ancient, lined, parchment faces, longing for the day when they would be called to a better world. It was the children who moved me most, though. They followed every detail of the service with grave expressions, intent on the actions of the priest. They were making the greatest sacrifice of all. As Catholics they would never be allowed to wear the red neckerchief of the Young Pioneers, for example. And in later life they would be barred from all positions of responsibility and excluded from worthwhile careers. I couldn't take my eyes off these angelic-looking youngsters. While the camera crew were busy filming, I knelt down in a pew at the side and crossed myself. Here in Hanoi I could listen to the Christians of Vietnam using the traditional Latin mass, calling to God *de profundis,* from the depths of their misery and rejection. *Quare me repulisti et quare tristis incedo, dum affligit me inimicus.* Nobody would have denied the congregation of St Joseph's belonged to the oppressed and silent church, but for me, as they knelt there in the flickering light of the candles, they were the true *ecclesia triumphans.* As a child I used to recite the 'Te Deum', a line of which now came to mind: *'Martyrum candidatus exercitus . . .'* 'the shining army of martyrs'.

At that time the Church in Vietnam was just beginning to find its feet again, albeit in a rather tentative fashion. To the surprise of Church leaders inside Vietnam, the Archbishop of Hanoi, Monseigneur Trinh Nhu Khue, had been allowed to travel to Rome to be ordained as a cardinal by Pope Paul VI. Nobody in St Joseph's that evening had any inkling that on 2 September 1976, the Vietnamese national holiday commemorating the revolution and the reunification of North and South, the Communist regime would formally invite the bishop onto the VIP rostrum. And that was where we filmed him, a frail, unassuming man in a threadbare black cassock. He stood on the edge of the row of guests on the balcony of the Ho Chi Minh Mausoleum, high above the sea of red flags and the endless procession of Communist jubilation, waving graciously to the crowd of loyal working men and women below: Monseigneur Trinh Nhu Khue, Cardinal of Hanoi.

The time for my departure was now quite near. There had been all sorts of last-minute complications because I had wanted to take the train from Hanoi to Peking. But the Vietnamese were none too happy about my crossing the sensitive border region with China. Meanwhile all kinds of rumours were circulating. There had been severe earthquakes in Manchuria and Peking and Tsientsin were said to have been affected. Yet the Chinese consul general in Hanoi issued a visa which I duly collected.

Two days before I left I was summoned to a high-level political meeting. It was quite late in the evening when the official car dropped me outside the garden of a magnificent colonial villa. A grey-haired Vietnamese with a lean, intellectual face stood waiting for me at the door. My host was Hoang Tung, editor-in-chief of the official party newspaper, *Nhan Dan,* and member of the central committee of the Communist Party. He had invited me round for a farewell chat. According to diplomatic observers Hoang Tung belonged to the inner circle of the leadership; some even described him as the Grand Inquisitor of the revolution. He was the chief ideologist of the party, a kind of Vietnamese Suslov. Hoang Tung took me warmly by the arm and led me up the stairs into a big room. We sat on a sofa, which had a white loose cover, and were served tea and beer. A portrait of Ho Chi Minh hung on the wall. In the villages of Tongking we always came across the same quartet of Communist leaders framed on the walls of local party offices: Karl Marx, Friedrich Engels, Joseph Stalin and Ho Chi Minh. In recent months the lionization of Stalin had been played down in deference to the wishes of Moscow. Mao Tse-tung had never been accepted as a member of the Vietnamese revolutionary canon.

Hoang Tung, who was also chairman of the propaganda committee, began by saying he wanted to be perfectly frank. He told me the Vietnamese held the German people in particularly high regard – after all, the founding fathers of dialectical materialism and Marxist philosophy had both been German. Germany was still the greatest power in Europe, even if it had been partitioned, but he was not prepared to hold the Soviet Union responsible for the present division of Germany into East and West. The discussion quickly degenerated into a polite sparring match. Whenever any question of political principle reared its head, all signs of affability would vanish from the face of the old ideologist. As the evening wore on Hoang Tung began to remind me uncomfortably of an ageing crocodile.

'We know there is still a great deal o be done in our country, and we're bound to make mistakes, especially now the two countries are reunited,' he said, changing the subject. He went on to explain that enormous problems lay ahead for Vietnam. Every year the population was increasing by 1.2 million, and by the year 2000 Vietnam would have 90 million inhabitants. Then there was the problem of public morality. Since North Vietnam had joined up with the degenerate South, some officials from the North had succumbed to corruption. At the next party congress delegates would have to get to grips with the problems of moral degeneracy and bureaucratic muddle. Secretary-General Le Duan had warned political commissars that the use of intimidation against the people would not be tolerated. There was still an enormous amount of work to be done in the South. He spoke about the 'three forces' who had refused to embrace the true path of revolution. Firstly, there were over a million former mercenaries from the days of the Thieu regime who would have to be re-educated. 90 per cent, he claimed, had had their full democratic rights restored to them. Only the generals and colonels of the 'puppet regime' would remain in detention camps. The second force consisted of the hundreds of thousands of members of the 'fair sex' who had previously worked as prostitutes and were now using their physical charms to try and subvert the morals of North Vietnamese troops. The third force was made up of the members of the middle-class intelligentsia who were too intellectually arrogant to comprehend the ideas of the party, and who rejected the principles of the worker-peasant democracy.

I asked him how long he thought it would take him to re-educate half the entire population of a country. The Grand Inquisitor gave me a searching look. 'If you want to explore and understand the ideas of Karl Marx you have to be prepared to study for a very long time,' he said. Karl Marx had evidently been accorded the status of Father of Church and chief prophet in Hanoi. Then Hoang Tung paused for a long moment. 'It's not just a question of stamping out the imported evils of French colonialism and American imperialism,' he went on. 'Possibly the greatest obstacle we have to face in creating a new society is Confucianism. I hear you're travelling to China the day after next. When you're in Peking, take a look at the problems the Communists are having there. They tried to launch an anti-Confucianism campaign but it never really got off the ground.'

He was very concerned about Sino-Vietnamese relations. Right up until the end Ho Chi Minh had never lost sight of his vision of a unified Socialist bloc, and he had used every means in his power to lessen the friction between Moscow and Peking. Hoang Tung felt apprehensive about the latest developments in China. He knew, of course, that Mao Tse-tung was dying, but what would happen after his death? Would China be divided up between powerful provincial rulers? Would its unity just disintegrate, as many Soviet experts had been predicting? A crafty smile softened his austere priest's face. 'Do you know what the Kuomintang clique on Taiwan say?' he asked. 'They claim Mao Tse-tung is the new Chin Shih Huang Ti. You know, of course, who I mean. He was the first emperor of the Chin dynasty and was the first person to impose any real unity on the Chinese empire. He did it over two thousand years ago, too. His aim was to abolish the doctrines of Confucius and push through a policy of centralized control. He had the Confucian scholars in China buried alive and made sure all their books were burnt, too. He was in many ways a very modern ruler. But his grand design came to grief in the end, and

277

Confucianism went on to dominate political and cultural life in China for the next two centuries. It's just malicious gossip on the part of the Taiwan Chinese to suggest that Chairman Mao is in any way like Chin Shih Huang Ti – or to predict that Maoism will be as short-lived as the emperor's early experiment in state control.'

Earthquake in China

Peking, late August 1976

The train puffed its way towards the Chinese border, leaving behind the flat lands of the delta region and heading towards the highlands of Kwangsi. All the passengers were pouring with sweat. I kept my eyes open for signs of troop movements but I didn't see anything. Once I caught a glimpse of a long row of wagons carrying rocket-launchers as we went past a siding, but that was all. My departure from Hanoi had been an emotional one. Madame Tu and Hong had taken me to the station, which had been hit by American bombs in 1970 and was still waiting to be repaired. In the days of the French there had been a tall building opposite the station that used to be a famous brothel. The block was still standing but when I thought of what used to go on there it seemed to belong to another world.

Madame Tu and Hong had presented me with a big bunch of wild flowers just before the train pulled out. The helpfulness and friendliness they had shown towards us, while still remaining faithful to their ideological principles, had been a better advertisement for Vietnam than all the speeches ever made by party officials and propagandists. One thing we had particularly appreciated during our stay was their sense of humour. We parted as friends, at least I hope we did, and as my train pulled out they stood waving on the platform until I was out of sight. Around noon, the train stopped at Lang Son in the scorching midday heat. The station there also bore the scars of the American war. Towards the end of the nineteenth century Lang Son had been the scene of a famous defeat, when a detachment of French colonial infantry had been surrounded and killed by the Chinese. The current prime minister of France, Jules Ferry, who had been

278

contemptuously nicknamed '*le Tonkinois*' by his political opponents, was forced to resign over the incident. Then in the autumn of 1950 the hasty evacuation of Lang Son by the expeditionary force had been the first ominous sign of defeat for France. The provincial capital was strategically placed between Vietnam and China. The train headed on towards the border. A little town with the delightful name of Dong Dang flashed past the window. Beyond it the landscape was bare and hilly. The sun beat down pitilessly on a gorge that had been christened Friendship Pass by Vietnam and China in the days when they were close allies. Under French rule it had been known by the prosaic but rather apt name Porte de Chine. Now we could see armed Vietnamese guards in green uniforms lining the railway track, looking as if they had been posted there to protect it from possible attack. There was no sign of bunkers or artillery positions in the surrounding hills; they had all been expertly camouflaged.

Just before we reached the border we had to change trains. On the other side of the platform spacious Chinese carriages were waiting to take us to Peking. The Vietnamese border officials had almost certainly been notified of my trip in advance, and they made a special point of being friendly. Their behaviour brought to mind a remark Madame Tu had once made: 'We feel closer to you Europeans than to the Chinese, you know.' A young Vietnamese girl in the perennial green army uniform ran up and down the platform between the trains, blowing her whistle as she signalled to the drivers. The jet-black hair under her pith helmet reached to her waist; on her belt she wore a holster with a heavy-calibre pistol sticking out. She looked as pretty as a picture, full of vitality and fun. She stood laughing and joking with the customs officials. Then, for the second time that day, I took my leave of Vietnam. I remembered I had left the bunch of flowers from Hanoi in the other compartment, so I dashed back to fetch them and presented them to the young Vietnamese girl. She looked at me in complete bewilderment, then burst into peals of laughter.

The journey from the Chinese border station of Ping-Hsiang to Peking took two days. The countryside shimmered in the stifling heat as it sped past my window: the strange brimstone cliffs of Kwangsi, the fertile rice plain of Chang Cha, the industrial area of Wuhan on the Yangtse Kiang. There was even a wider range of goods on sale in the station kiosks than there had been in Hanoi. On the third morning the air became dry, and the countryside now was yellow. Three camels walked along a dirt road, carrying heavy loads. We were approaching the capital of the People's Republic and already you could sense how close we were to the steppes and deserts of Central Asia.

Among the small circle of foreigners in Peking the subject on everyone's lips was the recent earthquake. The big industrial town of Tang Shan in Manchuria had been flattened by a terrible earth tremor that had struck without warning. There was talk of as many as 100,000 dead. Peking had also felt the quake and its streets were littered with debris. The people had been told to leave their brick houses and camp out on the streets. They were sheltering under tents and boxes and lengths of nylon sheeting. Millions of people had been left temporarily homeless, but there had been no sign of panic or disorder. Some had torn up the wooden fencing around the massive excavation works going on in the city centre to make temporary huts. The excavations were part of a major programme to build an underground transport system and, more importantly, a network of tunnels designed to withstand a nuclear attack. Now the works lay totally exposed, and the highly secret project lay exposed to any passer-by who cared to stop and look.

A strange feeling of doom pervaded the imperial city. Even a foreigner could sense it. It was almost as if the end of the world was near. An Australian press agency had reported that Chairman Mao had died, but the story was hastily denied the same day. And yet everyone knew that the days of the Leader were numbered. At noon that day our van had been stopped not far from Tien An Men Square to let through a long line of buses. The passengers seemed to be soldiers and miners, all of them wearing red paper flowers pinned to their tunics. Curious passers-by stopped to clap them as they drove past, and they joined in the applause, Chinese-fashion. It turned out the men were relief workers from the disaster zone in Tang Shan who had been singled out for special mention and brought to the capital for an official award ceremony. Towards evening a silent mass of people began gathering between the station and the Square of Heavenly Peace. Militiamen wearing distinctive white badges controlled the traffic and barred the entrances to the People's Palace. Soldiers from the People's Liberation Army came running up at the double, carrying folded seats under their arms. Word began to spread that government and party leaders had gathered to honour the Tang Shan relief workers. The people of Peking were not so easily fooled, though. They fixed their eyes on the lofty entrance to the Forbidden City, where two sentries from the People's Liberation Army stood guard, entirely motionless. Behind the big arch and the wall bearing the inscription 'To Serve the People' lay Mao Tse-tung's apartments. Had the time come for the father of the People's Republic of China to 'go to meet Karl Marx', as he himself used to say? The evening sky was bathed in violet light. Everything looked mysterious and strangely unreal. Inside the Forbidden City with its blood-red walls and golden roofs the portrait of the dying man hung over a series of archways, repeated like an echo. Beyond the arches a little temple on a hill silhouetted against sulphur-yellow cloud. It was on this very spot that the last emperor of the Ming dynasty hanged himself when his kingdom collapsed under the onslaught of the conquering Manchu armies. He knew his time had run out: the Mandate of Heaven had finally been revoked.

During that unforgettable evening I had a strange meeting behind the grey brick walls of a little house in the old part of the city. The area had survived the tremor, and when I got there Father S was waiting for me in his tiny garden. Father S was a former German missionary. He had spent years in prisons and punishment camps because of his faith. In the depths of his loneliness and suffering this Catholic priest had married a Chinese nun, and the couple had had two daughters. One had been allowed to emigrate to Australia. Her sister was fully integrated into Chinese society and refused to learn a foreign language. She greeted us with a brief but friendly '*Ni hao*', then left us when we started talking. Father S bore the scars of his years of imprisonment. He and his Chinese wife made a very harmonious and devout couple. Both were prematurely aged. On the table in the little room stood a crucifix flanked by two pictures of saints. The old man still looked like a priest: *Sacerdos es in aeternam.*

Needless to say he was better informed than any foreigners about the mood of the people. He told me they believed the catastrophe at Tang Shan to be a bad omen. 'You see they still remember all the old geomantic rules that had to be observed in ancient China every time a new building or excavation was started. If the rules weren't followed there was a risk you might bring down the wrath of heaven on your head, or disturb the dragons in their underground caves. It's no accident that the party propagandists have launched a big campaign against all forms of superstition. You hear people in the street complaining that far too many holes have been dug in the ground without proper precautions being taken. They say the rules and laws of the old order have been broken.' Reports of bad omens were coming out of the disaster zone in Manchuria. In some places black water was supposed to have gushed out of the cracks in the earth: the people believed the water was the blood of the dragons. It was nature's way of announcing the end of an epoch. Now the Chinese people were anxiously wondering whether the time had come for Mao Tse-tung to relinquish the Mandate of Heaven.

My visa expired and I drove to Peking airport as the Great Leader was on the point of death. A giant portrait of him gazed down on the empty runway. I was practically the only passenger on board the four-engined plane. Before we took off a young Chinese official checked my papers for the umpteenth time. He could speak a little English, and when he saw my German passport with the Vietnamese visa stamped in it he asked me one or two questions about the strength of the West German army. Then he brought up the subject of the reunification of Germany. He said he was all in favour of it, and said that in a way we were fighting a common enemy. Then he backtracked and asked abruptly: 'Were you in Hanoi then? Are there many Russians in Vietnam?' Then he left, and the plane taxied down the runway. 'The East is Red' sounded over the loudspeakers. On this occasion, however, it was evening, and the sun was setting in the west in a blaze of red light.

Conflict in Cambodia

The Thailand-Cambodia border, February 1979

So this was the third Indochinese war. We were barely fifteen kilometres from the smooth tarmac road linking the Cambodian border town of Aranya Prathet with Bangkok, but already we were in the depths of the jungle, plunged in its murky green aquarium light, enveloped by the hot, fetid smell of its endless cycle of decay and growth. Once again we found ourselves walking along behind little, slit-eyed men with brown skin and wavy hair. Although the shopper's paradise of Thailand was only a few kilometres away, they were dressed in rags and had nothing on their feet. Most were carrying antiquated rifles from World War II slung over their shoulders, but quite a few of them were armed only with shotguns. They had red, betel-stained mouths and ugly stumps of teeth, and they spat out the guttural noises of some strange Cambodian dialect. These village guerillas were, in fact, Khmer, even though they lived on the Siamese side of the frontier. They were being paid a few baht by the Thai government to fight between the new front lines of South-east Asia.

Early that morning we had travelled to a narrow strip of land jutting out into Cambodia south of Aranya Prathet which we christened the 'Parrot's Beak' after a similar tongue of land sticking out into Vietnam, far away to the east. We had gone there to try and find out what the chances were of crossing the frontier into Cambodia. We had set out from Bangkok late in the evening in an air-conditioned limousine driven by Joe Prasat, a well-built Thai guide from the Oriental Hotel. I had worked with Joe for ten years now; he had accompanied us to the Laotian border at Vientiane and been with us to the Golden Triangle. Joe wasn't his real name, but he used it to make life easier for foreigners. He had managed to drum up a contact for us in Aranya Prathet, a freelance reporter by the name of Seksan who knew the border crossings like the back of his hand. We found Seksan, who spoke no English, standing waiting for us by a Chinese food stall. He looked worried. After driving out to the 'Parrot's Beak' along a bumpy dirt road that threw up clouds of yellow dust (it was the dry season), we came to the burnt-out ruins of a Thai village. The dry rice paddies had been left untended and were overgrown with reeds. Little blue and white Thai flags fluttered in the tall tree-tops on the edge of the clearing. 'That's the border,' Seksan whispered. 'Cambodia is just on the other side. But this isn't a good place to cross – the Kemelush have laid mines and planted poisoned bamboo stakes all round the area.' The Kemelush were the Khmer Rouge.

It was the Kemelush who had been responsible for the devastation we saw on the Thai side of the border. They had descended on the village with fire and sword and the survivors had fled long ago. Most attacks by the Cambodian Communists were completely random, but every now and then they would carry out planned reprisals. The area south of Aranya Prathet had previously been the hide-out of the last pathetic band of supporters of Lon Nol, who had gone to ground with the so-called Khmer Serei, or Free Khmer. But the gang of jungle fighters didn't stand a chance against the blood-thirsty automatons of the Pol Pot regime.

Since the beginning of the year the strategic picture in South-east Asia had changed dramatically. After the second Indochinese war the battle-tried North Vietnamese divisions became involved in repeated border skirmishes with Khmer Rouge guerillas and made regular incursions into Cambodian territory. Then, out of the blue, Hanoi stopped playing games; at one stroke they exploded the fiction that the Communist nations of Indochina were united in brotherly harmony. They removed the mask and revealed the true face underneath – the face of naked aggression. What the Vietnamese really wanted now was power over the entire former territory of French Indochina. With astonishing matter-of-factness the Vietnamese – until recently an oppressed colonial people – took a leaf out of the book of their old colonial rulers and claimed the frontiers arbitrarily drawn up by the hated foreign oppressors as their natural birthright. On 9 January 1979 the first tank columns of the Vietnamese Chief of Staff, Van Tien Dung, inheritor of the mantle of Giap, rolled into the deserted ghost town of Phnom Penh. The North Vietnamese promptly set up a Cambodian puppet regime headed by a man called Heng Samrin. The only facts known about the new head of state were that he came from Kompong Cham and had once commanded a Khmer Rouge division there before falling out with Pol Pot and his gang. Now the élite troops of the 5th Vietnamese division, having overcome sporadic resistance around the capital, were making for the border with Thailand.

We walked behind Seksan in single file until we came to an abrupt halt on the steep bank of a wide *klong*, or canal. It was overhung on the Cambodian bank by thick clumps of bamboo. 'We have to cross here,' said Seksan. All the time we had been walking he hadn't laughed or joked once, which was most unusual for a Thai. He told us we could probably get hold of a small boat if we were willing to pay. Once we got to the opposite bank we would have to make our own way, though – no local scout would be willing to take us into Khmer Rouge territory. We would have to keep our eyes open for mines and booby traps on the jungle path. If we carried on walking for another seven kilometres we would eventually come to the old colonial road near the town of Nimit. He had heard that Vietnamese and Khmer Rouge forces were in the area and regular outbreaks of fighting were reported between the two. Usually the Vietnamese would start firing in the daytime, then the Cambodians would take over at night.

Our original plan had been to try and find some of the scattered Khmer Rouge units in the area, trusting to luck that they would be less hostile towards foreigners from the West now that the

Westerners had been defeated and left. No foreign journalist had been able to make contact with this ghost army. According to military attachés in Bangkok, the Cambodian forces were at least 30,000 strong, though most were boys between twelve and eighteen.

Seksan's wooden, expressionless voice was suddenly interrupted by sounds of fighting coming from the west. At first it was just the rattle of infantry fire, but then we heard the sound of tank guns. It would be suicidal to go wandering off into an unknown combat zone with a fully equipped camera crew. Word seemed to have got round that we were in the area, because just at that moment half a dozen Thai press photographers and cameramen appeared in the clearing. They were riding Hondas and had come from Aranya Prathet. They were obviously hoping to film us crossing the border – and possibly even being shot at. A week later I read in the *Bangkok Post* that a group of Thai journalists had, in fact, managed to cross the border at the place where we had tried. They had spotted a few black-clad Khmer guerillas in the distance but had been fired on by snipers almost immediately and had to run for their lives back across the canal into Thailand. In the mad dash for safety a photographer had stepped on a mine and been killed.

The Vietnamese had made a blitzkrieg attack on Cambodia and completely overrun it. General Van Tien Dung's green-uniformed troops had charged westwards in Russian tanks and armoured vehicles captured from the Americans. I could well imagine the satisfaction they felt as they threw themselves into mobile warfare, having spent thirty years crouching in tiny foxholes and tunnels. At last Vo Ngyen Giap, the Minister of Defence, was able to deploy his armour-plated cavalry – to do as his hero, Napoleon, had done when he sent in Murat's hussars against the enemy flanks. But sceptics were hinting that Giap no longer had the same gift for strategic planning now that he was getting to be an old man. They also claimed that Dung, his deputy, was too heavily influenced by Soviet-style conventional warfare.

The Vietnamese conquered Cambodia with ten to fifteen crack divisions and nearly 150,000 men. But when they got there, what did they find? Deserted towns, empty villages, blown-up bridges, impassable roads: a country with no agriculture, no industry and no currency. The Khmer Rouge had taken to the jungle, fleeing before the Vietnamese juggernaut. The people of Cambodia, greatly reduced in number, persecuted and demented by Pol Pot's reign of terror, no doubt looked upon the Vietnamese army of occupation as by far the lesser evil. It surely couldn't be worse than the hideous sufferings inflicted on them by their own countrymen in applying their particular brand of stone-age Communism. And yet the Cambodians could not feel any sympathy for their ancestral enemy, the conquerors from the east. Besides, even if they had wanted to fraternize, there was still the threat of the terrible reprisals being taken by Pol Pot's black-clad guerillas against all collaborators. These reprisals, like all the other atrocities, were carried out in the name of the 'national liberation struggle'. Ironically, the Vietnamese fought an American-style campaign in Cambodia; it was rather as if they were following in the footsteps of the old enemy. They would go into a locality and occupy it, then take control of the major roads. They would crush any organized resistance by means of napalm, bombs and artillery. They used helicopter support to reinforce their isolated outposts and support their tank manoeuvres. They were fighting a rude band of highly mobile, self-sufficient jungle fighters who were using Viet Cong tactics to challenge General Dung's mechanized divisions.

Pol Pot, the Red tyrant, was forced to retreat to the Cardamom Mountains with a small band of followers. The jungles he hid in stretched westwards as far as the border with Thailand and south to the Gulf of Thailand. His Chinese advisers and technical experts only just managed to escape the Vietnamese invasion. The Cambodian war was a blatant act of provocation that Peking could not ignore. She had seen her only ally in South-east Asia brought to its knees by the Vietnamese desire for hegemony. The Chinese risked losing face over Cambodia. It was essential for Peking to keep Khmer Rouge resistance alive by regular deliveries of arms and equipment. The Vietnamese were, China knew, hardly in a position to fight the kind of protracted war the Americans had got bogged down in.

During the early days most commentators in Europe and the United States emphasized the massive superiority of the North Vietnamese in men and arms, a superiority due in part to the colossal amount of hardware that had fallen to them when the Americans pulled out in 1975. Very few mentioned the deficiencies of Vietnamese maintenance, the shortage of spare parts, the damage inflicted by laterite roads and monsoon rains. The captured American weapons and tanks still fit for use at the start of the campaign were rapidly reduced to a heap of metal on the roads between Svay Rieng, Kratie and Battambang. The sole remaining source of supply of much-needed equipment was the Soviet Union.

American CIA agents in Bangkok could report back, with some satisfaction, that a new war by proxies had got underway in Indochina: the Vietnamese and the Cambodians were doing all the fighting, but it was Moscow and Peking who were chalking up the score. One agent said to me: 'The Khmer Rouge would have everything going for them if they would only stick to the good old Maoist rule of living among the people "like a fish in water". But,' he said, roaring with laughter, 'the Khmer Rouge fanatics have alienated their own people with mindless killings and atrocities. They've ended up throwing the baby out with the bathwater, and now there's nothing left for them to swim in.'

Sporadic firing continued in the Nimit area. I asked Seksan whether the two sides might run out of ammunition. He told me the Pol Pot snipers were very careful with cartridges – in fact the Khmer Rouge used sticks and shovels to carry out their mass executions. They had devised a new method of execution which involved tying a plastic bag over the victim's head and making sure no air could get in. It was only in very special cases that they actually used guns. The other day he had heard about a particularly horrific incident from an old Muslim, a refugee from the Cham community. A delegation of Cambodian Muslims had petitioned Pol Pot's regime asking that the ban on religion be waived to allow them to carry on certain ritual observances. The Muslim community in China had been allowed to continue observing their dietary laws and the Cham were asking for the same privileges to be granted in Cambodia. The Red commissars had apparently invited about 1500 Cham Muslims to talks in a big clearing in the jungle. When they had all assembled at the chosen spot they were ambushed and mown down by machine-gun fire.

Beyond the tree-tops, where the Thai flags fluttered in the breeze, lay a land in the grip of unimaginable horror. I knew the area very well from a trip I made there in the autumn of 1972, when I drove by car as far as Aranya Prathet. On that occasion I had walked across the border without a guide. When I got to the Cambodian town of Poipet, I had had a look round to see if I could find any transport to take me further. There were at least two dozen Peugeot 404 taxis waiting for customers, so I picked out a reasonably roadworthy vehicle with a reliable-looking driver. The journey took me to Battambang via Sisophon. It was absolute hell.

My chauffeur drove like a maniac. And the road surface was terrible – the battered stretch of tarmac with its huge potholes was worse than a dirt track. Traffic between Poipet and Battambang was very heavy. We kept passing huge petrol tankers on the Thailand–Phnom Penh run lying on their sides in the ditch. We saw no signs of security precautions or troop movements by the Lon Nol army. Battambang province had had a Communist-backed peasant revolt in Sihanouk's time, and was said to favour the Khmer Rouge. Yet this rich border province, which Sihanouk once described as 'our Alsace-Lorraine' (Thailand claimed sovereignty over it), had been supplying rice to both warring factions, so for the time being it was enjoying a brief period of peace.

The small town of Battambang, with its neat, well-cared-for streets, dozed peacefully in the tropical sun. I had gone there to meet two French archaeologists, Jean and Antoine, who had fled to the area after the Khmer Rouge took over Angkor Wat. They were now trying to prevent the Khmer temples and Hindu gods of nearby Prasat Sneng from gradually crumbling away. After searching all over the place I eventually came across them in a typical Cambodian pile village on the edge of the jungle. By the time I got there dusk had fallen and the two young Frenchmen had lit Davy lamps. The village had no electricity. It seemed Jean and Antoine were trying to revert to a state of nature and innocence. They were wearing the traditional *sampot*, or sarong. They ate the same food as the locals and they spoke their language fluently. They had built themselves a kind of small menagerie – perhaps Noah's Ark is a better description. Their collection of fauna included some bright-feathered birds, one or two strange-looking monkeys and the odd jungle snake. Jean and Antoine had got to know some of the local people, who all belonged to typical extended families, and had even managed to find themselves a woman each. Their mistresses were brown-skinned peasant girls with beautiful faces and shapely legs.

They had no illusions about the state the country was in. 'Cambodia has had it,' one of them said. 'We know our paradise here could collapse round our ears any day now. Our colleagues back in Paris think we're harbouring evil colonialist tendencies. The way they see it we're just nostalgic fools – we've fallen into the trap of thinking that just because these people are simple and don't ask much out of life, they must be happy,' said Antoine. 'But we think we know the Khmer as well as any white man can, and we can

288

vouch for the fact that before the war they were as happy as it's possible for any human beings to be. But it won't last much longer, because any day now the Khmer Rouge will arrive and start causing havoc.' Jean would have liked to see Henry Kissinger tried as a war criminal. 'You can just about forgive the Americans for getting mixed up in the Vietnam war,' he said, 'but there's no possible excuse for the attack on Cambodia. That was sheer bad faith on the part of Kissinger.' I asked them whether Buddhism might offer some way out. 'What was it brought down the great empire of Angkor? Why did the military skills and statescraft of the Khmer decline in the Middle Ages?' asked Antoine. 'It was all because of Buddhist ideas of worldly renunciation and contemplation. Buddhism preaches redemption of the soul, but in a totally self-absorbed way; there's no sense of responsibility to one's fellow human beings. A few centuries of Buddhism would send any empire into decline, I reckon. Maybe the same thing will happen to the Thai eventually. It's all very well to sit murmuring sutras and burning joss-sticks and giving alms to monks in peacetime – there's no harm in devoting all your energies to achieving nirvana and breaking out of the vicious circle of reincarnation then. But when you're under attack from a ruthless, hostile enemy who's hell-bent on promoting collectivization at the expense of the individual, then the only thing to do is to recognize Buddhism for what it is, the opium of the people. Though possibly not quite in the same way Lenin meant it.'

Jean went on. 'The Cambodian Communists could never have come to power on their own. Sihanouk would have got in their way, and so would basic Buddhist inertia, for that matter. Thailand was just a peaceful country before, quietly minding its own business. Then the Americans and the North Vietnamese came along and completely destabilized it. It's not as if either of them got much out of it in the end, either. All they've succeeded in doing is to turn the spotlight on all sorts of nasty fringe elements nobody had ever heard of before. So now Cambodia is in the hands of a few crackpot intellectuals who came back from the Latin Quarter having completely lost sight of the political realities of their country. Now they are trying to build their utopia on a mountain of corpses. That's one side of the Khmer Rouge. On the other hand you've got the primitive jungle tribes. They were the indigenous peoples who were driven up into the jungle centuries ago by the Khmer invasion. Now they're mostly confined to remote provinces like Ratanakiri and Mondulkiri. Last of all you have the Cambodian tribesmen whose whole lives revolved around the jungle. They used to make primitive, frightening clay statues of the Buddha and worship them like fetishes. It's this combination of left-Bank pseudo-Marxist waffle and primitive *sauvagerie* that's the secret behind the Khmer Rouge.'

Before the two men took me back to my hotel, Antoine sent someone to fetch a girl from the village. 'Here's an example of local hospitality for you,' he said. 'Can you afford to pass up the chance of sleeping with the living image of a Khmer goddess from the classical Chen-La period? She's got all the right features – a square skull, a straight forehead, almond eyes, sloping shoulders. And her skin looks just like black bronze, doesn't it? The only thing that's not quite right is her smile. It's too innocent.'

All that was seven years ago, but it seemed like an eternity. On the way back to Aranya Prathet that day we came across two armed men on bikes. They told us to take another road running south. This was the first Thai army roadblock we had encountered. The soldiers' uniforms and weapons were American and they looked just like the troops of General Thieu or Marshal Lon Nol. They casually waved us through. We hadn't gone very much further when we had to abandon the car because of the dense undergrowth on both sides of the track. Two kilometres further on we came across a few huts in the middle of a jungle clearing. Inside the huts were a dozen or so Cambodian guerillas who greeted us amicably enough. They appeared to be working for the Thai authorities and presumably belonged to the anti-Communist Khmer Serei. In exchange for a few hundred baht they offered to help us out. They heaved our camera equipment onto their backs, taking care not to let go of their shotguns or machetes, and we all set off. It seemed to me that these small, undernourished men would never be able to take on the rapacious Khmer Rouge, let alone the battle-hardened Vietnamese.

We were getting close to the Cambodian border again. The last village before the frontier had been abandoned, and the big wooden pagoda of a Buddhist monastery stood empty nearby. The monks had all fled. Inside the temple everything was thick with dust. The altar and sacred objects had been piled up in a corner like disused stage props. The whole place smelt musty and unused. It looked as if a magician had walked off and left his paraphernalia behind. A big wooden Buddha stood in a corner. It was an ugly statue with a long, pointed nose and a high forehead; it had a Western face. It reminded me of a particularly malicious clown.

A canal marked the border. The water here was thick and yellow and it had a putrid smell. The rotting jungle vegetation all around us was matted and tangled. Processions of big red ants marched over crumbling logs with a horribly purposeful air. We sank up to our ankles in mud, shuddering at the thought of the countless worms and insects crawling round our feet. A slippery tree-trunk lay across the canal so we slithered along it until we reached the opposite bank. We were on Cambodian soil at last.

One of the guerrillas – he might have been the leader, though he was as shabbily dressed as the rest of them – took a small bundle of pointed bamboo darts out of his bag with a grin. 'He says you've to keep your eyes open for these from now on,' Joe explained. 'The Khmer Rouge have stuck them all over their old emplacements so the whole place is bristling with them. Some are smeared with poison so watch out where you put your feet.' In the green, murky light of the jungle we could dimly see the outlines of a row of bunkers and approach trenches. It was from here that the Khmer Rouge had made their sorties into Thailand. Forced to retreat by the Vietnamese, they had vanished into the depths of the jungle, making for hide-outs only they knew. We all felt a strange sense of impending doom as we walked along. I kept picturing what it would be like to die out here in the jungle, alone. I thought of the myriads of insects and larvae that would batten on to my dying flesh. It would be a horrible end.

By the time we got back to Aranya Prathet the sun had sunk low. Earlier in the day we had driven past the neat Thai customs' building and made to carry on towards Poipet, but the barrier was down and we could go no further. A lieutenant from the Thai army waved us over. After we explained who we were, he said: 'If it was up to us we'd be happy to let you make your way to the Cambodian border station on foot and film there. The Vietnamese haven't taken Poipet yet – if you look you can see there's no flag flying from the mast. But the last few hundred metres are being watched by our Border Patrol Police, and they won't stand for anyone nosing around. You know how difficult it is with the BPP.' As it happened, we did know about the constant in-fighting between the army and the Thai border police. We were surprised by the soldiers, though. Considering they were supposed to be defending their country from imminent danger they seemed quite relaxed, to say the least. They had swapped their uniforms for shorts and T-shirts, and they seemed to be either playing volleyball or cooking rice. We didn't see a single armed sentry anywhere, not even in the ramshackle sandbagged bunker. The Border Patrol Police weren't much better. It was then five o'clock, time for them to go off-duty. Six of them walked a little way towards us. They wore spotted camouflage uniforms and carried M-16 rifles. They gave us a friendly wave, then disappeared into their billets at the back.

I wondered whether the Thai military had any idea of the storm that was brewing on its eastern frontiers. Their nonchalance seemed to border on lunacy. Unfortunately it was too late now for us to go looking for the refugee camp at Ta Phraya, where between 2000 and 3000 Cambodians had found short-term asylum behind barbed wire. It was proving impossible for the authorities to tell which refugees were sympathizers and which were victims of the Khmer Rouge. When they arrived at Ta Phraya, the Thai immigration officers would sort them out after a fashion and try to keep the two sides separate, but it was a hit or miss process. Every time armed groups of black-uniformed guerillas appeared out of the undergrowth at the border, the troops would hastily send for an escort of BPP. The border police would take the intruders about thirty kilometres to the north or south, then send them back into Cambodia at crossing-points not yet captured by the Vietnamese. The situation was becoming a lot trickier as the Vietnamese pressed ahead with their mopping-up operation in the provinces of Battambang and Siem Reap. How much longer would the Vietnamese High Command be prepared to stand back and do nothing while Pol Pot guerillas cut off in Thailand found shelter and asylum inside the country? Once again the North Vietnamese found themselves in the position of the Americans who for years had fumed as the Viet Cong took advantage of inviolable sanctuaries on the east Cambodia border.

Joe kept insisting we head back to Bangkok. I wondered whether the area really was unsafe after dark, as he claimed, or whether he was simply in a hurry to get back to his wife or girlfriend. The trip back to Bangkok was long and dreary. Only once did we sight some rocky hills bordering the straight tarmac road. Apart from that the scenery consisted of a monotonous succession of ricefields, lotus pools, and flat, barren countryside. The towns and villages looked identical. The wooden Siamese houses had been replaced by ugly concrete blocks. Garish-coloured advertisements everywhere proclaimed the rampant consumerism of Thai society, and neon signs flickered continually out of the dusk. Petrol filling stations were probably the main feature of Thailand's conversion to Western material values. The nearer we got to the capital, the more hopelessly congested the queues of cars and lorries became. The centre of every small town was done up like an American Main Street. The only note of contrast, and a fairly bizarre one at that, came from the extravagant architectural whims of the rich Chinese businessmen, who decorated their concrete houses with elaborate scrolls and twirls. The State had built new pagodas everywhere, all made out of cement and cast from an identical mould. The gables were decorated with tiny glass fragments that glittered in the light. Even the mythological beasts were artificial, lit up with red and green neon lights like a funfair. The sacred statues of the Buddha you saw everywhere had been mass-produced in response to a demand from the king and the government for the promotion of religion throughout the country. They were as stereotyped and unimaginative as the Lenin memorials in Soviet Russia.

And yet it was very pleasant being driven along in our air-conditioned car, listening to sickly Siamese pop tunes on the radio. By this time we had reached the city boundaries of Bangkok. At street corners candles and oil lamps burned outside the little temples of the Hindu gods which the people still worshipped with a naive, childlike faith. For centuries now these gods had been allowed to exist side by side with Buddhism, the religion of tolerance. And yet these humble tokens of traditional faith were completely submerged by the brash, oversize invitations to spend and acquire the status symbols of the new, affluent Thai society. Gigantic posters showed radiantly happy Thai families, from great-grandmother down to tiny tot, lined up on an idyllic beach, Coke bottle in hand. Cinemas wooed their audiences with sex and violence. We passed numerous massage parlours, brightly-lit and glass-fronted. Disco music blared from countless all-night bars. Cars were jammed bumper to bumper, it was impossible to move. A popular joke doing the rounds went as follows: 'If the Vietnamese ever invade Thailand with tank divisions, they'll get stuck in the traffic in Bangkok.'

The cool room and soothing music in the Oriental Hotel made me quite euphoric after a hot, tiring day. Several storeys below the lights of the city were mirrored in the dark waters of the Menam River. I soon fell asleep, to be woken at dawn by a telephone call. It was Rolf Schreiner, an ex-legionnaire who had become a successful businessman in Thailand and married a delightful Thai girl from a good family. 'Have you heard the news?' he asked. 'The Chinese launched a border attack against Vietnam this morning. The fighting seems to be in the same sector you and I spent some time in a few years ago. It looks as if it's going to be a big one.'

Holding the Vietnamese Tiger by the Tail

Bangkok, February 1979

The terrace of the Oriental Hotel was one of the few places in Bangkok where you could still sit and feel nostalgic for the old Siam. Practically every one of the picturesque canals had been drained and concreted over. The terrace looked out onto the Menam River. The wide-bottomed boats rode high out of the water when they travelled upstream, while on the way downriver to the ocean they were almost level with the surface of the water, weighed down by their heavy cargo of rice. The ferries plied back and forwards all day, non-stop. The gold of the monks' robes gleamed among the bright parrot plumage of the other passengers. In the distance, between the skyscrapers and the chimney stacks, the tiled towers and stupas of the royal pagoda of Wat Phra Keo faded into the milky-white morning sky.

Since the American débâcle in Vietnam, Bangkok had become the focal point of South-east Asian politics, the centre of speculation and intrigue, the new playground of the world's secret services. News of the Chinese offensive against Vietnam caused the same frenzied reaction among Indochina-watchers as someone treading on an anthill. The new combat zone between Tongking, Yunnan and Kwangsi was reported to be covered by a thick cloud layer so that even the pictures sent back by satellites were of poor quality. The rumours became more and more contradictory and confused. The Thai capital, which for almost ten years had been a 'rest and recreation centre' (or, less euphemistically, a gigantic brothel) for American GIs on short leave from Vietnam, seemed to have turned into a vast playground for tourists from the affluent societies of the West. They would land in their chartered jumbo jets in battalion strength at Don Muang airport. Their first port of call would be Pat Pong district, with its massage parlours and go-go bars. There were, of course, perfectly respectable tourists in Bangkok who genuinely came in search of relaxation and culture. They would religiously do the rounds of every pagoda in Chiang Mai, pausing to take in the elephant circus of Surin, then finally go in search of excitement and thrills to Mei Sai, in the heart of the Golden Triangle. The people they would meet would be brown-skinned, giggling, friendly and – outwardly, at any rate – simple. Visitors to the country were not to know that the Siamese are one of the most unfathomable and unpredictable races in the whole of Indochina, far more inscrutable than the Vietnamese, for instance, who acquired some Western reflexes in the course of their thorough-going colonization by the French.

The High Command of the Chinese People's Liberation Army had published an official announcement: it did not seek to make permanent territorial gains in its offensive against the Vietnamese. The campaign was intended as a small-scale, short-term punitive action against the Vietnamese 'revisionists' and 'troublemakers'. Peking's troops would administer a short, sharp lesson to the Vietnamese, then withdraw to their bases across the border. The statement concluded by saying that the Chinese army had no intention of advancing on the heartland of Tongking, the Red River Delta, or Hanoi. But where had the Chinese actually attacked? How far had they got? How successful had the Vietnamese defence been? No-one had any answers to these questions. Even the Americans were quite clearly in the dark over the whole business. However, with an instinctive need to justify themselves, they assumed that since the Vietnamese army had successfully defied the might of the American war machine, it was bound to be a match for the Chinese troops.

When we stayed in Bangkok we often used to go for a stroll through the streets and back-alleys of Sempang, the Chinese district. The Sons of Heaven remained outwardly calm, but behind the facade they were plainly worried about what the future held for them. Disaster had already struck the Chinese community in Vietnam. The wholesale nationalization of the retail trade in March 1978 had led to systematic repression of all Chinese residents in South Vietnam. It could be said in defence of Hanoi that the majority of the Chinese were traders or shopkeepers who stubbornly resisted all attempts to integrate them into the new Socialist state and were understandably hostile to the idea of being deported to the barren wastes of the New Economic Zones. In North Vietnam, too, the government was actively working towards the expulsion of all Chinese residents within its territories by adopting a policy of systematic harassment and, in some cases, actual pogroms. Even those Chinese who had performed many years of loyal service in the army and administration fell victim to the excesses of a political system that tended to use the argument of the class struggle as an excuse for indulging in xenophobic nationalism of the most virulent kind. There were detailed reports in Bangkok about refugees who spent weeks camping on the border between Vietnam and China before Peking would allow them in. Far more tragic was the fate of the middle-class Chinese in Cholon who managed to procure themselves exit permits by bribing officials with a few pieces of gold, then set out in frail, unseaworthy boats to brave the perils of the South China Sea – the typhoons, the pirates and the sharks. While many thousands made it to Hong Kong and other countries, a frightening number either died on ship or drowned.

Inside the Democratic People's Republic of Laos events had taken a less dramatic course. Most of the Chinese living there had escaped across the Mekong without too much difficulty, and once in Thailand they found refuge among their kinsmen and fellow Chinese. The reports from Cambodia, however, were grim indeed. The alliance between the Pol Pot regime and Peking had not prevented the Chinese community becoming the prime target of the Khmer Rouge's frenzied hatred of foreigners. The question now was whether this wave of anti-Chinese feeling would spread to the rest of South-east Asia. It came as no great surprise to any of the Chinese in Bangkok that the mighty People's Republic had hardly lifted a finger to save the hard-pressed Chinese people of Indochina. Only a tiny minority of the expelled Chinese wished to settle in their former homeland. The vast majority wanted to make their way to the United States, Canada, Australia and possibly Europe. They were not at all keen to live under Communism.

Looking further afield, there was a danger that the experiences of the Chinese in Indochina would set an ominous precedent for all overseas Chinese nationals. The Chinese business community had vivid memories of the race riots in Indonesia following the abortive putsch by left-wing officers in 1965. What would happen if Indonesia began expelling the four million Chinese living there? And what if the Federation of Malaysia, which ruthlessly pushed the exhausted Vietnamese boat people back into the sea, suddenly took it into its head to solve the acute and hitherto insuperable problem of its Chinese minority (nearly 40 per cent of the total population) by stripping them of their legal rights and deporting them? Nobody was particularly surprised when the Singapore Prime Minister, Lee Kwan Yew, the Chinese leader of a predominantly Chinese nation, lashed out at the Vietnamese Communists in a bitter attack on their policies. By pursuing its ruthless programme of deportation, Hanoi was threatening the stability of the whole of South-east Asia.

Finally there were the three million Sons of Heaven living in the kingdom of Thailand itself. In contrast to the 'Bumipatra' Muslims of Indonesia and Malaysia, whose religion made cultural assimilation with the Confucian immigrants impossible, the Siamese had coped with the massive influx of Chinese surprisingly well. Over the years some intermarriage had taken place, and many Chinese had adopted Thai names. Little by little, a reasonably flexible accommodation had been reached. Yet there was still a certain amount of antagonism and resentment below the surface. Every Thai knew, for instance, that the Sons of Heaven were increasing in numbers and hoarding up the wealth of the country. A very large number of the Thai establishment now had Chinese blood in their veins. Whenever you found yourself dealing with a particularly dynamic or competent Thai, you could be reasonably sure he was at least 50 per cent Chinese. The ruling Chakri dynasty of King Bumiphol owed its throne to a Chinaman from Fukien called Taksin, who successfully put a stop to the constant invasions and marauding by the Burmese in Ayuthya in the eighteenth century.

Quite a few familiar faces surfaced in Bangkok in the aftermath of the Chinese invasion of Vietnam. Peking and Hanoi had closed their frontiers, which meant that Bangkok, close to Laos and Cambodia, was now the best place to come to report on a conflict that threatened to engulf the whole of Asia. Military attachés and secret service agents met for regular discussions. The rendezvous were either held in the de luxe French restaurants of the international five-star hotels, or in the quiet back-rooms of Chinese eating-houses. The most sought-after people at these gatherings were the smiling Chinese diplomats. Now that the pragmatic Deng Xiaoping (Teng Hsiao P'ing) line had become the order of the day these Peking envoys, whom you rarely ever saw in Mao tunics now, had adopted a completely new tack. They worked on the principle that it doesn't matter what colour a cat is, so long as it catches the mice. Even when they were obviously putting forward official lies, they now did it with a disconcerting frankness. The Chinese embassy in Bangkok was clearly entrusted with the task of sending secret aid to the Khmer Rouge to support them in their fight against the Vietnamese army of occupation. To help in this the diplomats called on the Chinese business community in Bangkok, which controlled the entire civilian transport system. The Peking envoys said that the real purpose of their military intervention was to force the Vietnamese to withdraw from Cambodia. In their view the Soviet-Vietnamese pact of November 1978 had prompted Hanoi to send its divisions into Cambodia. The successors of Mao Tse-tung must have interpreted the alliance between Hanoi and Moscow as an act of provocation and an attempt to further the Soviet Union's policy of isolating China.

The Chinese representatives actively sought the company of their Western colleagues, yet quite a few diplomats felt they were publicizing their solidarity with the Atlantic Alliance rather too ostentatiously. Only a few days previously, Deng Xiaoping had returned from a trip to America. While over there he had posed for photographers in the inevitable stetson and generally submitted to all the public relations stunts dreamed up by his American hosts. But although the main purpose – and achievement – of his visit had been the strengthening of ties between Washington and Peking, he had repeatedly stated that China was no longer able to avoid teaching the Vietnamese a harsh lesson. At the time Washington hadn't taken his words very seriously, but the experts of the State Department were belatedly discovering the significance of his remarks. The repeated oblique threats the Chinese had directed at Hanoi while in America had, in fact, been calculated to persuade Moscow that the incursion into Vietnam had been drawn up, or at the very least agreed, between China and the United States.

It wasn't long before I established contact with a high-ranking Chinese informant. Our meetings usually took place in a restaurant. Sometimes we would sit in the Normandy Grill of the Oriental Hotel, gazing out over the grey sea of houses on the far bank of the river. At other times we would meet in the red-lacquered private room of a Cantonese restaurant, dining off South Chinese specialities. Mr Q, as I shall call him, was fifty-three but looked much younger. He was powerfully built for a

Chinese, and his red cheeks gave him a jaunty air. He had fought against the Americans in Korea, where he had held the rank of battalion commander. In short, Q was as unlike a mandarin as it was possible to be. His narrow eyes may have communicated a permanent crafty gleam, but what he said was always direct, clear and forthright. All the time we talked he would keep slapping me on the thigh in a characteristically hearty gesture. The Thai waiters would always bow respectfully to this influential man, who was an important member of the Chinese hierarchy in Bangkok. They had not forgotten that the kings of Siam had once been vassals of China and until the nineteenth century had paid a symbolic tribute to the emperor.

Mr Q admitted that the military action on the northern border of Vietnam had not gone exactly according to plan. Peking had hoped that the first reaction of the Vietnamese High Command would be to send its four divisions in Tongking into the combat zone. The People's Liberation Army could then have systematically destroyed Giap's strategic reserves while the bulk of the Vietnamese troops were tied down in the South by the Cambodian campaign. But General Giap was too crafty to fall into a trap like that. Instead he tried to contain the Chinese attack using his regional troops and militias. His task was made somewhat easier by the fact that the Chinese themselves had publicly announced their intention to limit their offensive to the belt of highlands north of the Tongking delta. Nevertheless, during the first days of the campaign the towns of Lao Cay, Cao Bang and Dong Dang had fallen into enemy hands – all vital strategic positions, as the French had learned to their cost. 'We had to take action,' explained Mr Q. 'We couldn't sit back and ignore the provocations of the Vietnamese any longer. There's still heavy fighting going on at the moment, and we certainly don't underestimate the strength of our opponents. But if we really wanted to we could be in Hanoi inside a week. The only thing that's stopping us is the public announcement we made of our short-term strategic aims. It's good for our army to have some practical experience of fighting a war. We haven't been in the field since Korea, and that's thirty years ago. So you see the campaign in North Vietnam is a useful exercise for us. We're learning something from it, and we're managing to hold the Vietnamese tiger by the tail now it's got its teeth sunk into Cambodia.' Mr Q was obviously very pleased with his metaphor because he burst out laughing. He conceded that Peking had had to consider the possibility that the Russians might intervene on behalf of their Vietnamese allies; but it was possible to exaggerate the risks. He knew what the 'Socialist-imperialists' were like from having spent four years living among them: if you showed them your teeth they would back off instantly. I asked him where the Chinese thought the Russians might strike, and he mentioned the Sinkiang-Uighur Autonomous Region, otherwise known as the 'Roof of the World', which stretches from the Gobi Desert to the Karakoram mountains. I then suggested that he might be able to secure a pass for my camera team so we could film a report on how the Khmer Rouge were coping with the Vietnamese invasion. But Mr Q shook his head gravely. It would be far too dangerous and he would not be able to guarantee our safety. In any case he was feeling very optimistic about the situation in Cambodia. There was no denying that the Pol Pot regime had committed major errors, but Peking was prepared to carry on backing the Cambodian patriots in their fight against the Vietnamese. Hanoi, he said, had got bogged down in a hopeless war of attrition, and it was going to be a question of who could hold out longest. Then Q asked, quite out of the blue, if I would like to interview Prince Sihanouk now that he was back in Peking again. 'Yes, of course, if you can get me a visa,' I replied. At that Mr Q put on his most roguish expression and gave me a hearty slap on the thigh.

The French and the Americans, needless to say, had differing views on the outcome of the Chinese offensive. By day two of the fighting the American diplomats were already talking in terms of a 'complete failure of strategic planning' and a 'major setback' for the Chinese. They were still smarting from the fact that they had completely failed to foresee this new confrontation in South-east Asia. They persisted in comparing the Chinese People's Liberation Army to their own over-developed war machine and had clearly learnt nothing from their experience in Vietnam. It never occurred to their military experts that they were witnessing an Asian conflict whose rules did not conform to the usual neat paradigm of Western warfare with its emphasis on speed and efficiency. As for the French observers, they were mainly either colonels who had won their spurs thirty years ago in Tongking, or youngish intelligence experts whose faces I remembered from my time in Saigon during the second Indochinese war. Neither of the French camps gave the Vietnamese much of a chance against the Chinese.

'This is the first time Giap has come up against an opponent who fights him with his own methods,' said one diplomatic adviser, who hid the seriousness of his role behind the facade of an easy-going playboy. 'Everyone knows the People's Liberation Army is desperately short of weapons, and the equipment they do have is pretty ancient. But then the North Vietnamese had exactly the same problem up to 1975. And make no mistake, the Chinese soldiers are every bit as long-suffering and determined and fearless as Giap's men. Heavy losses don't mean a thing to the Chinese. There's no Congress or National Assembly hanging round the necks of the Peking military demanding to know why so many young men are being lost in the fighting. And Peking has the advantage of being near its home ground. It's a case of 900 million Chinese against fifty million Vietnamese. Then you've got to take into account the fact that South Vietnam is passively resisting the Hanoi regime. One thing we mustn't do is to underestimate the tremendous stamina and patience of the Chinese. They work on a completely different time-scale to us in the West; things just take longer to happen for them. No, this time the Vietnamese have definitely got their come-uppance. They're already having to use Soviet Antonov planes to pull their élite units out of Cambodia and get them north in time. The Vietnamese have shot their bolt with this campaign, and now the Chinese are waiting for them to run out of troops and equipment. By the way, did you hear on the radio just now that the Japanese are saying Lang Son has fallen? If it's confirmed it means the Chinese have captured the key position in the North in an incredibly short time. Once they are in Lang Son they can march straight into the Tongking delta and Hanoi, though it'd mean heavy losses of course. I'm not saying the Chinese haven't made any serious errors so far. For one thing, they haven't really been able to pin down any of the Vietnamese forces, at least none worth mentioning. But just imagine what it'd be like in France if the enemy captured Lille, Metz and Strasbourg in a minor border incident!'

The question now was whether it really mattered any more what the French and the Americans thought about South-east Asia. France was no longer a potent force in the Far East, and since the Vietnam fiasco the United States had lost any active say in the affairs of Indochina. The crucial thing was what the Asians themselves thought of Peking's intervention. The Thai, for one, had greeted China's 'punitive action' with a sigh of relief. Officials in Bangkok showed the utmost discretion and restraint, of course, but the pro-government newspapers didn't mince their words. The Siamese had genuinely feared that Hanoi's revolutionaries would march right into Thailand. After all, there were active Communist cells in nearly every one of Thailand's outer provinces. However, now that the Chinese had nipped Vietnam's desire for hegemony in the bud with such spectacular success, the Thai were hoping to return to the old political balancing-act in Indochina. This policy had kept them independent of the French and the English in the nineteenth century, and it helped them survive in World War II, when they were caught between Japan and America. With luck it would come to their rescue again in the current crisis between Peking and Hanoi. The South-east Asians sensed intuitively that the Chinese dragon would win out over the Vietnamese tiger. For two centuries the technological superiority of the West had relegated China to the status of a backward and subject nation. Now this particular stage in China's relations with the West was drawing to a close. The outposts of Chinese capitalism, places like Taiwan, Singapore and Hong Kong, had already shown the world what the efficiency and intelligence of the Han people could achieve. The Siamese didn't need Napoleon to tell them that when the sleeping Chinese dragon awoke, the whole earth would shake.

The first thing that usually struck a visitor to Bangkok's main square was a huge monument erected in honour of the 'conquest' over French Vichy troops in 1940, when Marshal Pibul Songram had annexed the Cambodian provinces of Battembang and Siem Reap. These days, though, the eye of the passer-by was automatically caught by an enormous poster outside a cinema in the square. It showed helicopters spitting flames and bombs exploding over Vietnamese peasants, and a larger-than-life-size American film star with a red headband pressing a revolver to his temple. I took my place in the queue outside the entrance, my curiosity aroused by the reviews I had read in the local papers which claimed that *The Deer Hunter* was proof that America had come to terms with the trauma of Vietnam. The film was a bitter disappointment. When the film described the experiences of the main character during his time as a prisoner of the Viet Cong, I was tempted to get up and walk out of the cinema (as the Russians had done at the Berlin Film Festival). Admittedly the Viet Cong guerillas were not exactly noted for mollycoddling their prisoners, and there is no denying that some torturing went on. But they would never have forced a prisoner to play Russian roulette, and they would certainly never have bet money on it. Whatever else anyone might think of the Vietnamese Communists, the crude slander perpetrated in this film was an outrage and a disgrace. Peter Arnett, who always struck me as one of the most enterprising US correspondents during the Vietnamese war, made a very apt comment on *The Deer Hunter*. He said that whatever technical or artistic merit the film might have had, the whole story was, as he put it, 'a bloody lie'. The chaotic scenes of the last days of Saigon (with the possible exception of the shots of US personnel escaping from the roof of the American embassy) were pure invention too. There were no dives in Saigon where Russian roulette was played, the Vietnamese were far too civilized for that sort of thing. Even the Binh Xuyen would have drawn the line at that.

Despite the lateness of the hour, the lobby of the Oriental was packed with Italian and German tourists, all sunburnt from their stay in Pataya further down the coast. When I got back there was a message for me at reception, saying Wilfred Burchett was waiting to speak to me on the terrace. Wilfred Burchett was famous thoughout the whole of East Asia. He was an Australian who had been an active member of the radical trade union movement and the Communist Party from his early youth. His career as a militant was said to have dated from the time he spent working as a lumberjack. Later he had gone on to make a name for himself as a journalist, always faithfully reporting the Communist view of things.

The first time I met him was in Korea in the summer of 1952, outside the hut in Panmunjom where negotiations were being held. At that time the Western press corps was fascinated by this man, the only journalist from the Free World who dared wear the green cap and uniform of the Chinese People's Liberation Army. He was also quite different from the East European war correspondents, who at that time were under the iron yoke of Stalinism and tended to avoid talking to Western journalists. Burchett, on the other hand, always sought out our company. The English and Americans called him a renegade, a turncoat and a traitor, and generally despised him. The American provincial press, in particular, showed the most naked hostility towards him, treating him like some kind of arch-fiend. In those days Burchett, the Communist propagandist, had seemed a slightly sinister figure. He was even prepared to trot out horror stories about the Americans using biological warfare in Korea. But you can't deny the man was both courageous and unswervingly loyal to his principles. When the second Indochinese war broke out, he

303

automatically took the side of the Viet Cong. In the early years of America's involvement he used to creep up to the outskirts of Saigon with an escort of Viet Cong comrades, at incredible risk to himself, and report on what was happening in the city. Now the new Far East war between China and Vietnam had galvanized him into action again.

The man I saw on the terrace was white-haired and bespectacled, with a florid complexion; he still looked full of life and vitality, despite his age. Wilfred Burchett told me he was on his way to Hanoi. Unlike a great many others who had tried to get into Socialist Vietnam, he had been granted an entry visa straight away. He had heard I was trying to get hold of material on Vietnam, and he had remembered meeting me once at a reception in Paris given by the North Vietnamese. He proposed selling me the film report he was to make inside Vietnam. We quickly made a deal, and the conversation drifted on to other topics. This Australian propagandist for world Communism turned out to be a genial old soul, given to bursting out into guffaws of laughter at regular intervals. He claimed to be suffering from several illnesses, but this didn't stop him downing more than his fair share of drink.

We soon started reminiscing about old times. 'I didn't intend ever coming back to Asia,' he said, going back to our earlier conversation. 'I thought once Saigon was liberated it would be the end of the story. But as you can see, it's not finished yet.' In recent years he had turned his attention to the revolution in Africa, and he had covered Angola, Mozambique and Ethiopia. The next morning he was intending to set out for Hanoi, and when he got there he would be greeted by the members of the politburo like the old friend and comrade that he was. Pham Van Dong had promised him an interview, and he was also hoping to meet General Giap, who still seemed to be rudely healthy despite reports to the contrary. Burchett also claimed to be impressed by the Chief of Staff, Van Tien Dung, whom most Western intelligence sources thought of as a fairly run-of-the-mill army man. He seemed surprisingly, and rather cynically, unperturbed by the fact that his old comrades-at-arms from the Korean war, the Chinese, were now at daggers drawn with Moscow and Hanoi. A lot of water had passed under the bridge since the summer of 1950, when Joseph Stalin handed the letter of authorization for the capture of Seoul to the North Korean leader, Kim Il Sung. In those days China and the Soviet Union had formed – outwardly, at any rate – a united ideological front. Burchett confessed that even when he had been following Mao Tse-tung's troops in his Chinese uniform, he had felt himself to be first and foremost a committed supporter of the Soviet party line. Today he found himself, of course, in the Russian – and hence the Vietnamese – camp. His battling temperament and his political commitment were as strong as ever. God only knows how he managed to hold the convictions he did and still remain such a likeable man. How different this down-to-earth Australian was from the Polish journalist I met a month previously in Paris. The Pole told me he had just turned down a commission to do a news report on Hanoi for his Warsaw office. 'And do you know why I turned it down?' he said. 'Because I'm too old to lie.'

Reinforcements for the Khmer Rouge

Kyon Yai, late February 1979

At four in the morning we were woken in our hotel rooms in Trat by the owner of the boat we had hired the evening before. In theory he should have been on his way to Kyon Yai by now, where we had arranged to meet him later, but apparently he had been unable to set out because of thick fog. The hold-up was a nuisance, because we had planned to travel to Kyon Yai by car first thing that morning, so we could get on board his boat without too many people noticing us. Now we were stuck here in this little fishing port in the far south of Thailand, right next to the Cambodian border, and we would have to start looking for another boat and set out to sea in broad daylight. At first we thought the boatman in Trat might have got cold feet through fear of the border police. But he gave us back all the money we had paid him in advance and drove us out to a bend in the road. And sure enough the river which flowed into the Gulf of Thailand looked as if it was covered in a layer of cotton wool.

Trat was one of those totally featureless towns that are rapidly ruining the face of the Thai provinces. On the evening we arrived we had wandered along the main street. There was the inevitable massage parlour, of course, enticing customers with a pink and green neon sign. Inside, girl masseuses in white mini-smocks were sitting like monkeys in a green glass cage. All in all it was a pretty depressing sight. Thanks to the indefatigable Joe, we found a reasonable Thai restaurant which also had a cabaret as a bonus. The 'cabaret' turned out to consist of two Thai girls singing in shrill voices that sounded like nothing so much as a couple of mewing cats. The girls had tarted themselves up in cheap-looking outfits for their act, and wore very short skirts and bright red boots that came up to their thighs. Their faces were heavily made-up. The caterwauling sound was accompanied by a deeper male voice, which came from a very intriguing individual. He was an Asian albino with pure white hair and pale skin, and his face was half-hidden by sunglasses; he wore a well-cut black suit, and the whole effect was like something out of a science-fiction novel. One of the girls came over to our table. She spoke a rather comical variety of English. The general ambience in the restaurant, which was full of prosperous Thai businessmen, was curiously light-hearted considering the Cambodian border was barely five kilometres away. Suddenly the singer stopped talking and her baby-face became almost grave. She asked in a low voice: 'Do you really think the war will come here? We're all so worried.'

On the road to Kyon Yai we drove past a refugee camp which seemed to be guarded by a detachment of Thai marines. After much pleading and arguing with the sentry, we were allowed through the wire-netting gate and taken under armed escort to see the commanding officer. He was extremely friendly and amiable, but he absolutely refused to let us have any contact with the Khmer refugees who had fled there to escape from Pol Pot's thugs. The same thing had happened when we visited the divisional headquarters of the marines at Chanthaburi and asked to film the men. We had met with the same courteous, smiling refusal from the officer in charge, who politely waved aside our official letter of recommendation. During these discussions we would all drink tea and grin at once another, trying not to speak too loudly (in Thailand it was considered the height of bad manners to raise one's voice). But basically we would just look foolish, and inevitably fail to get what we wanted. The friendliness of the natives could be like a rubber wall sometimes. Whenever you saw an Asian in Thailand really lose his temper and start shouting and screaming, you could be pretty sure he was Chinese.

In Kyon Yai, Joe dropped us off at a Chinese restaurant while he went off to organize the boat trip. From our table we had a magnificent view over the narrow canal where the fishing boats lay at their moorings, packed together like sardines in a tin. The tiny harbour was full of life and bustle. The shops on both sides of the canal were crammed with every imaginable type of product, from fridges to TV sets to electric toothbrushes. Laid out on the jetty were fish and shellfish in profusion. I asked the restaurant owner where the Cambodian border lay. He pointed to a ridge of wooded cliffs that sealed off the bay about a kilometre to the east. Beyond that ridge lay the murderous hell of the Khmer Rouge, the ruthless killing of brother by brother, a world of unrelieved misery, hunger, torture and horror. Yet here, down by the harbour, within sight of the Cambodian outposts, we looked upon simple scenes of happy Asian life. Chubby-cheeked children tweaked the hair on our arms and shrieked with laughter. The old people busied themselves gutting and scaling fish. The people of Kyon Yai reacted to the threat on their doorstep by pretending it didn't exist.

There seemed to be virtually no policing of the border in this area. This was the most southerly promontory in Thailand, jutting far into Cambodia, yet at the end of it there was only a barricade and ten sandbags. A platoon of marines lay dozing in their hammocks in the shade of the trees. A police patrol vessel lay rusting in the canal, its gun unused for years. Still, we didn't want to take any risks; and once we had freed our hired cutter from the tangle of boats in the harbour, we took care to keep our heads down as we sailed past the seemingly deserted police vessel. Soon we were chugging out towards the open sea. The Gulf of Thailand lay at our feet, as smooth as a silver platter. Our fishing boat glided through the water, leaving a gentle furrow in its wake. The owner, who lived on board with his wife and little son, went forward to the bows and lit two joss-sticks. 'That's for the spirit of the boat,' said Joe. 'Every ship has its own spirit watching over it.'

Prem, the fisherman, was a grey-haired, quiet old man. He had been reluctant to agree to our plan, but in the end Joe had made him an offer he couldn't afford to refuse. We wanted to go inside Cambodian territorial waters. We especially wanted to have a look at the island of Ko Kong, which was still in the hands of the Khmer Rouge. We had heard rumours that it was being used to transship supplies from China destined for the Cambodian troops, and we wanted to check out the story for ourselves. Prem knew the coast like the back of his hand. Now that the authorities in Phnom Penh could no longer enforce their territorial rights in these remote waters, hordes of Thai fishermen had sailed into the bays around the Cambodian coast where the catches were better than on the Thai side. It was nearly midday. The heat had drawn a veil of mist over the water, but we could see the Cambodian mainland about three kilometres away. Beyond the white shoreline lay the edge of the jungle, which soon gave way to a rugged, mountainous landscape. 'Prem doesn't want to go too close to the island,' said Joe. 'He's heard the Khmer Rouge have got artillery – well mortars, anyway – and you never know how they're going to react. But he seems more worried about the Vietnamese navy corvettes. He says they patrol the area regularly. They fly the flag of the Vietnamese-backed Heng Samrin regime, though there aren't any Cambodians on board. Prem was stopped by one of these vessels last week. They went through everything looking for arms and contraband; they even ripped out the beds in the cabins. Then they gave him a warning and sent him back to Kyon Yai. Next time they said they'd confiscate the boat. Just imagine what would happen if they stopped him today and found foreigners on board.'

In the distance we could see a dark green rock rising out of the sea. 'That's Ko Kong island,' said Prem. The Thai fishing boats had fanned out across the bay and were busy pulling in the nets they had paid out during the night. They seemed to have quite a good haul. During the night they sometimes came across motor vessels with their lights extinguished, trying to escape detection by the patrol boats. These were the clandestine carriers who had been hired by the Chinese middlemen in Chanthaburi and Trat to ship arms and ammunition to Ko Kong. Recently however, the Vietnamese had captured the harbour at Kompong Som after fierce fighting, and since then things had been getting more dangerous for the arms smugglers.

It gradually began to dawn on us that Ko Kong was not, in fact, the major transit camp the Thai authorities had made it out to be. What was actually happening was that the Pol Pot guerillas still fighting in the area were being supplied overland with the tacit connivance of the Thai Border Police, though nobody in Bangkok was prepared to admit it. Hanoi had long ago realized what was happening and had threatened reprisals. We offered Prem extra money to sail closer to Ko Kong, but he was adamant. He turned the boat round in a sweeping curve, and we headed back up the coast.

We arrived in Pataya just as it was getting dark. The carnival atmosphere of this famous Thai beach resort and the blatant trade in sex hit us like a slap in the face. Pataya was no more than 200 kilometres away from the Khmer Rouge lines and the tank columns of the Vietnamese army. Yet here, nobody seemed to give a thought for the fighting and dying and suffering. The one, crowded street in the resort seemed to be filled with a bewildering array of prostitutes offering their services to passers-by. These girls had tried hard to look sexually attractive for their clients – mainly Europeans, Americans and Japanese. They had all come up with a similar sort of uniform; hot pants and thigh-length boots, tiny mini-skirts and low-cut necklines that plunged to below the waist at the back. There were all sorts of ingenious variations on this basic theme, though. Some were obviously trying the Lolita look, while others were done up like footballers in striped socks and sneakers. A prostitute in a flowing white dress and a maharani's turban drifted towards us. 'Be sure and watch out for the ones with heavy make-up and long dresses,' Joe warned us. 'They'll be transvestites. She'll be a he, in fact.' Crowds of males thronged the street outside the seedy fish restaurants and blaring discotheques, dazzled by the wealth of talent on offer. It wasn't long before the men wandered off on the arm of dusky beauties. There are two kinds of European tourist here,' said Josef Kaufmann, the cameraman. 'On the one hand you've got the single men who come on their own and get picked up by a Thai girl almost straight away. You can tell them by the satisfied smirk on their faces. Then you've got the ones who come out here with their wives and have to stand and watch the others having a good time, feeling jealous and frustrated.' Steve, our sound engineer, laughed. All this erotic bliss would probably only last for about three days, he said, then the lucky Lotharios would have to rush off to the doctor's and get some penicillin jabs.

Even Joe, who was usually game for anything in the enjoyment line, shook his head as he watched the crowds of tourists. Then he turned to me. 'Do you remember the Americans who used to come here on leave from Vietnam for R and R? It really makes me wonder what's going to become of this country when I see this sort of thing.' He paused for a moment. 'And yet you can make something of yourself in Thailand if you work hard and know what you're doing,' he said. 'Since the last time I saw you I've bought my own taxi. But the Westerners who come here to enjoy our women have no idea what goes on in Thailand. They don't realize the poor peasants in the north and the north-east sell their daughters to the brothels in the south for money. They see us smiling, but they don't realize a coolie in Bangkok is lucky to earn 40 baht a day.' (Forty baht was roughly the equivalent of 80p.) I asked Joe about the Communist rebels in the border provinces. He told me the Thai Communist Party had been weakened and split by the conflict between China and Vietnam. The situation was still fairly dicey in the capital and the countryside, though. In Thailand you can hire a killer for a few thousand baht to get rid of a business rival or a political opponent.

Back at the Royal Cliff Hotel a phone message from the German embassy was waiting for us. The government of Laos had issued us a joint visa and film permit. In three days time, if it was possible, we were to go to Vientiane.

Monks and Cocktails in Communist Laos

Vientiane, March 1979

In the Laotian capital of Vientiane hardly an evening went by without some diplomatic cocktail party or reception. Of course it was a very small world, and you inevitably kept bumping into the same old faces all the time. The Asians outnumbered everyone else by a long way and definitely dominated the social scene. The last time I had visited Vientiane in the summer of '76 on my way to Hanoi, the French ambassador had still been refusing to acknowledge the existence of the Communist revolution, and was hanging on defiantly, a proconsul stripped of his powers. This time, however, there wasn't a single representative of the Quai d'Orsay left in the Democratic People's Republic of Laos. It wasn't just the arrogance of this one diplomatic adviser that had led to the French legation being closed down. Officials of the Revolutionary People's Party, as the Communist Party of Laos was known, had obviously been determined to try to end the cultural influence of France. Then a mysterious National Committee for the Liberation of Laos had been set up in France, and this had merely confirmed the suspicions of the Communist leadership that Paris was actively encouraging all manner of reactionary plots to topple the regime. The deciding factor had probably been Hanoi's strong hint to the Laos government that it should show the old colonial power the door.

Social life in the capital of Communist Laos had recently been taken over by the diplomats of the ASEAN countries (ASEAN stood for the Association of South-east Asian nations). Its members included Indonesia and the Philippines as well as Thailand, Malaysia and Singapore. The extent to which this rather loosely-knit association of states had developed a new sense of solidarity, born of a mutual instinct for self-preservation, since the threat of Vietnamese dominance came to the fore in South-east Asia, was remarkable. The ministries of Bangkok and Jakarta, Manila and Kuala Lumpur were now sending some of their best people to this previously insignificant little town on the banks of the Mekong. Laos, in fact, was now a key factor in the much-discussed Domino Theory of the political upheavals taking place in this part of Asia.

At the reception I attended that evening I got talking to a tall Burmese colonel whose experiences in his own country made him probably better placed than anyone else in the room to assess the risks of civil war and factional strife in this Asian trouble-spot. He was reputedly a close friend of the Burmese president, General Ne Win. When I spoke to him he was critical of the Chinese military intervention on the North Vietnamese border. The Burmese were supporting Hanoi, not so much on ideological grounds as out of fear of possible Chinese aggression on their own frontier. It was, after all, a well-known fact that up until the nineteenth century the last kings of Mandalay had been forced to recognize the emperor of China as their feudal lord.

To everyone's surprise, the Americans had recently set up an embassy in Vientiane. Hanoi, which was anxious to normalize its diplomatic relations with Washington, took full advantage of the Vientiane link. The top American diplomat, who was being kept under close observation by the local security police, was a former officer in the marines who had spent several years in Vietnam and was married to an extremely inquisitive Vietnamese woman. The British had sent along a specialist who made up for his low ranking with a profound knowledge of Asian affairs. But more important than the envoy from St James's Palace was the head of the Australian legation. Australia, although it was not an Asian country, was a respected partner and a major influence in the

ASEAN alliance. The Swedes also occupied a special position in Vientiane. The Swedish chargé d'affaires, who had recently arrived from Stockholm, had started turning up at every official do wearing the Laotian national costume, a fluttering white silk shirt that buttoned up to the neck. He was a typical example of the Swedish desire always to be on the side of the 'progressives' in the non-European world, even if it involved a sacrifice of principle. Western diplomats in Vientiane were still highly indignant that one of the last acts of Olof Palme's administration had been to rush vital technical and economic aid to the Laotian Communists. The ostensible purpose of this aid was to help extend the road link between the Mekong and the Vietnamese coast, but its effect was to increase Vientiane's dependence on Hanoi, and hence make Laos even more of a satellite state.

For all the attempts of the Swede to ingratiate himself, there was no hiding the fact that the role of the West in Laotian affairs had dwindled to virtually nothing. On the banks of the Mekong, the white man's burden Kipling once talked about had become light as a feather. The new leading and medium-rank powers in Asia had already taken up the mantle of the West. Hence the Japanese, for instance, had made a point of staffing their embassy with an extremely personable young diplomat who had learned flawless French at the Sorbonne and acquired a liking for the good life you didn't often find among his compatriots. The 'Great East Asian Co-Prosperity Sphere' which the Japanese failed to establish by force during World War II was, everyone knew, now being realized though discreet trade deals and economic diktats; Japanese businessmen had even taken the lead in Vietnam. Nor had it escaped the Asians that Japan's colossal industrial base provided the potential for a massive re-militarization of the country.

The Indians also enjoyed considerable prestige and respect in Laos, a country deeply influenced by Hinduism, and Buddhism, the official religion of Laos, had originally taken root on the banks of the Ganges. More important still, in demographic terms India was the only real counterweight in Asia to the Chinese colossus. Behind the serene eyes of the Indian officials, behind the social poise and agility, lay the inheritance of thousands of years of civilization, the dismissive arrogance of a deep-rooted belief in caste. There was virtually no contact to speak of between the Indians and the Chinese in Vientiane. Memories died hard: when Mao Tse-tung's troops defeated Jawaharlal Nehru's élite regiments in the Himalayas in 1962, the Indian press had loudly denounced the 'barbaric Chinese hordes'.

That evening I found myself gravitating towards the table of the Chinese military attaché, an old man with thin grey hair and a friendly face who towered above all the Laotians in the room. According to unofficial sources, the military attaché was a general. He didn't speak any foreign languages and his wife had to translate into English for him. This lady wore a brightly-coloured flowered blouse. Her eyes shone with intelligence, and her fine features and confident manner marked her out as a daughter of the old Chinese aristocracy. The general was successfully playing the role of the naive old warhorse. 'All he can talk about is the weather,' complained one of the embassy wives. Earlier that day news had come through that the Chinese army, after capturing the stronghold of Lang Son, had halted its advance and was about to start its planned withdrawal across the border. When I questioned the military attaché about it his face was transformed by a broad grin. 'You mustn't get the wrong idea about our punitive action against the "Cubans" of Asia,' he said. 'It was a limited and fairly small-scale military operation. But we couldn't just sit back and do nothing while Hanoi continually provoked us and needled us. The Vietnamese had to be taught a lesson, and now it's over. Believe me, nobody in South-east Asia will ever accuse us of being a paper tiger again.'

He refused to be drawn out on the latest tensions between Laos and China. In fact the Chinese embassy in Laos was in a rather tricky situation at that particular time. The Communist government in Vientiane had declared its wholehearted allegiance to Vietnam, and had also asked Peking to withdraw its road engineers from the north of the country. The Chinese liaison office in Oudomsay had also been shut down without warning. The Democratic People's Republic of Laos, following in the wake of Vietnam, was set on a collision course with China. A buffer state of three million people was taking on a nation of 900 million inhabitants. The government in Vientiane were obviously undeterred by statistics or laws of probability. The Laotian Communists, whose Secretary-General, Kaysone Phomvihane, had been acting as prime minister since the takeover, must have been staking everything on the strategic superiority of the Soviet Union. The Land of a Million Elephants was on the brink of becoming a province of Hanoi and, more crucially, a military jumping-off point into South-east Asia for Moscow.

The Vietnamese never attended any of the social gatherings in Laos, no matter who was giving them; they were anxious to play down their presence in the capital. The Russians, on the other hand, were ostentatiously throwing themselves into their role as the new patrons in South-east Asia. They were as reluctant as the Vietnamese to join in the sophisticated round of cocktail parties and dances, but they would occasionally send along a token representative, a rather hard-boiled KGB man. Otherwise they were content to let themselves be represented by the more polished Cubans, who obviously enjoyed the relaxed conviviality of these gatherings. The Hungarians also felt quite at home in this informal atmosphere, but East Germany, which had sent a particularly dour team to Vientiane, was completely overshadowed socially by the West German legation. This was all mainly thanks to Wasserberg, the highly unorthodox ambassador from Bonn who always steered clear of ideological squabbles. He had recently gained a great deal of extra clout in the diplomatic community by taking charge of French interests in Laos. The other reason for the social success of the West Germans was the ambassador's beautiful wife, who managed to combine an almost provocative sense of chic with typical Rhineland ebullient good humour. Eva Wasserberg was the most coveted dinner guest in Vientiane.

The Laotian foreign office had sent along a few officials. They all spoke impeccable French and quite unconsciously aped the mannerisms of their former colonial masters. One of them was actually married to a French woman, and his children were living in Paris. To look at these men now you would never have thought they had just spent a couple of years fighting as guerillas in the caves of Vieng Xai. During discussions at the bar these high-ranking comrades never strayed outside the conversational limits laid down by the party, yet somehow they managed to convey to the other foreigners that Marxism in Vientiane had a more human face than the brusque Vietnamese equivalent.

When I first arrived in Vientiane I was immediately struck by the number of Buddhist monks you could still see on the sleeping streets of the capital, drifting from one monastery to the next in their ceremonial robes. The pagoda of Ong Tu housed the biggest school in the capital, and the monks were closely involved in the teaching there. I was eager to know whether the Communists had put Buddhism to the service of the revolution – or, more accurately perhaps, subverted it to the requirements of Marxist indoctrination. The new ideological syncretism of the regime clearly involved, at some level, translating the concepts of Buddhism into Marxist terms. A French couple who had taught in Laos and been deported from the country wrote an article in *Le Nouvel Observateur* in which they elaborated a whole theory on how the new, post-revolutionary system worked. According to them, in political seminars the Buddhist notion of *kaona*, or 'spiritual edification', was equated with the internalization of party slogans. The Buddhist meditation known as *sati*, which was originally intended to resolve all the contradictions inherent in man, now became a tool for learning how to examine one's (ideological) conscience and practise self-criticism and revolutionary vigilance. The Buddhist idea of *dhamma*, which was once used to mean man's sense of harmony with his fate, now became the hallmark of the enlightened revolutionary who had successfully embraced the new doctrine and was able to distinguish between good and evil. Conversely the Buddhist notion of *adhamma* corresponded in Communist theology more or less to the idea of the 'damned', in other words all those opposed to the wonderful new regime that was to bring happiness to mankind. The commissars of the Revolutionary People's Party, some of whom were former monks, were now trying to teach the followers of Buddhism that the great Gautama had revealed himself in a new reincarnation and was manifesting himself in the guise of material progress and human brotherhood. It was impossible to tell whether the followers of Buddhism actually swallowed this line. All we do know is that a third of the monks in Laos fled across the Mekong when the Communists came to power.

The atmosphere in Vientiane seemed relaxed and easy-going compared to my last visit during a stopover in the summer of 1976. On that occasion the car from the German embassy had been stopped on the way from the hotel to the airport by gangs of armed youths sporting red armbands who had searched us for arms, clearly enjoying their new role as militiamen. The capital now seemed to be far better supplied with food and basic consumer goods than it had been three years ago. The reason for this was the apparently unrestricted flow of contraband coming from across the border in Thailand. The regime had also made certain pragmatic concessions – for example, granting the US dollar quasi-official status and treating it as a second currency to be used for all monetary transactions with foreigners, for buying everything from a plane ticket on the domestic airlines to a bottle of beer in the Lane Xang Hotel. Generally speaking, it was difficult to tell how the local people were coping with all the changes. Rice was on sale at 45 kip per kilo in the state distribution centres; on the black market the same quantity cost 500 kip. Anyone who wanted to buy petrol (and there were still quite a few Hondas and one or two private cars left in Vientiane) had to go about it in a roundabout way by applying to the Army, which supplemented its meagre budget by selling fuel.

The big central market near the massive triumphal arch which the Royalists had built as a war memorial had come to life once more, and there seemed to be plenty of fresh vegetables and chickens on sale. However, the old shopping centre in the Rue Samsenethai was completely deserted and most of the shop windows were covered with iron grilles. The Chinese shopkeepers had cleared out long ago; the only traders left were a few enterprising Vietnamese flogging old Meo silver, bronze Buddhas and ugly Talmi jewellery to the tourists. The Russians eagerly bought up this cheap rubbish; Vientiane seemed to be a shopper's paradise for the Soviet technical experts and their families. The Vietnamese advisers working behind the scenes in every ministry in the city kept a very low profile and were rarely seen on the streets. Similarly the Vietnamese troops standing by outside Vientiane were stationed in secret billets and kept strictly isolated. The Russians didn't seek to maintain a discreet presence, and you saw them all over the capital. Aeroflot had taken over from Air France and was advertising holidays on the Black Sea. Most of the Soviet technical experts lived in a row of scruffy apartment blocks on the road to the airport. The Russian females were notable for their dowdiness and general lack of chic; they contrasted greatly with the pert Laotian women. The new puritanical Communist regime had banned the wearing of jeans and ordered all women to don the uniform of the *sin*, the traditional Laotian dress with coloured braid round the hem. Whereas the women of Cambodia had been forced to cut off their black hair to just below the ears, the Laotian women were simply forbidden to wear their hair bobbed or in a fringe. Such was the variety of the great Asian revolution.

The Communists had tightened up on morality in the city. They had closed down all the opium dens and sex parlours and replaced them with a 'leisure centre', a depressing dump that masqueraded under the name of a night-club. Here beer and lemonade were served beneath a huge red star and hammer and sickle. The fun-loving Lao girls were forbidden to 'play around' with married men on pain of being sent to a labour camp. The young men were promptly arrested if they were caught dancing to Western music or wearing their hair long. If they infringed the law a second time they were sent to a rehabilitation camp. However, the situation was different to Vietnam in that it was very easy to escape from Laos. All a refugee had to do was swim or sail across the Mekong and because the river was so shallow you didn't have to be a champion to make it safely to the opposite bank. The river border between Laos and Thailand stretched for hundreds of kilometres and there was no way the authorities could seal it off effectively. An added attraction was the knowledge that on the opposite bank were people who belonged to the same race and spoke the same language. According to official sources in Bangkok, there were currently 130,000 Laotians in refugee camps in Thailand. About a tenth of the entire population of three million people had fled the country, and a half of these had gone to ground abroad. During the summer of 1976 you could hear shots being fired by the border patrols down by the waterfront practically every night. Once an Australian diplomat got a bullet in the leg from an AK-47 while he was out water-skiing. Apparently a rather simple-minded soldier had been somewhat puzzled by the sight of this new-fangled sport. Now, three years later, the authorities seemed more resigned to the position. People in offices could be heard saying: 'If the capitalists and middle-men and all the other enemies of the Socialist revolution want to leave the country, then let them go.' What was more worrying was the fact that the peasants in the countryside had begun fleeing the country. This was because the Laotian Communists, spurred on by their Vietnamese task-masters, had set about trying to transform traditional, family-based rural village communities into Soviet-style agricultural cooperatives.

We had given up going out to eat at the Tam Dao Vien, the last Chinese restaurant in town where you could still get decent food. Instead we had slipped back into having our meals in the Lane Xang hotel, where the service still functioned after a fashion. Rather surprisingly, the swimming pool had been newly painted and cleaned up for foreign visitors. Whereas in the old days you used to get CIA agents coming there, you now saw Russians in swimming trunks sitting round it, playing chess in the shade of the trees, for all the world as if they were back home in one of their 'parks for culture and recreation'. Behind the counter in the bar, which was nearly always empty, a proverb dating from the days of the French still hung on the wall: 'Alcohol takes a long time to kill you, but never mind, we're in no hurry.'

One evening we took a taxi to visit the Tat Luang pagoda. It had just been newly whitewashed and looked bright and clean; you could see its golden pointed roof glistening in the evening sunlight from a long way off. Next door, the authorities had put up a monument to the men who had died fighting for the revolution. It was wedge-shaped and very ugly, and consisted of a red star painted on a white plaster background. Beside the war museum that no foreigner was ever allowed to enter, a pair of sentries stood guard in front of a particularly tasteless victory memorial. It showed a triumphant soldier and peasant standing with feet planted squarely on a bomb that carried the letters US.

At five o'clock the evening rush-hour started in Vientiane. Everyone would start pouring out of the government offices, and the wide avenue that passed the triumphal arch, built for some inexplicable reason in honour of the Royal Laotian troops, would suddenly be thronged with bicycles and scooters. Then the bustle would die and the streets would be quiet once more. Beside a crumbling stupa next door to the foreign ministry, water buffaloes grazed peacefully. In the Buddhist monasteries the monks were hanging out their saffron robes to dry. The sun was setting rapidly. The creeks of the once-mighty Mekong shone between the sandbanks like molten iron, glowing red in the evening light. On the far bank you had a clear view across to the Thai customs' house at Nong Khai. Once it got dark it wasn't advisable for Laotians to leave their homes, and foreigners had to take cover behind the privileges, and consular number-plates, of the diplomatic community.

On the second day of our visit to Laos we had to abandon any idea of being allowed to travel round the north of the country. Since the outbreak of the Sino-Vietnamese conflict even the Plain of Jars, which Western journalists were being allowed to visit only a year ago, had been declared a no-go area. We were told, unofficially, that a heavy build-up of Vietnamese troops had been reported in this strategically important area. According to reports from diplomatic sources, Hanoi currently had between 20,000 and 35,000 men in Laos. During the last three years the Boi Doi had systematically weeded out all the pockets of resistance among the Meo tribesmen in the north of the country, and destroyed their villages with napalm. Some Thai sources even claimed that poison gas had been used. After one last heroic struggle the Meo had been forced to retreat with their families to their stronghold at Phou Bia. Now they were desperately trying to get to the Thai border. They knew very well, of course, that they were not exactly popular in Thailand. For years the Thai army had been fighting a local war against a splinter group of rebellious Meo tribesmen living a nomadic existence in Nan province.

The foreign ministry had given us strict orders not to go beyond the limits of the Nam Ngum reservoir on the road to Luang Prabang. We set out first thing in the morning, still congratulating ourselves on the official escort assigned to us, a man called Mongkhul. He was definitely a cut above the average run of guides and interpreters. You could tell from his round, light-skinned face and his aristocratic self-assurance that he came from the Laotian upper crust. It wasn't until a few days later that he told me his father had served as prime minister for a time in the fifties under King Sisang Vatthana. Mongkhul himself had been dean of the law faculty in Vientiane before the upheaval. He had studied as an undergraduate in Paris. Like me, he had attended the Fondation Nationale des Sciences Politiques. The memory of our days there created an instant bond between us. No-one who had studied under men like André Siegfried, Raymond Aron, Maurice Duverger, and Pierre Renouvin could fail to be steeped in liberal ideas.

After travelling for about 100 kilometres, passing several military checkpoints on the way, we came to the Nam Mgum reservoir, which had partly been funded by aid from West Germany. We noticed manned anti-aircraft batteries in the surrounding hills; obviously the only enemy the Laotians were expecting to turn up here was the Chinese air force. In 1973 we had flown over this reservoir in miserable weather on our way to Long Chen. This time, however, the lake looked beautiful, a sheet of silver in the blazing sunshine. The tree-stumps were still sticking out of the water, but somehow they no longer looked eerie; if anything they seemed to heighten the romantic atmosphere of the place. We were once again due to be shepherded round the local re-education centres for prostitutes, drug addicts and vagrants. We were taken from one camp to the next in a ferry boat, and we did the obligatory rounds of sad-eyed girls and listless young men. They were obviously not being harshly treated, and from what we could see the camp attendants seemed reasonably humane. In theory the detainees were meant to be kept on the islands for a year until they were ready to go back into Socialist society. I could see further islands shimmering on the horizon and asked the camp commander if any political prisoners were being held there. He said he couldn't give me a definite answer; he had nothing to do with that side of things – that was the province of the army and the state police.

We had already tried to find out the number of political prisoners in the country when we were in Vientiane, but without success. There were always wide discrepancies between the figures given by foreign observers in the capital. It was generally assumed, or hoped, that most of the opponents of the regime – high-ranking officials from the previous administration, staff officers and generals from the Royal Laotian Army, recalcitrant capitalists, and so on – had escaped across the Mekong in time. Those who hadn't were sent to the northern provinces, where they were forced to live like poor hill peasants and plant manioc in the mist and rain. The Communist bully-boys had even arrested the peace-loving King of Laos, Sisang Vatthana, and dragged him away from his secluded residence in Luang Prabang to the inhospitable countryside around the Plain of Jars. There had been stories that a resistance group was planning to help him escape to Thailand. The king was meanwhile being held under close arrest in Vieng Xai, the old Pathet Lao stronghold. I wondered whether he still found time to pursue his major passion, the study of Proust's *A la Recherche du temps perdu*, surrounded by the cold, drizzling rain of the north. In Vieng Xai, the Neo Lao Haksat, the Communist Front for National Reconstruction, was rumoured to be active again. According to some reports they were busy completing the massive defence system of caves and tunnels that ran for kilometres through the steep limestone mountains. The tunnel system was designed to cope with all eventualities of war.

On Peace Island the Socialist state had built a hotel for foreigners visiting the detainees, and at midday we stopped there to eat. In January the Thai Prime Minister, Kriangsak Chovanan, had been a guest at the hotel. At the time of his visit the bombshell of the Hanoi-Peking conflict had yet to erupt. It was generally agreed that, in General Kriangsak, Thailand had finally got a prime minister who was worthy of the name. The dark-skinned, elegant man with the slight wave in his hair was in a completely different class from his predecessors, both military and civilian. At last here was someone who could command respect and inject some dynamism into the government of the country. After the

Vietnamese launched their offensive in Cambodia they encouraged the Laotian Communists – for compelling economic and strategic reasons – to adopt a more conciliatory attitude towards their neighbour across the border. Hanoi hoped that a lessening of tension between Laos and Thailand would help relieve its own critical position in Phnom Penh and possibly also strengthen the neutralist trend in Bangkok. General Kriangsak had skilfully played along with the idea. He had caused something of a stir on his visit to Peace Island by bringing along a group of Siamese dancers. The general impression at the time was that the prime ministers of Thailand and Laos had got on extremely well. Yet when I spoke to the Laotian prime minister a few weeks later in Bangkok, during his return visit to Kriangsak, it was quite plain to me that the much talked-about friendship between the two men could only have been a front. The strong man in Vientiane, prime minister and Communist party leader Kaysone Phomvihane, clearly felt inhibited and out of his depth amid the glitter and opulence of Siamese hospitality. He was wearing a dark grey suit. Every so often he would give a rather forced smile and awkwardly drink to the health of his host, who remained, as ever, utterly poised. The more Kaysone tried to look at home in Bangkok, the more alien he appeared; like it or not, he was a true son of Vietnam. (In Vientiane he always went around with a group of burly-looking bodyguards to protect him from journalists.)

During our trip we were constantly told that one day Peace Island would attract tourists from all over the world. But presumably before that happened the authorities would have to get rid of the two re-education camps on Production Island and Independence Island. We had a strong suspicion that the camps for political prisoners were actually located on Peace Island itself. The name of this Laotian equivalent of the Gulag Archipelago was clearly a masterly piece of Orwellian doublespeak. At least as far as its prisons were concerned, the capitalist world had always been more honest than the Communist states. At the time of Captain Dreyfus and, later on, Papillon, the authorities in French Guiana had at least called a spade a spade and sent the most recalcitrant prisoners to Devil's Island.

On our return from the islands we had driven for about fifty kilometres when Mongkhul drew our attention to some square straw huts by the roadside. Unlike the typical Laotian dwellings these were not built on piles. 'A group of Meo tribesmen came down from the mountains and settled here in the plain,' he told us.

'The Meo didn't all fight on the side of the CIA during the war. The vice-president of the Front for National Reconstruction, Fay Dang, is an influential Meo chief from the Xien Kuang area.' He was silent for a moment, then he asked: 'Is it true the French shipped a few hundred Meo to French Guiana and dumped them in the middle of the jungle?' I told him this was, in fact, what had happened. The Meo tribesmen he was referring to (or Hmong, as the ethnologists call them nowadays) had been employed by the French overseas department as woodcutters and planters, and the experiment had proved a huge success. The efficiency and enthusiasm of the new settlers contrasted with the work-shy 'Creoles' of Cayenne. These long-established immigrants, mainly mulattoes and blacks, idled away their days in semi-retirement, indulged by a liberal state. From what I, could remember of Guiana and its parasitic social set-up, the French government would have done better to ignore the protests of the 30,000 Creoles and allow the refugees from Indochina to colonize the jungle areas. It would have been the best thing that had ever happened to the country.

One evening as we sat drinking Scotch in the house of the German ambassador we learned that Souphanouvong, the Red Prince who had been appointed Republican head of state after the abdication of the king, was intending to fly to Phnom Penh in the next few days. The aim of his visit was to sign a pact of friendship and mutual assistance with Heng Samrin, the pro-Vietnamese prime minister of Cambodia; it would be on roughly similar lines to the pacts signed between Hanoi and Vientiane. The Vietnamese were tightening their net. Hanoi's vision of a united Indochina under the leadership of Vietnam had at last become a reality. The honours heaped on Souphanouvong could not hide the fact that effective political power had, in reality, been taken from him and placed in the hands of a small clique of faceless, unscrupulous party men. Once the Red Prince had been exploited as the figurehead and frontman for the Revolutionary Front of the Pathet Lao. Now he had served his turn. 'Why don't you look up Souvanna Phouma?' suggested Gunther Wasserberg. 'Maybe he'll invite you round for a game of bridge.' As it happened the ex-prime minister of Laos, who was also half-brother to the Red Prince, was now living peacefully in his white villa on the banks of the Mekong. He had once played an important role in the political affairs of his country, first as a neutralist and then as an ally of the United States. Now he spent his time making insincere protestations of loyalty towards the new regime and cultivating his Soviet and Vietnamese friends. He may have been secretly waiting for things to take a turn for the better, but he was alone in this naive hope. Prince Souvanna Phouma was, as he saw it, placing his patriotic opportunism at the service of the Laotian people. If he felt disillusionment at the way things had turned out he did not let it show. Perhaps he was too old and played out to give the security services of Kaysone Phomvihane much to worry about.

The Deserted Royal Way

Pakse, March 1979

An invitation had come out of the blue from the Laotian foreign ministry to visit the province of Champassak. Since 1975 this triangle of Laotian territory, sandwiched between Thailand and Cambodia, had been a notorious stronghold of anti-Communist resistance. Four years later the influence of the two great feudal families, the Boun Oum and Sananikone, seemed to be as strong as ever in the area. During the early years of the takeover by the Pathet Lao the Patikan, or 'reactionaries' as the Laotian Communists always called them, had received discreet backing from Thailand. Their ranks had thinned considerably since regiments of Vietnamese regulars had entered Laos and started hunting them down. Some estimates of the remaining strength of the Patikan put their numbers at as low as 1500, and they were rumoured to have only three hundred rifles between them. When the French writer Larteguy, who covered both Indochinese wars as a reporter, tried to make contact with them once, he fell on a pointed bamboo stake. He didn't wait for a second warning, but turned round and headed for home without more ado.

The last time I had visited the provincial capital of Pakse had been in 1966. Returning there in 1979, I found the town to be a pale shadow of its former self. Two thirds of the original population had already fled, leaving about 10,000 inhabitants still there. We were put up at a government guest-house on the outskirts of the town and kept under close surveillance by Pathet Lao troops. Everywhere we went we had the pleasure of the

323

company of these stocky, dark-skinned Kha soldiers. The government was obviously still worried about the possibility of a Patikan attack. In the afternoon we were taken to see work at an irrigation scheme that would one day enable the agricultural cooperatives around Pakse to harvest two rice crops a year. As we filmed we wandered about quite freely among the men and women labourers. They worked away tirelessly chatting and laughing among themselves. At five o'clock on the dot they downed tools and headed for home. Thankfully the Khmer Rouge system hadn't caught on here.

Later we strolled through the dusty streets of Pakse, still with the AK-47s of our guardian angels at our elbow. Many of the houses had been abandoned by the owners and were beginning to look dilapidated. Most of the shops were bolted and barred and the main street was lined with wrecked cars. The most impressive ruin of all, however, was the enormous castle of Prince Boun Oum. Its white concrete walls and curved roofs thrust skywards, dominating the plain like Dracula's castle. During the early sixties the prince, backed by the CIA and the Thai secret service, had plotted against Prime Minister Souvanna Phouma, and for a brief period had even managed to topple him. I couldn't help feeling Boun Oum must have suffered from delusions of grandeur when he inflicted this architectural monstrosity on the beautiful landscape. We picked our way through echoing halls and piles of rubble and climbed up to the battlements. The view from the top was breathtaking. To the west lay the hills of the Thai border region, profiled against the sky. Just below us the fishing boats sailed past on the Senone River, making glistening curves in the dark-green water. Back inside the castle we found a clumsy inscription in French written on a pillar. It said something about *amour, départ,* and *tristesse.* (Boun Oum had gone into exile in Paris, hence the nostalgia.) The prince must have invested the bulk of his fortune in this ridiculous palace. Mongkhul told us the Communists were toying with the idea of turning this feudal relic into a palace of culture for the people. This didn't strike us as being a particularly bright idea, given the depopulated state of the town.

The heat in the plain was almost unbearable, and evening brought no relief. The broad ribbon of the Mekong wound its way sluggishly southwards. In this region of Laos the river did not actually form the boundary with Thailand; the strip of wooded country we could see over on the west bank was still part of Champassak province. The Vietnamese were rumoured to have built one of their big training camps for Thai Communists in the jungles on the west bank of the river. A similar camp for budding guerillas had been set up north of Luang Prabang in Sayaburi province, also on the far bank of the Mekong. In his recent talks with Prime Minister Kriangsak, Kaysone Phomvihane had given a pledge (after reciprocal assurances from Bangkok) to withdraw all support from the bands of Communist guerillas who had been active on the north-east of Thailand for years. This promise did not, in fact, cost him that much because most Thai Communists followed the Maoist line. At that time the 'Voice of the Thai People' still broadcast from Kunming, capital of the Chinese province of Yunnan, and would regularly send out appeals to the Siamese people to rise in revolt against the 'rule of the military' and the 'tyranny of the capitalist exploiters'. Once the Sino-Vietnamese conflict began, Hanoi was no longer interested in the Maoist rebels in the eastern Thai provinces, some of whom had joined forces with the Pol Pot regime. In fact the Vietnamese would have been quite happy to see them completely wiped out. Long before the outbreak of the war, Hanoi had instructed her Laotian allies to do their utmost to block all deliveries of arms being sent from China to Thailand via the new all-weather road system. The Chinese, for their part, had recently decided the Thai monarchy should be strengthened to form a bulwark against the expansionist ambitions of the Vietnamese. The conquest of Cambodia had been a clear warning to the countries of South-east Asia. Peking knew that Vietnamese plans for an Indochinese Federation threatened that the expansionists in Hanoi were intending to annex sixteen north-eastern provinces to the Democratic People's Republic of Laos, all of them chiefly inhabited by Lao. At the height of the Cambodian crisis, when General Dung's tank divisions had been heading towards the Thai border, China had given Thailand an official pledge of support in the event of an attack by Vietnam.

The Thai Communists had had the ground cut from under their feet. The peasants among them would probably drift back to the land while most intellectuals from Bangkok, who had fled to the jungle after the collapse of the student revolt in 1976, would take advantage of the amnesty offered to them by Kriangsak. But a small nucleus – disillusioned with Maoism and its legacy – had yielded to the blandishments of the Vietnamese. This group had been prepared to recognize the regime of Heng Samrin, installed in Phnom Penh by the Vietnamese. Now the converts sat waiting in their guerilla camps in Champassak and Sayaburi, hoping for better days and preparing to resume the struggle against imperialists of every shade.

Next day we travelled to the Boloven Plateau, again under armed escort. There had been reports of firing in the area a few days previously, but we enjoyed an uneventful drive through the long elephant grass. We stopped in the town of Paksong, which had been razed to the ground by American bombs during the war. We stayed in a luxury guest-house reserved for party officials and other privileged members of the regime. The sky had clouded over, and it became noticeably cooler once we arrived on the high plateau. The authorities had obviously brought us here because they wanted to demonstrate the collapse of Patikan resistance in the area. We couldn't think of any other reason for taking us up there – they certainly couldn't have been hoping to impress us with the farming project they showed us. The so-called agricultural 'reconstruction' was pretty depressing. Where the old French plantation owners had once grown the best tea and coffee in Indochina, the new Socialist cooperatives were still struggling to plant a few beets. We met a small group of officials and officers who had previously served under the old royal Laotian regime and had been sent out to the remote Boloven Plateau by the revolutionary authorities to start a new career as tea-planters. On the state-run farm of Long Hien about sixty-five people were minding 400 lean-looking cows. Under the Socialist regime of the Democratic People's Republic of Laos, agricultural output seemed to have dropped to appallingly low levels. The local school in Long Hien was housed in a shed. Inside, two dozen Kha children were lined up in front of the blackboard, waiting to welcome us in song. The words went: 'The soldiers guard us so we can work to build up the land; together with the soldiers we are fighting against the reactionaries and the imperialists.'

In Pakse we were told that our planned helicopter trip to Khong Island, on the Cambodian border, had been cancelled 'for technical reasons'. Instead we were invited along to a Women's Day festival in the town. Some 3200 women and girls were assembled in the stadium. Our arrival was greeted by enthusiastic applause. The revolutionary women read out resolutions and speeches on the themes of Socialist renewal and – at significantly greater length – the threat from the Chinese 'reactionaries' in the north. The female propagandists, looking suitably deferential, went on to emphasize the vital role played by a strong, united

326

Vietnam in safeguarding the achievements of the Laotian revolution, in much the same way as SED party officials in East Germany used to pay lip-service to the 'glorious Soviet Union'. The Vietnamese living in Pakse were represented by a small delegation of women. Their aristocratic, rather severe beauty contrasted with the cuteness of the Laotian dancers whose singing and graceful movements followed the flood of speeches, much to the delight of the crowd. The Chinese community, formerly the largest foreign ethnic group in the town, was conspicuously absent from the gathering. Before we left, the organizer of the festival bade us farewell with much bowing and scraping. His name was Koni, and I had been struck by his thin lips and his gaunt, cerebral face, which gave him something of the air of a priest. Mongkhul later told me that Koni had spent twelve years in a Buddhist monastery before joining the Pathet Lao early on in the war. In his final address to the women Koni had spelt out three imperatives for the province: an increase in productivity, a speeding-up of collectivization and a relentless struggle against the Patikan and the 'International reactionaries' (another reference to the Chinese).

To make up for our cancelled visit to Khong Island we were allowed to travel 100 kilometres south of Pakse to see the ruins of Wat Phou on the west bank of the Mekong. The temple, which dated back to the seventh century, was an early example of the classical style of the great Khmer civilization that reached its apotheosis 500 years later in the empire of Angkor. The dark red walls and columns of Wat Phou were partly hidden by roots and lianas, and were beginning to crumble in places. Yet somehow this made the view from the top of the massive stone staircase all the more impressive. The upper temple was decorated with moss-covered sculptures and reliefs showing the gods of Hinduism paying homage to Shiva, the Destroyer. The voluptuous figures of the aspara maidens were frozen for eternity in the ritual movements of their sacred dance. The hieratic, almost Assyrian figure of the royal founder Wat Phou stood guard at the foot of the steep cascade of steps. The head of the left Naga snake at his feet was still perfectly preserved. These masterpieces of the early Chen-La empire were marked by a slight heaviness and lack of refinement.

In the inner courtyard of this Hindu temple the stamp of the Buddha was everywhere. Here the lingam, the symbol of eternal procreation and fertility, had been supplanted by the statue of a crude, yellow-painted Buddha in contemplative pose. There were even a few monks living in the adjacent temple and they allowed us to film them kneeling at prayer. Mongkhul was in his element here, and started giving us a lecture on the building. 'In Wat Phou you can somehow see the beginnings of the vast power that was to develop in the Middle Ages, when the Khmer empire stretched far beyond the frontiers of present-day Cambodia and took in most of Indochina. At that period Champassak was probably part of a cultural link between the two Khmer peoples, the Mon and the Cham. There was still no sign of the Vietnamese or the Thai or the Laotians at that time. They all lived in the far north.' Mongkhul picked up a carved stone that had fallen from the temple wall. 'Here we're on the northern edge of the *Voie Royale*, the "Royal Way" André Malraux wrote about in his novel. Malraux's hero, Perken, who was half-German and half-Danish, wanted to retire here. He dreamed of building his own kingdom around Wat Phou. But on the way here he died from the wound he received from the Stieng, the savage tribesmen living in the area.'

We talked a little about the globe-trotting Malraux who, as a young man, tormented by his genius had wandered through the jungles of northern Cambodia, plundering temples and embroidering the facts. 'It's a funny thing about Europeans,' said Mongkhul. 'They all seem to want to build their own empires. Have you ever come across Pierre Schoendorffer, who wrote that book about Borneo called *L'Adieu au Roi*?' I had only briefly met Schoendorffer, who used to be a correspondent with the French army, but I knew his book very well. I pointed out that Schoendorffer was only one in a long line of empire-builders, and reminded him of the Kipling short story *The Man Who Would Be King,* set in the Afghan region of Kafiristan. Then Mongkhul brought up Joseph Conrad's *Heart of Darkness,* a powerful story set in the African Congo. I told him the Americans had taken over the Conrad character of Kurtz the ivory hunter, who is worshipped as a white chief by primitive black tribesmen in one of the darkest corners of Africa; he had now been turned into a contemporary film hero, played by Marlon Brando. I summarized the script for him in a few sentences. 'Colonel Kurtz has set up his own little kingdom in a remote swamp in Indochina. He's living there surrounded by primitive natives, and rules by means of cruelty and white man's magic. Then the US command in Saigon decide it's time to hunt down this weirdo, who has obviously "gone savage". The CIA officer who's given the job of finding Kurtz ends up killing him; by this time he's become a kind of

Moby Dick of the Indochinese jungle. The film's called *Apocalypse Now*. And you needn't worry,' I went on, 'the old Royal Way that used to go from Europe to Asia and Africa is deserted now. There are no more white empire-builders on it.'

During our three days in Champassak we had kept our eyes open for signs of Vietnamese soldiers, but we had seen nothing. Obviously the troops had been instructed to stay in their quarters while the Western television crew were filming in the area. However, on the day of our departure, someone must have made a slip-up somewhere along the line. We were on our way to Pakse airport when we came across an entire convoy of Vietnamese troops. It was easy to tell they were Bo Doi as they were wearing green combat helmets with the red cockade and the yellow star, but for obvious reasons we refrained from filming them just at that moment.

Crisis on the Mekong

Vientiane, March 1979

The atmosphere in Vientiane had changed drastically during our three-day absence. There were large numbers of armed soldiers in the town centre again. Refugees on the banks of the Mekong were being shot at. All sections of the population were being mobilized for mass rallies where Chinese 'aggression' against Vietnam was denounced. The Revolutionary People's Party of Laos had, under the uncompromising rule of Kaysone Phomvihane, broken its last remaining links with Peking. Immediately after my return I was called to an interview with the minister of information, Sisane Sisana. He was a strange man with an elusive quality. He had none of the characteristics of a Laotian, and I tried in vain to identify his racial type. He certainly wasn't a Kha either. Sisane Sisana had a very genial manner. He led me over to a map and pointed out an area on the border between the provinces of Phong Saly and Yunnan where the Chinese were reported to have bombed a Laotian village. 'The Chinese are concentrating troops in this region,' said the minister. 'We have to be ready for a possible attack any day now. The Peking reactionaries have begun their retreat from the Vietnamese border region under pressure from our Vietnamese friends. Now they're looking for a new front.' He had ready a whole series of charges against the 'Peking clique', or 'Fascists' as he sometimes called them. Their spies would, he claimed, infiltrate Laos and incite minority groups to revolt. The people, he said, were ready to fight for their independence and defend their territory.

The first conscription of young soldiers had been announced. The small Pathet Lao army of 30,000 soldiers was to be reinforced with another 15,000 men. It was also confirmed that a Laotian contingent had been sent into action on the side of the Vietnamese against the Khmer Rouge in Cambodia. It was hardly surprising, then, that the young people of the capital, who had no desire to die for this Socialist satellite state, had already begun a new exodus to Thailand.

Sisane Sisana was already well known to the French Secret Service. As early as 1945 he had fought on the side of the Lao Issara against the former colonial power. In the second Indochinese war he had held out with his Sahai in the caves of Vieng Xai for many years, and he had survived the American bombing. I suddenly remembered what I had been told confidentially in Bangkok: the grandfather of this Laotian revolutionary had been a Corsican living in the Mekong. This was probably the reason for his resentment towards the arrogant foreigner who had once ruled Indochina. On closer inspection, Sisane began to look almost familiar. He had the features of a member of the Union Corse, the organization which Paris, with some exaggeration, claims is the Mafia of Corsica, and which played an important role in the underground movement during the Algerian war.

There was great alarm in the embassies of the Western alliance and the SEATO countries. Vietnam had announced a general mobilization for all males between the ages of fifteen and forty-five. A wartime regime had been imposed: eight hours work, eight hours military training and eight hours rest. The French Press Agency reported that this was not quite as dramatic and efficient as it might appear. Nevertheless, the effect on the political atmosphere in Vientiane was devastating. The short spring of limited freedom in Laos was soon over. The report of the Chinese raid on Laotian territory was probably a total fabrication, the news in any case having first been made public in Moscow and Hanoi before being repeated in Vientiane. Nevertheless the Secret Service expected that, in the event of a renewed flare up of border clashes between China and Vietnam there would be a strong Chinese attack on Lai Chau, the seat of administration of the military region of Viet Tay, which borders directly on Laos. The loyalty of the ethnic minorities in this region to Hanoi was extremely uncertain, as had been shown during the recent action of the Chinese army. In the first days of their offensive the Chinese had got within twenty kilometres of Lai Chau and had overrun the Thai village of Phong To, my Shangri-La of spring 1951, a second time.

I thought about my conversations with Mr Q, my Chinese source in Bangkok. He had openly admitted that the People's Republic would soon be just as hostile towards Laos as it now was towards the regime of Heng Samrin in Cambodia. An underground campaign by the rebel mountain tribes in north Laos was already underway. In Vientiane there was talk of growing unrest among the remaining Meo, but also among the Yao, the Lolo and the Khmu. Some 4000 partisans, so it was rumoured over cocktails, had already joined with Peking allies in a so-called Lanna Division. Mr Q, for his part, had questioned me about the Meo general, Vang Pao, who had fought on the side of the CIA. He was plainly disappointed when I informed him that the corrupt old warrior could scarcely be expected to exchange his cattle farm in Montana for an extremely precarious new military career. Nor could China expect the support of the neutral Colonel Kong Le, who had remained loyal to the French and was now living in France. 'In that case we'll just have to look for other Laotian patriots,' Q had answered, laughing. In fact, Peking was now supporting the Laos Socialist Party.

The situation on the Sino-Vietnamese border was still shrouded in mystery. Information trickled into Vientiane at an amazingly slow rate. The indefatigable Josef Kaufmann telephoned daily to the Vietnamese embassy in Bangkok, where he had applied for a visa. It was almost impossible to get an interview with the Vietnamese diplomatic mission. The only evidence of their presence was a display at the entrance gate of their building, which showed the wreckage of Chinese tanks and the Bo Doi advancing victoriously. In fact, with the conquest of Lang Son, which had only been won after bitter fighting, the Chinese army had accomplished what it wanted to and had demonstrated that it could advance all the way to Hanoi. The Chinese were, however, denied the psychological advantage which would have come from the encirclement and capture of considerable numbers of élite

Vietnamese units. Hua Kuo Fang's soldiers, as promised, now withdrew towards the north, according to plan, and the Vietnamese were pursuing them energetically. The Peking leadership had already proclaimed to the world at large that a second attack on Vietnam would be launched if Hanoi did not mend its ways. Deng Xiaoping, whose threats had been taken seriously since his trip to America, had sent a similar warning to the Secretary-General of the UN, Kurt Waldheim.

Our reporting mission in Communist Laos had come to an end. We had received the coded message from Bangkok that the Chinese authorities had granted us a visa. I also received an invitation to dine with Prince Sihanouk in Peking the following Monday. We had four days until then. On our last evening we had a celebration in the German residence. Back in Germany the carnival season had ended two weeks before, and at the Wasserberg's house we did our best to make up for having missed it. Josef Kaufmann told how one of his colleagues from West German radio had once covered the visit of Walter Ulbricht to the Aswan Dam. The broadcaster had taught the fellahs of Gamal Abdel Nasser the carnival song 'Humba humba tatara', claiming it was the national anthem of East Germany. And sure enough the father of East Germany was greeted with a rhythmic chorus of 'Humba humba'. Now Steve was busy teaching the Laotian staff, who were participating fully and learning how to enjoy themselves Rhineland style. Soon a chorus of 'Humba humba tatara' resounded from the kitchen.

Mulling over the War

Hong Kong, March 1979

I didn't have a particularly enjoyable stopover in Hong Kong. The hills of the New Territories were shrouded in mist and a cold rain fell on the town centre. The young Chinese in Hong Kong seemed to be getting increasingly insufferable, and the patently insincere, exaggerated politeness of the hotel staff was really just a thinly-veiled insult. The older generation of Chinese were easier to get on with, though. 'We're so glad our fellow-Chinese on the mainland are beginning to show some sense at last,' I was told by a backstreet tailor. (I had had to dash out and order myself a winter outfit, because the temperature in Peking was still below freezing.)

The consul-general invited me to tea along with some of the most distinguished China-watchers in town. His residence was situated on Victoria Peak and in fine weather the view from the house was magnificent. Now, unfortunately, everything was obscured by grey mist – the kind of atmosphere you find in those spy stories that always seem to be set in Hong Kong. There were three journalists there apart from myself, two of whom were strangers to me – a Dutchman who spoke perfect Chinese and was married to a Taiwan woman, and an American who had an intimate knowledge of Chinese affairs. The third guest, Russell Spurr, I had had a meal with six years before, in Phnom Penh. He was English, and a very experienced Far East correspondent.

During the past few days Central Chinese Television, the main TV station on mainland China, had been broadcasting film of the fighting going on around the southern border. The commercial TV station in Hong Kong had recorded these reports and re-broadcast them. We had all seen the films but reactions differed. The touching scenes of camaraderie between the local Vietnamese and the departing Chinese troops seemed to have made a particularly strong impression on some people. The film had shown soldiers of the People's Liberation Army in Vietnam carrying the old and infirm on their backs, distributing rice to local families, repairing the straw roofs of village huts, feeding hens, and even sweeping the street before they pulled out. The civilians in the occupied zone, who belonged to ethnic minorities in the main, were moved to tears by all this kindness and were seen warmly embracing the departing soldiers. If the film was to be believed, the 'oppressed' Vietnamese would have been quite happy to let their new masters stay on.

The Dutchman kicked off the discussion. 'Personally I think these pictures are fake and utterly crass. Talk about laying it on with a shovel!' he said. 'But maybe we're wrong to judge them by European attitudes. My wife's no Maoist but even she was moved by the scenes in the film. What seemed to me to be a terrible piece of ham acting came over as perfectly normal to her.'

The conversation then touched on Peking's policy towards ethnic minorities in the southern provinces of China. The American, sucking hard on his pipe, said: 'They're going to have to shake up their ideas a bit if they want to win over the Meo and

333

the Yao and the Mountain Thai – and that's just a few of them. The Chinese will have to take a different approach if they ever want to get the ethnic minorities on their side against Vietnamese nationalism. The Han have always had a strong sense of their own cultural superiority, and it's bound to get in the way of any rapprochement.' I had always been struck by the close phonetic resemblance between the tribal name Meo, or Man (pronounced 'Miao' in Chinese), and the word Moi, the name the Annamites used to describe their primitive hill-tribes. (Moi meant 'wild men' in Vietnamese.) The Chinese characters for the name of this people (the Meo were supposed to be of mixed Tibetan and Burmese origin) hinted at some animal in their ancestry. I remembered discovering on my trip to Lai Chau in 1951 that the Meo regarded the cat as a sacred object, while the Yao claimed descent from a legendary dog. 'The officials in the Ministry for Ethnic Minorities in Peking have introduced new ideograms for the various peoples, but of course that's not the end of the story by a long chalk,' said the American. 'Peking and Hanoi are playing for high stakes here. There are at least three million Meo living south of the Yangtse Kiang. That's more than the entire population of Tibet. The Chinese could really put the wind up Hanoi and Vientiane if they decided to exploit these minorities.'

The talk inevitably came round to the failure of the Soviet Union to take any positive action in the war. Despite all protestations to the contrary, the Vietnamese were bitterly disappointed by the lack of support from their allies. The Russians had admittedly sent a sizeable contingent of its Far East Fleet into the South China Sea. They had organized an enormous air-lift from Vladivostok to Hanoi. They had delivered the very latest weapons and flown in military advisers. The rapid transfer of the North Vietnamese élite units from Cambodia to the Chinese border could never have been carried out without the aid of Soviet planes. But the very least Hanoi had been hoping for was that Soviet marine commandos would land on the disputed Paracel Islands, just to teach the Chinese a lesson. Moscow's failure to come forward at the crucial moment lost her a good deal of prestige, not just in the eyes of the Vietnamese but throughout the whole of South-east Asia. Although nobody would go so far as to accuse Russia of being a paper tiger, the Asians had suddenly begun to see her as a white superpower whose capacity to react was hampered by the burden of her international obligations. In short, the Russians had become 'Red Americans' overnight.

'We should be very wary of jumping to conclusions,' continued the American. 'Right now we're all assuming that Peking and Moscow are going to be at each other's throats forever, that they're inevitably building up to total war. But I'd be more cautious about the whole thing. Do the Chinese really hate the Russians as much as that? From what our sources tell us, it looks as if there'll soon be a dialogue started between the two superpowers. Of course that could just be Deng Xiaoping trying the old dodge of "talk, talk – fight, fight". But at least the Chinese have a powerful lever to use against the United States. If Washington ever tries to attach too many conditions to its pact of economic cooperation with China, then the new leaders in Peking might conceivably take it into their heads to flirt with the Kremlin, just to strengthen their own position. Don't forget the pact between Stalin and Ribbentrop. In the long term there's probably bound to be a fundamental clash between whites and Asians some day, but remember we operate on a completely different time-scale from the Chinese.' I chipped in at that point with a quotation by de Gaulle. In one of his press conferences in February 1964 the general had spoken about the 'threadbare coat of ideological unity', and how the fundamental differences between Moscow and Peking were beginning to show through. From the Hindu Kush to Vladivostok, Russia was interested only in consolidating its territorial assets, but China was bent on expansion and the acquisition of yet more territory.

Everyone agreed that Deng Xiaoping's new, moderate government had enormous problems to solve. The Dutchman and his wife had just got back from a trip to the remote provinces of the People's Republic, where they had seen terrible deprivation among peasants. 'What do you think of the horror stories being put out by the Vietnamese?' asked Russell Spurr. According to Radio Hanoi the Chinese soldiers had run amok in North Vietnam, burning villages, raping women, killing children, torturing men, even tearing the hearts of captured Vietnamese troops out of their bodies while they were still alive. Everyone condemned the stories as grotesque lies. The American said: 'It's one of the hallowed precepts of the People's Liberation Army that you should treat the local population in an enemy country as courteously as possible and try to win them over with propaganda. I'm certain nothing's changed on that score. As for the stories of rape, we mustn't forget that for the last thirty years Chinese troops have been conditioned to be sexually continent, prudish, even. Rape? They probably wouldn't even know what the word meant.'

335

On the other hand there had been reliable eyewitness reports from two French AFP correspondents in Hanoi claiming that the Chinese army had blown up a conquered zone before they pulled out – streets, bridges, industrial installations, public buildings. They had even blown up the brand-new Pernod factory the French had just built in Lang Son (the star-anise tree which is essential to the manufacture of pastis, grew in the area). Ho Chi Minh's hermit cave on Kac-Mac Mountain, regarded by the Vietnamese as a sacred revolutionary shrine, was rumoured to have suffered a similar fate. All bunkers and fortifications in the area were also destroyed. The devastation extended to a distance of 500 kilometres.

As we left, Russell Spurr pressed a written message for Prince Sihanouk into my hand.

The Dragon and the Polar Bear

Peking, March 1979

In Peking a pale, clear, spring sun was shining out of a soft blue sky. It was a Sunday, and the people were crowding round the gates of the old imperial palace, the civilians still in their blue winter outfits, the soldiers in green. The war was an eternity away, 2000 kilometres in fact, somewhere far away to the south. The only place I had noticed large numbers of troops had been at the airport. None had been wearing army insignia, but you could tell the high-ranking officers by their self-confident manner and – just occasionally – their bigger build.

Each time I saw the Forbidden City again, its yellow-tiled roofs and its blood-red walls, its sheer scale and breathtaking harmony, I felt a sense of awe. Anyone who ruled all this must have felt himself the centre of the world, the Son of the Dragon. The emperor of China had simply to sit there and look towards the south to feel the rays of the Yang, the force of light and creation and masculinity flooding through him. Standing in this square, I saw the current border conflict with Vietnam in quite a different light. This was, indisputably, the centre of the universe, the mirror-image of divine order – an empire that needed no other

336

confirmation of its own superiority, that acknowledged no equal on this earth. Far away to the south, where China ended and the barbarian, uncivilized world began, a tiny vassal state was rising in revolt – a state whose whole heritage, whose very name (Vietnam means 'land of the south') proclaimed it an outpost of the great Chinese empire.

On my very first morning in the Nationalities Hotel I received a visit from the top men in Chinese television. They talked about the recent conflict. 'The Vietnamese seriously believed they were invincible. They were behaving as if they were the third-ranking military power in the world after the Americans and the Russians,' they said. 'We really showed them, though, and what's more, the "Socialist imperialists" in the north didn't so much as move a muscle. They're just like barking dogs – throw a stone at them and they run away with their tail between their legs.' Most business meetings in China took place in hotel bedrooms. My opposite numbers didn't seem in the least bit put out by the sight of my unmade bed. They confirmed that I was to turn up at Prince Sihanouk's residence on Monday evening at six o'clock (people ate early in Peking). They gave us a completely free hand to organize our time-table for filming in the capital. The atmosphere was a good deal more cordial and open than the last time I had visited China, when Madame Chiang Ch'ing's cultural policies had still been very much to the fore. The border conflict with Vietnam had (so my TV chiefs told me) ended with the People's Liberation Army winning a major victory. The soldiers had shown what they could do, and now they were all safely back on Chinese soil. 'If we have to – that is, if the Hanoi clique ever challenge us again – we're prepared to go on fighting until the Vietnamese finally see reason.' The rebel upstarts had to be taught a lesson, and there was to be no quarter. The thing that most upset the Chinese was the 'ingratitude' of Hanoi. We heard, for the first time, how 300,000 men from the People's Liberation Army, mainly engineers and support troops, had fought on the side of the Vietnamese during the French and American wars. A thousand Chinese had lost their lives and 10,000 had been wounded in the fighting. Even the victory of Dien Bien Phu would never have taken place had it not been for the active support of China.

My visitors were very cagey when I tackled them on the problem of the Vietnamese Chinese refugees who were beginning to make the headlines in the West. China was supposed to have initially granted asylum to about 200,000 of those expelled from North Vietnam, but after that Peking evidently felt she had fulfilled her humanitarian obligations. Where would we be, I heard several people ask, if all states who harboured dissidents decided to forcibly expel them? The British had probably had a foretaste of what it would be like when Idi Amin persecuted the Indian business community in Uganda and drove them into exile.

Western diplomats in Peking were still chuckling over a story that had gone the rounds at the time of Deng Xiaoping's visit to the United States. President Carter had asked his guest what the position on human rights was in China: could dissidents get a permit to leave the country if they wished to? The Chinese vice-premier replied, with a deadpan expression: 'No, we certainly wouldn't create any difficulties in a case like that. In fact if you're willing to take them in I'll send you ten million Chinese tomorrow.'

The border conflict was officially over by now, so the authorities – who in any case didn't seem particularly anxious for us to go wandering off to the southern 'front' – decided to show us the films made by their own correspondents. We assembled in a freezing cinema for the screening. After a brief taste of spring, winter had returned to Peking. It was below zero and the vast expanse of Chang An Boulevard was deep in slushy snow. Our escorts (including Fang, our interpreter, who turned out to be a godsend) were all wearing at least three jumpers under their thick quilted jackets. Our teeth were chattering with cold as we sat and watched the battle scenes unfold before us. It dawned on us that what we were seeing was not just a skirmish or a clash – it had been the real thing, a full-blown war. This time the Chinese divisions had not rushed into the attack in a human wave, as they had done in Korea against the Americans. Instead they had adopted a strategy of making commando-style raids on enemy bunkers and emplacements. They had waited till nightfall, then had gone in and knocked out enemy positions, hurling everything they had at them, bazookas, the lot. Time and again they had had to resort to fierce hand-to-hand fighting. Not everything had gone according to plan, of course: I heard from American sources that two divisional commanders had been demoted for incompetence.

We were also shown the rather soppy scenes of fraternization that had so amused my colleagues in Hong Kong. The closing shots of the film showed the triumphant return to Kwangsi province. Tanks, artillery, lorries full of soldiers, even a captured

Vietnamese T-54 tank, rolled past in triumphant procession. The soldiers of the People's Liberation Army, wearing big red paper flowers, marched in immaculate formation beneath the huge grey stone arch that was once called Friendship Gate in the days when Vietnam and China were allies. (The French had given the same arch the rather prosaic name of Porte de Chine, and before Mao came to power it had been called Gate of the Domination of the South.) Jubilant crowds lined the road, waving and cheering, pressing flowers and drinks and sweets upon the returning heroes. Children wrapped their red Pioneer neckerchiefs round the barrels of the tank guns. The air was filled with the din of crashing cymbals and exploding fireworks. Huge masks of bald, laughing, rosy-cheeked old men – supposed to bring long life and happiness – swayed in and out among groups of dancers dressed in the vivid costumes of ethnic minorities. In China they still knew how to celebrate a military victory. On the faces of the soldiers you could read a kind of new Asian spirit. This army of proletarian samurai had not only completely broken with the Confucian anti-war tradition, they obviously didn't care how many of their friends and comrades had been killed in the fighting. True, the Vietnamese border forces and militias on the northern front had been more or less wiped out, but the Chinese casualties were still disproportionately heavy. In Peking people were quoting unofficial figures of around 12,000 dead. The Americans were even putting round a figure of 50,000.

The first time I met Erwin Wickert, the West German ambassador in Peking, had been three years before. But when I saw him this time I had read his book on the Taiping Rebellion, *The Mandate of Heaven*. The book gives the reader a rare insight into the East Asian mentality and reveals the author's profound love and knowledge of history. The Taiping Rebellion in the nineteenth century was led by its mad prophet Hong Xiu Quan, who claimed to be a younger brother of Jesus. It had several interesting, and to me, significant features. It was, for instance, a nationalist uprising against the Manchurians, the foreign rulers on the Dragon Throne; it was grounded on a rather misconceived notion of Christianity, which it assimilated in a somewhat haphazard and amusing fashion. These aspects of the rebellion seemed to me to prefigure, in a series of remarkable coincidences, the great Communist convulsion of the twentieth century. Taiping – the 'heavenly kingdom of eternal peace' – was, like Maoism and all previous revolutionary movements in Chinese

339

history, rooted in the peasant population: it had all the classic features of the agrarian revolt. Yet the Taiping Rebellion was also marked by a degree of ideological confusion and religious hysteria you would scarcely have believed possible in a down-to-earth, hard-headed race like the Chinese. At the same time many of the pronouncements of Hong Xiu Quan, the self-appointed Emperor of Heaven and brother of Jesus, revealed all the peculiarities and preoccupations that were to characterize the worst excesses of the great Cultural Revolution a hundred years later. There was the quasi-Communist egalitarianism Hong Xiu Quan imposed on his disciples; the equal rights he granted to women; the emphasis on hard physical labour, which Confucius had always despised; the sexual prudery; and finally, the emphasis placed on the Bible which anticipated the idolization of the famous Little Red Book. Had the Taiping Rebellion been successful, and the whole of China been converted to this faintly absurd form of Western Christianity, then there would presumably have been no soil for Maoism to take root in. According to the sober accounts of British eye-witnesses of the period, this movement, and its eventual suppression, cost thirty million lives in all. The frenzy of blood-letting that took place can only be compared to the 'auto-genocide' introduced by the Red Anabaptists of Cambodia in the name of their perverted Marxist doctrines.

In Peking diplomats had given much thought to the avenues open to the Soviet Union to take the pressure off its Vietnamese allies. Of course, some observers and military attachés scoffed at the old-fashioned equipment of the Chinese forces and felt, quite rightly, that their rigid adherence to Maoist strategy was outmoded and obsolete. But the more serious experts among the Americans and Japanese no longer gave the Kremlin much chance of waging a successful and lightning campaign against China. Moreover, the best time for a preemptive nuclear strike had effectively passed now that the Chinese had built so many rocket-launching silos in the mountains and deserts of Central Asia; the Russians now could no longer be certain of destroying them all, and their hands were tied. And the threat of an atomic strike by China hung over Siberia. The upshot of all this was that during the recent conflict virtually no-one in Peking had seriously thought there was any chance that the men from the Kremlin would have been prepared to shoulder the responsibility, and the incalculable risk, of a nuclear war.

On the other hand there was a great deal of speculation about the possibility of a Russian invasion of Manchuria. A sizeable part of China's economic infrastructure and oil production was concentrated in this north-eastern province. The Soviet army could make a lightning knock-out strike to weaken their opponent then swiftly withdraw to their bases on the Amur and Ussuri Rivers. Peking's High Command had brought up massive concentrations of troops and artillery to the area near the Soviet far-eastern province and the naval stronghold of Vladivostok in order to forestall just such an attack. If the Russians did strike, they would find a second Port Arthur waiting for them – and it was worth remembering that the highly-equipped American forces had been crushed by the Chinese juggernaut in Korea. Finally, and this was the most likely scenario, the Soviet polar bear might conceivably launch an attack against the vast, desolate desert province of Sinkiang in the extreme west of China; once there, she could occupy a small corner of territory – by way of collateral, as it were. What made this theory appear even more attractive was the fact that Sinkiang was mainly inhabited by ethnic minorities – mostly Muslim Turks, Uigurs and Kazakhs, all of whom had suffered a great deal because of the policies and the militant atheism of the Han officials in Urumchi.

In the event of any of these hypothetical events coming to pass, the Chinese High Command had discreetly let it be known that the People's Liberation Army would not simply stand by but would seek 'territorial compensation' along the undefendable 7000 kilometre border with the Soviet Union. In other words, Peking had indicated to the Kremlin that any form of armed military intervention in the northern region of China would inevitably involve the Soviet Union in a protracted conventional war. 'The Russians might just get as far as the Hoang Ho River,' was the latest Chinese thinking on the subject. 'If the worst came to the worst, we could always fall back on Szechwan province, where Chiang Kai-shek successfully held out against the Japanese.'

Whether the Soviet General Staff was impressed by these calculated indiscretions was quite another matter. To find that out we would just have to wait until the next Chinese punitive expedition into Vietnam. Of course the list of bold strategic options outlined by the Peking experts inevitably smacked of war games to some extent, given the complete impenetrability of Chinese motives to Western observers. But they did bring to mind a visit I once made to a museum in Khabarovsk. In the summer of 1973 I spent three days travelling east from Irkutsk in the Trans-

Siberian Express. Passing through the autonomous region of Birobidzhan, where Stalin had once planned to settle the Soviet Jews, I had noticed that the stations still had signs in Hebrew. Once I got to Khabarovsk I had stood on the steep river embankment and watched the waters of the Amur and the Ussuri flowing into one another. Far off in the distance I could dimly sense the flat expanse of Manchuria. I had wandered through the local museum, stopping to look at some display cases of utensils and shaman costumes used by the original Siberian peoples, nomadic tribes very similar to the Canadian Indians. Then suddenly I found myself staring at a huge oil painting. It was a nineteenth-century portrait of Khabarov, the tsarist admiral who had given the town its name. It showed a bearded giant of a man with wide gold epaulettes and rows of medals on his chest. Spread out in front of him was a map of Siberia and Manchuria. On the other side of the table crouched an ugly little Chinaman wearing the magnificent costume of a high-ranking mandarin at the Peking court. With a haughty air and a regal sweep of the arm, the Russian was drawing a red line across the map – the new border between Russia and China. The picture I saw in the museum in Khabarovsk was a celebration of Russian ambitions and Chinese inferiority. I imagined it had probably stayed up on the wall even during the period when Stalin and Mao were allies.

Sihanouk's Guest

Peking, March 1979

Prince Norodom Sihanouk stepped forward to greet us with his head completely shaven: according to rumours circulating in Peking, he had decided to devote himself to Buddhism. Was he, I wondered, trying to work out a new political role for himself through spiritual meditation, or was it, as I suspected, simply a gesture of protest? Monseigneur was back living in the former French legation in the old foreigners' district. The heavily guarded entrance looked out onto the Fom Di Lu, the Street of the Struggle against Imperialism. The ex-head of state of Cambodia showed no apparent sign of the strains he must have been under during his three years of house arrest under the Khmer Rouge in Phnom Penh. He had hardly aged at all, and his spirit was far from broken: he was as full of vitality as ever. His wife, Princess Monique, stood at his side to greet their dinner guests – a handful of journalists from France, America and Britain. Monique, who was half-Italian, was still a beautiful woman. In Phnom Penh there had been hints of scandal surrounding her name, but now she looked the *grande dame*, a sadder and a wiser woman after her recent ordeal. She and Sihanouk were very much the happy couple, two people bound together by the vicissitudes of fate.

Sihanouk refused to be interviewed, but in the course of the evening he came out with a stream of comments on political affairs. He was still the same irrepressible clown, hiding his deep sadness behind the mask of the comedian. 'You're being served a French menu tonight, gentlemen,' he said as we sat down to table. 'I've given the cook instructions on what to prepare. I never let my cookery books out of my sight. Even when I was in prison in Phnom Penh I kept them beside me, and I have annotated all the best dishes.' His personal secretary, who was wearing the traditional Cambodian sampot, brought in a yellowing, tattered cookery book, which Sihanouk held aloft in triumph. Every time the secretary approached her former ruler, the descendant of the kings of Angkor, she knelt humbly before him.

'You no doubt want to know what I think about Chinese politics,' said Sihanouk coming straight to the point. While he was speaking he would frequently start giggling for no apparent reason. 'Now, the Chinese and I are the best of friends, and Chou En-lai was my great mentor. But needless to say I'm not 100 per cent in agreement with their policies. The People's Republic of China is still supporting the Khmer Rouge and the Pol Pot regime toppled by the Vietnamese. I, on the other hand, have every reason to detest this gang of thugs and murderers. They have persecuted and massacred my people in the most hideous ways. Some of the closest members of my family have been killed. Two sons, two daughters, and ten of my grandchildren have disappeared in the Khmer Rouge terror. But the Chinese are dependent on Pol Pot's guerillas – who are about 35,000 strong – if they want to carry on armed resistance against the Vietnamese occupying force. I happen to know that the present leadership in Peking has very little time for the bloodthirsty stone-age revolutionaries. But they are useful, vital even, to China. The Khmer Rouge will go on fighting for ever if they have to. Deng Xiaoping has personally told me China is supplying the guerillas with arms and ammunition via Thailand, and the whole operation seems to be running smoothly.

'I must confess to having a sneaking sympathy for the Chinese strategy in Cambodia. They're operating on two levels simultaneously – they're holding two trump cards in their hand, if you like. In a sense they're committing political bigamy since they're keeping two wives at the same time, Sihanouk and Pol Pot. As I said before, I'm not making any criticisms. When I was a Buddhist I used to practise polygamy and I loved all my wives – that is until I met Monique and fell under her spell.' At that he paused for a moment while he and the princess exchanged loving smiles. 'In Phnom Penh I even wrote a song for Monique,' he said fondly.

His mood changed abruptly and he plunged into bitterness. The broad face, like something from an ancient frieze in a royal temple, contracted into a mask of pain. 'When I spoke in defence of my country in front of the United Nations, Fidel Castro called me a stage prince. If that's true, then he's just a stage beard.' He went on to speak about the three years he spent as a prisoner of the Khmer Rouge. He said he had been comparatively well treated, thanks to the protection of his Chinese allies. He had lived in a wing of his old palace and had always been given enough to eat. Physically he'd hardly suffered at all, in fact. Monique leant over to me. 'Psychologically our position was almost intolerable,' she said in a low voice.

Sihanouk then gave us a rapid outline of the personalities behind Ankar, the secret organization behind the Khmer Rouge. The last head of state of Kampuchea Democratique, as the Khmer Rouge liked to call themselves, had been Kieu Samphan, one of Sihanouk's own ex-ministers. 'At least Kieu Samphan is an educated man,' said the prince. 'He was a student at the Sorbonne. He was the one who showed most kindness towards me and my wife. He even let me have a transistor radio so I could keep up with world events.' Sihanouk waved his hand and the secretary brought in the radio. 'But after 1975 Kieu Samphan had to take a back seat in Ankar. He was just a token presence, almost a puppet, really. The strong man of the regime was Pol Pot, a former Buddhist monk, whose real name is Saloth Sar. He's a fanatic, but there's no denying he's a brave man – he personally leads his guerillas into action nowadays. The worst of them all by a long chalk was Ieng Sary, who's still acting foreign minister. Ieng Sary lives in Peking. The Chinese keep denying it, but it's true. You'd never catch him going into the jungle and fighting. He's too much of a coward for that – he's utterly despicable. The first time I stayed in Peking, from '70 to '75, he was my constant watchdog. The Gang of Four had him spying on me day and night. I avoid all contact with the Khmer Rouge nowadays.' His eyes were full of naked hate as he spoke.

Raising aloft the remains of his glass of champagne, Sihanouk proposed a toast. 'I invite you all to Phnom Penh some day, to a new, happy Cambodia!' But then he broke off. 'Of course I realize there's no way I can ever keep that promise.' The corners of his mouth turned down again in a sad smile. Then suddenly he was cheerful again. 'Come and have coffee in the drawing-room and I'll introduce you to Miko.' Miko was a little white poodle that rushed up to Monique as we entered the drawing-room. Sihanouk picked it up and petted it fondly. Then he picked up two bottles, one of Taittinger champagne, the other of hock. 'You see, I've got everything I could possibly want,' he crowed in his high-pitched voice, then giggled. After this quick bit of clowning he became serious once more. 'I've started writing my memoirs. I'd like to really go to town on the chapter about the part Kissinger and Nixon played in the destruction of Cambodia.'

We asked him what his thoughts were on the future of his country, and he became thoughtful. The Chinese border action against Vietnam hadn't really altered the situation in Cambodia, he said. The Vietnamese would be able to hang on for a long time in Phnom Penh, even supposing the Pol Pot resistance held out and the new recruits from South Vietnam turned out to be no good. The only thing that might bring about a change for the better would be an international conference. The best venue he could think of would be Geneva, but everyone would have to be invited – the Americans, the Europeans, the ASEAN countries, the Chinese, of course, and the Vietnamese and Russians. From what he could see, Heng Samrin, the Vietnamese puppet, was a complete nonentity and would never be able to unite the people behind him. Sihanouk was in favour of free elections, and if that ever came about he would put himself forward as candidate for the all-important office of mediator and peace-maker. But before things got to that stage, the international community had to tackle the Cambodia question properly. The United Nations shouldn't just pass resolutions, they should send in armed 'blue helmets'. 'Right,' he said suddenly joking again, 'I'm in favour of the military occupation of my country by foreign contingents of UN troops. We'll have a different nationality in every province. You

345

could send the Algerian Socialists to Svay Rieng, for instance, next door to Vietnam, and you could send the Moroccan Royalists to Battambang, next door to the Kingdom of Thailand. But the main thing is to see that nobody – not even the Vietnamese – loses face.' The jester had given way to the statesman.

Norodom Sihanouk was clearly tired of sitting in his golden cage in Peking while the Cambodian community in exile waited in vain for a figurehead to rally round. He owned a house in Mougins, on the Côte d'Azur, but otherwise seemed to be in dire financial straits. The prince, who had once held an entire kingdom in trust as his personal property, had been too preoccupied with his personal mission to have time to acquire a bottomless Swiss bank account or vast amounts of foreign real estate – unlike so many others on the political scene. Norodom Sihanouk was no Shah of Iran. With a note of genuine despair in his voice, he talked to us about the fate of the Cambodian refugees who had received far less coverage in the Western press than the Vietnamese boat-people. 'My people are threatened with extinction,' he said, with a catch in his voice. 'Hundreds and thousands of them are wandering about the jungle, living off leaves and barks and worms. Hanoi is already sending its peasant-soldiers into the depopulated provinces of our country.'

To round off the evening Sihanouk took us through the grounds of the residence to an adjoining building. His Chinese hosts had built him a heated, ultra-modern swimming pool with a small indoor sports centre next to it that could also be used for showing films. 'As you can see, I have everything I could possibly want,' he laughed. 'All the same I'd be far happier back among my friends in Europe.' It was never really made clear during the evening why he didn't just pack his bags and leave for Europe. We sat in the comfortable, well-upholstered cinema seats. 'We're going to see a film I made myself. I'll give you a running commentary on it.' The first pictures appeared, pictures of a peaceful, rich, happy country, the land of the Khmer under the strong, wise leadership of an enlightened ruler, Prince Norodom Sihanouk. The prince and his wife were not the only ones to feel sad at the sight of these scenes. Everyone in the cinema felt overcome by a deep sense of melancholy. As we watched, pre-war Phnom Penh came to life once more, with its bustling markets, its modern university, its cheerful inhabitants, its beautiful temple-dancers. Then the strains of a sentimental ballad were heard. 'That's my tribute to Monique. I wrote it myself,' whispered Sihanouk.

They stood on the doorstep for a long time, he waving goodbye with his little chubby hand, Monique shivering slightly in the chill air. The cloud had lifted, leaving the night sky clear and with stars. It was ten o'clock, and the Street of the Struggle against Imperialism was deserted. Although nothing original had been said, we were all agreed that Cambodia's last hope of survival lay in Prince Norodom Sihanouk.

Wall-Posters and Western Fashions

Peking, March 1979

At the Xi Dan crossroads, just a few hundred metres from the Forbidden City, a huge traffic jam was forming. It was an unusual sight in Peking. Thousands of cyclists had got off their bikes and were blocking the vast breadth of Chang An Boulevard. Lorries were boxed in among them, but the drivers seemed to be making no attempt to move. They sat riveted in their cabs staring straight ahead. The blue-uniformed policemen, who only had limited powers anyway, were making futile efforts to get the traffic moving again with their whistles and loudhailers. Nobody was paying the slightest bit of attention to them. Pedestrians were standing in a bunch in the middle of the road, adding to the congestion. Everyone was huddled together in their quilted jackets and felt boots, their caps pulled down over their ears to keep out the icy wind blowing from the northern steppes.

This amazing scene was taking place in front of the Wall of Democracy, where for months now the citizens of Peking had been airing their grievances and criticisms and suggestions for debate on a series of wall-posters that laid end to end would have stretched for a very long way. At the corner of Xi Dan a huge poster with white characters on a red background, left over from the days of the Gang of Four, towered above the crowd. 'In industry we learn from Taching; in agriculture we learn from Dachai. The people and the whole country are learning from the People's Liberation Army, and the People's Liberation Army is learning from the people of the whole country.' Such was the gist of the message on the poster, a quotation from Chairman Mao. A

347

dissident voice had covered over the bottom row of characters with a question which read: 'Is Liu Shao-shi a man or a devil?' (Liu Shao-shi had been Mao Tse-tung's great rival before the Cultural Revolution; since then he had been denounced as a Chinese Khrushchev.) Someone had written underneath: 'Liu Shao-shi is no devil, and Mao Tse-tung is no god.'

It wasn't these political comments (which a year ago would have seemed utterly blasphemous) that were making the citizens of Peking stand there and boggle, jostling and open-mouthed, like a crowd watching a travelling showman. The scene they were so mesmerized by was unusual and eye-catching even by Western standards. In front of the huge Mao poster, in front of the accumulated poverty of this Asian crowd, a procession of models from a big Paris fashion house were strutting up and down, parading their most colourful and way-out creations. We had already met Pierre Cardin's models at the Great Wall of China, where these long-limbed, beautiful creatures had posed half-naked for photos, exposing themselves to the icy blast from Mongolia and the startled glances of soldiers. We had given these casual, free-and-easy Paris models a drop of *mao tai* to try and warm them up; after all, they were heroines of work, in a way. But the scene now taking place in the centre of Peking, in front of the Wall of Democracy, in sight of the Square of Heavenly Peace, beggared description and bordered on provocation. For most of the crowd these models walking up and down and turning pirouettes, might as well have been visitors from Mars. They wore slit skirts that opened to the hips, low necklines that revealed the whole of their naked backs. The collection of exotic silk creations featured loud, vibrant colours that made an almost indecent contrast to the washed-out greys, blues and greens of the dingy clothes of the crowd. And behind all this display of Western chic and decadence, behind the spectacle of these pampered racehorses being put through their paces for a shameless, materialistic, alien society, the characters on the red wall asserted that Liu Shao-shi was no devil and Mao Tse-tung no god. It was a remarkable moment indeed. At the same time it was an outrage that left even us Western spectators feeling thoughtful, almost apprehensive, after the initial reaction of amused surprise. It was an Asian Twilight of the Gods taking place against a background of Parisian *haute couture*.

Our camera team and a man from *Paris Match* snapped away delightedly. Then an oldish-looking man came out of the crowd and addressed me in English. He was wearing tattered old clothes and looked like a beggar. His pale face was ravaged by physical hardship, yet he spoke fluent English. He must have been an intellectual of some kind, because he had apparently done a long stretch in a labour camp. He was not the least bit interested in the fashion show. He pointed to the Wall of Democracy. 'You see those posters? That's real progress,' he said. 'Of course all criticism is kept in check and carefully channelled in the right direction. But things are gradually getting less rigid. There's just one thing, though – you people in the West should never fall into the trap of believing that China can ever attain Western concepts of freedom and parliamentary democracy. Just go and visit some of the country districts where you hardly ever find any foreigners, and you'll see how much poverty there still is in China. You've probably heard of the four 'modernizations' laid down for the people – the modernization of agriculture, industry, research and defence. But the men at the top forget about the fifth and most important modernization of all – the modernization of attitudes. We're really still living in a kind of Marxist feudal society, and the provinces will eventually be ruled by Communist warlords and mandarins. In twenty years' time, so they tell us, we can achieve significant material progress. Do you believe what they say? And what do you make of Marx and Socialism?'

There it was, the $64,000 question, Chinese-style. I didn't answer, but put a question in return. Was it true, I asked, that a few days ago two wall-posters had condemned the Chinese intervention in Vietnam and demanded an end to the war? I had been told by an informant that they had been taken down as soon as they went up. 'I really don't know,' replied the stranger, 'but I can tell you one thing. We were all in favour of the punitive expedition against the Hanoi troublemakers. We may criticize a lot of things in present-day China, but we're still patriots when it comes to the crunch.'

The man had said his piece in a quiet, rather tired voice. Only very occasionally did he have to stop and reach for an English word. During our conversation spectators had gathered around. There were almost certainly officials from the security services among the crowd, but it hadn't inhibited the stranger at all. He shook my hand, turned on his heels, and was instantly swallowed up by the crowd.

The Wheel Turns Full Circle

Kunming, March 1979

Strolling through the streets of Kunming, I felt a marvellous sense of exhilaration. It wasn't just because of the mild weather here in this Land of Four Springs (the Chinese name for Yunnan, their most southerly province). It wasn't just because of the air, which was heady like champagne (we were 1700 metres above sea level). No, my feeling of exhilaration sprang from my memories. I kept thinking back to that spring in 1951 when I set out from Lai Chau in the western highlands of Tongking to find the last remnants of Kuomintang troops cut off in the foothills of China. At that time a vast, ideologically united empire lay between the Indochinese border river of Nam Kum and the Elbe. Stalin and Mao still represented the twin faces of world revolution, the Janus head of Communism. In Korea the Americans had just been driven back from Jalu, on the 23rd parallel, by the army of China, a million strong. In those days I would never have imagined, not even in my wildest dreams, that one day I would be invited to the capital of this cold, remote province of Yunnan as an official guest of the Communist government in Peking. It would never have entered my head either that the reason for my trip would be a feud between comrades, with the heirs of Mao Tse-tung in one camp and the inheritors of Ho Chi Minh and Stalin in the other. Nearly thirty years had passed since my first visit to China and much had changed.

In Kunming the only sign you saw of the nearby border conflict was the odd army lorry. The vast parade ground, built in the style of Tien An Men Square, was dominated by huge portraits of Mao Tse-tung and Hua Guofeng. It was deserted apart from one or two old men who moved in slow motion, practising a kind of shadow boxing rather like T'ai chi. The back streets with their brown tiled roofs were full of bustle. You saw more and more women in brightly-coloured dresses on the streets now. The girls had prettier smiles than in the north – you could see echoes of the graceful Indochinese women, their neighbours across the border. The people thronging the town displayed an air of sunny, calm contentment, a typically southern *joie de vivre*. There seemed to be fewer problems with supplies of food and consumer goods than in the huge, poverty-stricken city of Canton which we had passed through two weeks ago. But most of all, life in Kunming was a hundred times better than under the Spartan regime in Hanoi. Our hotel was packed with Japanese and American tourists, and every bed in the place was taken. Even at the height of the conflict this stream of foreign visitors had never once dried up.

In the afternoon we visited the West Mountain, climbing up the steep steps and narrow passages leading to the rocky summit. At every turning in the path Taoist shrines had been let into the wall, and we occasionally saw joss-sticks burning in front of them. The goddess of mercy, Kwan Yin, shown here with a red-painted face, gazed down benevolently on a long queue of Chinese tourists; among them were members of the Yi people, one of China's ethnic minorities. The atmosphere was very jolly, almost like a family celebration. From the top of Yu Feng Shan you could gaze out over Lake Tienchih and see the soft reflections in its still waters. The beauty of the view was marred by an irrigation system and a large brown polder which the supporters of the Cultural Revolution had drained with their own hands. The Red Guards had decided it was more important to raise agricultural output than to pander to the aesthetic sensibilities of mandarins. We were told that when Chou En-lai had stood on the balcony of the Ruyen temple to view the scene, he had been outraged at this act of vandalism.

We spent most of our time filming and looking round the bamboo temple of Qiong Zhu Si. Inside a cave-like building we found every possible variation on the motif of the Luohan, the five hundred enlightened beings in Buddhist and Taoist mythology. Around the walls was a confused, grotesque welter of gold figures – Buddhas and Bodhisattvas, Fo and Pu Su, mythological creatures and Tantric demons, temple guards, nymphs, saints, philosophers, monsters, the fat grinning She of prosperity and long life – all intertwined in a tangled frieze of images that gleamed in the half-light. Above the entrance to the pagoda was a red banner which Fang translated for us. 'We salute the great victory won on the occasion of our action of self-defence,' it said.

In the fourteenth century a Mongolian prince built his summer residence beside this temple, reinforcing the powerful presence of the Yuan dynasty that had already left its mark on the area around Kunming. Chinese dominance in the remote province of Yunnan had begun under the reign of Kublai Khan, the great Mongol emperor. In the thirteenth century he brutally curbed the autonomy of the local aristocracy, a family belonging to the Bai people. The same Kublai Khan who set in motion the migration of the Thai peoples from Yunnan into Indochina was shortly afterwards to meet with disaster in the battle of the Bach Dang River, when he tried to bring the ancestors of the present-day Vietnamese people under his yoke.

The mountains of Yunnan provided a refuge for twenty-two ethnic minorities who made up about a third of the total population of thirty million people. Western journalists had had a lively discussion about the expansionist tendencies of the Han, the main ethnic group in China. One widely accepted theory states that the Chinese are not conquerors by nature, but that the great campaigns to win territory all took place under foreign dynasties, mainly the Mongols or the early Manchu. The main objection to this is that the final assimilation of Yunnan into the dominion of the Han took place under the Ming dynasty, which was solidly Chinese. For over 2000 years the Sons of Heaven fanned out from their original homeland between the Hoang Ho and the Yangtse Kiang Rivers. They scattered their new settlements throughout their newly-claimed territories and either subjugated or as-similated the foreign races that stood in their way. Moreover the emperors of the Han, Tang and Ming dynasties did not hesitate to undertake wars of conquest against the barbarian hordes when they had to. The policy of bringing into line the autonomous fringe regions of Mongolia, Tibet and Sinkiang currently being pursued by the People's Republic today is a modern example of this permanent expansionist drive that makes China's neighbours so anxious about their future. The radical militancy which Maoism sought to instil into the masses in every single area of their lives has already made considerable inroads into traditional Confucian attitudes, and particularly the old, contemptuous rejection of war and all things military. Who can guarantee that the successors of the Great Leader – freed at last from their humiliating role as poor relation to other military superpowers – might not themselves acquire a taste for imperialism one day?

The authorities in Yunnan had invited us along to an information session. Correspondents were there from Britain, Italy, France, West Germany and Japan. Americans had not been allowed to come on the trip as the US embassy in Peking was still not officially opened. Correspondents from the Eastern bloc countries were naturally excluded. The propaganda chief for the province, a canny old man called Pan Chuan He, told us we would start out next day for the south to visit a camp for Vietnamese war prisoners in Pan Qi. Pan Qi was, he told us, about 250 kilometres away, half-way between Kunming and the Vietnamese border town of Lao Kay. Pan Chuan He then proceeded to answer our questions, surrounded by a whole army of assistants. No, he said, peace was not yet restored to the Vietnam border area. There were still incidents and skirmishes taking place, and there had even been outbreaks of shooting. Although clear border lines had been agreed and drawn up in the nineteenth century between the French colonial power and the then ruling Ching dynasty, under the auspices of the so-called Li-Fourlier Commission there were still about sixty square kilometres of disputed territory. I asked him how far apart the boundary markers were, remembering my own experience of crossing the border in 1951. 'The boundary stones are placed at intervals of fifty to sixty kilometres,' he replied. If this was the case, then it was surely splitting hairs to quarrel over sixty square kilometres of jungle and mountain terrain; if there was the slightest desire for compromise on each side a dispute over such a small area could easily be settled.

Pan Chuan He went on to tell us that two delegations from the central committee had arrived in Yunnan to congratulate the troops. The official slogan for this visit was: 'We must always be ready to win more victories.' In the event of further provocation, he said, the People's Liberation Army would not hesitate to strike again. When asked about the situation in Laos, he was unable to clear up the confusion over what was happening in the north-ernmost provinces of Phong Saly, Hua Pa, and Nam Tha. Yet the Japanese correspondents had managed to find out that the Vietnamese were currently raising the strength of their garrison in Laos to 50,000 men. In the meantime about 2000 Russian military experts had arrived in Laos. The former CIA stronghold of Long Chen, where the Meo leader, General Vang Pao, had put up a fierce struggle against the North Vietnamese divisions, had now been turned into a Soviet intelligence base. A North Vietnamese squadron of MiG-21 fighters had also been stationed there. But the place all eyes were focussed on was the mountain region of the Black Thai, half-way between Hanoi and the Laotian end of the Mekong plain. Here the North Vietnamese were reported to be fortifying a strategically important hollow in the hills, which would eventually become a key base for Hanoi's élite units. The name of the valley had an ominous ring to it – Dien Bien Phu. The Indochina war had come full circle.

Not surprisingly, perhaps, we couldn't get any inside information from the official Chinese spokesman on the most recent power-struggles going on inside the Hanoi politburo. Once again the Japanese journalists seemed to know more about what was happening than anyone else. According to their sources, the moderate Pham Van Dong had been ousted by the militant pro-Soviet duo of Le Duan and Vo Nguyen Giap. People were already beginning to talk about the prime minister's political authority being seriously undermined. The chief spokesman for the pro-Chinese line, politburo member Hoang Van Hoan, who had once been Ho Chi Minh's right-hand man, was now being kept under close scrutiny. I was concerned to hear that our old friend General Chu Van Tan, the Grey Tiger of Viet Bac, had been arrested. The charge against him was not political deviation – even the Hanoi party men would have had to concede that Chu Van Tan was a loyal party man. But as a member of an ethnic minority inhabiting both sides of the border, he had too many links with China.

Next, a small group of soldiers were ushered into the conference room. Their faces were expressionless under the green caps with the red star: the faces of automatons, in fact. They introduced themselves to us as 'heroes' of the People's Liberation Army who had distinguished themselves in the recent conflict. The soldier heroes had obviously been well rehearsed. The first one said: 'The revisionist Le Duan clique in Hanoi has claimed that one Vietnamese soldier is worth thirty Chinese troops. We have shown the troublemakers that they are paper tigers.' The men then went on to describe in detail scenes of hand-to-hand fighting that had taken place. One NCO had captured a machine-gun from an enemy cave with his bare hands while it was being fired. His fingers had been badly burnt in the process. The crucial commando raids had been carried out under cover of darkness. We asked them how they would have behaved had they been taken prisoner. The reply came back: 'I would have tried to escape by any means possible. If that had been impossible, then I would have committed suicide, but I would have tried to kill a revisionist enemy first.'

I was the oldest among the group of journalists, apart from one of the Japanese from the Kyodo agency. He looked as if he had seen quite a few changes on the mainland of Asia in his time. Despite his grey hair, I could just picture him kitted out in the brown boots and tall peaked cap of Tenno's army. The Japanese reporter kept smiling at me as if we were old buddies. He was probably a little bewildered by all the upheavals that had taken place, all the shifting fronts and realignments. We raised our wine-glasses in a toast and downed the drink in one gulp.

The evening air in Kunming was as soft as silk on your cheek. We went for a stroll along the broad, tree-lined avenues in the direction of the town centre. All the locals seemed to be out and about, enjoying the mild weather. The tourists were all on the streets, too, taking the air. The American couples in their Hawaiian shirts and bright dresses attracted little crowds everywhere they went. There was always one Chinese student keen to try out his English on them. We were curious to know what they found to talk about. We managed to eavesdrop on one or two of these rather halting conversations, which concerned rather ordinary topics. The Chinese tended to ask questions about the standard of living and wages and prices in the USA, while the Americans were interested in the mundane details of everyday life in China. Only a few years ago the Yankees had been painted as capitalist monsters by the Chinese propagandists, yet here they were finding instant acceptance among the inhabitants of Kunming. Back in Peking I had been struck by the emphasis the authorities placed on cultivating friendship between China and the United States. If you were European you felt an outsider in Kunming, a bystander excluded from this dialogue between the two giants on opposite sides of the Pacific. Without their being at all aware of it, the tourists from Missouri and Illinois had become missionaries, spreading the gospel of the American way of life. They were following in the footsteps of Pearl Buck, whose sentimental and naive writing suddenly appeared to me in a completely new light.

We passed quite a few lovers out for a stroll that evening, walking along with their arms tightly round each other. A new era really did seem to have dawned in China. We heard jazz coming out of a side-street, and through a half-drawn curtain we saw young Chinese teenagers clumsily trying out the latest Western dance-steps and having great fun in the process. As soon as they realized we were watching the party came to a halt, and we walked hastily on. By this time we had come to a district of yellow-washed villas built in the French colonial style, once the homes of French engineers working on the Hanoi–Kunming railway. The French construction workers had called this gruelling stretch of mountain track the lace railway, on account of the hundreds of viaducts and tunnels along its length. At the time it had been built, just before World War I, the warlords of Yunnan were still trying to assert their independence from the tottering Manchu dynasty in Peking, while the French were seeking to enlarge their colonial dominion in Indochina to include a protectorate reaching as far north as Kunming. '*Sic transit gloria mundi*,' was the comment of a French journalist who had tagged on to our group. Those were exactly the words de Gaulle had quoted in Rio de Janeiro on hearing of the fall of Khrushchev.

Companions for Thirty Years

Pan Qi, March 1979

We were travelling through a pitted, scarred landscape the colour of a lion's coat. We had turned off the tarmac road and our convoy of cars was throwing up clouds of dust in its wake. Down in the valleys below us the ricefields had shrunk to tiny green dots. The people we passed on the road were carrying heavy loads or leading buffalo teams, and wore blue costumes with red braid trimming. They belonged to the Yi people, better known in Tongking as the Lolo. The region was wild and desolate. The enchanting, picture-book Asia was behind us now – the villages of the Han Chinese with their noise and bustle, the houses with their curved gables, the pagodas built like tall lighthouses, the ancestor's graves among the soft green of the ricefields. Now we were travelling through a harsh, remote land, the autonomous district of the Yi, where no white man had set foot for at least a generation.

It would have been far simpler to take the main road from Kunming to the Vietnamese town of Lao Kay, but it seemed that there was some fortification or radar installation on that particular stretch of road, so the organizers had sent us on this detour. At the side of the gravel road ran a pipeline, which had originally supplied the North Vietnamese army with petrol. Now the fuel was being sent to the forward tank units and columns of the Chinese Army along the Tongking front. We passed very few military vehicles, all of them camouflaged with netting. Our detour via Lu Nan district had allowed us to make an overnight stop in the guest-house near the 'petrified forest' of Shi Lin. The evening sun was setting like a huge red Chinese lantern over an incredible maze of cliffs and rocks. It was a scene so larger than life, that no Chinese landscape artist would have dared to paint it. Later we were entertained by a dance troupe of Yi peasants wearing blue and black costumes with red embroidery. The stocky little girls wore coloured hoods decorated with a pair of red devil's horns. We watched the same familiar movements and listened to the same monotonous, shrill singing. The songs, as usual, were about Socialist reconstruction and the wonderful leadership of Mao Tse-tung. 'Delightful savages,' commented a blasé Englishman.

The gravel road suddenly fell away steeply into a fertile valley. Far below us, at the bottom, a narrow river wound its way through the ricefields. Parallel to its eastern bank ran the lines of the old Yunnan railway. We eventually arrived in the commune of Pan Qi in Huaning district and were immediately led off to a barracks where a regiment of Chinese border guards had been stationed before the war. We were struck by the small number of sentries round the camp; not all of them seemed to be carrying AK-47s either, which was unusual. The barracks contained a row of long, solidly built brick huts. The whole place was spaciously laid out and spotlessly clean. The gravel path was lined by shady trees, and there were beds of vegetables and lettuce. There were no watchtowers or high barbed-wire fences protecting the camp perimeter. In the middle of the camp we came across a large playing-field that was also used as an exercise ground. We were promptly issued with an invitation to stay for lunch, regular mealtimes being one of the hallowed conventions of revolutionary China. Then the commander of the First Prison Camp of the Border Guards of the People's Liberation Army in Yunnan province invited us to a briefing. We were shown to a row of comfortable wicker seats in a shady courtyard.

Political Commissar Wang Yu Qing had clearly grown old in harness. His weather-beaten, lined face radiated good-natured calm and cunning. 'There are no flies on him,' muttered someone. The commissar started off by giving us a few details about the camp. There were about 220 Vietnamese prisoners in Pan Qi, of whom 109 had been serving as Vietnamese regulars, mainly in Divisions 316A and 345. Eleven of the men were from the border guards and thirty-seven belonged to the armed militia. There were also sixty-six wounded who were kept under medical supervision in two special huts. All the prisoners had been captured around Lao Kay and Hoang Lien Son province. The Chinese had taken 1500 Vietnamese prisoners in all. 'We are following the Maoist

357

principle of showing leniency and clemency towards our captured adversary,' continued Commissar Wang Yu Qing. 'Our first rule must always be to practise revolutionary humanity. We respect the human dignity of our opponent.'

The Vietnamese were kitted out with new uniforms as soon as they arrived at the camp. Their food allowance – thirty kilos of rice per month – was very generous: Chinese troops and labourers had to make do with twenty. Nearly all the prisoners – young men aged between seventeen and thirty-six – had gained two to three kilos in weight since they arrived at Pan Qi. They were allowed to write letters to their families. According to the commissar, the prisoners had been very wary of their Chinese captors at first, and had refused to have anything to do with them. This was because they were the dupes of the horror stories put out by their own propaganda machine, he said. But gradually the Vietnamese had seen what things were really like, and had found out about the true aims and motives of the People's Republic of China. The Le Duan clique had turned their backs on the long-standing friendship between Hanoi and China, but the two peoples had to come together again some day. We were interested that the Chinese were making out that Secretary-General Le Duan was the chief culprit behind Hanoi's anti-Peking stance. Prime Minister Pham Van Dong tended to get off more lightly. It bore out Japanese reports that Pham Van Dong had opposed the aggressive stance the leadership was taking towards Peking and criticized it for being too dependent on Moscow. For the first time in thirty years of war signs of a rift were appearing among the Hanoi quartet.

The main purpose of the camp seemed to be to subject the prisoners to a constant stream of propaganda. When we put this to Commissar Wang, he sidestepped the question. 'We don't force anyone to take part in our political instruction classes or our "truth sessions". Once the prisoners return to their homeland the authorities may well take reprisals against them, and we don't want to cause any difficulties for them. But they listen regularly to our radio broadcasts in Vietnamese, and they can read our revolutionary literature if they want to.' Before inviting us to visit the prisoners he mentioned the harsh measures the Vietnamese authorities had taken against suspected collaborators – particularly those belonging to ethnic minorities – after the Chinese Army had pulled out. 'Quite a few of them actually sought refuge with us,' he added.

So we did the rounds of the camp. We were allowed complete

freedom to wander round and talk to people. Down by the big playing field we came across some Vietnamese prisoners in blue uniforms playing football and volleyball. For the third time in my life I was seeing Vietnamese prisoners of war, though in very different circumstances. For thirty years now I had been haunted by the tragedy of this country. The Bo Doi were almost certainly better off under their Chinese captors than they would have been in the two preceding wars. The prisoners of war taken by the French had not had an easy time of it. Rations behind the barbed wire had been meagre, and methods of interrogation brutal. The Americans had taken very few prisoners in their military operations against the Viet Cong. Anyone who was lucky enough to survive was handed over to the South Vietnamese military authorities, which inevitably meant systematic ill-treatment and torture. Under the Chinese things were definitely more humane. The People's Liberation Army was well-versed in the art of revolutionary warfare. They were really only interested in one thing – working their prisoners over ideologically, as opposed to physically. The French and the Americans had very quickly realized the futility of their fight on the Asian mainland, and had lapsed into embittered resignation. The Chinese, by contrast, were utterly convinced both of the justice of their cause and of the certainty of their ultimate victory over Hanoi. Time was on their side, and their revolutionary path was, so they believed, the only true one. There was no question of them being plagued by doubts, and even less danger of them succumbing to the morbid defeatism that passes for pacifism in the West. Their aim was to send the prisoners back to their families as soon as possible to spread the word about Maoist thought and Chinese generosity.

From what we could see, life in Pan Qi seemed almost idyllic. Undoubtedly the Asian talent for adaptation to new and difficult situations was an important factor in this apparent harmony. All the same, these well-fed Vietnamese peasant lads looked far from unhappy. They sat around their spotless huts, where each man had his own camp bed, playing Chinese chequers and a form of halma. They were even allowed to cook their own meals, we were told. When we asked them if they were being well treated they replied that they were. But when we tackled them on political issues, they immediately became self-conscious and started answering us in clichés. They told us the friendship between the Vietnamese and the Chinese peoples should be constant. They felt happier talking about the close friendship that had existed between Hanoi and Peking in the days of Mao and Ho Chi Minh. Our questions about the relative strengths of the two enemy camps were answered by one NCO with the terse comment: 'There are fifty million of us, and 900 million of them.' At one point we surprised a prisoner who was reading Mao's writings and he quickly hid the book under his bed. Portraits of Mao and Hua Guofeng looked down from the walls of the room. Wherever we went there were always green-uniformed Chinese soldiers present – during sports, leisure activities, political instruction classes – but they were always unarmed.

We did hear complaints and protests from some of the prisoners, and these were faithfully translated for us by our Chinese interpreters. 'The prisoners you see here are nothing like the soldiers in our People's Army,' said one angry young Vietnamese. 'We were really just peasants, quietly minding our own business, before we were caught by the Chinese attack.' He admitted to having been trained as a militiaman. A Vietnamese NCO complained that the prisoners were being used as guinea pigs for Chinese propaganda techniques. The interpreter relayed these statements to us without batting an eyelid. On the wall of one hut someone had painstakingly written a Vietnamese poem in Roman script. It was dedicated to the new friendship between the Vietnamese and Chinese peoples, and it even had one or two drawings of flowers on it. We noted one verse in particular. 'This much I know: if I refuse to take up arms and fight against the Chinese, my family will lose their rice ration and will have to starve.' From time to time the guards left us alone with the prisoners. Of course the language barrier meant there was no chance of us having a proper conversation with them. So I tried telling the young peasant lads the names of the Vietnamese towns I had visited on my previous trips to Indochina. They caught on straight away and seemed highly delighted at this unexpected reminder of home. Their honest-to-goodness peasant faces lit up, and all of a sudden I thought I recognized them. They were just like the Bo Doi troops we had spent so many evenings with in the jungle north of Saigon in 1973. I felt a strong sense of affinity with these captured Vietnamese soldiers. Although I had always been on the opposite side of the fence from them, these men had, in effect, been my companions for the last thirty years.

Sitting there in Pan Qi, I could well imagine what the exchange of prisoners at the Sino-Vietnamese border would be like. As it happened, I was able to witness these scenes two weeks later when

I was invited to do a film report for French Television. The moment the Vietnamese prisoners caught sight of the grim faces of their own political officers their expressions froze. It was only a short time since they had parted company from their Chinese guards, wreathed in smiles. Now, however, they launched into a chorus of invective against the Peking reactionaries, tearing the blue prison uniforms from their bodies, and throwing the farewell presents the Chinese soldiers had given them into the ditch with a great show of disgust. Others threw away their crutches, as if they were contaminated. For a moment it even looked as if the wounded were going to remove their bandages. The Vietnamese military authorities stood stony-faced, while the Chinese official escort and medical staff watched the histrionics with sardonic smiles. Then it was the turn of the Vietnamese border guards to escort their Chinese prisoners to the checkpoint. The Sons of Heaven proved to be at least as talented as the Vietnamese when it came to acting. With much groaning and agonized grimacing, they limped north across the border and promptly began complaining to the French camera team about the terrible treatment they had received. They said they had been starved in prison, and claimed the only food they had had to eat was millet. They had been subjected to brutal brainwashing and repeated beatings. In short, it was the Chinese who emerged as having the greater dramatic gifts in this classic piece of Asian play-acting. The Peking Opera certainly had a lot to answer for. When I was back in Paris watching the scene on television, I was reminded of the time I witnessed the exchange of French and Vietnamese prisoners on the Thanh Hoa coast in the summer of 1954. I remembered most of all how pathetic and helpless the French survivors of Dien Bien Phu had looked when confronted with their adversaries' well-rehearsed routine.

Dusk was beginning to settle on the valley of Pan Qi. We were coming to the end of our tour of the camp when we came across a badly-wounded Vietnamese political commissar, apparently a captain in the border guards. The man was extremely reticent, but even he praised the efficiency of the medical staff. He told us he had fought against the Americans in the Hue area during the second Indochinese war. I asked him if there was any comparison between the American and Chinese methods of fighting a war. Back came the answer: 'The Americans had more weapons, but the Chinese had more people. The Americans were more scared than the Chinese.'

Our interpreter took us to see a collection of armed weapons –
automatic pistols, mortars, ancient Russian machine-guns
mounted on wheels. As arsenals went, it wasn't very impressive. A
woman officer from the Chinese army drew our attention to the
Soviet, American and Chinese manufacturers' names on the guns.
'The Vietnamese are not able to produce any of their own weapons
themselves. They are parasites,' she said emphatically. There
came to mind a particularly withering remark by Mao Tse-tung
when he described Hanoi's big four – Pham Van Dong, Vo
Nguyen Giap, Le Duan, and Truong Chinh – as 'four begging
monks, forever holding out their bowls and asking for more'.

The Vietnamese prisoners were drawn up in two blue squares
on the exercise ground. At a given command they sat back on their
heels in the typical resting posture of the Asians. Four hours a day
were set aside for political instruction. Everyone had been got
together to listen to a long Chinese broadcast in Vietnamese: it was
evidently all part of the re-education programme. However,
before the piercing voice of the woman announcer sounded over
the loudspeaker system a young, fresh-faced prisoner jumped up
and raised his arm. The Vietnamese then launched into a song that
had been etched indelibly on my memory. I remembered it from
the days I spent as a prisoner of the Viet Cong in the jungle, from
my visit to the 'hoc lap' camps in Ho Chi Minh City, from the
concert by disabled ex-servicemen in the French Opera House in
Hanoi. The familiar chorus of 'Vietnam, Ho Chi Minh!' rang out
across the playing field of Pan Qi. 'Vietnam, Ho Chi Minh!' The
refrain swelled in intensity and became an impassioned patriotic
utterance, a defiant declaration of faith in the Vietnamese
revolution and the Vietnamese nation.

After we had listened to the radio broadcast and finished our
evening meal, a big canvas screen was unrolled at one end of the
playing field, rather like a drive-in cinema. In front of it squatted
an informal, mixed audience made up of soldiers of the guard,
Chinese officers' families, Vietnamese prisoners and journalists.
The film showed the capture of Shanghai by Mao Tse-tung's
troops. It had been banned during the reign of the Gang of Four,
apparently because the Communist general who led his troops to
victory on the banks of the Wang Pu River had fallen out of favour
during the Cultural Revolution and had only recently been
reinstated by Deng Xiaoping.

The train coming from the Vietnamese border pulled into the
station, right on time. The valley of Pan Qi lay shrouded in

moonless darkness, but the station itself was brightly lit up. It looked exactly like a provincial French station. The sleeping compartment was spick and span and comfortably fitted out, though our colleagues put this down to the fact that the last passengers to use the sleeper had been the delegates on the central committee. The woman guard wore a dark-blue cap over her long pigtail. We clattered our way north through the inky black night. I felt oddly moved by the events of the day, and I lay awake a long time before drifting off to sleep. The regular clicking of the rails beat out in my brain. I found myself humming the song of the Vietnamese prisoners in time to the rhythm: 'Vietnam, Ho Chi Minh . . . Vietnam, Ho Chi Minh . . .' Somehow I couldn't get it out of my head.

Marx and Mohammed

Kunming, March 1979

We pulled into Kunming station as dawn was breaking. We had a few hours to kill before our plane took off for Kweilin, so we went and filmed the town. In the middle of the shopping centre we came across the local equivalent of the Wall of Democracy. Here, too, the wall-posters were mostly preoccupied with the campaign of the 'four modernizations'. The general tone was more cautious than in Peking and the criticisms put forward were all fairly constructive. The latest directives from the central committee were all there as well: it hadn't taken long for them to filter through to this remote southern province. There was a warning from the top-ranking party committees that there could be no question of allowing young men to grow their hair long, or letting young girls wear jeans. The order of the day was not to slavishly copy the ways of Western decadence but to acquire the benefits of Western technology. In other countries false liberalism and so-called democratic freedom were simply a cover for capitalist exploitation of the masses. The Chinese people had to hold on firmly to their belief in Marxism-Leninism and the thoughts of Chairman Mao. Underneath this stern pronouncement someone had scrawled: 'Those are the words of the Gang of Four.'

363

Fang pointed out a flat building tucked away behind a wall. 'That's the big mosque you were asking me about,' he said. 'There are also a couple of smaller mosques still open in the town.' Unlike the Christian churches in Kunming, which had all either been torn down or turned into warehouses, the Muslim temple in the centre of town still held regular services of worship. In the inner courtyard squatted a grey-haired imam with a straggly white beard. He greeted us shyly with the traditional '*Salam aleikum*'. Inside, the mosque was furnished with straw mats and cheap carpets. The prayer corner faced west towards Mecca. The mosque had a curved roof, and the sayings from the Koran on the walls were decorated with every conceivable Chinese motif – excluding, of course, dragons and other mythological animals. Beneath the canopy was a primitive painting showing the Kaaba, the black meteorite of Mecca, the chief shrine of Islam.

Our guide from the information services was a cultured man with the aloof manner of a mandarin. His Mao tunic was well cut and he spoke fluent French. 'Islam has played an important role in the history of Yunnan,' he began. 'Even today there are 50,000 Muslims among Kunming's 900,000 people. In the past it was assumed that the Muslim immigration was started by Kublai Khan's troops; the Mongol emperor raised a large part of his army among the Turkish peoples of Central Asia. Marco Polo was one of the first foreigners to point out the large number of "Saracens" in Yunnan. Another theory claims Islam was imported here from Canton, where there was a strong Muslim tradition in the Middle Ages.' He said that in the fifteenth century the Muslim admiral Zheng He, who originally came from Yunnan, brought all the coastal countries under Chinese domination. Then in the nineteenth century, the Muslims in Yunnan joined in the Taiping Rebellion against the Manchu dynasty. The Muslim potentate in Kunming, the Sultan of Da Li, was only finally defeated when French colonial forces were brought in.

Peking must have been getting increasingly worried by the Islam question. In the summer of 1978 I was visiting Tehran at the time Chairman Hua Guofeng was on a state visit to the Shah of Iran, paying his respects to the Peacock Throne. At that time there was already serious unrest in the bazaar area among opponents of the Pahlevi dynasty. The Chinese had misjudged the Iran situation just as badly as the Americans had done. When I flew back with the Ayatolla Khomeini from Paris to Tehran in January 1979, the members of the Shi'ite leader's entourage were still incensed at what they saw as China's blatant political opportunism. Now Peking was having to tackle the thorny problem of the huge Muslim minority – mainly Uigurs, but also Kazakhs and Kirghiz, among others – living in the strategically vulnerable western province of Sinkiang, across the border from the Soviet republics and their Muslim Turkish populations in Central Asia. The revolutionary awakening of Islam went far beyond the frontiers of Shi'ite Iran. Inside pro-Soviet Afghanistan, for instance, a holy war had broken out. In Pakistan, Bangladesh, Indonesia and Malaysia, militant Islam was on the march. In the south Philippines the Muslim Moros were fighting a fanatical campaign against the Marcos dictatorship in Manila.

Our guides were waiting for us when we got to Kunming airport. We sat in the departure lounge in front of a huge white plaster bust of Mao Tse-tung, standing out against a red background. In the noonday heat the spring sky over Yunnan was tinted in soft pastel shades. A ripple ran through the tender green of the ricefields at the edge of the runway. Planes of the Chinese air force – based on Russian MiG fighters – landed and took off continuously. They would taxi down the runway in close formation, one behind the other. On landing the pilots released a coloured brake parachute which would billow along behind like a huge scarlet poppy. Were they, I wondered, rehearsing for the next round of the third Indochinese war?

Epilogue in Europe

Paris – Bonn, August 1979

There was the usual chaos of holiday traffic at Roissy-Charles de Gaulle airport. Noisy, colourful crowds of travellers were queuing up outside the entrance to the transparent Plexiglass tubes, where escalators would take them up to the concrete and aluminium departure points. Some of the holiday-makers seemed nervous and irritable, others were enjoying the whole thing. The summer day had dawned cool and grey in Paris, but hot beaches, blue sea and green woods lay in store at our journey's end. The tourists waiting for the charter flight took hardly any notice of the group of

Asians sitting huddled together. All they had with them were a few possessions, pitiful little bundles which they clutched to them. Their dejected, silent mood contrasted sharply with the cheerful hubbub all around. They had brown faces, almond eyes, and jet-black hair. They were Cambodians and they shivered slightly in the draughty expanse of the glass-walled lounge, wrapping themselves tighter in the blankets and shawls they had been given. These Khmer refugees, who had flown from Bangkok, were some of the privileged few who had managed to escape a wretched death in the jungle or the degradation of an internment camp.

Earlier that same morning, a scheduled flight from Ho Chi Minh City had landed in Charles de Gaulle airport. This particular group of official emigrants were lucky to have had connections and family ties in France; when they came out of the customs exit, relatives stepped forward to meet them, weeping. These latest arrivals from Vietnam would have relatively few problems in adjusting to a new life in France; they would soon make a fresh start, even if it meant having to make do with fairly humble jobs at first. Shoppers in the middle-class areas of Paris had soon got used to seeing young Asians serving in their local supermarkets. The new recruits made up for their lack of French by the keenness and speed with which they learnt. Elsewhere, in the staunchly Communist districts of Paris, the situation was quite different. There, the survivors of the Vietnamese labour camps were a constant source of embarrassment to the local officials of the French Communist Party. The majority of these refugees almost certainly came from the Chinese districts of Saigon and Cholon, and so probably belonged to the *compradores*, the despised capitalist exploiters. Apart from the Chinese in North Vietnam who had been herded into boats and forced out to sea by the Red commissars, there were at least two to three million native South Vietnamese desperate to grab the chance of fleeing the country, even if it meant risking their lives and leaving behind everything they possessed.

Who would have thought, all those years ago, when the *Andus* transported the first reinforcements for the Expeditionary Force to Indochina, while the legionnaires on board sang their old Wehrmacht songs – who would even have dreamed then that the ripples from the Vietnam conflict would one day spread over the whole of Western Europe. Only three years ago, just as the second Indochinese war was coming to its inglorious end, press commentators deplored how short-lived the interest of the reading public was, how its appetite had to be constantly fed by sensation. They had thought then that they could safely banish the subject of Vietnam from the headlines for ever, but now this remote country on the edge of South-east Asia was in the news again. Vietnam had once more forced its way to the forefront of world events.

With hindsight it was possible to see the Indochina question for what it was, not just a flashpoint in Far Eastern affairs but a kind of political acid test. Big-power politics and the ideological struggle had been fought out in a patch of jungle and ricefield between Hanoi and Saigon. It had all started with the French. Their defeat in 1954 in Indochina had marked the beginning of the end, had paved the way for the loss of their entire empire. In the Viet Minh prison camps, in the contact with the great Asian revolution, the spark was lit that flared up in Algiers in May 1958. The seeds that led to the fall of the Fourth Republic and the second era of Gaullism had been sown on the banks of the Red River.

The clash between the American giants and the little yellow men from Hanoi demonstrated the limits of United States power. America's self-confidence never recovered from the shock. Johnson's resignation, Nixon's Watergate scandal, the creeping paralysis that overtook Washington under Gerald Ford and, to an even greater extent, under Jimmy Carter – all these events could be traced to the humiliating defeat the Viet Cong had inflicted on the mighty Uncle Sam. The military power, credibility and reliability of the United States were cast into doubt by the retreat from South-east Asia. In the United States the second Indochinese war unleashed a new wave of political consciousness. It also unleashed a feeling of helplessness and moral uncertainty, a sense of rage and disgust. The deep-seated psychological trauma that affected the mass of the American people following the Vietnam débâcle appeared far more significant to social analysts than the short-term consequences of the fiasco.

Even the putative victors had little to rejoice about. The third Indochinese conflict between the Vietnamese and the Cambodians and the Chinese and the Vietnamese punctured the myth of 'World Communism' for ever. Henceforth no propagandist could refer to 'international proletarianism' or the 'mission' of Marxism-Leninism to unite and pacify the peoples of the world, without exposing himself to ridicule. The first Communist religious war to take place on Indochinese soil was every bit as cruel and ignoble as the armed confrontations of the despised imperialists that had gone before. Pol Pot instituted a regime of horror in Cambodia that had only been surpassed in modern times by Hitler's extermination camps.

Even the Russians had cause for anxiety at the thought of the South-east Asian alliances they had become embroiled in. The propaganda value to Moscow of Hanoi's military successes against France and the United States was offset by the revelation of the Socialist Republic of Vietnam as a rapacious war machine, a 'cold monster', an instrument of Stalinist repression. Since the Sino-Vietnamese border conflict of February 1979, and possibly even before, Moscow has found herself involved in the dubious venture of war by proxy, committed to sending lavish amounts of aid to Hanoi for an indeterminate period. The Soviet empire – a sixth of the surface area of the globe – constitutes a direct provocation to the masses of Asia in these post-colonial times. Despite her commitment to back the ideological crackpots and charlatans in the Third World, Moscow will inevitably end up leading the white vanguard of Europe in Central Asia, Siberia and the Far East. As de Gaulle once prophesied: 'The Russians will find out one day that they are whites, too.'

As for the People's Republic of China, since February 1979 and the capture of Lang Son the Chinese have shown the world that, in their book, pacifism equals weakness. The Chinese dragon lost a great deal of international prestige and goodwill when it showed its claws in Vietnam. But why should this empire with its vast population – soon to pass the 1000 million mark – be bothered if a few theoreticians in the West dismiss China as a world force? In the West there has been a failure to grasp the fact that the fundamental, outstanding problem of the Chinese revolution is its clash with Confucianism.

I had been dogged by my memories of Indochina that day at the airport, but there was to be another encounter in store for me that evening in Bonn. I chanced upon a TV programme that featured a local choir of Vietnamese children. The girls were wearing well-cut *ao dai* made of gold-coloured silk. They mostly belonged to the Chinese Hoa people. They looked clean, intelligent, well-behaved and enthusiastic. A couple of these young Sino-Vietnamese answered routine questions in what was already fairly fluent German. I felt somewhat moved, yet something was being deliberately played down. The audience was being reassured; they were being reminded of the kindness and humanity they had showed towards the immigrants. The appearance of these survivors of a cruel blow of fate, these children rescued from the sinking fishing boats and the degradation of the transit camps in Thailand and Malaysia, was organized to encourage people to give further practical aid. Unfortunately, however, the serious intention was in danger of being trivialized.

A young German conductor stepped up in front of the choir and raised his hand and the Vietnamese children launched into a well-known song. 'Ein Jäger aus Kurpfalz, der eitet Durch den grünen Wald . . .' The Asian voices sounded a little shrill, but the song was faultlessly sung. The girls in their *ao dai* smiled the Confucian smile of the well-brought-up child. Yet as the TV cameras moved in on them I thought I detected in their almond eyes a look of fear and sadness, as if these children of Saigon and Cholon were recalling the warm evenings, the bustling streets, the majestic rice plains, the well-ordered family life of their lost homeland. 'Ein Jäger aus Kurpfalz . . .' The chorus started up again and the audience joined in. In Hanoi and Ho Chi Minh City they are singing a very different song.

Chronological Table

1940
September. After defeat of France in Europe, Japan moves into northern part of French Indochina and later completely occupies area.

1945
March. Japanese forces arrest French colonial officials and intern remaining French troops in country.

August 16. Surrender of Japan.

September 2. In Hanoi, Ho Chi Minh proclaims independence of all of Vietnam.

October. First French units land in Saigon, with British aid, and reaffirm France's colonial rights in face of armed resistance.

1946
March 6. Paris recognizes Vietnam as autonomous state within French Union.

March 9. French troops land in Tongking.

July. France presses for separation of Cochin China from rest of Vietnam.

September 14. Franco-Vietnamese conference in Fontainebleau ratifies Vietnam's place in French Union. Ho Chi Minh consents to French military presence in Tongking.

November. Following series of incidents, French bomb harbour town of Haiphong.

December. Ho Chi Minh issues call for general uprising against French. Rebellion begins in Hanoi. French army launches military campaign against Viet Minh.

1948
June. France hands over running of Vietnam to ex-Emperor Bao Dai.

December. Mao Tse-tung's armies conquer southern Chinese province of Yunnan and reach northern border of Tongking. Viet Minh now enjoy full support from Chinese Communists.

1950
June 25. Outbreak of Korean War.

October. Evacuation of border fortress town of Cao Bang by French troops.

October 20. Evacuation of Lang Son on border with China.

December. General de Lattre de Tassigny takes over supreme command in Indochina.

1952
January. Death of de Lattre de Tassigny.

February. Town of Hoa Binh, previously encircled by Viet Minh forces, is evacuated.

April. General Salan takes over as Commander-in-Chief of French forces.

1953
May. Viet Minh advance into Laos and are repulsed by French troops.

May. General Salan replaced by General Navarre.

July 27. End of Korean War.

1954
May 7. Jungle stronghold of Dien Bien Phu, encircled for many weeks, surrenders to Vietnamese Commander-in-Chief, Vo Nguyen Giap, after heavy fighting.

April to July. Geneva Conference on Indochina. On July 21 final Declaration on Indochina conflict provides for end of hostilities in Cambodia, Laos, and Vietnam; provisional regrouping of both armies on either side of demarcation line (not a frontier) along 17th parallel; withdrawal of French troops from the North; general elections to take place in July 1956 under international supervision; Cambodia and Laos to be totally self-governing and refrain from joining any military alliances.

1955
Stepping-up of American military aid to Saigon. Prime Minister Ngo Dinh Diem proclaims republic in October and deposes Bao Dai.

1960
December. Formation of National Liberation Front for South Vietnam (Viet Cong).

1963
November 1. Prime Minister Ngo Dinh Diem toppled and killed. Further coups follow.

1964
Early August. Incident in Gulf of Tongking. North Vietnamese patrol boats fire on US destroyer. American bombers begin retaliatory strikes over North Vietnam.

1965
February. US air strikes over North Vietnam continue. American ground troops land in Vietnam. Total maximum reached: 500,000 men. General Nguyen Van Thieu appointed leader of committee of national leadership and head of state of South Vietnam.

1968
January 29. Viet Cong and North Vietnamese launch Tet offensive.

Late March. Partial cessation of US bombing raids over North Vietnam.

May. Start of Paris talks between Washington and Hanoi. Later Saigon and National Liberation Front for South Vietnam (Viet Cong) join in talks.

1969
May. Richard Nixon, US President, proposes eight-point peace plan for Vietnam.

June 10. Viet Cong announce formation of Provisional Revolutionary Government for South Vietnam.

1970
March 18. Prince Sihanouk, head of state of neutral Cambodia, toppled by army. General Lon Nol takes over with American backing. Factional strife breaks out.

Late April. Large contingents of South Vietnamese troops advance into Cambodia, supported by American air and ground troops.

October. Lon Nol proclaims republic in Cambodia.

1972
May. Major new offensive by Communist divisions on 17th parallel and in Cochin China. Americans retaliate by resuming all-out air attacks over North Vietnam and starting partial blockade.

July. Resumption of Paris peace talks. Saigon opposes substantial areas of agreement worked out between Washington and Hanoi.

December. Resumption of massive air strikes on Hanoi and Haiphong provokes worldwide protest. After cessation of bombing at end of year, Hanoi agrees to reopen negotiations.

1973
January 27. Vietnam ceasefire agreement signed in Paris. Plans for a Council of National Reconciliation set out in this agreement are never put into practice.

February. Ceasefire in Laos agreed.

Late February to early March. Vietnam Conference in Paris attended by signatories of ceasefire agreement plus People's Republic of China, USSR, France, Great Britain and representatives of International Control Commission.

Late April. Withdrawal of remaining American troops from Vietnam.

1974
July. New offensive by Khmer Rouge against Lon Nol regime in Cambodia.

December. Offensive by North Vietnamese in Vietnam–Cambodia border area.

1975
March. After fall of military bases in highlands of Annam, South Vietnamese forces retreat and Communists begin continuous advance. Coastal towns of Hue and Da Nang occupied by North Vietnamese.

Mid-April. Resignation of President Nguyen Van Thieu. Flight of remaining Americans from Saigon. Communists enter capital. South Vietnam surrenders unconditionally.

1976
Effective reunification of North and South Vietnam.

Spring. Start of first border conflicts between Communist troops of Vietnam and Cambodia.

December. Fourth Congress of Communist Party of Vietnam (formerly Lao Dong Party).

1978
November 3. Soviet Russia and Vietnam sign pact of friendship and mutual aid.

December. Major Vietnamese offensive launched against Cambodia.

1979
January 7. Vietnamese troops conquer Phnom Penh. Flight of Pol Pot government.

February 17 to March 5. Chinese launch attack against Vietnam border area then immediately withdraw.

July 21–22. Conference on Vietnam refugees held in Geneva.

Index of Names

377